PRIVATIZATION AND
PERFORMAN

PRIVATIZATION AND ECONOMIC PERFORMANCE

Edited by

MATTHEW BISHOP
JOHN KAY
COLIN MAYER

OXFORD UNIVERSITY PRESS

1994

Oxford University Press, Walton Street, Oxford OX2 6DP

Oxford New York
Athens Auckland Bangkok Bombay
Calcutta Cape Town Dar es Salaam Delhi
Florence Hong Kong Istanbul Karachi
Kuala Lumpur Madras Madrid Melbourne
Mexico City Nairobi Paris Singapore
Taipei Tokyo Toronto
and associated companies in
Berlin Ibadan

Oxford is a trade mark of Oxford University Press

Published in the United States
by Oxford University Press Inc., New York

British Library Cataloguing in Publication Data
Data available
ISBN 0–19–877343–9
ISBN 0–19–877344–7 (pbk.)

Library of Congress Cataloging in Publication Data
Data available
ISBN 0–19–877343–9
ISBN 0–19–877344–7 (pbk.)

Typeset by Hope Services (Abingdon) Ltd.
Printed in Great Britain
on acid-free paper by
Biddles Ltd.,
Guildford and King's Lynn

PREFACE

In 1986 Colin Mayer, David Thompson, and I edited a collection of readings *Privatisation and Regulation—the UK experience*. At that time, privatization was still a novel idea and Britain's new style of utility regulation was only two years old. Now, privatization is a policy which has aroused not only interest but imitation around the world, and we have learnt that regulation introduces many new problems as well as solving old ones. The explosion of what was then a very limited literature in the field has now justified two separate volumes on Privatization and Regulation respectively. The articles they contain have been written and revised at various dates, and while some authors have brought their analysis or conclusions up to date at the time of going to press, others have preferred to leave their views as they stood.

The editors are indebted to Barbara Lee for assembling the material and putting together the manuscripts.

J.K.

CONTENTS

CONTRIBUTORS

JONATHAN AYLEN is Senior Lecturer in Economics, University of Salford.

MICHAEL BEESLEY is Professor of Economics, London Business School.

MATTHEW BISHOP is Journalist with *The Economist*.

SIMON COWAN is at the Institute of Economics and Statistics, University of Oxford.

DAVID DE MEZA is at the University of Guelph, Guelph, Ontario, Canada.

JOHN DODGSON is Senior Lecturer, Department of Economics and Accounting, University of Liverpool.

SIMON DOMBERGER is Professor at the Graduate School of Business, University of Sydney.

SAUL ESTRIN is Associate Professor of Economics, London Business School.

RICHARD GREEN is at the Department of Applied Economics, University of Cambridge.

PAUL GROUT is Professor of Economics, University of Bristol.

JONATHAN HASKEL is at the Department of Economics, Queen Mary and Westfield College, University of London.

TIM JENKINSON is Stock Exchange Fellow in Economics, Keble College, University of Oxford.

JOHN KAY is Chairman of London Economics, and Professor of Economics at the London Business School.

STEPHEN LITTLECHILD is Director-General, Offer.

FRANCIS McGOWAN is at the School of European Studies, University of Sussex.

COLIN MAYER is Professor of Economics and Finance, Warwick Business School.

SHIRLEY MEADOWCROFT is Economist, Office of Telecommunications. At the time the paper was written, was a Research Officer at the Institute for Fiscal Studies.

JOHN PIGGOTT is at the Department of Economics, University of New South Wales.

CATHERINE PRICE is at the Department of Economics, University of Leicester.

KEN ROBBIE is at the Centre for Management Buy-out Research.

DAVID STARKIE is Director of Putnam, Hayes & Bartlett Ltd.

STEFAN SZYMANSKI is at the Imperial College Management School, University of London.

DAVID THOMPSON is at the Department of Education. At the time the paper was written, was a Senior Research Fellow at the Centre for Business Strategy, London Business School.

STEVE THOMPSON is Senior Lecturer in Business Economics, UMIST, Manchester.

INGO VOGELSANG is at the Department of Economics, Boston University.

JOHN WINWARD is Director of Research, the Association of Consumer Research.

MIKE WRIGHT is Professor of Financial Studies, and Director of the Centre for Management Buy-out Research, School of Management and Finance, University of Nottingham.

GEORGE YARROW is Fellow and Tutor in Economics, Hertford College, University of Oxford.

TABLES

FIGURES

Introduction: Privatization in Performance

MATTHEW BISHOP,* JOHN KAY,† and COLIN MAYER‡

One of the most enduring legacies of the 1980s has been the programme of privatizations that the Thatcher government set in train in the first half of the decade. Whole sectors of the UK economy which were formerly part of the public sector were sold to the private sector. Some were bought out by their employees; others were bought by the public at large. Some public services were contracted out to the private sector; others were placed on a more commercial footing. The UK privatization programme had an influence on economic policy throughout the world. Privatization programmes were initiated in Asia, South America, and Africa, as well as in Europe and North America. The most recent to experiment with privatizations have been the East European countries which have seen privatization as the fastest route to move from socialism to capitalism.

The purpose of this book is to stand back and examine what has been learnt from the extensive programme of privatization that the UK government has completed and to consider what elements of privatization remain to be achieved. This book attempts to evaluate systematically the privatizations that have been undertaken in different sectors of the UK economy over the past ten years. It examines what has happened and why, where have been the successes and failures, what lessons can be learnt for the design of privatization programmes elsewhere, and what the UK government can still usefully do in this area.

This introduction gives an overview of these issues. It begins in Section 1 by describing the objectives that lay behind the privatization programme. It argues that there are essentially three factors that can justify privatizations: finance, information, and control. The *financing* of both government and the firm is affected by privatization. The government raises finance in the process of disposing of assets; firms are free to raise finance from capital markets. *Information* is of relevance in setting prices. Competition ensures that prices are consistent with efficient allocation of resources and lowest costs of supply. Even in the absence of competition it has been suggested that privatization may allow prices to

* Journalist with *The Economist*.
† Chairman of London Economics, and Professor of Economics at the London Business School.
‡ Professor of Economics and Finance, Warwick Business School.

be imposed that encourage greater efficiency of supply. Where price mechanisms alone are not adequate then *control* is of relevance. Changes in ownership are most directly associated with changes in control. Privatization programmes in principle involve a weakening in control exerted by the state and a transfer of control to private investors. It is this aspect of privatization that is the most important to East European countries which regard the elimination of state control as a primary objective.

Section 2 evaluates the performance of the UK privatization programmes in these three regards. The main conclusions are:

Finance

- Private capital markets have not been a central source of funding of privatized enterprises and equity markets have been largely irrelevant.
- The effect of privatizations on the public-sector accounts has been negative.
- Assertions to the effect that 'public-sector assets were sold too cheaply' are largely meaningless.

Information

- Privatization programmes have encouraged the precise identification of the public-good aspects of state enterprises.
- Performance has significantly improved where competition has been introduced.
- The UK privatization programme frequently failed to identify opportunities for introducing competition.
- Surrogate competition through yardstick comparisons is a poor substitute for actual competition.
- However, even where competition has been limited or absent there have been significant improvements in efficiency.
- The information conveyed by stock-market prices has been important in monitoring performance and improving managerial incentives.

Control

- Capital markets have exerted little control over privatized companies either through the threat of take-over or bankruptcy.
- The power of both state and trade unions has been significantly reduced by privatization.
- The regulator has replaced the state as the single most powerful external body.
- Regulatory control is inefficient, ineffective, and unduly expensive.

The implication is that privatization is an important aspect of corporate restructuring. Its primary relevance lies in the greater transparency that it allows in monitoring corporate performance. Where competition can be introduced then performance can improve substantially.

Even where competition has been absent there have been gains to privatization. Contrary to what was originally anticipated, privatized utilities have displayed significant improvements in efficiency even where there has been little or no competition. The incentive effects of share prices have been an important spur to efficiency. However, they have come at a cost: in the absence of direct competition regulation is required. Efficient and effective forms of regulation have not as yet been identified and may not exist. As the companion volume on regulation describes, the failure of the UK government to establish appropriate structures of industries prior to privatization has left a lasting legacy of inefficiency in many of the privatized utilities.

1. THE OBJECTIVES OF PRIVATIZATION

There were three primary sets of objectives associated with the UK privatization programme. The first was concerned with finance (Section 1.1), the second with information and the setting of incentives (Section 1.2), and the third with control (Section 1.3).

1.1 Finance

The UK privatization programme evolved out of the sales of council houses and small state-owned enterprises at the beginning of the 1980s. Initially, a major motivation behind the sale of state-owned enterprises was to help fund a large public-sector deficit. Over the period from 1984 when the first large privatization of British Telecom (BT) occurred to the end of the 1980s, the UK government raised a total of £37 billion. This is approximately the same as the entire UK public-sector deficit in 1992.

The sale of BT introduced the notion of wide share ownership and popular capitalism. There was a firmly held belief amongst financial advisers to the UK government that it would not be possible to sell a company as large as BT to institutional investors alone without attracting a large subscription from individual investors. 49 per cent of the shares in BT were to be sold for £3.9 billion. In total, the private sector raised just £1.4 billion from new equity issues in the same year so that the privatization dwarfed anything that the stock-market had previously encountered. A heavy promotion of the privatization to individual investors was therefore initially viewed as a necessary requirement for a successful flotation, not a desirable objective in its own right.

In the event, the flotation was an overwhelming 'success'. It was five times oversubscribed and investors were well satisfied by the 86 per cent premium that they received on the first-day trading price over the (partially paid) issue price. Such was the popularity of the issue that thereinafter wide share ownership became a central plank of the UK government's privatization programme. The UK government pointed to a huge success in widening share ownership in the UK from 7 per cent of the adult population in 1981 to 22 per cent in 1992.

Perhaps still more significant than the public-sector revenues was the belief that privatization could help alleviate constraints on financing under which the companies themselves were operating. The incoming UK government was committed to a programme of restraining government expenditures and reining back the borders of the state. One of its main mechanisms for achieving this was the imposition of tight financial constraints on public-sector enterprises. The notion that capital appraisals by public-sector enterprises should be undertaken on the basis of real required rates of return (test discount rates) had already been abandoned in the 1978 White Paper on Nationalized Industries. This introduced external borrowing limits that were set in nominal terms. The idea behind these was that real required rates of return had failed to provide an effective control on the expenditures of public-sector enterprises. Financial borrowing controls were required to impose limitations on public-sector enterprise expenditures.

By the early part of the 1980s, public-sector enterprises were complaining that limitations on their ability to fund necessary capital expenditures were being imposed. One of the most vociferous exponents of this view was BT. At one stage, the UK government contemplated experimenting with novel forms of financing, such as BT specific bonds (to be known as 'Busby bonds'). However, it was persuaded that in practice it was impossible to create bonds of public-sector enterprises that could compete on fair terms with those of private-sector enterprises because there was an unavoidable implicit guarantee that public-sector enterprises would not default. The government would therefore be unable to restrain the borrowing activity of state-owned enterprises and the public-sector deficit could not be separated from that of its enterprises. The only way in which these enterprises could be allowed to raise external finance on fair terms was if they were privatized. The desire to avoid the imposition of unwarranted financial constraints on public-sector enterprises was therefore a primary impetus behind the privatization programme.

1.2 Information

One of the main objectives of privatization was to improve the efficiency of public-sector enterprises. Central to this was the notion that the market encourages efficiency by providing incentives to managers and workers. Competition encourages efficiency by allowing consumers to purchase from lowest-cost suppliers. It achieves *productive efficiency* by encouraging firms to minimize costs and *allocative efficiency* by bringing consumers' demands in line with marginal costs of supply. To the extent that privatization allows state-owned monopolies to be broken up and competition to be introduced, privatization clearly offers considerable scope for efficiency improvements.

Even in the absence of competition, privatization may improve efficiency. Firstly, if prices are regulated then private-sector monopolies have incentives to minimize costs. By lowering costs, they are able to increase profits and raise incomes of managers and workers whose pay is related to corporate performance. Secondly, privatization permits the introduction of incentives that are unavailable to public-sector enterprises. In particular, managerial and worker incomes can be related to the market value of enterprises in the form of shares and stock options. Share prices provide independent assessments of the current and expected future performance of firms. They can be used to justify corporate restructurings and replacement of management. Thirdly, private-sector enterprises are subject to threats of take-over and bankruptcy. Firms that do not minimize costs risk being subject to hostile take-overs by predators that believe that they can supply services at lower costs. Firms that fail to restrain costs risk the possibility of bankruptcy. Fourthly, privatization encourages the explicit costing of public services. Subsidies for the provision of specific services, for example, rural bus, telephone, and other utility services, are made transparent. Fifthly, the public-good element of utilities' activities are separately identified from the remainder. Consideration of where competition can and cannot be introduced involves evaluation of where scale economies create natural monopolies. For example, the pipeline system of a gas company may be a natural monopoly; the trading and supply of gas are not. The electricity grid may be a natural monopoly; the generation and supply of electricity are not. While public-good aspects of utilities' activities require regulation, the remainder do not. Finally, the information on which to base regulation of natural monopolies may be improved. It may be possible to introduce elements of yardstick competition through comparisons of costs of firms supplying different areas and different customers. For example, the costs of water, electricity, and gas companies supplying different areas of the country can be compared and prices can be set on the basis of average or lowest costs of supply.

In summary, in some cases privatization permits the introduction of unregulated competition. Even in the absence of competition, it allows more powerful incentives (market-value related incentives, take-overs, and bankruptcy) to be introduced. It separates public- and private-good elements of supply, and provides more information on which to base the regulation of the public elements.

1.3 Control

In addition to affecting incentives, privatization alters control. Most obviously, state control is reduced and control by private investors is increased. As noted above, private-investor control may come from take-over and bankruptcy as well as direct intervention. The UK privatization programme had the objective of reducing the power of trade unions as well as that of the state. Under public ownership, the government was unable to restrain the bargaining power of unions of essential public services. It was thought that the private sector would be able to impose more credible budgetary limits.

2. THE PERFORMANCE OF THE UK PRIVATIZATION PROGRAMME

This section evaluates the performance of the UK privatization programme on the three criteria described in the previous section. Section 2.1 considers finance; Section 2.2 discusses information; and Section 2.3 examines control.

2.1 Finance

As noted previously, the UK privatization programme has raised large amounts of revenue for the government. However, this has come at the expense of the disposal of assets. A comprehensive system of public-sector accounting would reflect the fact that there is an offsetting item to revenues raised from sales in the form of reduced holdings of public-sector assets. Since public-sector enterprises were sold at a substantial discount below their market value, as revealed by the market capitalization of the public-sector enterprises one day or week after privatization, the net effect on government's balance sheet was negative rather than positive. In addition, large costs were incurred in disposing of the assets, in the form of advertising expenditures, fees to advisers, etc.

It has also been asserted that the subsequent strong performance of shares of many privatized companies since privatization is evidence of underpricing. This is incorrect. Subsequent performance has been affected by numerous factors, in particular the behaviour of regulators. As discussed below, the UK system of privatization has left regulators with considerable powers of discretion. Evidence that regulators are taking a tougher line in restraining prices charged by privatized firms to their customers results in share-price falls and evidence of more lenient behaviour by the regulator creates share-price rises. Share prices at the time of privatization reflected the expected behaviour of regulators; share-price movements subsequently are therefore in large part a re-evaluation of the attitude of regulators and have little to do with the 'intrinsic value' of assets.

The costs of issue have been justified on the basis of the success of the privatization programme in encouraging wider share ownership. In fact, the success of the programme in this regard is far from clear. While it is true that the number of individual shareholders has increased markedly on account of privatizations, the value of shareholdings by individuals has continued to decline relative to that of institutions. Since 1981, the proportion of UK equity held by individuals has fallen from 25 to 20 per cent in 1992, while the proportion of institutional shareholding has increased. Furthermore, individual shareholdings are in general very concentrated in a small number of shares: most individuals have bought just one privatization issue and no other shares.

It was noted above that one of the main objectives of the UK privatization programme was to free public-sector enterprises from the constraints of public-sector external borrowing limits. Some companies, such as British Telecom and British Gas, have raised appreciable amounts in bond issues since privatization: British Telecom has made fourteen issues, and British Gas has made twenty-two. However, in other cases companies have made few or no issues. There is a good reason why there has been little external financing by privatized companies. In setting the price limits on the amounts that privatized companies could charge their customers the government took account of their effects on the financial position of firms. In effect, prices were set at such a level as to ensure that they yielded both an adequate return and sufficient cash flow to meet financing requirements. The most striking example of the influence of financial considerations was the water industry, where price limits were set at a level well above that required to yield a return equal to the cost of capital in the early years after privatization. This reflected the high expenditures that water companies were required to make on renewing the water-system's infrastructure.

While previously public-sector utilities funded their investments from government tax receipts and borrowing, they now largely fund investment from charges levied on customers. This has conferred considerable powers on regulators; however, the reduced external borrowing requirements of privatized companies suggest that if anything weaker financial control is now being exerted over privatized companies. The only difference between this and a less stringent public-sector external borrowing limit is that costs are now borne by consumers rather than the tax-paying public. This has significant distributional implications.

2.2 Information

One of the more striking consequences of privatization is the extent to which it has made the behaviour and performance of privatized companies more transparent. Previously, public-sector enterprises were submerged in the depths of government ministries and accountability for performance was almost impossible to establish. After privatization, distinct enterprises have been created with clearly defined lines of responsibility.

Share prices provide more objective measures of performance than have been available hitherto and it has been possible to provide higher-powered incentives to managers and workers in privatized enterprises. Cost cutting has been a feature of several privatized firms even where competition has been quite limited. The most pronounced example of this is the electricity generators: despite the fact that they effectively operate a duopoly they have both undertaken large-scale manpower shedding programmes. Likewise, costs have been reduced in water, gas, and telecoms. While incentives have been improved, this has not come about through threats of either take-overs or bankruptcy. Most of the large privatized companies are effectively protected from the threat of either of these. In the water industry, for example, the regulator has stated that he would be opposed to mergers between water companies unless there were very clear economy of scale cost benefits. The reason for this is that mergers reduce the number of comparable companies that can be used in yardstick comparisons. Similar considerations apply to the Regional Electricity Companies.

In principle, it is possible for privatized companies to go bankrupt. In practice, an insolvency that was likely to have a highly disruptive effect on a key industry could not be allowed to happen. The way in which this eventuality is in practice avoided is through the regulator setting prices that ensure that firms earn sufficient revenues to meet their financing and investment obligations. Privatized firms are some of the most highly financially protected firms in the UK: they do not face serious threats of financial distress.

One of the most important consequences of privatization has been the attempt to identify specifically the public-good elements of firms' activities. Nationalization was originally justified on the grounds of large economies of scale, networks, distributional considerations, and national importance. However, privatization has revealed that these considerations only in general apply to a limited segment of firms' activities. Electricity and gas illustrate this principle clearly. Their nationalization was justified on the grounds that the creation of national grids for distribution required co-ordination between different producers. Co-ordination in turn created a monopoly which justified public ownership. It is indeed true that the national grid or transmission system of gas and electricity are natural monopolies: they are networks where competition cannot be readily introduced. However, there are several other aspects of both services that are not natural monopolies. Competition in generation of electricity and production of gas is perfectly practical. Competition in trading and supply is also feasible. Likewise, competition in the provision of bus and coach services is possible even where competition in the provision of terminals is not.

One of the most important aspects of a privatization programme is to separate those components of services which are subject to natural-monopoly problems from those that are not. In general, the natural-monopoly elements are associated with core networks, such as transmission and grid systems. Real improvements can be made where competition can be introduced into at least a part of a formerly integrated public-sector enterprise. Where privatization programmes encounter most difficulty are precisely in those industries in which the separation of core monopolies from the remainder is most difficult. Examples of these are railways, where the performance of one train operator has significant effects on the performance of others, and postal services, where the network comprises a substantial proportion of the total service provided.

Privatization has also made transparent subsidies that previously existed. The most striking way in which these have been revealed has been in the discrepancy that existed between the market- and current-cost book value of privatized companies. At the time of privatization, British Gas was sold for £5.6 billion; its market capitalization at the end of the first week of trading was £6.1 billion. In comparison, the current-cost value of its assets was £18 billion. The water companies were in total sold for £5.2 billion; their market capitalization at the end of their first week of trading was £6.4 billion. The current-cost value of their assets was £110 billion. Similarly, the regional electricity companies were sold at well below the current-cost value of their assets. The reason for the discrepancy between market and current-cost values is that the prices that they charged for services were well below those required to earn a normal return on the current-cost value of assets. In the case of gas, this reflected a deliberate policy of subsidizing the use of gas. In the case of water, no serious attempt was made prior to privatization to determine true-cost charges. As a consequence, in the absence of substantial adjustments to charges levied on consumers, the amounts for which privatized companies could be sold was considerably below their current-cost values. In the case of electricity, privatization has also made transparent the scale of subsidies paid by generators to the coal industry. Users and distributors wish to purchase fuel from cheapest sources, for example, gas generators as against coal-powered stations. However, market-determined fuel-procurement policies have devastating consequences for the coal industry. Similarly, the failure of the government to sell nuclear-powered stations and the requirement that a nuclear levy be imposed on the rest of the electricity industry revealed the extent of the implicit subsidy of nuclear power.

The main failure of the UK privatization programme was to identify sufficiently precisely the areas where natural monopolies existed, to separate those from the remainder of the industry and to introduce competition elsewhere. One of the most striking examples of this was British Gas. Despite the possibilities for competition mentioned above, British Gas was sold as a single integrated company. Its subsequent performance has been disappointing and the Monopolies and Mergers Commission has recommended a fundamental restructuring of the industry.

The extent to which competition was introduced into the electricity industry was limited by the government's preoccupation with the nuclear stations. It was thought that the successful disposal of the nuclear stations required the retention of sufficiently large generating stations to be able to absorb the costs and risks of operating nuclear generators. In the event, as mentioned above, the government was unable to dispose of the nuclear stations and it was forced to leave them in public ownership. However, by the time that this was decided it was too late to split up the generating companies and two generating companies were privatized. This has left the market for electricity in England and Wales seriously distorted by the presence of a duopoly, and an uneven duopoly at that.

Even where it has not been possible to introduce direct competition, privatization has allowed surrogate competition to be established in the form of yardstick competition. The ten water and sewerage companies have regional monopolies. Competition is administered by the regulator that undertakes comparisons between their performance. Efficiency levels in terms of inputs, unit costs, and quality of services are compared and, in principle, prices can be set on the basis of lowest costs and highest standards of provision. Similar comparisons are made of the twelve Regional Electricity Companies. In practice, both costs and quality of services are heavily influenced by local factors that differ across regions. For example, delivery of water and disposal of sewage are affected by density of population, access to water sources and sewage outlets, the age and quality of infrastructure, etc. Attempts have been made to control for these factors by estimating cost and production functions.

However, there are two few observations and too many factors to estimate such functions with a high degree of precision. To date, the degree
of yardstick competition has been limited. There is therefore a marked
difference between areas in which privatization has allowed competition
to be introduced into at least a segment of an industry and areas where
this has not been possible. Yardstick competition is a poor substitute for
actual competition. The information conveyed by share prices is valuable but the ability to restructure industries into competitive units is
unquestionably the greatest potential benefit of privatization.

2.3 Control

One of the most important questions raised by privatization was the
extent to which it would reduce control by government over 'essential'
public services. The answer to that is not yet clear. While it is true that
the day-to-day involvement in the running of firms has been significantly reduced, periodic interventions to undertake substantial restructurings of industries are likely. These have already occurred in telecoms
with amendments to the licence to permit freer entry. Major restructuring of British Gas to break up the monopoly created at the time of privatization has been proposed by the Monopolies and Mergers
Commission. Similarly, restructuring of the electricity industry seems
inevitable at some stage to introduce greater competition into electricity
generation. Thus where serious structural mistakes were made at privatization, government intervention is almost inevitable. This reinforces
the importance of ensuring that correct structures are established before
privatization.

Control by trade unions has also been weakened. The large-scale
shedding of labour in electricity would have been inconceivable under
the old Central Electricity Generating Board without considerable dis-
ruption and serious strikes. There have been very few disputes despite
substantial reductions in labour in many of the privatized firms.

Control has been transferred from the public to the private sector.
However, as mentioned above this is not exerted in the form of threats
of take-over or bankruptcy; nor has it for the most part come from direct
investor intervention. UK financial institutions are noted for their pas-
sivity in monitoring and managing their investments. There are good
reasons for this: their portfolios of investments are widely diversified
across a large number of companies. They have little incentive to manage any one company since most of the benefits accrue to other
investors. In most privatized firms, management has therefore been
given a free rein. As noted above, they have improved incentives to perform efficiently; however there is little direct external control exerted by
investors. External control does, however, come from another source.

While privatization has reduced the direct involvement of the government, this has in large part been transferred to the regulator. Privatization has conferred considerable powers on regulators to control the activities of privatized firms. The activities and powers of regulators are broadly defined. They were granted a high degree of discretion in evaluating the performance of firms, in setting prices, and imposing obligations to supply services on firms. Regulators have been more active monitors and controllers of privatized firms than the capital markets.

In effect then privatized companies have come to view one of their main objectives as minimizing interventions by the regulator. Most privatized companies have established regulatory departments, whose primary objective is to deter interference from the regulator and ensure that best possible outcomes can be negotiated with the regulator. A large industry of 'regulatory games' has therefore emerged in which firms evaluate the objectives of the regulator and optimize their behaviour conditional on the assumed response function of the regulator. The amount of management time that is devoted to 'fighting' the regulator has been a serious cost of privatization. The area in which this is most clearly seen is in relation to investment. Obligations to supply impose investment requirements on firms. As noted above, obligations to supply were not, and could not have been, clearly specified at the time of privatization. Required capital expenditures have therefore at least in part been at the discretion of regulators. The question that then arises is what return should firms be allowed to earn for these investments. As the accompanying volume on regulation describes, the determination of rates of return is complicated by the system of price regulation that has been introduced. Rates of return are unspecified and subject to considerable negotiation.

Disputes between regulators and privatized companies can be taken to the Monopolies Commission. Ultimate jurisdiction over the behaviour of regulated utilities lies with the Secretary of State. This is a formal and cumbersome system of arbitration and thus far the Monopolies and Mergers Commission has been called upon only once to act in this capacity. The system of regulation that the UK has established has introduced too much conflict between regulator and firm. It is costly and introduces too much uncertainty.

What has been the overall effect of privatization? There is little doubt that the efficiency of firms that began the 1980s in public ownership has improved considerably. Profits generally rose in the years following privatization and investors have earned substantial returns over and above those on the stock-market as a whole. However, where firms enjoy monopoly power, profits are not a good guide to efficiency: profits can rise because monopolies are exploited. Productivity measures such as labour productivity (output per employee) and total factor productivity (output per representative unit of capital, labour, and other inputs) rose sharply when measured against the same firms' performance during the 1970s. Labour productivity significantly outstrips total-factor productivity growth, highlighting the success of the control over trade unions: efficiency improved by substituting more productive capital for less productive labour. This is confirmed by a fall in employment in most of the utilities and, in firms like BT where there has been a rapid growth, by a relative reduction in the work-force. Prices are another indicator of efficiency. During the 1980s, prices charged to residential customers fell by 0.4 per cent per year in air transport, rose by 1.5 per cent per year in British Gas, and by 0.2 per cent in electricity, and were unchanged in BT. In each case this represents a decline in real terms.

On the face of it, this is an impressive performance. However, many of the most significant improvements in total-factor productivity in the monopoly utilities took place before privatization. They resulted from the imposition of hard budget constraints by the government, clear commercial goals, performance pay, and decentralized and accountable management. Privatization had little effect. Indeed in some cases, notably British Steel and British Airways, it was these improvements that actually made privatization possible. Similarly, changes in pay and employment can be traced back to events that preceded privatization, in particular to a series of costly and lengthy industrial disputes that may well have not been endured by the management of a private-sector firm.

3. CONCLUSIONS

This introduction has identified three main effects of privatization: finance, information, and control. On finance, the article has concluded that privatization has had only modest effects. The same shift in burden of financing between consumers and investors could have been achieved by raising consumer prices under public ownership. The capital markets have not been a primary source of external finance and wider share ownership has not altered the structure of capital markets in any substantial way. In regard to information, greater transparency has been argued to be an important benefit of privatization. The association of performance with identifiable corporate entities is an important source of incentive. Share prices do provide information on performance that is relevant in setting incentives.

It has been argued that one of the most important aspects of privatization is the separation of those aspects of corporate activities that have public-good elements associated with them from those that do not. The UK privatization programme has not always been as successful at doing this as it should have been and there have been several missed opportunities to introduce competition. Even so there are a number of areas in which competition has been successfully introduced. Yardstick competition has been harder to operate than was anticipated. As a consequence, surrogate competition is little substitute for the real thing. Even so, regulators have probably exerted more of an influence over corporate performance than the capital markets. The free rider problems in information collection in financial markets are serious and neither take-over nor bankruptcy provide effective sanctions over corporate performance.

On control, there clearly has been a weakening of control exerted by the government. However, the failure to establish appropriate industrial structures at the outset has meant that periodic government intervention to restructure has been and will continue to be necessary. Fundamental changes of this sort are difficult to achieve after privatization and introduce considerable uncertainty into corporate activities. Uncertainty has also been created by the adversarial relation between regulator and firm. Regulators have considerable discretion in the way in which they affect corporate activities. Investment in particular is harmed by this 'regulatory uncertainty'.

Privatization has contributed to the rebalancing of control between trade unions and management. In the absence of tight external control by capital markets, control over privatized companies essentially lies with management. Weakening of trade union power has allowed management to achieve remarkable reductions in employment without provoking disruptive industrial disputes.

In summary, even if the UK privatization programme can be faulted in many respects, it has identified the way in which privatizations can be successfully achieved. In questioning the extent to which the public control over corporate activities is warranted, it is likely to have enduring effects.

The articles in this volume reflect a mixture of aims: historical record, analysis of what has happened, and suggestions about what might—and should—be done in the future. It begins with a piece by Michael Beesley and Stephen Littlechild that first appeared in 1983, but is included here without 'updating', both because of its substantial impact on the shape of many subsequent privatizations and the continuing relevance of its ideas. Likewise, the survey of economic literature on the theory of privatization, by Simon Domberger and John Piggott (Chapter 2) and the study by Simon Domberger, Shirley Meadowcroft, and David Thompson, of the effects of competitive tendering on local authority refuse collection (Chapter 8), were first published in 1986.

1

Privatization: Principles, Problems, and Priorities

MICHAEL BEESLEY* AND STEPHEN LITTLECHILD†

1. INTRODUCTION

What principles should guide a further programme of privatization? What kinds of problems will be encountered, and where should the priorities lie? Economists have not written much on these issues. We hope to provide an explicit structure in which relevant questions can be identified and answered.

'Privatization' is generally used to mean the formation of a Companies Act company and the subsequent sale of at least 50 per cent of the shares to private shareholders. However, the underlying idea is to improve industry performance by increasing the role of market forces. Many other measures can contribute to this, notably freeing of entry to an industry, encouraging competition, and permitting joint ventures. Market forces can also be increased by restructuring the nationalized industry, to create several successor companies which may be publicly owned. To secure maximum benefits, a whole set of measures must be designed for each industry, including privatization as a key element.

In this paper we seek criteria to decide:

- whether a particular nationalized industry is a serious candidate for privatization;
- how the industry should be structured and the regulatory environment designed;
- what the priorities should be for privatization among the industries.

2. CRITERIA FOR PRIVATIZATION

It is helpful to structure the problem as a cost–benefit analysis. In principle, one might examine the effects of each alternative privatization

* Professor of Economics at the London Business School.
† Director-General of Offer.

This article was first published in *Lloyds Bank Review*, July 1983; it was written before the 9 June 1983 General Election was announced. Reprinted by permission of the authors.

proposal on different interest groups such as existing and potential customers, taxpayers, suppliers of labour and capital, etc. Trade-offs between these interest groups could be established and decisions made accordingly.

We propose to short-circuit this procedure somewhat by specifying a single criterion, namely the present value of aggregate net benefits to UK consumers. This is measured primarily by lower prices of currently available goods and services (offset by any price increases). Effects on the level of output, the quality and variety of goods and services available, and the rate of innovation will also be important. Typically, there will be release of resources, benefiting the consumer in other ways. Changes in the distribution of benefits (e.g. by geographical area) and effects on employees, suppliers, exports, and taxpayers must also be considered. None the less, the criterion of aggregate net benefit to consumers seems a simple and appropriate starting point. Unless this promises to be considerable, the political costs of change will scarcely be worth incurring. (Public opinion on privatization is probably changing. Political 'costs' may prove significantly less than they once appeared.)

We do not assume that privatization is desirable in itself. Respectable arguments support such a view—for example, that political freedom depends on private property, or that government intervention should be minimized, because the larger the government sector, the larger the threat to liberty. Here, privatization is strictly an economic instrument. Privatization in certain industries (or parts thereof) could be ruled out as simply not beneficial to consumers.

Our criterion excludes the stock-market value of the successor company or companies. This value could clearly be artificially increased (e.g. by granting a monopoly or announcing lesser restrictions on entry), but this would be counterproductive to consumers. Similarly, the (alleged) poor proceeds of sale, realized or in prospect, should not in themselves deter privatization. The right sale price is simply that which investors are prepared to pay, once conditions and timing of sale have been determined by the criterion of consumer benefit.

Though it should not influence the decision to privatize, the sale value is not unimportant. The proceeds are the price at which the present owners of the company's assets (viz. the taxpayers) transfer these assets to the future owners (viz. the shareholders). The method of flotation should aim to minimize over- or under-subscription. There is no merit in making a gift to 'stags' or imposing losses on underwriters. The difficulties of estimating future stock-market prices are great, as witness Amersham, Britoil, and Associated British Ports. There is therefore a strong case for supplementing professional advice by the organization of some form of futures market, e.g. by distributing to customers limited quantities of shares to be traded in advance of the main flotation.

The criterion of benefit to consumers should be used to design the privatization scheme as a whole. Consider some of the things to be decided in order to write prospectuses for floating one or more successor companies:

- the number of companies, the assets and liabilities of each, and their intended aims and scope of business;
- the structure of the industry in which the company (or companies) will operate, especially the conditions of new entry;
- the regulatory environment, including competition policy, efficiency audits, controls (if any) on prices or profits;
- non-commercial obligations (e.g. with respect to employment, prices, or provision of services) and sources of funding for these obligations (e.g. direct subsidies from government or local authorities);
- the timing of the privatization scheme, including the flotation date and the times at which new competition is allowed and/or regulation instituted;
- future levels of government shareholding, and ways in which the associated voting power will be used.

Potential investors will translate this package, which is designed to maximize benefits to consumers, into a stock-market price. Successful flotation requires an accurate forecast of this price, and a limited futures market in the shares can help.

3. BENEFITS AND COSTS

Our criterion involves benefits for two sets of consumers: actual or potential consumers of the industry; and other consumers, who benefit from savings in resources which may accompany privatization. Thus, if lower subsidies are paid, other consumers will benefit via lower taxation. Subsidies represent real resources which could be consumed elsewhere.

Privatization will generate benefits for consumers because privately owned companies have a greater incentive to produce goods and services in the quantity and variety which consumers prefer. Companies which succeed in discovering and meeting consumer needs make profits and grow; the less successful wither and die. The discipline of the capital market accentuates this process: access to additional resources for growth depends on previously demonstrated ability. Selling a nationalized industry substitutes market discipline for public influence. Resources tend to be used as consumers dictate, rather than according to the wishes of government, which must necessarily reflect short-term political pressures and problems of managing the public sector's overall demands for capital.[1]

But gains are not all one way. Privatization is intended to change motivations of management towards profit-making. A privately owned company will have greater incentive to exploit monopoly power commercially. To the extent that this is not limited, consumer benefits from privatization will be less than they might be. Second, a privatized company will be less willing to provide uneconomic services. The resources so released will be used more productively, but particular sets of consumers will lose by the change. This raises the question of how such losses, often thought of as social obligations, should be handled. Third, eliminating inefficient production and restrictive labour practices means the release of resources. This will benefit taxpayers and consumers outside the industry, but some employees and suppliers will suffer. The short-cut criterion does not explicitly recognize these losers. Ways of coping with these three problems are discussed below.

Some have argued that ownership is largely irrelevant. But could the benefits of privatization be obtained without the change in ownership? We have already argued that ownership *does* matter because consumers in general will be better served. Also, for political reasons, privatization may be a necessary accompaniment to competition. The additional liberalization of entry into telecommunications announced in February 1983 would not have been politically feasible if the transfer of British Telecom to private ownership had not by then been in process. Furthermore, competition policy is (or certainly could be) more effective against a private company than against a nationalized industry.

Alternative ways of increasing market pressures are politically limited. The benefits of privatization derive partly from the ability to diversify and redeploy assets, unconstrained by nationalization statutes. These statutes might be relaxed without transferring ownership, but rival firms and taxpayers fearing government-subsidized competition or uncontrolled expansion would undoubtedly oppose this. Again, efficiency might increase if governments refrained from intervening in the industries, but as long as the industries are nationalized, such self-restraint is implausible. The industries might be asked to act commercially, but nationalization itself delays inevitable adjustments to market forces. The substantial reductions in overmanning in BA and the nationalized manufacturing industries could surely not have been achieved if the intention to privatize had not already been expressed.

Nationalized industries were deemed appropriate vehicles for a wide variety of social policies. But most consumers' interests were adversely

---

[1] To support this argument, there is growing empirical evidence, mainly from the USA, that privately owned companies make more efficient use of labour, capital, and other resources, and are also more innovative. See, for example, De Alessi (1974*b* and 1980).

affected, and nationalization often proved inadequate for the social purposes too. It is now necessary to reform the industries while meeting social needs. This is always a politically difficult exercise, and impossible with nationalization. Privatization properly designed makes it possible to decouple the two tasks, and to focus social policy more effectively.

4. COMPETITION

Competition is the most important mechanism for maximizing consumer benefits, and for limiting monopoly power. Its essence is rivalry and freedom to enter a market. What counts is the existence of competitive threats, from potential as well as existing competitors. The aim is not so-called 'perfect' competition; rather, one looks for some practical means to introduce or increase rivalry. The relevant comparison for policy is between the level of competition that could realistically be created, and the present state of the nationalized industry.

Certain features of nationalization need attention whatever the ownership form finally adopted. The artificial restrictions on entry embodied in the statutory monopolies granted to most of the earlier nationalized industries should be removed. Government-controlled resources (e.g. wayleaves and radio spectrum; airspace, routes, and landing rights; harbour facilities; mineral rights on land and sea; etc.) should be made equally available to new entrants, without favouring the incumbent nationalized concerns.

The starting structure for the successor private company or companies is extremely important. In some cases, different parts of the industry could compete if formed into horizontally separate companies. Resources or assets could be transferred to potential entrants. Vertically separating the industry into different companies would also generate rivalry at the interface. If, for example, British Telecom's International division were separated from the Inland division, each would encourage alternative sources of supply (including self-supply).

Splitting up an organization might involve sacrificing economies of scale or scope. Increased costs of production or transacting may offset the gains from increased competition. This argument is dubious for present nationalized industries, since they have been determined largely by political or administrative, not market, forces. However, in the absence of competition, one cannot know in advance precisely what industry structure will prove most efficient. Therefore, as far as possible, the future growth of the industry should not be fixed by the pattern established at flotation. Companies should be allowed to expand or contract, diversify or specialize, as market forces dictate. Where there are very few existing outside competitors, or none at all, the starting structure should be designed to create effective competition. When in doubt, smaller rather than larger successor companies should be created, and allowed to merge thereafter, subject to rules of competition policy discussed below.

5. REGULATION AND COMPETITION POLICY

Even the introduction of such competition as is feasible may still leave the incumbent with significant monopoly power in some industries. How should this be dealt with? Government will no longer have the direct and indirect control associated with nationalization, but alternative means of influencing or regulating conduct are available (besides the promotion of competition).

One favourite idea is to influence the successor company's prices by limiting the profits earned, expressed as a rate of return on capital. The USA has had much experience of this; the result has generally been higher rather than lower prices. Some defects are well-known: disincentives to efficiency, a 'cost-plus' mentality, and expensive enforcement. Other defects are gradually becoming better understood: the vulnerability to 'capture' of the regulatory commission by the regulated industry, and the associated tendency to limit competition among incumbents and to restrict new entry. In fact, US regulation embodies a philosophy similar to nationalization, with similar effects. Rate-of-return regulation should not be thought of as a relevant accompaniment to privatization.

There is considerable pressure for efficiency audits or value for money audits, on the grounds that monopoly industries will have inadequate incentive to increase efficiency. Without sanctions for non-compliance, such audits are likely to be ineffective. However, if they are used for setting tariffs and controlling investment plans, the system essentially amounts to rate-of-return regulation, itself defective for the reasons just indicated. Pressure of competition and the firms' own incentive not to waste resources are likely to be more effective inducements to efficiency than the creation of a government 'nanny'.

Another possibility is to limit prices directly by means of explicit tariff restrictions. For example, it is proposed that the price of a bundle of telecommunications services should not increase by more than X percentage points below the retail price index (the RPI–X formula) for a period of five years. This could be applied to any set of services, perhaps weighted as in the bills of a representative consumer. The level of X would, in practice, be the outcome of bargaining between BT and the Government; an exhaustive costing exercise is not called for.

The purpose of such a constraint is to reassure customers of monopoly services that their situation will not get worse under privatization. It 'holds the fort' until competition arrives, and is inappropriate if competition is not expected to emerge. It is a temporary safeguard, not a permanent method of control. The one-off nature of the restriction is precisely what preserves the firm's incentive to be efficient, because the firm keeps any gains beyond the specified level. Repeated 'cost-plus' audits would destroy this incentive and, moreover, encourage 'nannyish' attitudes towards the industry.

A preferable alternative to detailed regulation of costs, profits, or prices is greater reliance on competition policy. Predatory competition should be discouraged, both to curb monopoly power and to allow new ownership structures to emerge after privatization. In the UK at present, potential anti-competitive practices have to be considered in turn by the Office of Fair Trading, the Monopolies and Mergers Commission, and the Secretary of State. In the case of hitherto nationalized industries a stronger and speedier policy is required. The main aim should be to protect existing and potential competitors likely to be at a disadvantage when competing with a dominant incumbent, who in the past has generally had the advantage of statutory protection, and who even now probably has significant legal and other advantages (e.g. rights of way). Certain practices (e.g. price discrimination, refusal to supply, full-line forcing) should be explicitly prohibited if they are used by the dominant incumbent to eliminate or discipline specific competitors. Parties adversely affected should be able to sue in the Courts, perhaps for triple damages.

The 1983 Bill privatizing British Telecom exhibits some awareness of the problem. Present monopoly control has been supplemented by an Office of Telecommunications, and BT's licence will require published tariffs and prohibit predatory price discrimination. However, encouraging future entry and reliance on competition policy instead of regulation have yet to be as firmly established as would be desirable.

6. NON-COMMERCIAL OBLIGATIONS

Nationalized industries provide various services which are uneconomic at present prices and costs. Not all are necessarily uneconomic and some could be made viable by a private company or companies operating with increased efficiency. However, there will also be attempts to raise certain prices and/or reduce certain services. Since a main aim of privatization is to guide resources to the most highly valued uses, the companies should not be prevented from doing so. Nevertheless, it may well be felt socially desirable or politically necessary to ensure that certain prices or services are maintained (e.g. in rural areas).

Procedures for establishing non-commercial obligations need to be clearly specified. Each privatization act should define which services are potentially of social concern. Any company claiming that such a service is uneconomic should be required to provide relevant financial data to support its case, accompanied by a request to withdraw unless a subsidy is provided. A specified public body (e.g. a local authority) will then consider whether the case is plausible, whether another operator is willing to provide the service, and whether a subsidy should be provided.

Where should this subsidy come from? One of the prime aims of nationalization was to facilitate cross-subsidies from more profitable services. However, cross-subsidization largely hides the extent of the subsidy and opens the door to political pressures. Also, it inevitably entails restrictions on competition so as to protect the source of funds: cross-subsidization and unrestricted competition are mutually incompatible. For these reasons, economists have long recommended that explicit public subsidies should be provided in preference to cross-subsidies.

What if the government is unwilling to do this? Explicit subsidies have admittedly not proved politically popular to date. Other possibilities have to be explored. In telecommunications it is currently envisaged that BT will charge an access fee to other networks; this will be used to finance emergency services, call-boxes, and certain loss-making services in rural areas. This amounts to a tax on telecom operators to support particular socially sanctioned outputs. So long as the scope of these 'social' services is narrowly defined, stringent tests of loss-making are applied, and the access fee is applied to all relevant operators, the tax will remain low and competition should not be seriously damaged. Such compromises may well have to be worked out for many cases of privatization in which protection of particular consumers is deemed important. They will reduce total net benefits to consumers; but political realities have to be faced. Unless safeguards are provided for adversely affected interest groups, privatization itself could well be jeopardized. Once again, the design of the privatization scheme is crucial.

Privatization is often opposed on the grounds that it leads to unemployment. But even state-owned firms cannot in practice finance overmanning over long periods. Large-scale redundancies have already occurred in those which have failed to match international competitors' efficiency. Where the effects of privatization promise to be severe generous redundancy payments should be made. However, remaining employees' prospects will be brighter in privatized industries, which have a superior ability to adapt, diversify, and grow.

7. PRIORITIES

We have argued that a nationalized industry should be privatized if the net benefits to consumers from doing so are positive. Many industries will meet this criterion, yet it would be impossible to privatize all of them at once, it only because of the constraints imposed by the parliamentary timetable. Which industries should then be given priority? Leaving aside political considerations, our criterion indicates those industries where the consumer benefits of privatization are greatest. How can this be determined?

First, other things being equal, a larger industry offers larger potential scope for savings. That is, if costs and prices can be reduced by an average of x per cent, an industry with a turnover of £2 billion offers twice the potential benefit of an industry with a turnover of £1 billion. Table 1.1 lists the nationalized industries in order of turnover. It shows that the largest three industries (electricity, telecommunications, and gas)

TABLE 1.1. Nationalized industries,[a] year 1981/2

	Turnover (£m.)	Capital employed (CCA basis) (£m.)	Work-force ('000s)	Percentage change in work-force since 1979/80
Electricity industry[b]	8,057	32,605	147	−8
British Telecom	5,708	16,099	246	+2
British Gas	5,235	10,955	105	0
National Coal Board	4,727	5,891	279	−5
British Steel	3,443	2,502	104	−38
BL	3,072	1,521	83[c]	−31
British Rail	2,899[d]	2,746	277	−7
Post Office[e]	2,636	1,347	183	0
British Airways	2,241	1,338	43[f]	−24
Rolls-Royce	1,493	992	45	−23
British Shipbuilders	1,026	655	67	−18
S. Scotland Electricity Board	716	2,817	13	−5
National Bus Company	618	508	53	−16
British Airports Authority	277	852	7	−7
N. Scotland Hydro-Electric	270	1,981	4	−3
Civil Aviation Authority	206	162	7	−2
Scottish Transport Group	152	157	11	−17
British Waterways Board	16	50	3	−2
TOTAL	42,792	83,178	1,627	

[a] These are the organizations classed as nationalized industries in the public enterprise division of the Treasury, as reflected in HM Treasury (1983), with the addition of BL and Rolls-Royce.

[b] Including CEGB, Council and Area Boards. Figures for CEGB alone are £6,364m., £23,357m., 55,000, −11 per cent.

[c] UK only; overseas approximately 22,000.

[d] Including government contract payments £810m.

[e] Including Giro and postal orders.

[f] Reportedly 37,500 as at March 1983.

account for nearly half the total turnover in the nationalized sector. At the other end of the list, there is relatively little to be gained by privatizing the smallest seven industries, whatever percentage gains each one could generate, since together they account for less than 6 per cent of total turnover in the nationalized sector. Of course, other things are *not* equal, and the industries offer significantly different scope for generating benefits, as we show in a moment. None the less, the criterion of size must be constantly borne in mind. For example, to match a 1 per cent saving in capital employment in the electricity industry, it would be necessary to achieve a saving of 2 per cent in telecoms, 5 per cent in coal, 13 per cent in steel, or 24 per cent in posts.

Second, industries will offer less scope for savings if they have already been subject to severe remedial action, and more scope if they are as yet relatively untouched. The last column of Table 1.1 shows the percentage changes in manpower over the last two years. By this criterion, the 'manufacturing' nationalized industries (British Steel, BL, Rolls-Royce, British Shipbuilders), plus British Airways and the bus companies probably have relatively small further savings to offer compared to the other industries, particularly since press reports suggest that yet more redundancies are already in train.

Third, benefits to consumers are likely to be greater in so far as competition rather than monopoly is likely to predominate. Competition could come from multiple ownership in the same industry, from abroad, or from rival products. However, in order to ascertain which industries, or parts of industries, are susceptible to competition it is necessary to examine more closely the demand and cost conditions under which the industries are likely to operate.

These ideas may be clarified by conceiving of each nationalized industry as located in a simple two-by-two matrix. Demand prospects for typical services and products are classified as Good or Bad, depending on long-term trends, and supply prospects are classed as conducive to Single or Multiple (competing) ownership depending on developments in technology. This of course over-simplifies the situation, but the contrasts between the industries are great enough for the divisions to be useful.

Figure 1.1 shows our own conjectures as to the quadrant in which each industry would be located *if appropriately privatized*. These are not necessarily the same quadrants as the one in which the industries would currently be placed. As we shall shortly argue, privatization may well be necessary in order to shift an industry from an 'inferior' quadrant to a 'better' one, i.e. to one which offers greater benefits to consumers (and, often, to employees also). In some cases, too, it is appropriate to place different parts of an industry into different quadrants (e.g. electricity production and distribution). We now consider each quadrant in turn—for convenience, in the order D, C, A, B.

DEMAND PROSPECTS

		Good	Bad
SUPPLY PROSPECTS	*Single*	A Electricity distribution (Areas Boards and Grid) Telecoms (local) Gas distribution Airports	B Rail Post (or possibly C?) Waterways
	Multiple	C CEGB (excl. Grid) Telecoms (excl. local) Gas production Coal British Airways	D Steel BL Rolls-Royce Shipbuilding Buses

FIG. 1.1. Classification of nationalized industries post-privatization.

(i) Quadrant D

Industries in this quadrant need present no problems of monopoly power, since multiple ownership is quite feasible within the UK. Moreover, the manufacturing industries among them—British Steel, BL, British Shipbuilders, and Rolls-Royce—are already subject to international competition, which secures prices as low as can be expected, given the current excess capacity on a world scale. Operating efficiency—or lack of it—in the UK industries is a relatively minor factor in determining prices. Labour monopoly power has surely been much reduced. There may be expansion as the depression ends, but there will probably be increasing competition from superior sources abroad, so these industries are always likely to occupy quadrant D. Thus, consumers in these manufacturing industries will gain little *directly* from privatization.

Consumers will, however, gain indirectly from privatization, notably as taxpayers. Private owners will be more willing and able than the government to identify and rectify inefficiencies and to exploit new opportunities. Privatization will reduce the liability to losses and free resources for better use elsewhere. It should not be deferred merely to get the industries 'into the black', by further subsidies, so that a 'respectable' flotation price can be achieved.

Of all the nationalized industries, bus operations are least suited to the scale of operations which nationalization implies. Nevertheless, the prospective gains are greater from encouraging competition than from privatization. An important element of NBC is long-distance traffic. Here deregulation occurred in 1980, leading to increased competition, better service, and lower prices. Further gains would follow from removing further obstacles to competition (e.g. by facilitating access to favourable terminal locations). In urban areas—the principal short-distance markets—quite different conditions prevail. The incumbent operators are owned by local authorities, and to a much lesser extent by NBC, and entry is still toughly regulated. Here, there would be a large gain from deregulation, not least in the redistribution of bus resources towards the more favourable routes. Methods of subsidy should also be changed to stimulate competition so as to promote efficiency among all kinds of operators (e.g. by shifting subsidies to users, not paying them to producers).

In sum, privatization of the manufacturing industries in quadrant D will yield positive but small net benefits to consumers, so a high priority is not indicated. In the bus industry, preference should be given to facilitating competition where it is at present restricted.

(ii) Quadrant C

Industries in this quadrant are characterized by good long-term demand prospects. They happen to be very large, and (with the exception of British Airways and British Telecom) are relatively untouched as yet, so they presumably offer considerable scope for improvements in efficiency. They need present no significant problems of monopoly power, because multiple ownership is viable. Thus they are prime candidates for privatization.

Interestingly, however, none of the industries is organized as if it were in quadrant C at present. The CEGB and British Telecom are each a single organization (though Mercury should begin to offer a challenge to the latter). The NCB is a single organization whose prospects in the absence of privatization are somewhat dim. British Airways is part of a multi-ownership industry, but again its prospects without privatization are unclear. Currently, these industries would probably be put in quadrants A, B, and D respectively. Privatizing them involves recognizing that, wholly or partly, they could belong to quadrant C, and that benefits for both consumers and employees can be secured without generating severe problems of monopoly power. However, careful attention needs to be given to their structure after privatization.

In the case of the CEGB, the national grid should remain in public ownership for the present, perhaps as a common carrier. (It might be integrated with the Department of Energy.) The generating stations should be sold to separate buyers, so as to establish competition in production. Firms would be allowed to bid for a group of stations (and coal-mines) so as to achieve economies of integration, but sufficient independent entities would be created to make competition workable.

Privatization of the British coal industry would follow a similar pattern. Consumers would benefit directly from the lower prices due to competition, including the removal of restrictions on imports. The prospects for the British coal industry itself would also be greatly improved. There are currently very dramatic differences in costs between different pits. Resources of capital and labour would be reallocated so that the more efficient pits—which would command the highest prices on privatization—would expand. There would also be benefits from a severe reduction in the monopoly power of labour. The relatively low capital–labour ratio (£21,000 capital employed per man in 1981/2) could profitably be increased. Because long-term trends in demand are favourable to coal (particularly when synthetic fuels become viable), and because Britain has many favourably placed locations for coal-mining, the industry could once again become an expanding one. Employment could then increase in the British coal industry as a whole. In practice, privatization seems necessary to secure these benefits. Of the pits which are presently extra-marginal, some would become viable as a result of more efficient management. Widespread closure of the least efficient pits would necessitate a generous policy to cope with social adjustment. As noted earlier, a merit of privatization is that it divorces the problem of industrial development from that of discharging society's debts arising from the past.

The 1983 Bill enabling the privatization of British Telecom does not envisage the restructuring of British Telecom. The present analysis would indicate the creation of several successor companies. Local distribution (which we place in Quadrant A) presents the chief monopoly problem. The Bill does explicitly recognize the need for developments in competition policy to prevent the exploitation of a dominant position, and the Government has concurrently announced limited measures to facilitate competition from new entry, though more could be done. Overall, most of the industry is prospectively in quadrant C.

The British Gas Corporation is already subject to competition in the discovery and extraction of gas. It has hitherto held a favoured position as sole buyer; this has recently been discontinued. Competition and efficiency would be further increased if some of the extremely valuable existing contracts were auctioned to new entrants, if the production side of the Corporation were completely separated from the national grid and local distribution, and if restrictions on gas exports were removed. Whether privatization of gas production would create direct as well as indirect benefits for consumers is not clear.

No special steps are necessary to achieve a competitive market structure for British Airways, though fewer restrictions on routes and allocation of airport landing slots on a more competitive basis would facilitate competition. However, as with the manufacturing industries, it is not clear that the further gains to consumers from privatizing BA would be substantial. Thus, in quadrant C, the prime candidates are the CEGB, British Telecom, and the NCB.

(iii) Quadrant A

The industries in this quadrant are characterized by good demand prospects but the supply prospects do not favour multiple competing ownership. Local distribution systems for electricity, gas, and telephones are characterized by high sunk costs. With the possible exception of telephones, they do not face much immediate technological challenge, and will be sustainable as local monopolies. Consumers are therefore at risk.

Cannot the market process be used even if successor entities are sustainable monopolies? Some have argued for auctioning franchises to private bidders, thereby encouraging competition for the monopoly privileges. Franchising would transfer the value of the inherent monopoly power to the seller—in this case the government. This benefits the tax-payer, but does little to help the consumer. There are practical snags, too, in awarding the franchise to the bidder offering the lowest price to consumers, as witness experience in the US with franchising cable TV. It is difficult to specify in advance the appropriate pattern and quality of output, and the costs of negotiating and monitoring contracts are substantial. Furthermore, it is difficult to sell a franchise on the premiss of sustainable (natural) monopoly alone. Bidders will usually demand statutory monopoly privileges, which will create formal exemption from risks of entry and engender a position from which to exact further concessions from governments. Though the franchising option is not ruled out, it needs far more analytic attention before positive recommendations can be made.

This does not mean that nothing can be done to generate benefits for consumers in these industries. Restrictions on new entry can be removed, so as to pare down the monopoly to a minimum. This has recently been done for gas and electricity, but entry into local telephone networks (e.g. by cable TV companies) is still highly restricted. Dividing utility distribution systems into regionally independent units would create market pressures on supplies of factors of production, not least in providing alternative opportunities for hiring and rewarding management talent, and would facilitate competition on the production side. Between airports, there is some, but not much, scope for direct competition for customers. It would be quite feasible, and beneficial, to organize the more important airports as separate entities.

To summarize, privatizing the industries in quadrant A will pose problems in curbing monopoly power. It would be more fruitful to encourage competition by removing restrictions on entry and restructuring the industries, even if the successor companies remain as nationalized, municipal, or other public bodies.

(iv) Quadrant B

The industries in this quadrant have declining demand prospects while their supply conditions favour a single organisation. Monopoly power may be a problem in some services, but it is generally not severe because the reason for the decline in demand is the emergence of substitutes preferred by consumers. Nationalization was seen as a means of resisting decline: it led to continued injections of new capital and the financing of losses. The aim of privatization would be to facilitate the movement of resources out of these industries and/or use existing resources more fully by developing new products and services. However, social and political problems will accompany the withdrawal of services. Privatization schemes will need to be designed with careful thought to non-commercial obligations.

As far as rail operations are concerned, British Rail would remain in quadrant B after privatization. These operations are not easily divisible below reasonably-sized and geographically separate sectors, such as the old regions. No one is likely to want, or to be able, to emulate such successor railway supply companies, so their monopolies will be technically sustainable. However, demand is adverse, and will increasingly be so. This particular combination of circumstances BR shares with British Waterways. But BR is marked off from the other nationalized industries by the exceptionally high alternative use value of its assets. Its territory is immense, and in many parts very valuable indeed. Privatization here would indeed be called an asset-stripper's paradise, not just for selling land, but for all the myriad deals which can be constructed, based on locational advantage.

In the case of a declining industry of high alternative use value, asset-stripping is very much in the general consumer's interest. However, railways are perhaps the most politically sensitive of all the nationalized industries. Wholesale withdrawal of services would not be politically acceptable. A practical compromise therefore presents itself. Successor companies could be floated which, in return for command over assets, would have to bind themselves to a minimum programme of rail output. This output would be heavily passenger-oriented and would, in effect, be financed by profits from other activities. Because of privatization, the required output would be achieved in a much more economical way than at present, thereby freeing up many stations, marshalling yards, and miles of track. The alternative use value of these assets is so great that a quite considerable passenger output could be insisted upon. The Serpell Report thought it necessary to curtail the rail network severely in order to achieve financial viability. With the present approach, a much higher rail output could be attained. Thus privatization would open up social solutions not possible under nationalization.

Demand for postal services is probably decreasing, partly because of more direct competition from telecommunications. However, there are attractive market possibilities in new forms of collaboration with new techniques. In fact, though most would now place the Post Office in quadrant D, there are opportunities for its eventual emergence in quadrant C. Mainly because it is so labour-intensive—capital employed is the lowest of all Table 1.1's industries at £7,360 per man—there is considerable scope for labour substitution and redeployment. The basic distribution network has great potential for development outside traditional Post Office work. A useful form of privatization would be a successor national company, or several regional companies, which essentially would franchise the local operations to individual small groups. One could therefore expect not only an improvement in postal services, but also a willingness to diversify into such services as security and delivery work.

8. CONCLUSIONS

Privatization is not merely a matter of selling shares in a nationalized industry. The underlying intent is to improve industry performance by increasing the role of market forces. To achieve this, other devices for promoting competition must also be adopted. Each act of privatization must be part of a whole scheme tailored to the particular conditions of each industry.

The following general considerations should guide policy:

- Privatization schemes should be designed to maximize net consumer benefits, measured primarily by lower prices and improved quality of service, rather than stock-market proceeds. A futures market for shares would facilitate floatation.
- The promotion of competition—by removing artificial restrictions on entry, making resources equally available to potential entrants, and restructuring the existing industries—is the most effective means of maximizing consumer benefits and curbing monopoly power.

- Stricter competition policy is preferable to rate-of-return regulation, efficiency audits, and related forms of government 'nannying'.
- Clear ground rules should be laid down concerning the criteria for providing uneconomic services and the sources of finance for these.
- Compensation should be paid for serious transitional unemployment, though in the longer run employees' prospects will be enhanced by privatization.
- Priority should be given to privatizing those industries where consumer benefits are likely to be greatest. Potential benefits will depend upon the size of the industry, whether it has already received attention, and whether competition rather than monopoly is likely to ensue.

The scope for privatization is substantially greater than is commonly believed. Consumers would benefit, directly or indirectly, from appropriately designed privatization schemes in industries covering over four-fifths of the presently nationalized sector. In the remaining industries, notably buses, airports, and local distribution of electricity, gas, and telephones, the main benefits would derive from restructuring into smaller units and facilitating new entry.

The announced intention to privatize British Airways and the manufacturing industries has already helped to increase efficiency, and privatization should not be delayed merely to increase the proceeds from flotation. Nevertheless, these industries are no longer first priorities. Greater benefits to consumers would derive from privatizing the Central Electricity Generating Board (excluding the national grid), British Telecom, the National Coal Board, British Rail, and the Post Office. Apart from British Telecom, these industries are seldom thought of as candidates for privatization. However, the bulk of the consumer benefits that can be expected to follow from privatization could be achieved by appropriately designed policies for these five industries alone.

References

De Alessi, L. (1974), 'An economic analysis of government ownership and regulation: theory and evidence from the electric power industry', *Public Choice*, 19, Autumn.
—— (1980), 'The economics of property rights: a review of the evidence', *Research in Law and Economics*, 2.
HM Treasury (1983), *The Government's Expenditure Plans 1983–84 to 1985–86*, Cmnd 8789, London: HMSO.

2

Privatization Policies and Public Enterprise: A Survey

SIMON DOMBERGER* AND JOHN PIGGOTT†

1. INTRODUCTION

In recent times, government policies involving the transfer of assets or activities from the public to the private sector have become prominent in the policy debate. 'Privatization', as this process has come to be called, is inevitably associated with the desire for 'smaller' government, and is thus a politically charged term. There is, however, a growing body of analytic and empirical research which explores privatization from a more or less dispassionate perspective, and which is already providing insights into the economic impacts of the process.

This survey aims to present a systematic treatment of this literature, which can be thought of as comprising the economic analysis of privatization. The term 'privatization' is on occasion used to describe almost any attempt to improve public-sector performance. We have deliberately chosen to keep our task tractable by restricting our analysis of privatization to policies designed to improve the operating efficiency of public-sector enterprises through increased exposure to competitive market forces. We do not address the broader issues of public-sector provision of merit and other goods or services (for example health or education) nor do we consider in detail hiving off and contracting out policies within the public sector generally. We also wish to distinguish privatization from US-style deregulation which applies essentially to enterprises wholly owned by the private sector. There is inevitably some arbitrariness in these dividing lines and other studies may cover different ground.[1] We believe, however, that our delineation of the topic permits

* Professor at the Graduate School of Business, University of Sydney.
† Department of Economics, University of New South Wales.

This survey has been prepared for the *Economic Record* following discussion with the Survey Editor. It was written while Simon Domberger was visiting the University of Sydney, and first published in 1986. We would like to thank Robert Fraser for his enthusiastic and able research assistance, and David Hensher and Austin Holmes for comments on an earlier draft. The usual disclaimer applies.

[1] The most authoritative international contribution is Kay and Thompson (1986), whose

a unified approach to be developed, while at the same time permitting analysis of the most important and relevant privatization possibilities.[2]

Limiting our survey in this way makes it natural to begin in Section 2 with a critical discussion of the economics of public enterprise. This provides an analytic context for subsequent discussion and introduces some concepts used later. Sections 3 and 4 compare the economic performance of public and private enterprises from both analytic and empirical perspectives, and identify the sources of possible gains in performance from privatization. Section 5 discusses issues surrounding the revenue gains from privatization while Section 6 examines alternative instruments of privatization and explores their implications. Section 7 draws some lessons from this analysis for Australia by means of an illustrative example, while Section 8 offers some concluding remarks.

2. THE TRADITIONAL ECONOMIC ANALYSIS OF PUBLIC ENTERPRISE

The traditional approach to the economic analysis of public-enterprise pricing and investment policy has a welfare economics orientation, and in particular is concerned with the issue of allocative efficiency. An allocation is said to be efficient if the existing resources in the economy cannot be reallocated without making somebody worse off even when lump-sum transfers are feasible. Necessary conditions for an efficient allocation include the well-known marginal equivalences consistent with a competitive equilibrium—for present purposes the most important of these is that output be priced at the marginal cost of production.[3] In a market economy, the assumption is conventionally made that competitive forces will generate a pattern of resource use which approximates an efficient allocation; this scenario provides a rationale for

focus is similar to ours. Legrand and Robinson (1983) include a number of papers on the privatization of welfare services. An early paper which influenced the UK policy debate is that of Beesley and Littlechild (1983). Survey-type contributions with an Australian orientation are currently being prepared by Forsyth and by Hensher. A bibliography on privatization has recently been released by the Research Service, State Library of NSW.

[2] Australia has a large number of public trading enterprises (pte's). We calculate that in 1976–7 the net capital stocks of pte's represented 35.2 per cent of Australia's non-dwelling capital stock (derived from Australian Bureau of Statistics, 1981, Table 29). In 1980–1 pte's accounted for 15.8 per cent of Australia's wages salaries and supplements (derived from *Australian National Accounts, National Income and Expenditure*, 1983–4, Tables 22 and 24). A list of Commonwealth pte's can be found in the ABS publication *Commonwealth Government Finance, Australia 1981–82*, ABS Cat. no. 5502.0, 2–3. State and local pte's are listed in *State and Local Government Finance—Australia 1981–82*, ABS Cat. no. 5504.0, 2–5. More recent listings are not available apparently because of changes to the Census and Statistics Act which makes release of such information a breach of its confidentiality provisions.

[3] These are spelled out in many standard microeconomics texts, for example Layard and Walters (1978: ch. 1).

central authority intervention when, in certain circumstances, the competitive market mechanism 'fails'.

Two important circumstances in which the market will fail in its allocative role are when increasing returns to scale exist in the production of particular commodities (electricity distribution is an example) and when externalities such as congestion exist (e.g. urban transport). In the first of these cases, the resulting 'natural monopoly' has been thought to induce profit-maximizing output prices set above marginal cost.[4] In the case of externalities, the marginal social benefit from mass-transport utilization exceeds the marginal private benefit, since the resulting reduction in congestion benefits all commuters. To put it another way, the marginal social cost of mass transport is less than the marginal resource cost alone because of the positive externality which flows from its use. In this case, the private market could be competitive but the private marginal-cost pricing which would follow takes no account of the positive externality, and the resulting allocation is therefore not efficient.

There have been two broad policy responses to these kinds of market failure. The first is the regulation of private monopoly: this is common in the US. The second is to resort to public production, a policy more commonly used in the UK, continental Europe, and Australia. We shall be concerned with the economic implications of this latter policy.

At first sight, public ownership of industry appears a straightforward solution to the allocation problem where industry technology or output is associated with market failure. The firm in question will be directed by the government, through its officials, to mimic the behaviour of a competitive firm, after making allowance for external effects.[5] In the simplest of worlds where all else in the economy is consistent with allocative efficiency, this would ensure that the allocative blemish associated with the market failure is eliminated. This appealing scenario has provided a strong economic rationale for public production, or nationalization.[6]

In practice, however, the public production experiment has been controversial and certainly less than completely successful. There are a number of reasons for this. First, as the assumptions outlined above are relaxed to give some realism to the public production model, optimizing

---

[4] This received wisdom has recently been challenged by the 'contestability' literature. We return to this issue in Section 6.

[5] The simplest rules might be the choice of cost-minimizing production techniques, with their implications for investment behaviour, and output prices set equal to marginal social cost.

[6] It should be noted that nationalization policy has been defended on other grounds as well, including in-kind redistribution (e.g. cheap power to the poor) and a political desire to acquire national ownership of the 'commanding heights' of the economy (e.g. motor vehicles). Rees (1984: 2) provides a comprehensive list.

rules become more and more complicated. It is by no means straightforward to provide a public enterprise with directives which will lead to allocative efficiency. Many of these complications are examples of 'second best' problems, which arise when some institutional or other constraint prevents the attainment of an efficient allocation through standard government interventions.[7] The absence of clear and simple economic principles for public production policy has in our view tended to contribute to the difficulties which surround the operation and direction of public enterprises.

A second and, in the present context, more central consideration relates to the nature of objectives, incentives, and constraints that confront public-trading enterprises. The nationalization of an industry necessarily isolates it from competitive market pressures. In the output market it is a monopolistic supplier of its product(s), and frequently enjoys protection from international competition as well. In the capital market, take-over is impossible, so management faces no threat of job loss from private entrepreneurship. Furthermore, bankruptcy is impossible, at least while the government is prepared to support the enterprise, so that labour employed by the enterprise can negotiate without fear of job loss through the firm going out of business. The absence of the competitive market pressure which applies through various channels to private enterprises can lead to inefficiencies of operation which are costly to the economy as a whole. In addition, the existence of public enterprises provides an irresistible temptation to governments to use public production to serve non-commercial objectives such as regional employment policy, and government procurement and other protectionist policies.

3. PUBLIC VS. PRIVATE ENTERPRISE: OBJECTIVES, INCENTIVES, AND CONSTRAINTS

The theoretical case for public ownership has traditionally rested on considerations of allocative efficiency—that is with the properties of resource allocation in the economy as a whole. In contrast, the case for private ownership rests on the incentives and constraints that the

---

[7] General rules concerning the determination of Ramsey (optimal second best) prices are not available except under very restrictive assumptions, even in the simple cases which we have so far explored. Rees (1984), for example, devotes close to half his text on Public Enterprise to issues related to the second best. Further complications result from considerations of uncertainty (Rees 1982), alternative financial constraints (Marchand *et al.* 1982), and uncorrected externalities (Rees 1984: 139 ff.). About the only generalization of significance is the proof by Diamond and Mirrlees (1971) that in a wide class of cases, productive efficiency (that is, cost-minimizing behaviour by public enterprises taking market prices of inputs) is optimal, provided an optimal set of taxes otherwise prevails.

market provides to promote efficiency within the firm. This type of efficiency, which is known as 'technical' or 'productive' efficiency, is synonymous with cost minimization for a given level of output. The traditional approach to public-enterprise economics has tacitly assumed that productive efficiency will be satisfied irrespective of the conditions of ownership or competition. Whether this assumption actually holds in practice is of crucial importance for two reasons. First, allocative efficiency will automatically be violated in the absence of productive efficiency. In other words the latter is a necessary condition for the former whereas the converse is not the case.[8] Second, much of the impetus for privatization has come from a perception that public enterprises do not behave in a cost-minimizing manner. We shall now consider whether such behaviour stems from the nature of objectives, incentives, and constraints facing public-sector management and labour.

There are three main reasons why we might expect that public-sector management will not behave in a way which is consistent with cost minimization. First there is the absence of a clear-cut profit objective which is the overriding goal of private enterprise. Profit maximization implies cost minimization and in the absence of the former objective the incentives to pursue the latter will be severely blunted. In these circumstances, and particularly where there is no ultimate sanction on poor performance given that public-enterprise deficits will generally be subsidized by the government, productive efficiency is not something on which the survival of the enterprise depends.

The second problem arises from the fact that public enterprises are often assigned a number of (sometimes conflicting) objectives amongst which cost minimization typically has low priority. More importantly, governments are generally willing and able to direct the management of public enterprises to pursue non-commercial objectives for political reasons.[9] Such political interference is strikingly at odds with the 'benevolent dictator' view of the government which is to be found in the welfare economics literature. It can and does lead public enterprise away from efficient modes of production. Perhaps the best example of such costly intervention is when national governments (notably the UK) induce public enterprises to buy domestically produced capital equipment even though, given free choice, such equipment would not be selected by the management on efficiency grounds.[10]

Finally, the incentives confronting public-sector management are not

---

[8] See Rees (1984: 15–16) for further discussion of this issue.

[9] Some of the more important non-commercial objectives imposed on public enterprises are outlined in Rees 1984.

[10] Pryke (1981: 132) suggests that British Airways' operating costs were significantly higher than they could have been as a consequence of the enforced purchase of domestically produced aircraft. Davis (1984: 80) points out that National Express had committed itself to a comparatively expensive 'buy British' policy.

compatible with the pursuit of efficiency in production since typically neither their earnings nor tenure are directly related to any measure of performance such as profitability. In addition, public-sector unions can be expected to put up stiff opposition whenever new working practices are proposed which, while enhancing efficiency, might also contribute to job losses. Such a stance by public-sector unions has often been supported by governments as a consequence of their political sensitivity to the unemployment issue. Thus, attempts by management to improve public-enterprise efficiency can involve confrontations with both government and the unions. Such attempts are thus incompatible with that ubiquitous managerial objective—the desire for a quiet life.[11,12]

Productive efficiency can be thought of as having two distinct requirements. The first is that the minimum quantity of any input be used to produce a given quantity of output, holding all other input levels fixed. The second is that those inputs be used in a cost-minimizing combination which can only be determined by reference to relative factor prices. In fact it is easily shown that for a given ratio of relative input prices there is a unique ratio of those inputs which is cost minimizing, given conventional assumptions on the production technology.[13]

Public enterprises often fail to fulfil the first of these requirements because of overmanning and over-capitalization in the absence of incentives to economize on inputs. Excessive expenditure on labour within public enterprise may arise because workers are underemployed (overmanning) and also because they are given generous fringe benefits over and above the competitive wage (feather-bedding). The latter effectively represents a redistribution of income from consumers to public-enterprise employees. In situations where the benefits associated with public-sector employment lead to rent-seeking behaviour, however, the value of these benefits will tend to be bid away by workers competing for such jobs, and the redistribution will thus evaporate in wasteful effort.[14] The second element of efficiency implies rapid adjustment of capital–labour ratios to changes in relative factor prices and here again

---

[11] The notion that the desire for a 'quiet life' can be an economic objective was proposed first by J. R. Hicks.

[12] In recent years the UK government has begun to recognize the importance of these incentive problems and has responded by setting the nationalized industries clear-cut financial objectives in an effort to improve productive performance. It is fair to say that these attempts have generally failed, partly because the new financial objectives conflicted with pricing and investment criteria which had been set earlier, and also because the temptation to interfere in the enterprises' activities for political reasons remains as strong as ever.

[13] We assume a strictly convex production technology. For a detailed analysis of the measurement and decomposition of productive efficiency as described above see Farrell 1957.

[14] Rent-seeking behaviour is a source of resource waste, since it uses inputs with a positive opportunity cost, and yields no gain to the economy as a whole.

public enterprises frequently face obstacles to such adjustment, particularly from strong public-sector unions as suggested above.

Advocates of privatization argue that private ownership restores incentives which promote productive efficiency and has a few more advantages besides. The threat of bankruptcy— which may be regarded as the ultimate sanction on inefficiency—is perhaps the most important. Private ownership, at least in principle, frees the enterprise from the prospect of political interference in managerial decision-making, and this must count strongly in its favour. Finally, with private ownership there is a clearly defined objective, namely profitability, and a clearly observable indicator of performance, namely the stock-market or share price. This contrasts sharply with the often confused and conflicting multiple objectives of publicly owned enterprise.

Private enterprise, however, does not always guarantee maximum productive efficiency. Under private ownership, incentives and constraints on managerial behaviour may be blunted by lack of competition in product markets combined with the divorce of ownership from control. The latter is typical of large modern corporations in which ownership is dispersed amongst a multitude of shareholders whilst control of the enterprises rests with a relatively small management group. This raises a potential conflict of interests—often referred to as the principal–agent problem—in that the pursuit of profitabiliity, which maximizes shareholder wealth, does not necessarily maximize managerial utility. Indeed, the empirical evidence suggests that managerial emoluments are more closely correlated with firm size than with profitability (see Scherer 1980: 29–41 for a summary of the evidence). This raises the possibility that management's dedication to the interests of the owners of the firm may be less than complete. Instead, managers may pursue their own objectives and this might involve discretionary expenditures which enhance their utility directly. This aspects of managerial behaviour could be particularly troublesome in circumstances where firms have dominant positions which make them potentially highly profitable and thus where management's discretion in pursuing less than maximum efficiency is greatest. The threat of bankruptcy would be minimal in this case, even if management behaved in a 'satisficing' rather than a profit-maximizing manner.[15]

A potential constraint on such 'managerial slack' is the threat of take-over, which exists under private but not under public ownership. Empirical research conducted in the UK and elsewhere suggests that the threat of company take-over increases as the 'valuation ratio' falls—that is the ratio of the stock-market value of a company to its book or accounting value. The work of Kuehn (1975) and Singh (1975) shows

---

[15] This is well recognized in the industrial economics literature. For a comprehensive discussion of these issues see Scherer 1980: 2.

that the probability of take-over is inversely related to the valuation ratio which implies that the capital market imposes some constraints on managerial behaviour. When shareholders express their dissatisfaction with the company's management by disposing of their holdings this process will, in due course, depress the share price sufficiently to make the company vulnerable to a take-over bid. A successful bid generally leads to a displacement of the existing management who will therefore regard the prospect of a take-over as a potential threat. Thus an efficiently working capital market would appear to provide some discipline on management whose interests diverge from that of the company's owners.

This discipline, however, is not especially rigorous. The empirical relationship described above is neither statistically strong nor independent of firm size. Specifically, the probability of take-over was found to be inversely related to firm size, *ceteris paribus*, which suggests that large firms can sustain a bigger fall in their valuation ratio than their smaller counterparts before they become candidates for take-over. Indeed, some companies may be so large that take-over is extremely unlikely,[16] and in this case capital market discipline would not be effective. This suggests that the case for private ownership is not entirely watertight.

It should also be noted that ownership transfer need not, of itself, generate any gains. Suppose for example that a publicly owned firm is privatized simply by transferring its equity at zero price to the nation's adult population on a per capita basis. If the financial viability of the firm remains guaranteed by the government, the tenure of labour and management remains secure, contracts and working practices are unaffected, and competition is excluded through restrictions on entry, then privatization has not generated any incentives to greater efficiency. Neither are there are revenue receipts: the assets have been transferred without charge rather than sold.

Efficiency gains from privatization arise essentially out of the interaction of product and capital-market pressures. Competition in product markets means that persistent under-performance will ultimately lead to bankruptcy. Competitive capital markets mean that if management is not successful in averting a downward performance trend, it will be displaced through take-over well before the company has reached the point of no return. Thus competition in product markets can be seen as the mechanism through which inefficiency is revealed and the capital market as a mechanism through which efficiency may be restored. For both mechanisms to work privatization must be accompanied by deregulation (or 'liberalization' as it is known in the UK), removing restrictions on entry to promote potential in addition to actual competition. Given

---

[16] This proposition is true in most cases, but it is nevertheless possible for small firms to take over much larger firms.

that capital-market pressures are often weak, as suggested earlier, the role of deregulation is likely to be of crucial importance in the privatization process. Whether competition plays a greater role than ownership in promoting productive efficiency is ultimately an empirical question to which we now turn.

4. PUBLIC VS. PRIVATE ENTERPRISE: EVIDENCE ON PERFORMANCE

Over the last twenty years a large number of studies have attempted to compare public- and private-enterprise performance. While this accumulation of evidence suggests certain tentative conclusions about the relative operating efficiency of private and public enterprise, there is no single study which is entirely compelling in its findings. This is because cost comparisons are rarely straightforward in the absence of a controlled experiment, and no such experiments exist for public enterprise. Among the methodological problems which arise are the difficulties of measuring capital and other costs and of standardizing outputs.

International Evidence

The inconclusive nature of this empirical literature is reflected in the two major international surveys. Borcherding *et al.* (1982), citing more than fifty studies from five countries, report that 'the findings in most of the studies . . . are consistent with the notion that public firms have higher unit cost structures' (p. 134). By contrast, Millward (1982), surveying the North American literature, and therefore analysing a somewhat differentiated sample of studies, finds 'no broad support for private enterprise superiority' (p. 83).

Our reading of the international literature is more in line with that of Borcherding *et al.* than with Millward, though we concede that we have had to rely on the surveys themselves in many cases, since a comprehensive firsthand examination of the international literature is beyond the scope of this paper. Borcherding *et al.* report that out of more than fifty studies surveyed, in only nine does private enterprise fail to outperform public enterprise.[17] A further four studies, examined by Millward but not by Borcherding *et al.*, also report this result.

The surveys agree that the presence or absence of competition may be an important determinant of a firm's economic performance. The studies cited in both surveys support this conclusion. In Table 2.1 we provide a summary of the thirteen studies in the combined survey total which

[17] In their paper, they cite nine studies (excluding a German Ph.D. thesis by Buschmann 1977) but report that only eight studies yield this result.

failed to find superior private-enterprise performance. In our view, the survey authors have judged six of these papers to have employed reliable data and procedures. In all six cases, the public firm faced a competitive market environment. This strongly suggests that opening up a market to competition is crucial in promoting improved economic performance. It provides tentative support for the belief, emphasized by Kay and Thompson (1986), that in at least some cases liberalization without ownership transfer will generate substantial improvements in productive efficiency. This belief is shared by Borcherding *et al.*: they conclude that 'it is not so much the difference in the transferability of ownership but the lack of competition which leads to the often observed less efficient production in public firms' (p. 136).[18]

Broadly, then, the international empirical evidence is consistent with the analytic material presented in Section 3. Alternative interpretations are, however, both possible and plausible. For example, it is frequently argued (by Millward, among others) that observed cost differences between public and private firms may well be due to the 'non-commercial' objectives which public firms are directed to pursue. If this hypothesis is correct, then productive efficiency will be promoted simply by abolishing non-commercial objectives. More specific results would allow us to discriminate between these alternative hypotheses.

One prediction of our earlier analysis was that while samples of public and private firms would both reveal distributions of economic performance, the public distribution would have a longer tail of poor performance. Persistent poor performance in the public sector cannot be eliminated by either take-over or bankruptcy. The absence of capital-market discipline may thus lead to lower average public-sector efficiency, even though many public-sector firms operate as efficiently as those in the private sector. A recent study of private and public electricity-generating firms in the UK in the interwar period (Foreman-Peck and Waterson 1985) provides indirect evidence of such a pattern, which would not be predicted by the 'non-commercial objectives' interpretation of the cost-comparison evidence. Further research along these lines for other industries would be of great value in helping to resolve these issues.

---

[18] Various other findings from the surveyed research are also reported by Borcherding *et al.* Public firms adopt cost-saving devices more slowly, if at all; give managers longer periods of tenure; realize lower and more variable rates of return; price less closely to imputable cost and with less regard to peak-capacity problems; favour voters to non-voters, business to residential users, and organized to non-organized political groups; and systematically over-capitalize.

TABLE 2.1. Summary of international evidence on the effects of competition on the efficiency of public enterprises

Industry	Study; country; (survey author)	Performance measure	Survey author's assessment of methodological approach	Effects of competition
Public provision most efficient				
Electric utilities	Meyer (1975); US; (B. and M.)	Operating costs per unit of output and per customer	Data deficiencies—limited application	Threat of competition improved cost efficiency—weak inference only
Electric utilities	Neuberg (1977); (US); (M.)	Average distribution costs per customer	Results dependent on cost of capital	Not applicable
Electric utilities	Primeaux (1977); US; (M.)	Total costs per unit of output	Reliable	Changed unit-cost curve to upward sloping. Lowered unit costs by approx. 10%
Electric utilities	Yunker (1975); US; (M.,)	Operating costs per customer and per unit of output	Results not statistically significant. Crucial variables neglected	Not applicable
Hospitals	Lindsay (1975, 1976); US; (B.)	Not available	Violation of *ceteris paribus*—difference in quality	Not applicable
Refuse collection	Edwards and Stevens (1978); US; (M.)	Prices	Crucial variables neglected	Not applicable
Refuse collection	Pier, Vernon and Wicks (1974); US; (B. and M.)	Capital and labour costs	Limited data coverage. Serious *ceteris paribus* violations	Not applicable

No difference in efficiency

Insurance sales and servicing	Finsinger (1981); West Germany; (B.)	Cost differences. Rate of return	Reliable	Competitive-environment promoted efficiency
Railroads	Caves and Christensen (1978); Canada; (B. and M.)	Total factor productivity	Reliable	Brisk competition between private/public modes and alternative transport. Inefficiency disappeared with removal of stringent regulations restricting competition
Refuse collection	Collins and Downes (1977); US; (B.)	Cost differences	Important variables neglected	Not applicable
Refuse collection	Hirsch (1965); US; (B.)	Average total collection costs per ton	Important variables neglected	Not applicable
Refuse collection	Savas (1977); US; (B. and M.)	Costs per household and per ton	Reliable	Private/public cost differential removed in time with introduction of competition
Refuse collection	Spann (1977); US; (B.)	Not available	Reliable	Competition promoted efficiency

B = Borcherding *et al.* 1982.
M = Millward 1982.

Australian Evidence

Australian evidence on the comparison of private- and public-sector efficiency is not, on the whole, as comprehensive in its coverage or as ambitious methodologically, as much overseas research. There is one study of the banking sector (Davies 1981) and two studies on buses (Poynton 1985; and Bus and Coach Association of NSW 1985). The one area which has been comprehensively researched is domestic airlines; both Australian and overseas scholars have tried to exploit the unique features of Australia's domestic two-airline policy to draw stronger conclusions than would otherwise be possible. Since the pioneering paper of Davies (1971), there have been at least twelve government and academic studies of comparative economic performance of Australia's two major domestic airlines. These are summarized in Table 2.2, which suggests striking differences in conclusions. Two tentative findings do emerge, however. First, both airlines are much less efficient than 'similar' North American operations.[19] Second, the private enterprise is somewhat more efficient than the public enterprise.

The remaining Australian evidence is sparse. A recent study by the transport consultants Travers Morgan (1985) commissioned by the NSW Bus and Coach Association suggested that private bus services can be provided for half the cost of the municipal bus system: the Urban Transit Authority's buses were found to cost $3.2 per km to operate whereas the figure for private buses was only $1.5 per km. Both private and public bus operators work within a highly regulated environment and do not compete directly with each other. Poynton (1985) reaches similar conclusions.

Davies (1981) compared the economic behaviour of Australia's public- and private-sector banks. He concluded that managers of government-owned banks hold a higher proportion of their banks' assets in low-risk and low-paying investments than do their private counterparts. Government firms, he found, grew more rapidly and had larger staffs, and monitored and organized work and workers less effectively, with resulting lower profit rates.

5. ISSUES RELATING TO REVENUE RECEIPTS FROM PRIVATIZATION

At first sight it may appear that a major economic gain from privatization is the revenue accruing to the government from asset sale. Further reflection suggests that this gain is illusory. If the sale value of the firm to be privatized is equal to the present value of its expected public ownership profit stream, then the public sector has not altered its net worth

[19] This finding is consistent with the international literature on the effects of regulation on performance.

through the privatization process.[20] On this view, real economic gains remain confined to productive efficiency improvements.

This proposition raises two related issues. First, to the extent that improvements in productive efficiency result from the privatization process, the present value of the expected profit stream after privatization will, *ceteris paribus*, be larger than the present value of the profit stream under continued public ownership. The firm's sale price will in some degree reflect these expectations and will be greater than the present value of the anticipated public-ownership profit stream. An increase in the net worth of the public sector will result. This anticipation of superior private-sector performance will not alter the overall gain to the economy from the privatization process. It amounts simply to dividing the gains of privatization between the public and private sectors.

Second, in an economy where lump-sum taxes and transfers are not feasible, an improvement in allocative efficiency[21] may result from the government's increased net worth from the sale of the public enterprise when improved performance is reflected in the firm's sale price. If the government either reduces taxes or reduces its debt issue to compensate for its lump-sum windfall gain from the sale (measured as the difference between the present value of the public-ownership profit stream and the sale value), then it is certainly plausible (though not theoretically necessary) that a reduction in the distortionary cost of taxation can be achieved. In the tax-reduction case, the gain is immediate. In the debt-issue reduction case, the gain will occur through the reduction in taxes that will result from reduced continuing interest payments on the government's debt.

Recent studies have found that the distortionary cost of raising marginal revenue can be as high as 50 cents to $1 per dollar raised, so the quantitative impact of this effect could be substantial.[22]

---

[20] This point has been recognized in the UK policy debate. See, for example, Kay and Thompson 1986.

[21] Strictly, an allocation is either efficient or it is not. The phrase 'improvement in allocative efficiency' is used loosely to refer to a change in aggregate distortionary or welfare costs between two allocations. In applied welfare economics, this idea is very close to the notion of a potential Pareto improvement. We are indebted to Robert Fraser for bringing this point to our attention.

[22] The welfare cost of distortionary taxes has traditionally been regarded as low. In the 1970s there was a received wisdom that, overall, the excess burden from taxation policy in industrialized countries was of the order of 2 per cent of tax collections. In recent years these magnitudes have been revised dramatically upwards. This has occurred partly because of new and higher econometric estimates of labour supply and savings elasticities, and partly because of rising marginal tax rates. But the crucial factor in this changed perception about the importance of excess burdens in tax policy assessment has been a focus on the marginal excess burden of taxes, as opposed to the average or total calculations which characterized the literature on this topic prior to 1976. A number of studies, both Australian and international, now estimate the marginal excess burden of tax revenue to be a substantial fraction of the revenue raised: estimates between 50 cents and $1 for each dollar of revenue raised are not uncommon. References include Findlay and Jones 1983, and Ballard *et al.* 1985.

TABLE 2.2. Summary of evidence on the comparative economic performance of Australia's two major domestic airlines

Study	Performance measure	Finding	Remarks
Albon and Kirby (1983)	Index of cost efficiency	Public/private both efficient	Costs above minimum achievable levels. Regulation causes 'cost padding'. Lack of competition (market entry) causes cost inefficiencies
Davies (1971, 1977)	Labour productivity measures	Private more efficient	Private firm 12–100% more efficient. Public ownership inherently inefficient—'property rights' approach
Department of Transport Domestic Air Transport Policy Review	Various measures	Public/private may both be inefficient	Insufficient information to make firm conclusions about absolute efficiency levels. May, however, be scope for improved efficiency. Recognizes international comparisons not infallible
Hocking (1977)	Physical units of inputs and outputs	Public/private both inefficient. North American firms more labour productive	Costs above minimum achievable levels. Regulation causes cost inefficiency
Forsyth and Hocking (1980)	Labour productivity measures	No difference in public/private performance. US firms markedly more productive	Regulation responsible for similar economic performance. Higher productivity in US associated with more flexible regulation and greater competition
Holcroft Report	Various measures	Public/private both inefficient	Regulated environment 'second best'. Regulation causes cost inefficiencies

Jordon (1981)	Not available	Similar public/private performance. North American firms more efficient	Regulation constrains operators to similar economic performance. Ownership has little effect. Competition associated with more efficient US operations
Kirby (1979)	Social welfare costs	Public/private both inefficient	Regulation of domestic air industry imposes welfare cost on community in the order of 50% of gross industry revenue
Kirby (1984)	Index of cost efficiency	Private marginally more efficient. US operations markedly more efficient	Public firms' operating costs 51% higher. Australian firms' operating costs 55% higher than equivalent US operations before deregulation
Kirby and Albon (1985)	Index of cost efficiency	Private more efficient	Difference in efficiency between public/private firms small in comparison to gross inefficiency in both resulting from regulation
Mackay (1979)	Operating costs per tonne-km and other measures	Private marginally more efficient. North American firms more productive and cost efficient	Regulation forces costs above minimum achievable levels. Recognizes international comparisons not infallible
Millward and Parker (1982)	Productivity	No difference in productivity	

The allocative efficiency gains referred to here will not of course be realized if the present value of the expected privatized profit flow does not exceed the present value of the expected public-ownership profit flow. That is, no allocative efficiency gain from a reduced tax-revenue requirement can be anticipated independently of an expected productive-efficiency gain.

6. ALTERNATIVE INSTRUMENTS OF PRIVATIZATION

Privatization policies can be divided into three broad types: asset transfer from the public to the private sector, generally through sale; deregulation or liberalization of statutory monopolies (with or without asset sales) and with particular emphasis on removal of entry restrictions; and, finally, franchising or contacting out the provision of marketable goods and services to private-sector firms.

Which instrument is to be used depends largely on the designated set of objectives and the type of economic activity under consideration. It is important to note in this context that there is a potentially serious conflict of objectives involved in privatization—specifically between the financial objectives (i.e. the realization of public assets) and efficiency improvements. The value of the public assets to be sold is greatest if the privatized firm retains its monopolistic privileges through statutory restrictions on entry. But in this case the allocative efficiency object will not be met since the private monopoly will be able to set prices at levels above marginal cost. Perhaps more importantly, the absence of product market competition will substantially reduce the pressure to improve productive efficiency. To pursue these arguments further, it is helpful to relate the alternative instruments of privatization to the policy objectives described above by means of Table 2.3.

Asset Sales

Asset sale is the instrument which has been most extensively used to date in the UK government's privatization initiatives. Typically it involves disposals of assets in public-sector firms and natural monopolies such as telecoms with no more than minimal relaxation of statutory protection from competition. Such disposals can be implemented in two ways: through offers for sales of shares at a set price (as was the case in the sale of British Telecom) or through share sale by tender. The main problem with the former method of sale lies in the determination of the share price—typically the shares offered for sale do not have a private counterpart from which inferences could be made about appropriate values. Moreover, the UK experience suggests that the risks of setting

TABLE 2.3. Objectives and instruments of privatization

Instruments	Objectives		Revenue receipts	Remarks
	Allocative efficiency	Productive efficiency		
1.1 Asset Sales (of monopolies)	No	Yes	Yes	Regulatory framework required to control monopoly abuse
1.2 Asset Sales (of companies in competitive product markets)	Yes	Yes	Yes	—
2.1 Deregulation (with asset sales)	Yes: provided market is competitive or contestable	Yes	Yes: but less than in 1.1 if incumbent's dominance is expected to be short-lived	—
2.2 Deregulation (without asset sales)	Yes: provided market is competitive or contestable	Yes: provided trading losses are not under-written by the government	No	—
3.1 Franchising (Chadwick-Demsetz Auction)	Yes: provided bidding is competitive	Yes: subject to contract being incentive compatible	No	Franchising authority required to monitor and enforce contracts
3.2 Franchising (Monopoly Rents Auction)	No	Yes	Yes	

the share price too high, so that underwriters are left with large quantities of unsold shares, are perceived to be greater than the risks of setting the price too low so that the issue is oversubscribed. As a consequence, asset sales at a set price in the UK have typically been associated with significant discounts.[23]

Revenue receipts to the government are guaranteed by the use of this privatization instrument—for example since 1979–80 asset sales by the UK government to the private sector raised £370 million. By the year 1983/4 the figure was £1.1 billion and the 1984 sale of half of the equity in British Telecom is expected to yield close to £4 billion. Any improvements in productive efficiency, however, are conditional on capital market pressures upon the management and its willingness and/or ability to recontract with labour to reduce overmanning and implement 'best practice' techniques of production. The effectiveness of these pressures cannot always be relied upon. In the case of British Telecom, for example, the threat of outright take-over is absent because the UK government retains ownership of 49 per cent of the assets. Hence the controlling management is likely to have considerable discretion in the stance it takes towards greater efficiency.

Where a privatized firm enjoys statutory monopoly status, allocative efficiency will be at risk in the absence of regulatory constraints on monopoly pricing. Privatization of this form, therefore, is likely to be followed by calls for regulatory controls, and it should be anticipated that some regulatory authority will need to be established.[24]

Deregulation

Deregulation (or 'liberalization' as it has come to be known in the UK) places a key role upon the removal of entry restrictions into the market. If the deregulated market is competitive, allocative efficiency gains can be expected. The recent theory of 'contestable markets' put forward by Baumol and his associated (1982) suggests that the removal of entry barriers will ensure socially desirable behaviour even in cases of natural monopoly—provided it can be shown that the monopoly is 'perfectly contestable'. In these circumstances, whenever the incumbent creates profitable opportunities for new entrants by raising prices above costs he becomes vulnerable to 'hit-and-run' entry. Hence, equilibrium in a perfectly contestable market implies that a natural monopolist will be making no more than normal profits. The policy implication of this new

[23] See Kay and Thompson 1986 for details of the extent to which the realized value of the assets sold fell below their post-privatization market value.

[24] In the UK this has in fact happened following the privatization of BT with the creation of OFTEL—the regulatory agency for the UK's telecommunications industry.

theory is that the removal of artificial entry barriers is a more powerful instrument for restraining natural monopoly than regulation.

However, the assumptions which need to be satisfied for perfect contestability are rarely met in practice. A crucial assumption is that entry must be costlessly reversible—that is, the entrant must be able to exit from the market at no cost when it is no longer profitable to remain. It can be shown that for entry to be 'free' in this sense there must be no 'sunk costs'—costs which cannot be eliminated upon cessation of production. Sunk costs are likely to be considerable however, whenever the fixed assets required for the operation are sufficiently specialized to have no alternative use or when there are no secondary markets where they may be realized.[25] Thus the main concern has been with the realism of the assumptions and, more importantly, with the implications for the theory of even minor violations of the assumptions. If the theory's assumptions are not wholly satisfied then contestability cannot be relied upon to secure allocative efficiency.[26]

As regards productive efficiency gains, much depends on whether deregulation is accompanied by asset sales. If it is not, then the possibility that the government will subsidize the losses of the deregulated enterprise could attenuate incentives to minimize costs. As previously outlined, efficient pricing none the less would be secured by actual or potential competition. Finally, revenue receipts to the government following asset sale are likely to be small if investors expect a deregulated enterprise's dominant position to be short lived. But where the incumbent's dominance is expected to be longer lasting, revenue receipts could be substantial and perhaps not much smaller than where deregulation is altogether absent.

Franchising

Franchising involves conferring rights in the supply or distribution of goods or services to a sole producer or operator for a specified period. It was essentially conceived as a mechanism for introducing competition *for* the market where competition *within* the market is neither feasible nor desirable. Natural monopolies would therefore be obvious candidates for franchising.

[25] A good example of sunk costs associated with entry are advertising expenditures which clearly cannot be recovered upon exit. Another important assumption is that entry can occur sufficiently quickly for the incumbent to be unable to reduce his price in time to eliminate its effect. This means that if the incumbent's price is set at a level which renders him vulnerable to entry, he is liable to suffer a catastrophic fall in demand if entry does occur. Hence the incumbent's entry-prevention and long-term survival strategy require that price be set at a level consistent with a normal rate of profit.

[26] For a stinging attack on the theory, see Shepherd (1984) and for a discussion for 'non-robustness' of the theory see Vickers and Yarrow 1985.

The principle was first enunciated by Chadwick (1859) but was promoted as a serious alternative to regulation or nationalization by Demsetz 1968. In a Demsetz auction, competition takes place through bidding for the franchise contract, and the winner is the contestant who bids the minimum supply price—that is, the contractor who undertakes to supply the good or service at the lowest unit price. Provided bidding is competitive, a Chadwick-Demsetz auction will reduce the operator's expected profit to the 'normal' competitive level by inducing bid prices which are equal to unit costs of production. In this way the worst pricing inefficiencies of natural monopoly will be avoided.[27]

An alternative award mechanism involves granting the contract to the producer bidding the highest capital sum for the franchise. Since the award of the franchise confers monopoly rights upon the producer, the values of bids under this scheme are likely to reflect contestants' expectations of the discounted stream of monopoly rents over the life of the contract. This scheme obviously provides revenue receipts to the government by transferring, at least in part, the expected future profits from the franchisee to the franchisor. However, unlike the Chadwick-Demsetz auction, it does so at the expense of allocative efficiency.

Franchising is particularly suitable in circumstances where the government wishes to control the characteristics of the service or product to be provided, or where provision is to be financed through explicit government subsidies. Bus and air transport services are likely candidates, and recent proposals in this context include local buses in the UK and airline services in Australia.

Nevertheless, franchising is not without some difficulties which need to be considered briefly. The first is that bidding must be competitive. Cases of collusive bidding have been recorded in the past (Schmalensee 1979) and this clearly would be a cause for concern. A second difficulty concerns contract specification: franchising is likely to work best for goods or services which can be specified with precision and without ambiguities about the characteristics of supply. A third potential problem is contract duration: identifying the optimal contract length can be difficult and yet may be crucial to the success of the franchise scheme. Finally it must be recognized that franchising requires some regulation: contracts have to be enforced and contractor performance monitored. In principle this involves a minimum of regulation but problems can arise when contractors' performance falls below the specified standard. Space precludes detailed analysis of these issues here (see Domberger 1986, for

---

[27] As an illustration, Demsetz (1968) considers the award of contracts for the supply of vehicle licence plates, the production of which is assumed to be subject to increasing returns. The contract is in force for one year, and is awarded to the producer bidding the lowest unit price. At the end of the contract period a new set of bids is considered and the contract goes to the lowest bidder once again.

further discussion) but it is clear that the success of franchising, as with the other instruments, depends on the way in which it is implemented.

7. PRIVATIZATION IN AUSTRALIA: AN ILLUSTRATIVE EXAMPLE

In recent years a number of studies have been prepared which advocate the privatization of various Australian public-sector activities.[28] All of these contributions recognize some of the advantages and difficulties of privatization but do not in general present a systematic account of the likely economic impacts of alternative privatization options. In this section we briefly examine the economic implications of alternative strategies for privatizing a publicly owned and administered urban bus service in Australia in an attempt to make concrete some of the analytic points of earlier sections. The specific firm to which these instruments will apply will be the NSW Urban Transit Authority which provides metropolitan bus services in the cities of Sydney and Newcastle. UTA is a relatively large firm—in 1983–4 it operated a fleet of 1,694 buses and had 6,227 employees.

In Australia private bus services have co-existed with public-sector operations for over a century. Sectoral-cost comparisons have found private operators to have significantly lower unit costs. This industry therefore would seem to be a potential candidate for privatization. In other States (for example Victoria), private-sector provision of bus service through contracting with the State authorities has been increasing. Moreover, the recent 1984 White Paper in the UK proposed a radical scheme for deregulation of local bus services in which Australian evidence on public/private performance was cited in support of the proposals.

The first privatization possibility would be straight sale of UTA assets—the bus fleet and depots—to the private sector within the existing regulatory environment. This would ensure that the present routes served would continue to be protected from competition. A difficulty with this proposal, however, is that the authority runs at a loss (Bus and

---

[28] These studies emphasize the telecommunications, postal, and electricity industries. A recent Treasury Economic Paper argues for increased private sector activity in the telecommunications and postal industries, but did not advocate asset transfer. Trengrove (1982) provides an analysis of the telecommunications industry in which he focuses on the reasons for monopoly in the industry. Albon (1985a) explores the possibility of establishing a competitive private postal system in Australia, and (1985b) examines cost inefficiencies within Australia Post. Swan (1981) analyses the implications of the lack of accountability of QUANGOS (quasi autonomous government organizations) such as SERV (State Electricity Commission of Victoria) and ELCOM (Electricity Commission of NSW). Other studies include Swan and Nestor (1983), who examine the question of cost inefficiencies in railways in Australia; and Clarke and Porter (1982) who present a general discussion of the advantages and disadvantages of privatization.

Coach Association 1985). For the financial prospects of the enterprise to improve either unit costs must be reduced or prices must rise or both. In the former case the existing labour practices would have to be reformed and one therefore would anticipate stiff opposition to such proposals from the unions involved. (It should be noted the wage levels and super-annuation payments tend to be lower in the private sector.) On the other hand it may be possible for a privatized UTA to make profits with exist-ing levels of manning and wage payments by increasing fares charged to passengers over the entire network. This is likely to generate a hostile response from urban commuters which may make this option politically unacceptable.

If the overriding policy objective is to improve the economic perfor-mance of the UTA, deregulation without transfer of ownership may be considered. In this case the routes would be open to competition from other (private) operators and to the extent that UTA does not operate efficiently, it would lose passengers and revenue to the private opera-tors. If limits were to be imposed on UTA subsidies then these competi-tive pressures would force the UTA to improve its performance or lose market share. However, there are two problems with a deregulation policy of this type. The first relates to the 'cream-skimming' argument: the UTA serves both potentially profitable and loss-making routes. The latter are operated on social grounds to provide services to low density outlying areas and in off-peak periods. If deregulation were to take place the private operator would move in on the profitable routes leaving UTA to service the loss-making ones. If UTA chose to abandon these routes, considerable political opposition would be likely to emerge.

The other problem is that the metropolitan bus industry may not in fact be contestable. If the incumbent UTA has significant advantages over potential entrants, deregulation will not achieve the desired results. A telling illustration of this problem is provided by the liberalization of the express coach industry in the UK. Prior to the 1980 Transport Act, the express coach industry, serving distances of 30 miles or more, was highly regulated: incumbents held monopoly over individual routes and operators seeking entry into these routes had to apply for a licence to the Traffic Commissioners. As might be expected, few such licences were ever granted because the incumbent operator and other interested par-ties (e.g. the railways) usually argued forcefully against new competi-tion. The National Bus Company, through its subsidiary, National Express, held monopoly rights to the largest number of express coach routes in the UK and was the dominant firm in this industry.

Following the 1980 Transport Act all restrictions on express coach ser-vices were removed with the exception of those relating to safety. Any operator, existing or potential, could enter any market segment without requiring a licence to operate a particular route. Since the express coach market was expected to be a perfectly contestable one, it generally was anticipated that new entry would follow closely the deregulation process. This is essentially what took place and entry by new operators was particularly widespread in the profitable inter-city routes such as between London and Manchester. There is little doubt that as a result of competitive pressures brought about by deregulation, the performance of the express coach industry showed a dramatic short-term improvement.

The longer term effects of the policy in this sector are, however, less clear-cut. Many of the early entrants left the industry and today National Express remains the dominant firm. Thus deregulation has had little effect on the structure of the express coach industry and whilst this in itself need not be a cause for concern, there is no evidence to suggest that economies of scale and/or scope are significant in this sector.[29] We therefore would not expect the emergence of a single dominant operator unless it enjoyed some other advantages over potential entrants. It turns out that National Express had one such advantage: the ownership of Victoria Coach station in London. This enabled it to deny its competitors access to the most important coach terminal facility in the capital, the result of which has been to ensure the continuation of National's dominant position and thus to blunt the impact of the deregulation policy.[30]

In situations such as the one described above, franchising may be preferred to deregulation. Two possible franchise schemes could be envisaged. In the first, private bus contractors would be invited to bid for a predetermined set of routes and frequency of service with the contract being awarded to the firm offering the lowest fare price (a Chadwick-Demsetz auction).[31] The alternative scheme would involve the franchising authority setting fares on the basis of social priorities. The bids would be positive or negative depending on whether contractors expected to make profits or losses from running the system as a whole. In this way the contract would be awarded to the operators bidding the maximum (possibly negative) sum for their monopoly rights.

Such franchising schemes would ensure that competition *for* the market is present, and thus that service would be provided efficiently. Subsidy payments would also be minimized. Moreover, public regulation of the level of service and perhaps also fares would not be affected. It should be obvious that the above is only the briefest sketch of the way franchising might proceed and cannot be viewed as a blueprint. Rather,

---

[29] Economies of scope imply that an operator providing a number of services can do so at lower cost per unit than operators providing a single good or service. For a rigorous definition of economies of scope see Baumol *et al.* 1982.

[30] For a detailed discussion of this fascinating case study of deregulation see Davis 1984.

[31] The fact that a multitude of fares may be involved can be overcome by publicizing a bid-price index which would be a franchisor-weighted average of all the relevant fares. For details see Domberger 1986.

it is suggestive of the way in which such a scheme might be formulated.

The discussion in this section does not provide firm conclusions on the most appropriate privatization instrument for the UTA bus system, and should not be interpreted as an argument for privatizing the UTA in any fashion. Rather, our objective has been to indicate the kinds of issues which need to be addressed when privatization is being considered in a specific context.

8. CONCLUSION

This paper has surveyed and analysed the literature relating to the economics of privatization, with special emphasis on public-trading enterprises. On this basis, we offer the following concluding remarks.

Privatization, as defined in this paper, can take place through asset sales, deregulation or liberalization of a protected or regulated market, and franchising. Each of these instruments can be used separately or in combination with others. The best choice of instruments will depend on the industry under consideration and the social objectives that the government is seeking to maximize.

Privatization through asset sale can in some circumstances be worthwhile, yielding a reduction in resource waste in the overall economy. This assessment is consistent with, but not overwhelmingly supported by, the international evidence on comparisons of private- and public-sector performance (Australian evidence is sparse). The waste reduction comes partly from improvements in the operating efficiency of firms following exposure to competitive product and capital-market pressures, including the threats of take-over and bankruptcy. Privatization may also permit a reduction in distortionary taxation and may reduce wasteful rent-seeking behaviour by workers seeking employment in public enterprises offering higher wages than and/or superior fringe benefits to their private counterparts.

Where a public enterprise operates in a highly protected or regulated environment, deregulation or liberalization of the market may generate a substantial improvement in public-sector performance, without ownership transfer. This assessment is strongly supported by the international evidence.

Privatization through asset sale without liberalization is likely to do more harm than good, since the firm will continue to be protected from competition while being relieved of the requirement to follow government directives designed to promote social aims.

Privatization appears particularly prone to exploitation by special interest groups at the expense of genuine gains in overall economic welfare. In particular, liberalization is likely to be resisted by management and labour, since it will threaten tenure and impose more rigorous performance requirements. There is also a conflict between liberalization and a government desire to maximize revenue receipts from asset sale. This is because the firm's sale value will be higher if restrictions on competition remain in force than if they are removed. UK experience suggests that these conflicts can lead to privatization outcomes such as that outlined in the last paragraph.

Where a public enterprise functions to correct a market failure (e.g. monopoly or externality), the anticipated benefits of privatization through asset sale should be set against the distortionary cost which may result from withdrawal of government control.

Franchising is an appropriate mechanism for privatization when the market is inherently monopolistic and/or when the government desires to retain control over output and/or price. Examples of industries where franchising may be appropriate include urban transport and domestic airline services.

This survey has focused on the privatization of public-trading enterprises. This orientation is in line with both the policy debate and the present literature on the subject. It is possible, however, that the privatization of non-traded publicly produced goods and services will yield greater gains. The 'contracting out' of such activities as laundry services for public hospitals, the provision of road transport services to bureaucracy and government, and the cleaning and maintenance of schools may offer considerable potential for cost-cutting. We surmise this because the incentives to efficient operation in non-trading bureaucracies appear to be even weaker than in public-trading enterprises. Research into this topic, however, is at an early stage internationally and is non-existent in Australia.[32] It is in our view a fertile area for further investigation.

References

Albon, R. (1985a), *Private Correspondence*, Centre for Independent Studies, New South Wales, Australia.

—— (1985b), 'The effects of financial targets on the behaviour of monopoly public enterprises', *Australian Economic Papers*, **24**, 54–65.

—— and Kirby, M. G. (1983), 'Cost-padding in profit-regulated firms', *Economic Record*, **59**, 16–27.

---

[32] The recently published proceedings of the Joint Economic Committee (US Congress 1985) offer cost comparisons of a number of activities presently undertaken by the US government, and suggest substantial cost savings would be realized if these were contracted out.

Ballard, C., Shovens, J., and Whalley, J. (1985), 'The welfare cost of distortions in the United States tax system: a general equilibrium approach', *American Economic Review* **75**, 128–39.

Baumol, W. J., Panzar, J. C., and Wiling, R. D. (1982), *Contestable Markets and the Theory of Industry Structure*, New York: Harcourt Brace Jovanovich.

Beesley, M. E., and Littlechild, S. C. (1983), 'Privatization: principles, problems and priorities', *Lloyds Bank Review*, **149**, 1–20.

Borcherding, T. E., Pommerehne, W. W., and Schneider, F. (1982), 'Comparing the efficiency of private and public production: the evidence from five countries', *Zeitschrift fur Nationalokonomie*, suppl. 2, 127–56.

Buschman, H. J. (1977), 'Frei-gemeinnutzige Krankenhauser: Eine Studie ihres Verhaltens mit Hilfe der Theorie des Eigentumsrechte', Ph.D. thesis, University of Konstanz.

Caves, D. W., and Christensen, L. R. (1978), 'The relative efficiency of public and private firms in a competitive environment: the case of Canadian railroads', Social Systems Research Institute, Workshop Series, Oct.

Centre of Policy Studies, Monash University (1982), *Energy Pricing Issues in Victoria: A Report Prepared for the Long-Range Policy Planning Committee of the Victorian Government*, Jan.

Chadwick, E. (1859), 'Research of different principles of legislation and administration in Europe of competition within the field of science', *Journal of the Royal Statistical Society, Series A*, **22**, 381–420.

Clarke, R., and Porter, M. G. (1982), 'State enterprise accountabilty: a contradiction in terms?', in *Quangos: The Problem of Accountability*, Centre of Policy Studies, Monash University, Special Study no. 3.

Collins, J. N., and Dones, B. T. (1977), 'The effect of size on the provision of public services: the case of solid waste collection in smaller cities', *Urban Affairs Quarterly*, **12**, 333–47.

Davies, D. G. (1971), 'The efficiency of public versus private firms: the case of Australia's two airlines', *Journal of Law and Economics*, **14**, 149–65.

—— (1977), 'Property rights and economic efficiency—the Australian airlines revisited', *Journal of Law and Economics*, **20**, 223–6.

—— (1980), 'Property rights and efficiency in a regulated environment: reply', *Economic Record*, **56**, 186–9.

—— (1981), 'Property rights and economic behaviour in private and government enterprises: the case of Australia's banking system', *Research in Law and Economics*, **3**, 111–42.

Davis, E. (1984), 'Express coaching since 1980: liberalisation in practice', *Fiscal Studies*, **5**, 76–86.

Demsetz, H. (1968), 'Why regulate utilities', *Journal of Law and Economics*, **11**, 55–6.

Department of Transport, *Domestic Air Transport Policy Review, Vol. 1: Report*, Canberra: AGPS.

Devine, P. J., Jones, R. M., Lee, N., and Tyson, W. J. (1974), *An Introduction to Industrial Economics*, London: George Allen & Unwin.

Diamond, P. A., and Mirrlees, J. A. (1971), 'Optimal taxation and public production. I: Production efficiency', *American Economic Review*, **LXI**, 8–27.

Domberger, S. (1986), 'Economic regulation through franchise contracts', in

J. Kay, C. Mayer, and D. Thompson (eds.), *Privatization and Regulation: The UK Experience*, Oxford University Press.

Edwards, F. R., and Stevens, B. J. (1978), 'The provision of municipal sanitation services by private firms: an empirical analysis of the efficiency of alternative market structures and institutional arrangements', *Journal of Industrial Economics*, **27**, 133–47.

Farrell, M. J. (1957), 'The measurement of productive efficiency', *Journal of the Royal Statistical Society, Series A*, **120**, 253–66.

Findlay, C. (1985), 'Forces for regulation and deregulation: the case of domestic aviation in Australia', revision of a paper presented to the Conference, *Flights of Fancy: Australian Aviation Policy into the 1980s*, organized by the Centre of Policy Studies, Monash University, 19 June.

Findlay, C., and Forsyth, P. J. (1984), 'Competitiveness in internationally traded services: the case of air transport', ASEAN–Australian Working Papers, no. 10.

—— (1985), 'International trade in airline services', Australian–Japan Research Centre, Research Paper no. 123.

Findlay, C., and R. Jones (1982), 'The marginal cost of Australian income taxation', *Economic Record*, **58**, 253–62.

Finsinger, J. (1981), 'Competition, ownership, and control in markets with imperfect information: the case of the German liability and life insurance markets', International Institute of Management, Berlin, mimeo.

Foreman-Peck, J., and Waterson, M. (1985), 'The comparative efficiency of public and private enterprise in Britain: electricity generation between the World Wars', *Economic Journal*, **95**, suppl. 83–95.

Forsyth, P. (1985), 'The economics of privatization', *CIS Policy Forum*, 10 Dec.

Forsyth, P. J., and Hocking, R. D. (1980), 'Property rights and efficiency in a regulated environment: the case of Australian airlines', *Economic Record*, **56**, 182–5.

Hirsch, W. Z. (1965), 'Cost functions of an urban government service: refuse collection', *Review of Economics and Statistics*, **47**, 87–92.

Hocking, R. D. (1979), 'The economic efficiency of the Australian airlines', App. A6.2 in Department of Transport, *Domestic Air Transport Policy Review, Vol. 2: Appendixes*, Canberra: AGPS.

Jordan, W. A. (1981), 'Performance of North American and Australian airlines: regulation and public enterprise', paper presented at the Conference on Managing Public Enterprises: Purposes and Performance, Vancouver, BC, 14 Aug.

Kay, J. A., and Thompson, D. J. (1986), 'Privatization: a policy in search of a rationale', *Economic Journal*, forthcoming.

Kirby, M. G. (1979), 'An economic assessment of Australia's two-airline policy', *Australian Journal of Management*, **4**, 105–18.

—— (1984), 'Airline economies of "Scale" and Australian domestic air transport policy', Paper 1, in Discussion Paper no. 112, Centre for Economic Policy Research, Australian National University.

—— and Albon, R. P. (1985), 'Property rights, regulation and efficiency: a further comment on Australia's two-airline policy', *Economic Record*, **61**, 535–9.

Kuehn, D. A. (1975), *Take-overs and the Theory of the Firm*, London: Macmillan.

Legrand, J., and Robinson, R. (1983, eds.), *Privatization and the Welfare State*, London: George Allen & Unwin.

Layard, R., and Walters, A. (1978), *Microeconomic Theory*, New York: McGraw Hill.

Lindsay, C. M. (1975), *Veterans Administration Hospitals: An Economic Analysis of Government Enterprise*, Washington, DC.

—— (1976), 'A theory of government enterprise', *Journal of Political Economy*, **87**, 1061–77.

Mackay, K. R. (1979), 'A comparison of the relative efficiency of Australian domestic airlines and foreign airlines', App. A6.1 in Department of Transport, *Domestic Air Transport Policy Review, Vol. 2: Appendixes*, Canberra: AGPS.

Marchand, M., Pestieau, P., and Weymark, J. C. (1982), 'Discount rates for public enterprises in the presence of alternative financial constraints', *Zeitschrift fur Nationalokonomie*, suppl. 2, 27–50.

Meyer, R. A. (1975), 'Publicly owned versus privately owned utilities: a policy choice', *Review of Economics and Statistics*, **57**, 391–9.

Millward, R. (1982), 'The comparative performance of public and private ownership', in E. Roll (ed.), *The Mixed Economy*, London: Macmillan.

Neuberg, L. G. (1977), 'Two issues in the municipal ownership of electric power distribution systems', *Bell Journal of Economics*, **8**, 303–23.

Pier, W. J., Vernon, R. B., and Wicks, J. H. (1974), 'An empirical comparison of government and private production efficiency', *National Tax Journal*, **27**, 653–6.

Pirie, M. (1985), *Dismantling the State: The Theory and Practice of Privatization*, Dallas: National Center for Policy Analysis.

Poynton, P. (1985), 'The urban bus transport industry. A comparison of costs: private vs. public', A.G.S.M., University of New South Wales, mimeo.

Primeaux, W. J. (1977), 'An assessment of X-efficiency gained through competition', *Review of Economics and Statistics*, **59**, 105–13.

Pryke, R. (1981), *The Nationalised Industries: Policies and Performance Since 1968*, Oxford: Martin Robertson.

Rees, R. (1982), 'Some problems in optimal pricing under uncertainty', *Zeitschrift fur Nationalokonomie*, suppl. 2, 63–78.

—— (1984), *Public Enterprise Economics*, London: Weidenfeld & Nicolson.

Report of the Independent Public Inquiry into Domestic Air Fares (1981), vol. 1: Report, Canberra: AGPS.

Savas, E. S. (1977), 'An empirical study of competition in municipal service delivery', *Public Administration Review*, **37**, 717–24.

Scherer, F. M. (1980), *Industrial Market Structure and Economic Performance*, Chicago: Rand McNally.

Schmalensee, L. (1979), *The Control of Natural Monopolies*, Lexington, Mass.: D. C. Heath and Co.

Shepherd, W. (1984), ' "Contestability" vs. Competition', *American Economic Review*, **74**, 572–87.

Singh, A. (1975), 'Take-overs, economic natural selection and the theory of the firm', *Economic Journal*, **85**, 497–515.

Spann, R. M. (1977), 'Public versus private provision of government services', in T. E. Borcherding (ed.), *Budgets and Bureaucrats: The Sources of Government Growth*, Chapel Hill, NC: Duke University Press.

Swan, P. L. (1983), 'The marginal cost of base-load power: an application to Alcoa's Portland smelter', *Economic Record*, **59**, 332–44.

—— (1983), 'The economics of QANGOS: SECV and ELCOM', in *The Economics of Bureaucracy and Statutory Authorities*, Centre for Independent Studies.

—— (1984), 'Real rates of return in electricity supply: New South Wales, Tasmania and Victoria', A.G.S.M. University of New South Wales, mimeo.

—— and Harper, I. R. (1981), 'The welfare gains from bank deregulation', in *Australian Financial System Inquiry. Commissioned Studies and Selected Papers, Part 1* (1982) Macroeconomic Policy: Internal Policy, Canberra: AGPS.

—— and Nestor, J. (1983), 'The railways: haemorrhage of the body politic', *IPA Review*, 64–9.

The Bus and Coach Association (NSW 1985), *The $90m Case for Private Buses*.

Treasury Economic Paper No. 10 (1983), 'Public monopolies: Telecom and Australia Post', submission to the Committees of Inquiry into telecommunications services in Australia and into the monopoly position of the Australian Postal Commission', Canberra: AGPS.

Trengrove, C. D. (1982), *Telecommunications in Australia. Competition or Monopoly?*, Centre of Policy Studies, Monash University, Special Study no. 4.

—— (1984), 'Improving the performance of state enterprises', Centre of Policy Studies in Office of Economic Planning Advisory Council, Discussion Paper 84/07.

US Congress (1984), *Hearings before the Subcommittee on Monetary and Fiscal Policy and Joint Economic Committee*, Ninety-Eighth Congress, Second Session, Part 1, May 1, 2 and 30, 1984, Washington: US Printing Office.

Vickers, J., and Yarrow, G. (1985), *Privatization and the Natural Monopolies*, London: Public Policy Centre.

Yunker, J. A. (1975), 'The economic performance of public and private enterprise: the case of US electric utilities', *Journal of Economics and Business*, **28**, 60–7.

3

Privatization, Restructuring, and Regulatory Reform in Electricity Supply

GEORGE YARROW*

1. INTRODUCTION

The privatization of the British electricity supply industry, accomplished during 1990 and 1991, was the most ambitious exercise in the whole UK privatization programme. Seventeen new private companies were created, significant organizational restructuring occurred, and a whole new regulatory framework was established. Most important, at least in so far as England and Wales are concerned, British public policy abandoned the traditional model of the horizontally and vertically integrated utility (i.e. the franchised-monopoly model), and opted instead for experimentation with an approach based upon competition in both electricity generation and retail supply of electricity.

In themselves, the ownership and institutional reforms associated with privatization neither changed the underlying policy issues nor resolved the fundamental economic trade-offs; rather they provided a different means of attacking the problems facing the industry. With the razzmatazz of stock-market flotation now largely a matter of history, it is perhaps already possible to see old, familiar problems of pricing, investment, and financial returns re-emerging, and to discern the implications of the new market and regulatory structures for the way these problems will now be tackled.

In this paper the focus will be on the likely consequences of the horizontal and vertical restructuring of the industry for competition and for pricing and investment. That is, attention will be directed to questions surrounding the transition from a monopolistic to a more competitive market structure. As a consequence, many other interesting and important issues will be bypassed, of which the most significant is the likely impact of environmental regulation on the industry (see Vickers and Yarrow 1991). A more comprehensive treatment would also take

* Fellow and Tutor in Economics, Hertford College, University of Oxford.

account of the interactions between monopoly and environmental regulation, and of the combined effects of these two types of regulation on pricing and investment. Similarly, the paper will deal only with privatization in England and Wales, since privatization in Scotland was not accompanied by industrial restructuring aimed at introducing competition.[1]

The paper is organized as follows: Section 2 discusses underlying issues of competition and economic efficiency, and the roles of horizontal and vertical reforms within the privatization policy as a whole; Section 3 briefly summarizes some of the main features of electricity privatization in England and Wales, including aspects of the new regulatory framework; Section 4 examines post-privatization competition and performance in the wholesale electricity market, focusing particularly on pricing in the power pool and on new entry into the market; Section 5 assesses initial developments in competition in retail electricity markets; Section 6 is concerned with pricing and investment issues in the naturally monopolistic parts of the industry, namely transmission and distribution, and with the implications of transmission/distribution pricing and investment for competition in generation and supply; finally, Section 7 sets out some concluding thoughts.

2. UNDERLYING ISSUES

The economic activities encompassed by the publicly owned electricity corporations can usefully be divided into four, vertical stages: generation of electricity (wholesale supply), high-voltage transmission, lower-voltage distribution, and retail supply. The 'transportation' activities of transmission and distribution are, in present market conditions and with current technologies, naturally monopolistic. On the other hand, both generation (wholesale supply) and retail supply are potentially competitive activities. For example, it is possible for a trader to be engaged in the activity of purchasing electrical energy in a wholesale market, paying for the use of transmission and distribution wires, and selling electrical energy to final customers such as industrial and commercial companies.

The case for competition in the generation and retail supply of electricity is, then, simply a version of the general economic case for competitive markets. With given cost conditions, competition can be expected

---

[1] Nuclear generating capacity was separated from other generating capacity and allocated to a new, state-owned company, Scottish Nuclear. This exercise, however, was the result of a failure to achieve the government's objective of privatizing nuclear power: it was not a measure aimed at promoting competition.

to lead to higher output and lower profit margins, and since neither activity is naturally monopolistic there is no reason why monopolization should produce substantial, compensating cost advantage (via economies of scale, for example). Indeed, when informational effects and dynamics are taken into account, over time it is competition, rather than monopoly, that is likely to lead to the lower cost base.

2.1 Externalities

There are, however, some complicating factors which arise from the physical nature of electricity supply systems. For example, at a given moment a group of generating companies may be operating at full capacity to meet a given demand, but if, a moment later, there is a signif-icant increase in demand, and if an additional generating set is not made available by some other company, there will be a supply failure. If the market does not clear properly, it collapses. Put another way, there is a very strong interdependence among the production and cost functions of generating companies, leading to economic externalities when rele-vant contracts take simple forms.[2]

Electricity supply systems tend to give rise to both horizontal exter-nalities, such as the one just described, and vertical externalities (see 2.2 below). In both cases, the chosen method of dealing with the problems is usually either internalization or complex contracts, or both. Internalization, in effect, means horizontal and/or vertical integration, and this option corresponds to the traditional 'franchised monopoly' approach to the industry. Contractual approaches to externality prob-lems are represented by 'power pooling' agreements, through which utilities seek to co-ordinate their behaviour.[3]

Since contractual approaches allow for the existence of distinct and independent companies, they also open up the possibility of competition among generating companies. The difficulty, however, is that the atmos-phere required to encourage effective formulation and implementation of, and compliance with, inter-utility agreements to co-ordinate behav-iour is likely to be an atmosphere more conducive to explicit or implicit collusion than to vigorous competition. Ideally, public policy would like to see inter-firm co-operation to counteract externalities associated with electrical disequilibrium, but not inter-firm co-operation to counteract

[2] An example of a 'simple' contract here would be one in which a generator agrees to sell a certain quantity of megawatt hours at some given price per MWh. The point is that the contract makes no reference to the behaviour of other generators, other customers, or any other market participants.

[3] 'The term power pool generally refers to formal and informal agreements among inde-pendent utilities to coordinate some or all of their investment and operating activities. The term incorporates a wide range of cooperative activities and very different degrees of interfirm coordination.' (Joskow and Schmalensee 1983.)

profit externalities associated with failure to reach a joint profit-maximizing price.[4] Consequently, there is a strong tension between 'co-ordination' (co-operation) and competition (Joskow and Schmalensee 1983).

2.2 Vertical factors

While the arguments for increasing competition at those stages of the electricity supply chain where it is feasible (i.e. generation and retail supply) are easy enough to understand, it is much less obvious why *vertical* integration and *vertical* relationships should be important policy issues.

In the context of electricity supply systems, which among other things typically require substantial investment in durable and specific assets such as power-stations and transmission or distribution lines, there are powerful arguments for vertical integration or vertical control through contractual agreements. The interdependences between electricity generation and transmission are particularly strong—for example, the net revenues of a particular power-station may be highly dependent upon whether or not a particular programme of transmission investment is or is not carried out—and the most commonly observed solution to the resulting co-ordination problem is the traditional, vertically integrated generation and transmission (G&T) utility.

General discussions of these vertical externality problems can be found in Williamson (1975), Tirole (1989), and Yarrow (1991), while Joskow and Schmalensee (1983) deal with the issues in the specific context of the electricity supply industry. Summarizing the literature, it can be said that there is no general presumption against vertical integration and vertical control as such. This is because, unlike in the case of horizontal co-ordination, correction of the vertical externalities among firms does not in general impose negative external effects (such as higher prices) on consumers.

It is possible, however, that in a restricted set of circumstances vertical integration and vertical control can have anti-competitive effects that outweigh the benefits from reducing or eliminating the externalities. These anti-competitive effects tend to occur as the result of an extension of market power: a firm with market power at one stage of production may be able to increase its profits by using that power to reduce competition at another stage of production.

In general, vertical integration and vertical control are unlikely to be problematic where there is significant horizontal competition at both

[4] When firms compete they impose negative profit externalities on each other. Collusion can be viewed as a means of overcoming those externalities, but it is a means that has the unfortunate effect of imposing rather larger externalities on consumers.

stages of the supply chain (for then there is no great market power to extend in the first case). However, even where there *is* substantial market power at one stage of production, stage A say, it remains difficult to justify any general presumption against vertical integration or control. The great bulk of the private benefits of the market power may well be available from the company's horizontal dominance of stage A of production, in which case preventing it from operating at stage B, say, will tend to yield little in the way of social benefits from increased competition but might lead to significant inefficiencies via the introduction of externalities.

Given the existence of potentially significant economic externalities when vertical integration and vertical control between generation and transmission are weakened, the case *for* weakening the vertical links must rest on the view that there is some source of substantial, offsetting benefits to be had from greater 'separation'. Yet, at first sight, it can be difficult to see how such an argument can be sustained. The core of the market power in electricity supply systems lies in the naturally monopolistic activities of transmission and distribution. If, therefore, transmission is separated from generation, that market power would be left substantially intact. That is, the reduction in market power achieved by separation would, at best, be relatively small.

2.3 *Regulation*

There is, however, a complicating factor, and that factor is regulation. In an unregulated electricity supply system it is likely that vertical separation between generation and transmission would be highly damaging. The monopolistic transmission entity would have almost as much market power as a combined generation plus transmission utility, and inefficiencies from loss of co-ordination benefits (i.e. the emergence of external effects) could be expected to be significant. On the other hand, once regulation is introduced the picture changes significantly.

Precisely because of the natural monopoly in transmission, public policy will usually seek to regulate transmission activities. Suppose initially that vertical integration between transmission and generation is permitted, but that only transmission rates are regulated. The integrated utility then has very strong incentives to reduce competition in generation, and those incentives have been created by regulatory intervention. Because the utility is prevented from setting high transmission charges and thereby benefiting fully from its monopoly position, it will have incentives to use its control of the transmission system to hinder competitors in generation, thus raising profit in the latter, unregulated activity. Putting this more generally, the firm has incentives to shift profits from regulated to unregulated businesses.

It can be seen, therefore, that the 'vertical problem' in industries such as electricity supply is but one aspect of a more general problem relating to the *scope* of regulated utilities. Transfer of profits from regulated to unregulated businesses of the same company could also occur, for example, where the two businesses make use of common inputs (head offices, corporate advertising, etc.). The businesses could be unrelated in market terms, as when a utility diversifies into activities unconnected with its core activities, in which case the negative economic effects of the profit transfer will tend to show up in inefficiency (e.g. excessive expenditures on certain joint inputs) rather than reductions in competition.

Where regulatory intervention to limit the scope for abusing market power at one stage of a supply chain creates strong incentives for the monopolist in question to seek to transfer profits to a vertically adjacent stage there are three main policy approaches that are available:

(a) Permit vertical integration, allow monopolization of the adjacent stage if this occurs, but regulate (via price controls) *both* stages of the integrated operation.
(b) Permit vertical integration, but regulate the monopolistic stage to prevent discrimination against non-integrated rivals.
(c) Prohibit vertical integration.

Solution (a) is the traditional, regulated, generation plus transmission (G&T) utility approach, familiar in most countries and corresponding to the pre-privatization position in the UK. Solution (b) seeks to 'ring-fence' the monopolistic activity by prohibitions against certain types of discriminatory business practices. Such 'regulated access' has characterized the approaches taken (i) in the telecommunications and gas privatizations in the UK, (ii) in relation to the (naturally monopolistic) distribution and (potentially competitive) supply businesses of the new Regional Electricity Companies (see 3.2 below), and (iii) by the 1992 EC Directive on liberalization of the electricity market (see Section 7).

Solution (c) is the one that has been adopted for generation and transmission activities in the post-privatization electricity supply industry of England and Wales.

3. THE UK REFORMS

Prior to privatization, the publicly owned electricity supply industry in England and Wales was divided into two parts. The Central Electricity Generating Board (CEGB) was responsible for generation and high voltage transmission of electricity, while twelve, regionally based Area Boards were responsible for distributing and selling electricity to final customers. The CEGB therefore had a monopoly over the wholesale market, while the Area Boards had regional monopolies over retail supply. The wholesale monopoly had persisted despite the introduction of the 1983 Energy Act, which had attempted to open the market up to new competitors.

The government's detailed plans for privatizing the industry were first set out in a White Paper published in February 1988 (Department of Energy 1988). Implementation of those plans was completed in 1991, with the exception of the White Paper's proposals for nuclear power. The initial intention to privatize nuclear power was abandoned in 1989 in the face of mounting practical difficulties associated with the anticipated unwillingness of private sector investors to purchase these power-stations, despite substantial subsidies in the form of a 'fossil-fuel levy'.[5,6]

In electricity distribution, government policy followed the structural and organizational conservatism manifested in the earlier privatizations of the telecommunications and gas industries. Thus, the twelve Area Boards were converted into twelve 'Regional Electricity Companies' (RECs) and privatized without further modification: restructuring options such as pre-privatization amalgamation of some Boards or (vertical) separation of distribution from some or all aspects of retail supply were rejected.

Upstream of distribution, however, in generation and transmission, privatization of the electric supply industry was characterized by a much more radical, structural approach. In particular, the CEGB was split both 'horizontally' and 'vertically' as follows.

3.1 Horizontal reforms

Generation assets were passed to three new companies: National Power, PowerGen, and Nuclear Electric. National Power and PowerGen received all the CEGB's fossil-fuel stations (plus a very limited amount of hydro capacity), while all the nuclear power-stations were transferred to Nuclear Electric, which has remained in the state-owned sector. The initial, post-privatization shares of generating capacity held by the three companies are shown in Table 3.1 (and the figures in parentheses show the capacity shares that would have resulted from the implementation of the Government's initial proposals, which called for the allocation of all nuclear stations to National Power).

[5] It is noteworthy that the information revealed by the attempted privatization led to a freeze in new investment in nuclear power (other than in connection with the completion of the Sizewell B station). Whether or not the nuclear programme is eventually resuscitated will depend in large part upon the future course of fossil-fuel prices, (international) progress in the design and construction of nuclear stations, and developments in environmental regulation.

[6] The fossil-fuel levy is a tax on the output of coal, oil, and gas power-stations, the proceeds of which are transferred to the operators of other types of power-stations, most notably nuclear but also including generation from renewable energy sources.

TABLE 3.1. Percentage shares of
generating capacity, 1991

National Power	52	(67)
PowerGen	33	(33)
Nuclear Electric	15	(–)

Source: Privatization prospectuses.

3.2 *Vertical reforms*

The transmission assets of the CEGB were transferred to a fourth new company, the National Grid Company (NGC). NGC is jointly owned by, but operates at arm's length from, the twelve RECs. Thus, the vertical separation (in terms of both ownership and control) of generation and transmission that characterised the state-owned industry was replaced by vertical *integration* (by ownership but *not* by control) of transmission and distribution.

Many of the co-ordination activities previously undertaken internally by the CEGB are now the responsibility of the National Grid Company. For example, NGC is responsible for the dispatch of generating sets,[7] the maintenance of system stability,[8] and the co-ordination of transfers of power across system interconnections (with Scotland and France). The conduct of these activities is governed by general agreements with the generating companies, the RECs, and other participants in the wholesale electricity market.

The RECs were also required by their licences (see 3.3 below) to keep separate accounts for their distribution and supply business. Thus, distribution and supply can be said to have been (vertically) separated in an accounting sense, but not by either ownership or control. To illustrate, whenever a REC uses its own distribution system to supply a customer, the REC's supply business must 'pay' its own distribution business for use of the relevant wires and equipment.

RECs must, however, make their distribution systems available to other suppliers on equivalent (regulated) terms to those upon which they provide services to their own supply businesses. Given entry of rival companies into the retail supply of electricity, therefore, the outcome is *partial*, rather than complete, vertical integration of distribution

---

[7] A power-station may comprise two or more generating units or sets, each of which can be operated independently.

[8] The electric equilibrium of the supply system may break down for one of a number of technical reasons, including a fall in frequency as a result of circumstances in which demand for power is increasing significantly faster than supply of power.

and supply. More specifically, RECs are monopolists in distribution but not in supply.[9]

3.3 Regulatory reforms

The new framework for the regulation of the electricity supply industry was set out in the 1989 Electricity Act which, among other things, established the post of Director General of Electricity Supply (DGES) and a new Office of Electricity Regulation (Offer). To operate in the industry a firm requires one or more of four types of licence: generation, transmission, public electricity supply, and second-tier supply. The first two are self-explanatory; public-supply licences are held by the RECs and authorize the supply of electricity to all premises in a given area; and second-tier licences authorize supply within one or more authorized areas to any premises specified. For example, a company other than a REC may be authorized by a second-tier licence to supply power to any premises in England and Wales with a maximum demand in excess of one megawatt.

The general duties of the DGES, and also of the Secretary of State for Energy, are:

- to secure that all reasonable demands for electricity are satisfied;
- to secure that all licence-holders are able to finance the carrying on of their licensed activities; and
- to promote competition in generation and supply of electricity.

The DGES is also responsible for monitoring compliance with licence conditions—including price controls—and ensuring enforcement. He can issue new licences and can alter existing licence conditions either by agreement with the relevant firms or by obtaining a recommendation for alteration following an investigation by the Monopolies and Mergers Commission (which investigation the DGES can initiate). In these latter respects the legislation and regulations closely follow the precedents set in the telecommunications and gas privatizations.

The general approach to regulation of the industry can be summarized as:

(a) price-cap regulation to prevent abuse of market power in the naturally monopolistic parts of the industry, namely transmission and distribution; and

(b) regulation to promote competition in the other parts of the industry, namely generation and supply.

---

[9] Although RECs have been granted temporary monopoly franchises in respect of supplies to small customers (see 3.3).

Thus, most of the revenues of the National Grid Company are subject to a RPI–X price cap,[10] as are the revenues of the distribution businesses of the RECs (including 'revenues' derived from provision of services to the REC's own supply business). In practice, however, the dichotomy between the two regulatory approaches just described is not quite as clean-cut as this. While supply of electricity is viewed as a potentially competitive area of activity, in the initial post-privatization period it too has in large part been subject to price-cap regulation. Customers with peak demands of less than 10 MW have been defined as 'right-to-tariff' customers. This means that the local REC is required to meet their reasonable demands at published, regulated prices. In this case, the price-control formula is of the $RPI - X + Y$ type, where the Y term reflects the cost to the REC's supply business of 'exogenous' factors such as wholesale electricity costs, transmission charges, and distribution charges. Price controls have, however, been removed completely for customers with maximum demands in excess of 10 MW.

The regulation of prices for tariff customers does not necessarily mean that competition in supply has been written off as a significant factor for all customers other than the largest. Right-to-tariff customers will also be free to seek supplies from sources other than their local REC. It is currently planned that all electricity customers will have this freedom after 31 March 1998. Until 31 March 1994, however, customers with peak demands less than 1 MW will not be free to seek competitive supplies— they can buy only from their local REC—and between 1994 and 1998 customers with peak demands less than 100 kW will continue to be confined to their local REC. Thus, it is intended that monopoly franchises will shrink over time and that the role of competition in electricity supply will gradually be increased.

Further recognition of the potential strength of competitive forces in the supply of electricity is implicit in some of the initial *restrictions* on retail competition that were applied in the run-up to privatization. Specifically, caps were imposed on the shares of the various regional, retail markets that could be captured by the two major generating companies, National Power and PowerGen, in the period up to 1998. These caps provide some protection to the supply businesses of the RECs against competition from major generators who integrate forward into retail supply,[11] and the fact that protection was deemed necessary is an indication of the strengths of the perceived competitive threats.

---

[10] The RPI–X price condition does not, however, apply to NGC connection charges, which cover the costs of equipment *specific* to the connection of individual customers to the high voltage network. These are regulated on a 'reasonable return' basis.

[11] Although there is a somewhat dubious counterargument to the effect that, by preventing monopolization of non-franchised retail markets by National Power and PowerGen, these quotas also have pro-competitive effects.

Like retail supply, the generation and wholesale supply of electricity is not, in itself, a naturally monopolistic activity, but, again like retail supply, it has been subject to explicit regulation. The regulation is not, however, of the price-cap variety: rather it takes the form of the imposition of obligations on companies wishing to participate in the wholesale market. The mechanism for this is the Pooling and Settlements Agreement, to which all the main players must belong.

Under the pooling agreements, generators must submit day-ahead bids to supply power to the system from each of their sets, and, on the basis of this and its information about demand requirements, NGC seeks to dispatch generating sets so as to minimize total supply costs.[12] The offer price of the marginal generating set operating in any half-hour is called the system marginal price (SMP). The pooling agreements specify that generators supplying power to the system will be paid a price per unit (kWh) equal to the system marginal price plus a 'capacity' element.

The capacity element is intended to remunerate capacity held for system-security reasons and is calculated as follows. Each day, and according to agreed procedures, NGC estimates the probability that capacity will, in any period, be insufficient to meet demand. This is called the 'loss of load probability' (LOLP). It is assumed that when load is lost the affected customers suffer a substantial economic loss as a consequence. The 'value of lost load' (VOLL) had been estimated in earlier exercises undertaken by the publicly owned industry and, on the basis of these results, was set at £2 per kWh when the pool was established in 1989. Its level in subsequent years increases with the general price level (i.e. it is indexed).

The price credited to generators for electrical energy supplied to the wholesale market, called the pool input price (PIP),[13] is defined as:

$$PIP = SMP + LOLP\,(VOLL - SMP).$$

It may be noted, however, that the capacity element is paid for all capacity that is declared available, whether or not the relevant sets are called upon to deliver power to the system. Power that is taken out of the pool is purchased at the pool output price (POP), where

$$POP = PIP + uplift.$$

Uplift is an adjustment that is made to cover the costs imposed by transmission constraints,[14] stand-by capacity, and so on.

---

[12] The actual dispatch calculations are quite complex, and, in addition to bid and demand information, need to take account of factors such as transmission-system constraints and requirements for standby capacity to meet sharp demand fluctuations.

[13] Generators are also paid for other services, such as operating on stand-by. These payments are covered by the 'uplift' applied to the pool input price.

[14] For example, when a particular transmission line is operating at capacity it may not be possible to meet increases in demand by dispatching the additional generating set with

The point to be noted about these procedures here is that they are effectively *imposed* by regulation. The regulatory structure may be attempting to mimic the operation of an unregulated spot market—for example, by seeking generators' bids that reflect short-run marginal costs and by setting prices on the basis of those marginal costs—but it would be wrong to regard it as *being* an unregulated spot market. This is most obvious in the capacity element of pool prices, where a key parameter, the value of lost load, is set by regulatory decree.

4. THE WHOLESALE MARKET

Following privatization, much initial public attention was centred on the behaviour of wholesale (pool) prices. Broadly speaking, it is to be expected that pool prices will be positively correlated with volumes of energy produced. As demand rises NGC will need to dispatch generating sets with higher offer prices, and when demand approaches available capacity the probability of lost load and value of lost load calculations will come into play. The capacity element of pool prices can be expected to be particularly volatile: with a value of lost load set at £2 per kWh, the maximum potential pool price per kWh, achieved when the system is at maximum stress, was approximately *eighty* times greater than the average pool price forecast for the immediate post-privatization period (around 2.5p per kWh). Given that minimum prices (in off-peak, low-demand periods) will be significantly below average, it can be seen that the regulatory framework was designed so as to accommodate a price swing (measured as the ratio of maximum to minimum price) of well over one hundred.

Pool prices did indeed show substantial volatility in the post-privatization period, and while the 'highs' inevitably drew complaints, it was perhaps the pattern of the movements, rather than the range of variation, that gave rise to initial concerns about the workings of the new wholesale market. For example, prices rose with demand through the second half of 1990, but then failed to fall back as demand declined in late winter and spring of 1991. There were very high spikes in prices in the late summer of 1991, a period when system demand was relatively low. Indeed, prices during this period were higher than at the demand peak of the previous winter.

The concerns about pool pricing gave rise to a review by the Director General in the autumn of 1991. He concluded that the major generators were, via their bidding strategies, manipulating prices to some extent,

the lowest offer price (since to do so might overload the power line). Where a higher cost set is dispatched instead, the increase in costs can be attributed to the transmission constraint.

and he made recommendations for changes in certain of the procedures set out in the Pooling Agreement. Radical remedies, such as a proposal to split National Power and PowerGen into smaller companies so as to increase competition, were rejected, although the DGES did hold out the prospect of direct regulation of pool prices if there was excessive exploitation of market power.

The post-privatization evidence on pool prices has been used to support the argument that the CEGB should have been split into a larger number of generating companies, say five to ten, before transfer to the private sector. Such proposals were widely advocated in the earlier debate on the best way to privatize the industry (see Henney 1987; Sykes and Robinson 1987). The logic here is clear enough. The pooling system is designed to replicate the properties of a perfectly competitive spot market, so that, for it to function effectively, there needs to be a sufficient number of bidders for each bidder to act (approximately) as a price taker. Privatization did not achieve that: horizontal restructuring was constrained by the attempt, later aborted, to privatize nuclear power. Taking the reasoning one step further, it can be argued that the DGES should now seek to remedy the failure by imposing further divestment of assets.

It is clear that both National Power and PowerGen can significantly manipulate pool prices, either directly via the effects of offer prices on SMP or indirectly through capacity availability declarations on the capacity element of pool prices (for a formal analysis, see Green and Newbery 1991). It does not at all follow from this, however, that simply creating a few more generating companies would produce a competitive market. Pool bidding is a repeated pricing game, played three hundred and sixty-five times a year. Even among otherwise unconnected players this number of repetitions offers considerable scope for the development of 'non-cooperative' collusion (Tirole 1989). Adding in factors such as the pressures toward co-operation when dealing with external effects in the supply system, the common (public sector) background of many of the industry's top personnel, and the spatial segmentation of the market (particularly if transmission and distribution prices are made cost reflective—see Section 6 below), the prospects for creating a fully competitive wholesale spot market are not encouraging.

This negative conclusion about pool pricing should not, however, be interpreted as implying a negative overall verdict on privatization in respect of the objective of promoting competition. In Vickers and Yarrow (1988) it was argued that it would be unwise to assume that effective price competition among incumbent firms could easily be promoted. Rather, it was stressed that the key to increasing competition lay in reducing barriers to entry. The point here was twofold. First, the major performance weakness of the state-owned electricity industry had been its inefficiency in power-station construction. Thus it was an investment deficiency, rather than an operational deficiency, that most required correction. Second, given that generation is not a natural monopoly, with appropriate regulation it should be quite possible to make entry threats effective, notwithstanding the failure of the earlier 1983 Energy Act.

The evidence to date shows that there has indeed been considerable activity on the entry front since privatization. By late summer 1991 there were over twenty plans by new entrants for power projects over 100 MW in size, adding up to a total capacity of over 13,000 MW. By autumn 1991, approximately 8,000 MW of this 'independent' capacity had been classed as committed by NGC (see Table 3.2), representing approximately 13.5 per cent of existing system capacity, and around 50 per cent of planned new capacity.

TABLE 3.2. Percentage shares of new capacity committed for connection to the national grid during 1991–1996, as at autumn 1991[a]

	All capacity	Fossil-fuel capacity
National Power	27.1	30.9
PowerGen[b]	10.4	11.9
Nuclear Electric	7.7	—
Scottish companies	4.6	—
New entrants	50.2	57.2

[a] The National Grid Company designates plant 'committed' upon conclusion of a connection and use-of-system agreement between itself and the generating company. If projects are abandoned thereafter the generators must pay financial compensation to the NGC for any expenditures incurred by the latter as a result of the agreement (e.g. on engineering work to connect plant to the system).

[b] PowerGen's share may be understated because these figures do not include 1350 MW of as yet uncommitted capacity planned for completion in 1995 and 1996.

Source: National Grid Company.

Of course, it will take time for this new capacity to come on stream, and the independents' combined market share will not be substantial for many years to come. But that is not the main point. Developing a perfectly competitive spot market in the pool is a chimera,[15] and in any case the big gains in efficiency lie in improving investment efficiency. Given this, the presence of the independents on such a scale should already be having major effects. Thus, even if National Power and PowerGen engage in substantial programmes of new power-station construction

[15] Virtually all product markets are imperfectly competitive in one way or another.

themselves (in order to prevent a rapid erosion of market share, say) they will be under competitive constraint to keep their capital costs down.

It is too early to make a quantitative assessment of the impact of privatization and competition on power-station construction costs, but it is significant that National Power and PowerGen have been compelled to abandon earlier plans for new coal-fired capacity and, like nearly all the potential new entrants, are now basing their investment programmes on combined-cycle gas turbines (CCGTs). Thus, competition has already led to a major, radical shift in the investment strategies of the incumbent companies.

In seeking to enter the market, new entrants do not appear to have been unduly deterred by relatively low pool prices in 1990 and 1991. One of the pre-privatization reasons for pessimism about the likely efficacy of entry threats had been the fear that National Power and PowerGen could manipulate pool prices to keep them below the price at which new CCGT capacity could earn a normal return on capacity, estimated at around 2.8p per kWh in 1990 prices. Average pool prices were well below this level in 1990—when the generators were still in the public sector— and despite later increases continued to be significantly below it during 1991.

Theory and evidence on this issue are, however, in accord: recognition that today's market prices do not provide a credible means of deterring entry was the starting point of modern theories of entry prevention.[16] Nor is it likely that National Power and PowerGen can credibly threaten a price war following entry. An entrant with a project based upon a take-or-pay contract for gas will have a private marginal cost close to zero in the post-entry period, and will therefore take a lot of driving out! Put another way, the ability to sign long-term contracts gives entrants a potential means of committing themselves in a way that counters threats from incumbents.

There is, however, one potentially negative feature of new entry that has to be weighed in the balance against its positive effects on the efficiency of incumbent generators. One reason why pool prices were low in 1990 and 1991 was the existence of excess capacity in the supply system, which meant that the capacity element of the pool price was low. New entry will, however, add to that excess capacity: in early 1991 NGC projections showed the reserve margin rising from 24.6 per cent in 1991/2 to 36.7 per cent in 1995/6 (see Table 3.3). By the end of 1991, NGC's projections envisaged the reserve margin rising to no less than 51.6 per cent in 1996/7, and even this took no account of an additional 3.7 GW of CCGT capacity committed in the early months of 1992.

---

[16] Signalling theories, in which today's low prices can deter entry by signalling a low-cost base, are probably not very relevant here because generation costs are reasonably well known.

This 'rush to gas' may lead to over-rapid displacement of older, coal-fired plant. That is, once the CCGT stations come on stream, coal-fired plant whose average variable cost is below the average total cost of CCGT plant may be abandoned. Alternatively, given the tendency toward take-or-pay contracts in the gas market, the contractual structure may lead to CCGT stations running at base load when, in opportunity-cost terms, they are displacing more efficient coal-fired plant.[17]

TABLE 3.3. NGC demand and capacity projections, based on data to end-March 1991 (GW)

Year	ACS peak demand	Capacity	Plant margin (%)
1991/2	49.2	61.3	24.6
1992/3	49.6	64.5	30.0
1993/4	50.3	65.7	30.6
1994/5	50.6	69.0	36.4
1995/6	51.0	69.7	36.7

Source: National Grid Company.

Given the record of new entry shown in Table 3.3, it can be asked whether it was the vertical separation of generation and transmission that has been the key ingredient in reducing barriers to entry. Prima facie, there are strong reasons for answering in the affirmative. In particular, when entry into the industry was nominally opened up by the 1983 Energy Act there was, unlike in 1990 and 1991, no rush to move into the industry.

There are, however, a number of other factors that have served to weaken the market power of incumbents and limit their ability to deter entry. Among these factors are:

- A shift, since 1983, in the relative costs of alternative generating technologies—due to developments in technology, fuel prices, and regulatory constraints—in a way that has favoured gas over coal and oil (upon which incumbents had traditionally relied).
- Changing environmental regulation (including expectations of future environmental regulation), which has also tended to favour gas over coal and oil on account of its lesser implications for acid rain and greenhouse gas emissions.
- The establishment of a completely new regulatory regime.

As will be argued below, the third of these appears to be of particular significance.

[17] Note, however, that these points ignore environmental considerations. Thus, accelerated scrapping of coal-fired plant may be desirable on environmental grounds.

5. RETAIL SUPPLY

Like generation (or wholesale supply of electricity), retail supply is not a naturally monopolistic activity, but just as generation had been bundled with transmission in the years before privatization, so retail supply had been bundled with distribution. Each Area Electricity Board was responsible for both distribution and supply in its own region and was therefore a monopolist in both activities.

Unlike generation and transmission, however, distribution and supply were not separated by ownership at the time of privatization. Thus, in terms of the list of three approaches set out in Section 2, in the downstream part of the industry the government chose the second option (regulated access) in preference to the third option (full vertical separation). This difference provides one means of assessing the relative importance of vertical reforms in reducing entry barriers.

Notwithstanding the fact that entrants into retail supply had to purchase a key input, namely the use of distribution wires, from an incumbent distribution monopolist which, initially, was also an incumbent supply monopolist, the penetration of the available market by competitors to the RECs was both substantial and rapid. The major entrants were the generating companies, particularly National Power and PowerGen, so that entry can be viewed here as a form of downstream vertical integration. Table 3.4 indicates both the scale and speed of the advance.

The point to be stressed here is that joint ownership of distribution and supply businesses did *not* enable RECs to so hinder access to their

TABLE 3.4. Percentage market shares of second-tier suppliers,
1 July 1990

Region	Non-franchised market	Total market
Eastern	16.0	3.5
East Midlands	19.2	5.7
London	39.0	7.0
Manweb	49.0	25.0
Midlands	33.0	9.9
Northern	57.0	26.0
Norweb	36.7	10.9
South-East	44.4	8.7
Southern	32.2	6.7
South Wales	71.0	36.0
South-West	62.6	13.6
Yorkshire	42.5	18.7

Source: RECs' privatization prospectuses.

distribution systems that entry into the unregulated parts of their supply businesses was blocked. In this case, therefore, the regulated access route has proved a success, at least when judged in terms of the goal of removing barriers to entry.

Why, then, did the regulated-access approach work for retail supply but not for generation (wholesale supply) in the period following the Energy Act 1983? In my view, the crucial factor was the difference in the regulatory environment. When the Energy Act was placed on the statute book little else in the industry was changed. In particular, nothing was done to ensure that the intentions of the legislation were translated into operational policy. Thus, even when the CEGB altered its tariff structure in ways that were obviously designed to discourage entry, the state-owned enterprise was not prohibited from doing so.

Following privatization the situation has been completely different. There is a formal regulatory structure, based around a Director General of Electricity Supply who is able to operate at arm's length from central government. Not only was the DGES given the power to take measures in the event of anti-competitive conduct by dominant firms, but he was also given the *duty* of promoting competition in the industry. Post-privatization, therefore, new entrants can operate in a regulatory environment where promises that they will be protected against monopolistic abuse carry some degree of credibility. Regulation of the industry has now become a serious and specialist business of its own.

The hypothesis that the change in regulatory framework has had a pivotal effect is supported by the evidence on pool prices presented earlier. In the short term, there is little doubt that, through their bidding strategies, National Power and PowerGen could increase pool prices significantly above current levels, and, as was pointed out earlier, the fact that they have not done so cannot easily be ascribed to the desire to deter entry (because current prices are weak instruments for deterring entry). The generators do, however, have incentives to refrain from monopolistic abuse in that the DGES can credibly threaten actions against them in the event that they operate in unacceptable ways. The threat of price control, contained in the DGES's review of pool pricing in autumn 1991, serves as an illustration of this factor.

Turning from new entry to pricing, it does appear that there have been some downward pressures on prices in the non-franchised market as a result of increased competition in retail supply. A survey of consumers with maximum demands of 1 MW and above, undertaken for the Major Energy Users Council, indicated significant switching of supplier in the year ending 31 March 1991, the first year of operation of the new industrial and regulatory structures (see Table 3.5). The same survey also indicated that the great majority of customers had been able to negotiate significant price reductions (see Table 3.6). The downward

TABLE 3.5. Switching of supplier by large consumers, 1990/1

Percentage of respondents who had:

Transferred entirely to supply from a generator	13.6
Transferred partly to supply from a generator	17.8
Transferred entirely to supply from another REC	3.8
Transferred partly to supply from another REC	17.4
Remained with the local REC	37.6
Switched to pool-related contracts	9.8

Source: Power in Europe 1991.

TABLE 3.6 Price changes for large consumers,
1989/90 to 1990/1

Percentage of respondents who reported:

Reductions greater than 20%	31.3
Reductions between 10% and 20%	44.6
Reductions under 10%	15.7
No material difference	6.6
Increases	1.8

Source: Power in Europe 1991.

TABLE 3.7. Changes in industrial prices since the same quarter
of the previous year

Size of load (GWh/year)	1992 (Q4)	1991 (Q1)	1990 (Q1)
<0.88	+11.9%	+ 2.8%	+13.1%
0.88 – 8.88	+ 2.8%	– 6.1%	+ 5.6%
8.88 – 150	+ 6.2%	–12.8%	+ 5.2%
>150	+14.5%	– 1.0%	+15.8%

Source: Energy Trends 1992.

pressure on prices to industrial users over the same period is confirmed by Department of Energy figures (Table 3.7).

Table 3.7 also indicates that price movements have varied somewhat by size of load. This was to be expected: state-ownership and an absence of competition tend generally to be associated with cross-subsidization, and one of the first effects of introducing competition in such circumstances is a rebalancing of tariffs as relative prices move closer to relative costs of supply. In respect of the position of the largest industrial users, it can be noted that these companies were the beneficiaries of special tariff schemes in the public-ownership days, schemes that were explicitly or implicitly supported by government. Privatization has brought the phasing out of these arrangements, a change that largely accounts for the relatively unfavourable price movements shown in the final row of Table 3.7.

Despite the generally beneficial (for consumers) changes in prices indicated in Tables 3.6 and 3.7, the first column of Table 3.7 indicates that the performance data needs to be interpreted with some caution. In the first place, most of the data relate to tariffs which were settled when the relevant suppliers were all state-owned enterprises (the RECs were privatized in November 1990 and the generating companies in March 1991). Particularly in the case of the generators, who were entering the retail market and were the force driving toward lower prices, shareholders' profits were not immediately at stake (cf. the history of lower-than-expected pool prices over the same period). As indicated by the first column of Table 3.7, industrial prices in the financial year beginning on 1 April 1991—the first full financial year following privatization—increased significantly.

Second, prices in the pre-privatization period were generally pushed up in anticipation of flotation (see Table 3.7). In the three or four years to the beginning of 1990, for example, the price of industrial electricity rose substantially *relative* to the prices of other industrial fuels such as coal, gas, and heavy fuel oil (see Table 3.8). Any assessment of the impact of privatization on prices must take account of this longer price history.

Third, the value added at the retail-supply stage accounts, on average, for only a small fraction of the final selling price (of the order of 5 per cent or less). Hence, even if competition led to major cost savings at the supply stage, the impact on final selling prices would, on average, be much less than the numbers quoted in Tables 3.6 and 3.7. To a first approximation, therefore, the initial impact of retail competition can be regarded as a change in price *structure*, rather than a change in price level (see the statistics for the ratio of domestic to industrial prices in Table 3.8). And while the development of a more cost-reflective price structure in industrial markets may be regarded as beneficial in terms of allocative efficiency, these changes inevitably raise questions about the broader price structure. That is, the price effects of privatization in industrial electricity markets cannot properly be analysed independently of its price effects in the domestic sector.

In the domestic sector, real prices of electricity were falling steadily in the period up to the 1988 White Paper (by nearly 14 per cent in the four years to 1987/8). Since then the downward trend has been checked (see Table 3.8), despite continuing falls in the real price of coal, the largest single cost component for the industry. As of 1992, therefore, it appears likely that privatization has had the effect of leading to higher domestic electricity prices than would otherwise have obtained.

TABLE 3.8. Index numbers of price relativities, 1986–1991

	Year					
	1986	1987	1988	1989	1990	1991
Industrial electricity to industrial:						
Coal	106	108	127	141	137	143
Heavy fuel oil	210	192	271	271	247	285
Gas	116	119	132	146	144	146
Domestic electricity to:						
GDP deflator	99	94	93	93	94	97
Industrial electricity	101	104	104	104	112	120

Source: *Energy Trends* 1992.

6. TRANSMISSION AND DISTRIBUTION

Although competition in transmission and distribution is largely infeasible,[18] regulation of these two transport activities is of crucial importance for the development of competition in generation and retail supply. It is also highly significant for electricity-pricing structures, as will be explained below.

6.1 Transmission

Broadly speaking, investment in transmission serves to facilitate competition in generation. Without transmission connections, electricity markets would be geographically segmented and consumers in a particular area would only be able to draw their power from local generating sets. Transmission opens up new connections and breaks down market segmentation. In Britain the existence of the national grid means that a local customer is physically connected to all generating sets throughout the country, including Scotland, and also to continental systems via the cross-Channel transmission link to France. The economic significance of these links depends, of course, on their capacity. Where transmission capacity is limited, market segmentation will re-emerge. Generators in region B may have lower costs than generators in region A, but consumers in region A may not be able to benefit much from these lower costs if transmission constraints place limits on the level of imports.

---

[18] The ability of electricity consumers to substitute out of these inputs does, however, impose some (albeit weak) competitive constraint. For example, high charges for electricity transportation can be expected to lead some industrial users to generate their own requirements on site.

Precisely because of substantial past investments in the national grid during the period of public ownership, transmission capacity was sufficient to accommodate many of the substantial, new demands for connection that emerged in the period after 1988 (see Section 4). New entry could not have been such an important factor in the market so soon after privatization had the transmission system been substantially weaker. There is, however, a potentially negative side to this pro-competitive effect of past transmission investment. As discussed in Section 4, the introduction of new generating capacity into the industry may be progressing at too rapid a pace from the point of view of economic efficiency.

To the extent that excessive entry occurs as a result of commercial misjudgments, there is no compelling reason why the industry's regulators should seek to intervene. Regulators are not necessarily very good at second-guessing market developments, not least because they typically have less at stake in getting their forecasts right than do the relevant firms. On the other hand, regulators clearly have an interest in ensuring that the pricing and investment policies of NGC do not seriously distort the market.

One initial problem with the structure of transmission charges in the immediate post-privatization period was that it did not reflect the differences in costs imposed on the system as a result of locational differences in power supplies and demands. The predominant pattern of power flows in the national grid is north to south, and post-privatization entry into electricity generation has tended to accentuate that pattern. Against this background, transmission charges for generators in the North should be significantly higher than charges in the South. Indeed, on a marginal or incremental cost basis, and excluding the firm-specific costs of making the actual connection to the network, it can be argued that transmission charges to generators in many parts of the South should actually be negative. The relevant short-run marginal costs tend to be negative because additional generation in the South reduces requirements for the transport of power from the North, thus reducing energy losses and tending to ease transmission constraints. The equivalent long-run marginal costs tend to be negative because of reductions in both energy losses and requirements for investment in north to south transmission links, the capacity of which is largely determined by the maximum expected flow from north to south.

NGC's initial use of system charges—which exclude firm-specific connection charges—did embody some degree of spatial differentiation (see Table 3.9), and it is noteworthy, for example, that the zonal infrastructure charge was zero for new generation in the London area. For a generating set supplying power to the system for approximately half the year, however, the maximum differential in generation charges

TABLE 3.9. National Grid Company's initial use of system charges, 1990/1.
System service charged levied on demand only: £3.372 per kW, plus local
infrastructure charge

Zone	Demand (£/kW)	Generation Capacity (£/kW)	Energy (p/kWh)
1 North-East	5.9578	3.1341	0.0249
2 Cumbria	5.9578	2.9826	0.0237
3 North-West	6.2030	1.7724	0.0141
4 Yorkshire	5.9578	1.9239	0.0153
5 E. & W. Midlands	5.9578	1.2490	0.0099
6 E. Anglia & Central	7.5638	0.5608	0.0045
7 Wales and West	6.4270	1.0768	0.0085
8 London	8.5497	0.0000	0.0000
9 South Coast	7.3550	0.8144	0.0065
10 South-West	7.2431	1.0350	0.0082
11 South-East	5.9578	1.3444	0.0107

Source: National Grid Company.

(between the North-East and London) was approximately £4.20 per kW, or less than 0.1p per kWh. This is, in fact, a relatively low differential when set against figures for marginal energy losses and for the construction of new power-lines and substations.

It can be argued, therefore, that inefficient pricing could have been a contributory factor to inefficient investment planning. Given what was, in effect, a cross-subsidy to generation facilities in the North,[19] the initial tariff structure contained incentives for inefficient location of new plant and, in so far as other factors tended to favour northern locations, may also have contained incentives for excessive new entry in general. Further, to the extent that any additional entry in the North did occur as a result, and that investments to strengthen the transmission system had to be made to meet the additional demand, it can be argued that the pricing structure also tended toward inefficient investment in the grid itself.

These general points are, however, somewhat moderated by the facts that (i) it is longer-term transmission charges that should matter for the entry and location decisions, and (ii) the DGES indicated in his first report that a review of transmission charges would be an early regulatory priority. The signals contained in NGC's first tariff structures were therefore inevitably muted.

---

[19] There was a corresponding cross-subsidy to demand in the South.

6.2 Distribution

Failure to reflect spatial cost differences in prices was even more obvious in distribution than in transmission. NGC's zonal structure for use of system charges did at least carry some spatial-cost information, with generation charges tending to be lower in importing zones than in exporting zones, and the reverse being true of demand charges. Differentiation in distribution charges, however, was based exclusively on non-spatial characteristics of supply (see Table 3.10). Given that both energy losses and capital costs are strongly and positively linked to the distances over which power is transported, initial distribution charges clearly embodied high levels of geographic cross-subsidies.

TABLE 3.10. Representative distribution charges, Eastern Electric, 1990/1 (p/kWh)

LV1 (low voltage domestic, non-night)	2.0009
LV2 (low voltage domestic, night rate)	0.3031
HV (high voltage)	0.4584

Source: Eastern Electric privatization prospectus.

It remains to be seen how far regulation will go in the direction of imposing cost-reflective spatially differentiated tariffs for electricity transmission and distribution. The arguments in favour are based chiefly on the efficiency case for marginal-cost pricing. On the other hand, geographic cross-subsidization may be a public policy objective in its own right (Peltzman 1989). Or, to put it another way, there may be strong political resistance to pricing structures that lead to very marked place-to-place variations in prices of commodities such as electricity, and in particular to local variations in prices to small customers (who account for the great bulk of the votes in elections).

7. CONCLUSIONS

As indicated at the outset, the analysis in this paper has concentrated largely on issues of competition, pricing, and investment. In terms of encouraging competition, it is not too early to declare the effects of privatization and the accompanying regulatory reforms a success. New entry on a significant scale has occurred in both generation and the retail supply of electricity, the two stages of activity where competition was deemed feasible.

It is true that significant problems concerning competition remain, most notably the question of the degree of competition among generators in the pool-bidding process. Given, however, that the pre-privatization performance weaknesses of the ESI had much more to do with inefficiencies in investment and power-station construction than with short-term operational efficiency, it is new-entry competition that is the more important. Moreover, the DGES has substantial powers available in the event of major abuses of market power in the pool.

Perhaps the most interesting question concerning competition is, what was it about the privatization exercise that produced such different results from the early attempts at liberalization via the 1983 Energy Act? I have argued that the failure of the Energy Act was a failure of regulation: no mechanisms were established for enforcing the provisions of the Act in ways that would achieve the intended effect. Put at its simplest, abuse of dominance by incumbent firms was largely unregulated. I believe that evidence is broadly consistent with this view, and that the key factor in privatization was therefore the establishment of the DGES and Offer, with their substantial influence over the operation of the relevant markets in general, and over the competitive conduct of incumbent firms in particular.

In contrast, alternative hypotheses about factors governing the level-of-entry barriers are quite difficult to square with the evidence. Privatization created two powerful incumbent privately owned generators—one of which, National Power, could be described as 'dominant', at least in the way that term is often used in competition law—but entry was not deterred as a result. Similarly, entry into retail supply against monopolistic incumbents (the RECs) indicates that market dominance *per se* was not the critical factor in preventing entry in the earlier period. Entry into retail supply also speaks against the view that full vertical separation between distribution, transmission, and non-naturally monopolistic activities is necessary to establish competition in the latter areas. RECs were allowed to operate as both distributors and suppliers of electricity, but entry was not thereby blocked.

Despite the criticisms of those who believe that the reforms accompanying privatization were not taken far enough in the direction of promoting competition, it remains true that, in electricity supply, the UK has gone much further down this particular road than has any other major economy. In comparison with UK policy, the 1992 EC Draft Directive on liberalizing the electricity market is an extremely cautious document, proposing, for example, that retail competition be allowed for the accounts of only the very largest of industrial customers and that integrated utilities operate their transmission activities as separate divisions. Indeed, on virtually all major issues of liberalization, UK policy had gone further by the beginning of 1992 than the positions the European Commission is seeking to reach by the beginning of 1996.

Turning to the pricing and investment performance of the industry since privatization, the judgement at this stage is necessarily more tentative. If it is accepted that the performance weaknesses of the publicly owned ESI were largely investment related, it is to be expected that it will take some time for the full effects of privatization and regulatory reform to be felt.

Competition in retail supply has already altered relative prices, although the extent to which it will continue to do so will depend heavily upon the regulators' attitudes to cross-subsidization in distribution. The effect of retail competition on *average* electricity prices, however, is limited by the small fraction of the final electricity price that is accounted for by the retail supply business.

Electricity generation accounts for a much higher proportion of the final selling price, and developing competition, particularly from new entry or the threat of new entry, can be expected to exert significant downward pressures on costs, particularly capital costs. This success may, however, be bought at the price of significant excess capacity in the industry or of premature retirement of existing plant.

This last point indicates how difficult it will be to evaluate the privatization exercise, even after a number of years have elapsed and the post-privatization data set is enlarged. The joker in the pack is environmental regulation. What may be deemed premature scrapping of existing coal plant on the basis of 1990 environmental standards may turn out not to be premature according to the standards of 1995. If that is the case, privatization will appear in a better light, even if the outcome is purely fortuitous. On the other hand, if nuclear power returns to favour at some point in the future (on account, say, of rising fossil-fuel prices induced by a 'carbon tax' aimed at reducing carbon dioxide emissions) then the negative impact of privatization on the nuclear power programme may be seen as a detriment.

Much will therefore depend upon the future balance between the regulation of market power and environmental regulation. Of the two, it is the environmental side that is likely to be the more important. For example, any beneficial effects of privatization on final selling prices of electricity—and as yet there are few signs of such effects—are likely to be dominated by the effects on prices of burgeoning environmental controls. Nevertheless, given its manifold implications for industry performance, regulation of monopoly can be expected to remain an important issue for the foreseeable future.

References

Department of Energy (1988), *Electricity Privatisation*, London: HMSO.

Department of Trade and Industry (1992), *Energy Trends*, newsletter, London: HMSO.

Financial Times (1991), *Power in Europe*, newsletter, London.

Green, R., and Newbery, D. (1991), 'Competition in the British electricity spot market', DAE Working Paper no. 9108, University of Cambridge.

Henney, A. (1987), *Privatise Power: Restructuring the Electricity Supply Industry*, London: Centre for Policy Studies.

Joskow, P., and Schmalensee, R. (1983), *Markets for Power*, Cambridge, Mass.: MIT Press.

Peltzman, S. (1989), 'The control and performance of state-owned enterprises: comment', in P. MacAvoy, W. Stanbury, G. Yarrow, and R. Zeckhauser (eds.), *Privatization and State-Owned Enterprises*, Rochester Studies in Managerial Economics and Policy, Boston: Kluwer Academic Press.

Sykes, A., and Robinson, C. (1987), *Current Choices: Good Ways and Bad to Privatise Electricity*, London: Centre for Policy Studies.

Tirole, J. (1989), *The Theory of Industrial Organization*, Cambridge, Mass.: MIT Press.

Vickers, J., and Yarrow, G. (1988), *Privatization: An Economic Analysis*, London: MIT Press.

—— —— (1991), 'The British electricity experiment', *Economic Policy*, **12**, 188–227.

Williamson, O. E. (1975), *Markets and Hierarchies*, New York: The Free Press.

Yarrow, G. (1991), 'Vertical supply arrangements: issues and applications in the energy industries', *Oxford Review of Economic Policy*, vii, no. 2.

4

British Airways:
A Turn-Around Anticipating
Privatization

RICHARD GREEN* AND INGO VOGELSANG†

Privatization has often been advocated as a means of improving the efficiency of state-owned companies. Government ownership is alleged to provide few incentives towards efficiency, compared to the disciplines which private ownership will impose. The large number of profitable privatized companies which had made significant losses under state ownership provides prima-facie evidence for this view. Almost all of them became profitable while they were still in the public sector, however, which makes the link between privatization and efficiency harder to discern. Did the companies become profitable under state ownership independently of the prospect of privatization, which only became possible once they were profitable, or did the prospect of privatization at last give the companies the incentives they needed? British Airways (BA) provides a good example of this puzzle—in 1980/1, the state-owned carrier made an operating loss of £95 million, and was widely regarded as badly overmanned and inefficient. In 1984/5, still in state ownership, the company made an operating surplus of £292 million, while one measure of productivity[1] showed a 40 per cent improvement on four years earlier.

This chapter looks at BA during the eventful period since 1979, chronicled in Section 1. The airline's performance, which depended upon both external events and the company's own efforts, is examined in Section 2, which reports a number of measures derived from BA's published accounts. One important influence on BA has been the regulatory

* Department of Applied Economics, University of Cambridge.
† Department of Economics, Boston University.

Much of the analysis of Section 2 is based upon research done for the World Bank, through its Comparative Divestiture Project. The project aims to calculate the costs and benefits of a sample of privatizations in developed and developing countries, and to draw appropriate policy conclusions. Research assistance from Manuel Abdala, and helpful comments from the editors, are gratefully acknowledged.

[1] Available tonne-kilometres (ATK) per employee rose from 154,000 in 1980/1 to 213,000 in 1984/5. This is a crude measure, concentrating on a single input and an undifferentiated output, but the dramatic improvement is undeniable.

system imposed by the countries between which it flies, and this has been changing throughout the period, with more radical changes expected soon. Section 3 describes these changes, and their impact on airlines in general, while Section 4 attempts to look into the future and predict the outlook for BA.

1. WHAT HAPPENED TO BA

The British Airways Board was created by the 1971 Civil Aviation Act, as the holding corporation for the British Overseas Airways Corporation (BOAC) and British European Airways (BEA). BOAC was created when the private-sector airlines created during the 1920s and 1930s (which had gradually merged to form Imperial Airways and British Airways) were nationalized in 1939. BEA and the short-lived British South American Airways[2] had been split off from BOAC in 1946, but the Edwards Committee, formed to consider the future of British civil aviation, recommended that the two airlines should be combined under a State Airline Holdings Board (HMSO 1969). Joint marketing arrangements paved the way to a full merger in 1974, when BOAC and BEA were dissolved, but the two airlines remained as separate divisions within BA until a reorganization in 1977. BA inherited a legacy of two different 'cultures' from its parents, and was widely perceived to be overmanned, and to suffer from bad labour relations—strikes in 1974/5 cost it an estimated £11 million in operating profits, and another £40 million was lost from disputes in 1977/8.

BA's first annual report stated that the airline's 'primary objective is to conduct its affairs on strictly commercial lines' (BA, 1973: 10), but in one crucial respect, it adopted a policy which at the least fitted in with political constraints, and may well have been dictated by them. This was the 'intention of the British Airways Board to rationalize the operations of BA without resort to staff redundancies' (ibid. 17). This intention was embodied in the ambitious corporate plan produced by a team under Roy Watts (Chief Executive 1979–83) in 1978. The aim was to solve BA's productivity problems by 1986, by nearly doubling its output, without a significant increase in staff numbers. The older aircraft, which would fail new noise regulations, would be replaced by a fleet of larger jets, requiring less labour per seat, which would cost £2.4 billion. Two-thirds of this could be found from BA's profits and depreciation, and the detailed plan was internally consistent. The planned growth rate, from 16 million passengers to 30 million in eight years, was higher than the govern-

[2] It was reabsorbed by BOAC in 1949.

ment's forecasts of the industry's growth,[3] but not impossible, given the assumptions on which the plan rested.

Unfortunately, these assumptions were soon overtaken by events. The price of aviation fuel doubled after the 1979 oil shock, while the number of scheduled passengers fell as the British economy (and then the world) went into recession. Sterling appreciated against many other currencies, which had the effect of increasing BA's costs relative to its revenues (Ashworth and Forsyth 1984). BA made a small profit in 1979/80, but an operating loss of £95 million in 1980/1, worsened to an overall loss of £141 million by interest payments. The North Atlantic routes between the UK and the USA are BA's most important, typically providing a quarter of the airline's revenue, and profits on these routes fell dramatically in response to entry by a new carrier. Laker Airways was given permission to operate its Skytrain, a cheap no-frills service, in 1977, and carried 5 per cent of UK–US passengers during the next two years. In 1980 and 1981, however, Laker's market share rose to more than 10 per cent, and the incumbent airlines responded by selling a large number of tickets at prices close to Laker's. Most of an airline's costs depend on its scheduled capacity, irrespective of whether that capacity is filled, which means that the marginal revenue from an extra passenger with a discounted ticket exceeds the marginal cost. Although this gives airlines an incentive to discount, their average revenue can then easily fall below their average costs. Laker had expanded too fast, and loans denominated in dollars became too great a burden when sterling depreciated after 1980 (Banks 1982). Laker Airways collapsed in February 1982, but was to haunt BA later, even after the price war over the North Atlantic had ended.

Before the downturn in BA's fortunes, its privatization had been announced. Proposed during the election campaign in April 1979, a Civil Aviation Bill to turn BA into a company, suitable for sale, was introduced in July and became law the next year. BA's worsening results made privatization in the near future impossible, and a new Chairman, Sir John King (now Lord King of Wartnaby) was appointed in February 1981 with the task of turning the airline around. In September 1981, a survival plan, based on large cuts in capacity, employment, and peripheral activities, formally ended the Watts strategy of expansion. Employment fell by nearly 20 per cent during the 1981/2 financial year, from 52,000 to 43,000, and the airline made a small operating profit. This was dramatically offset by extraordinary provisions for redundancy and supplementary depreciation which produced a net loss for the year of £541 million, so that liabilities exceeded assets by £257 million. The size of the provisions was partly to concentrate all the bad news into a single

[3] BA planned for a 90% increase in passenger numbers; the government expected growth of between 42% and 78% (Green 1978).

year (Campbell-Smith 1986: 30), and although £44 million of the £198 million set aside for redundancies was written back in later years, the accounts' gloomy snapshot did show BA's position at the time.

A snapshot does not necessarily show the direction of movement, and BA's position was improving rapidly. In 1982/3, operating profits of £185 million were large enough to allow a post-tax profit of £90 million, even after paying interest on the debts acquired during the recession. Operating profits rose again the following year, and BA's net worth returned to a positive value. Privatization was scheduled for early in 1985, and lobbying about its consequences started. This was headed by British Caledonian Airways (BCal), BA's main rival in scheduled services, which had been created as a 'second force' by a merger in 1970, following a recommendation of the Edwards Committee. BCal alleged that a privatized BA would dominate the British airline industry to an unhealthy extent, and proposed that BA's domestic routes should be transferred to regional airlines, and some of its international routes should be sold to BCal, reducing BA's market share (among the UK airlines) from 80 per cent to about two-thirds. The government asked the Civil Aviation Authority to enquire into the matter, and it proposed a smaller set of transfers (CAA 1984). BA would lose its routes to Zimbabwe and Saudi Arabia, its Gatwick services, and services to Europe from provincial UK airports; 7 per cent of its revenues in total. A forceful campaign by BA followed, and the government decided on a limited swap of routes—BA gave up its profitable services to Saudi Arabia, and gained BCal's loss-making South American routes (Department of Transport 1984). BA remained the dominant UK airline, but even the original BCal proposals would have had a limited effect on competition on individual routes, since international agreements restrict the number of airlines serving the vast majority of scheduled destinations from the UK. The government chose a solution which gave BA a greater value than the other two proposals, and secured the support of its management in the run-up to the sale.

Until November 1984, the sale was expected in February 1985, but BA was one of several co-defendants in a lawsuit brought by Laker's liquidator, who was claiming damages that would be tripled to $1.05 billion under US anti-trust laws. A criminal investigation was dropped under political pressure from the UK, but the government could not insulate BA from the risks of the civil case—had the government agreed to bear BA's costs, it might have inflated the value of any settlement, while an outstanding case would certainly have reduced the value of BA, and might make it unsaleable. The flotation was accordingly postponed in November, and the case was eventually settled out of court for $69 million, half paid by BA, in July 1985. The sale was rescheduled for July 1986, and then postponed again, because negotiations between the

UK and the USA on transatlantic services, which could materially affect BA's profitability, were in progress at the time. These postponements make it difficult to determine the point beyond which any behavioural changes could be ascribed to privatization. An attractive option is to take the 1984/5 financial year as the break-point, since BA would have been privatized then, but for the Laker lawsuit, and was operating independently from the government by that time.[4]

BA was finally sold in January 1987, nearly eight years after the sale was announced. The 720 million shares sold, at a price of 125p, gave the company a value of around £900 million, and the government received approximately £850 million after the costs of the issue and of various incentive schemes. On the first day's trading, the partly-paid shares closed at a premium of 68 per cent on the first instalment, giving a rise in value of £317 million. Part of this was planned, but the government had underestimated the demand from small investors (so that the allocation to institutions was reduced), and the general level of share prices rose between the day when the price was set and the first day's trading, both of which pushed up the price of BA shares (National Audit Office 1987).

Soon after privatization, in July 1987, BA ran into controversy again, when it announced an agreed take-over of BCal. The smaller airline had not been strengthened by the 1984 route transfers; ironically the South American routes improved as memories of the Falklands conflict receded, while the slump in oil prices reduced traffic to Saudi Arabia, so that BA got the best of the deal. BCal had been expanding into more competitive markets during the 1980s, while losing the cost advantage inherited from its charter predecessors (Cronshaw and Thompson 1990), and with the slump in transatlantic traffic in 1986 (following the Chernobyl explosion and the bombing of Libya), the company made a loss. The companies argued that the merger was required because BCal no longer had a realistic future as an independent airline, and that investment by a foreign company might jeopardize BCal's route licences, which were only valid for a 'British' airline. The take-over was referred to the Monopolies and Mergers Commission, which approved it, on condition that BA gave up a number of route licences to destinations that were previously served by both airlines, and a number of take-off and landing 'slots' at Gatwick (Monopolies and Mergers Commission 1987). By this time the Scandinavian airline, SAS, had expressed interest in taking a minority stake in BCal, to create a

[4] The government was able to issue instructions to the BA board, which were not published. However, if the government had been in tight control of the company, it is extremely unlikely that it would have allowed BA's high-profile lobbying campaign over the CAA's 1984 report, which ensured that the government's decision over the future of the airline industry would be highly controversial.

'twin-hub' network around Copenhagen and Gatwick. This proposal could well have been viable, and BA was forced to raise its offer for BCal before winning control at the end of December 1987, for a price of £246 million.[5] In March 1988 the European Commission forced BA to make further concessions on the surrendered route licences, and to use no more than 25 per cent of the slots at Gatwick for four years, a reduction of 10,000 a year from its former level.

BA was highly successful in its first years under private ownership, increasing its operating profits in each year, and earning a final profit of £246 million, its highest ever, in 1989/90. Its results in 1990/1 were less impressive on paper, for the airline's operating profits fell by more than half, and the profit after tax was reduced to £95 million. In context, these results look better, for the Gulf War caused a dramatic decline in air travel, and the effects of recession kept passenger numbers down after it ended. BA responded with a programme of cost-cutting, and in 1991/2 its profits recovered most of the ground they had lost in 1990/1. Even though they slipped back again in 1992/3, shareholders' profits still approached £200 million. Many other airlines have made large losses over the past few years; in nominal terms, the recent losses are greater than the sum of all the profits earned by the industry since 1945. Of the industry's former giants, Pan Am has ceased trading, and a restructured TWA is a shadow of its former self, while some other large American carriers are technically bankrupt. BA's performance in these circumstances looks relatively strong, but its future prospects will depend crucially on the regulatory system. This is changing rapidly, and will be examined in Section 3, following the next section's analysis of BA's performance since 1979.

2. WHAT CHANGED AT BA

This section draws heavily on a World Bank Report (Vogelsang and Green 1994) on the privatization of British Airways, which used data from BA's annual reports, and other published sources, to describe the changes in BA's profits, costs, and outputs, and to provide an explanation. That report used data from 1979/80 to 1989/90, including five years before the first firm date for the flotation, in 1984/5, and five years after it. The series have been extended to 1992/3 for this chapter, although with less disaggregation.

BA's annual reports provide accounting data, which must be transformed into appropriate economic categories. This is best seen with the figures for profits, given in Figure 4.1. Private profit is based upon BA's

---

[5] Fees, reorganization expenses, and the need to absorb BCal's net liabilities of £10m., raised the total cost of the acquisition to £353m.

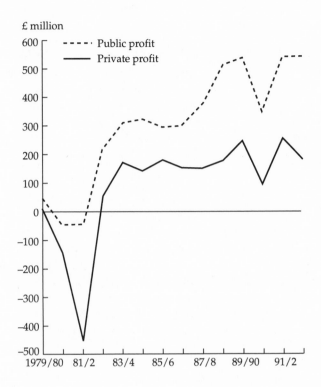

£ million

Fig. 4.1. British Airways' profits

published shareholders' profit:[6] dividends and retained earnings. It falls dramatically in the early 1980s, but then rebounds from 1982/3

[6] Our figures are slightly different from BA's figures between 1981/2 and 1984/5, because BA's accounts for 1981/2 contained a provision of £198.8m. for redundancy payments while £100.4m. was spent in that year, leaving £98.4m. as a future provision. Of this, £31.7m. was written back in 1983/4 and 1984/5, which raised reported profits in those years, while the results for 1981/2 were depressed unnecessarily. We attempted to assign the costs to the years in which they were incurred, and assumed that an equal amount was spent in each of the three years from 1982/3. Our results are £98.7m. better than BA's in 1981/2, £22.7m. worse in 1982/3, £43m. worse in 1983/4, and £32.7m. worse in 1984/5. This makes the improvement in BA's profits somewhat less marked than in the published accounts. An alternative to the assumption that an equal amount was spent in each year would be that most of the £66.7m. was spent in 1982/3. This alternative would give lower profits in that year, and higher profits in the subsequent years, which means that we may have overstated the improvement in 1982/3, as BA's figures do, and understated the subsequent improvement.

onwards. During the rest of the period private profits fluctuate around a fairly constant level, although 1989/90 and 1991/2 are significantly higher, and 1990/1 significantly lower, than in the rest of the period. Private profit is affected by changes in taxation and the treatment of depreciation, and an alternative measure may give a better idea of how well the airline is using its assets.

The measure we use, which attempts to give the total returns to BA's fixed operating assets, is called public profit. It is defined as the gross profit earned by the company, including interest payments and taxes, without deducting depreciation, but excluding non-operating returns, and deducting the opportunity cost of working capital. It corresponds to the positive entries that would be made in a cost-benefit analysis of a project, once the project is operating. In a cost-benefit analysis, all sums will be discounted to a common date, and the cost of investment, at the time it takes place, gives the total opportunity cost of fixed capital. The annual opportunity cost of working capital is deducted from public profit, on the assumption that another use could readily be found for liquid funds, while other assets are bygones. Non-operating returns are excluded because they are not 'earned' by the company from its main operations; a *ceteris paribus* argument would imply that changes to the company's performance would not affect these benefits. An alternative expression for public profit, operating revenues less the cost of labour, intermediate inputs, and the opportunity cost of working capital, leads to the interpretation that they are 'short-run variable profits', or quasi-rents. With this interpretation, it is important to relate public profits to the capital that had to be invested to obtain them; even more than with private profits, profitability, or the return to capital, is a better guide to a company's performance than the level of profits. For a number of companies, we have found that movements in public profitability parallel changes in total factor productivity, although we cannot offer a theoretical justification for this empirical regularity.

Public profits do not decline by nearly as much as private profits in the early 1980s. This is mostly because the extraordinary depreciation which depressed private profits in 1981/2, and the increasing burden of interest payments,[7] are not deducted when calculating public profits. Because the results for 1981/2 are better, the turn-around in the following year is less pronounced, but still exceeds £260 million. The mid-1980s show little change, although there is a slight upward trend, and public profits reach a significantly higher level after 1988/9 (except for 1990/1), after privatization and the acquisition of BCal. That merger, which raised the level of profits, in part because more assets were in use, highlights the need to consider rates of return and capital employed.

---

[7] Interest payments came to £35m. in 1979/80, £120m. in 1981/2, and £130m. in 1982/3, and remained at about £110m. until 1985/6, when they fell to £39m.

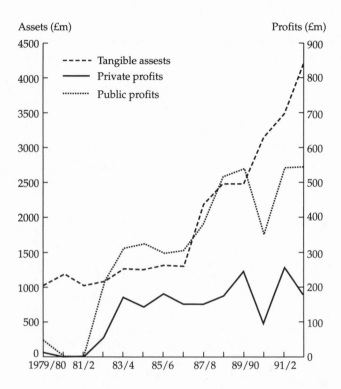

Assets (£m)   Profits (£m)

Fig. 4.2. British Airways' assets and profits

Figure 4.2 repeats our two measures of profits alongside BA's net tangible assets, taken from their annual reports. The book value of BA's capital stock increased slowly until privatization, and rapidly thereafter. Measured at constant replacement cost, BA's capital actually fell throughout the period preceding privatization. The sudden addition of BCal in 1987/8 reversed this trend,[8] and further investment in new aircraft during the early 1990s doubled the book value of the capital stock inherited on privatization. Profits are graphed against the right-hand axis, and the scale implies that the lines would coincide if the company earned a 20 per cent return on book value. It can be seen that the

[8] The net book value of BA's fleet was also increased by nearly £300m. in a revaluation in March 1988.

increases in private profit from the mid-1980s have been much smaller than the increases in capital employed, and so the company's rate of return will have been falling. Public profit kept up with the capital stock until 1989/90,[9] but fell with the Gulf War, and the recovery in the level of profits has not been enough to maintain the rate of return.

Figure 4.3 emphasises that BA's public profits are the difference between two large flows, giving the value of its sales and of its variable costs. The figure shows that the recovery in current price profits in 1982/3 and 1983/4 came from holding costs down while sales rose (particularly in the first year), and that the fall in profits in 1990/1 came from a faster increase in costs than in sales. The trend rise in both sales and costs is partly the result of output growth, and partly that of cost and price inflation. To the extent that many costs and some prices are outside BA's control, a graph which uses constant prices may give a better picture of the airline's efficiency.

Figure 4.4 deflates the major categories of BA's inputs and outputs by appropriate price indices (or uses volume measures such as employee numbers) to produce series at constant 1984/5 prices. At these prices, the airline never makes a 'loss', implying that they were more favourable than the prices faced at the beginning of the period. The real level of output declined until 1983/4, and profits fell at first because the airline did not reduce its inputs in consequence. The recovery in 1982/3 came about once the airline started to cut costs. From 1984/5 onwards, output at constant prices has risen in every single year. The smallest increase came in 1986/7, when there was a reduction in transatlantic travel associated with the US bombing of Libya, and the explosion at Chernobyl. BA did not reduce its capacity to match that decrease, and so its constant-price profits declined in that year, but they have risen in every subsequent year. In the early 1990s, BA responded to the problems facing the world airline industry by reducing its costs in real terms, despite increasing output, and there was no more than a small increase in costs in 1992/3, when output rose by more than 10 per cent.

These changes in volume are combined with the actual changes in profits in Figure 4.5, to give the implied effects of price changes. At the very start of the period, the rising price of oil harmed BA, as did the appreciation of sterling (see Ashworth and Forsyth 1984). Prices then moved in BA's favour as sterling depreciated, so that the airline could obtain more revenue without raising the prices of tickets to foreign travellers. When favourable price and quantity movements coincided in 1982/3, the airline recorded its largest ever rise in public profits. A favourable price movement also occurred in 1986/7, when oil prices fell,

---

[9] The gap between public and private profit increases in the late 1980s, which is a natural consequence of the greater capital stock and its increased depreciation, since public profit is a gross measure, and private profit is net of depreciation.

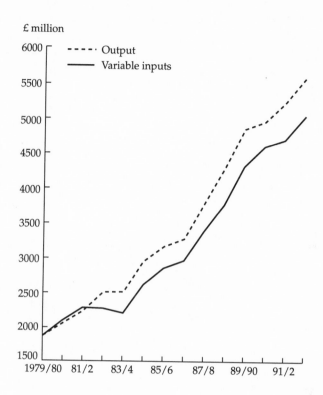

£ million

FIG. 4.3. British Airways: current-price data

offsetting the unfavourable quantity changes in that year. Since that time, all of the major price movements have been unfavourable to BA, as costs have risen, and increasing competition has made it harder for the company to increase its ticket prices.

Figure 4.6 shows our estimates of BA's total factor productivity, which rises irregularly over the period. As with other studies (for example, Encaoua 1991; Forsyth *et al.* 1986; Windle 1991) the change in BA's total-factor productivity is less than in its labour productivity. We do not attempt to compare BA with its competitors; given the problems of compensating for different route structures, other authors have produced a wide range of results. A common theme is that BA's position relative to its competitors improved during the 1980s, but that BA remained behind the most efficient airlines.

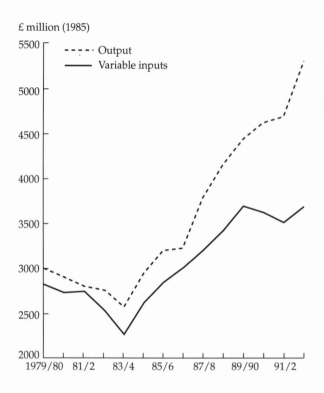

Figure 4.6 also shows BA's load factors, the ratio of capacity (available tonne- or seat-kilometres) to output (revenue tonne- or seat- kilometres), for its scheduled flights and for all of its flights. Productivity and load factors both have an upward trend over the period, although the movements in particular years are not well correlated. Since many costs depend on the level of capacity offered, an improvement in load factor will inevitably tend to reduce the ratio of inputs to outputs. Although the improvement in BA's load factor will have helped to raise its productivity, it should not be treated as a purely exogenous factor. The increase in load factor may well reflect improvements in product quality, and should be seen as the result of improvements at BA, rather than

something that has helped to improve the productivity figures, without any real change in BA's inputs per unit of capacity offered.

The World Bank study found two major breaks in BA's performance, one in about 1982, and one in 1987, while the cost-cutting from 1990/1 onwards might count as a third. There does not seem to have been any visible immediate announcement effect of the privatization, in that 1980/1 is worse for BA on almost any measure than 1979/80,[10] but this is not due to events at the airline alone. It had embarked on an expansionary policy just as demand for air travel was about to decline, and the

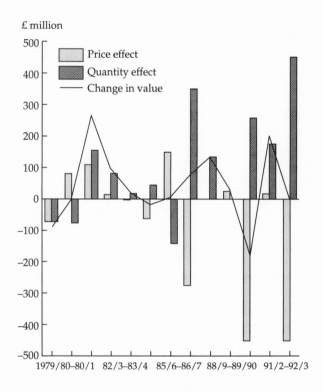

Fig. 4.5. Changes in BA's public profits

[10] In turn, profits were lower in 1979/80 than in 1978/9, so the announcement effect did not come in that year, either.

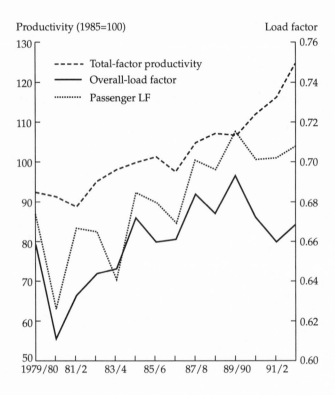

Fɪɢ. 4.6. British Airways: productivity and load factors

price of fuel to double, so that bad results were only to be expected. The wisdom of the Watts strategy can be questioned with hindsight, but the political constraints against reducing overmanning via redundancies were tight. By 1981, the position was so bad that the Watts strategy had to be abandoned, and cost-cutting had become an acceptable alternative. BA's position got better, again according to almost any measure, although the improvement in terms of constant-price public profit is not nearly as marked as for private profit, due to the favourable effects of price changes upon the latter, and the differences in depreciation. The managers and staff who achieved this improvement may have been inspired by the prospect of privatization, especially at the more senior levels, but it is difficult to say that the changes were directly due to that prospect.

The change in profitability following privatization is much more pronounced in the constant-price figures than in current prices. The shift in
the constant-price figures is certainly large enough to require explanation: the problem in providing one is that privatization and the acquisition of BCal occurred in the same calendar year. Although our data are
based on financial years, the act of privatization would have had its
effects in 1986/7 and 1987/8, and the acquisition would have affected
1987/8 and 1988/9. Untangling the one from the other is therefore
extremely difficult, especially as 1986/7 already suffered from freak
travel patterns. It is probable that a large part of the increase is due to
the acquisition of BCal. BCal was generally perceived to have lower
costs than BA, and so the merger would reduce BA's observed costs to
the weighted average of the two airlines' costs, even if there were no
gains in efficiency.[11] However, BA was able to convince the Monopolies
and Mergers Commission (1987) that substantial 'synergies' existed, and
that benefits from these would outweigh any risks from reduced competition. The large increase in the level of output, relative to the quantity of
inputs, helps to confirm the existence of these synergies, as does the fact
that BA shed 2,500 jobs from the newly merged airline during 1988 (BA
1989: 6). At the same time, the reduction in competition probably helped
the airline to raise its yields in 1988/9 and 1989/90, even though BCal's
services had initially had lower yields than BA's.[12] Overall, a large part
of the improvement in the late 1980s may have been due to the take-over
of BCal, rather than as a direct consequence of privatization. Of course,
the take-over would have been almost inconceivable had BA remained
in the public sector, since another suitor (SAS) was willing to rescue
BCal.

The third possible turning point is 1990/1, when BA responded to
adverse conditions in the world air travel market with a cost-cutting
programme which helped to raise total-factor productivity by more than
15 per cent in three years. The airline has remained profitable when others have failed to cut their costs to match the tougher market conditions,
and have made huge losses. BA might have found it more difficult to cut
costs if it had remained in the public sector, although there were fewer
redundancies than in 1982/3, when it had successfully regained profitability under state ownership. The one area in which its private-sector
status has undoubtedly helped BA is in forming alliances with foreign
airlines, positioning itself in an increasingly competitive market-place.

[11] It should be noted that the evidence on BA and BCal's relative costs is not unanimous; for example, Windle (1991) found that BCal had higher unit costs than BA in 1983,
and if this had persisted the merger would have raised BA's observed costs in the absence
of other changes.
[12] The lower yields of BCal's services is suggested by a decline in output prices in
1987/8, and confirmed by Cronshaw and Thompson 1990.

The future of the air travel industry is being shaped by changes to the way in which it has been regulated, and we now turn to these.

3. REGULATION AND BA

When BA was formed, international scheduled air travel was tightly regulated. An airline serving an international route has to meet the provisions of the bilateral air service agreement (ASA) for that route, which is negotiated between the governments at each end. Further treaties give rights to overfly the intervening countries. Until the early 1970s, almost all of these ASAs tended to restrict competition. In some cases, only one airline would be allowed to serve the route, and very few ASAs allowed more than one airline from each country. There were often strict limits on the total capacity that could be offered. The revenues earned on a route would often be pooled between the airlines serving it, and sometimes the costs as well. If a route was served by only one airline, the other country's home airline would often participate in the cost- and revenue-sharing agreement, earning profits without ever flying the route. These pooling agreements could be justified on the argument that airlines could concentrate on providing an efficient level of capacity, while competition might mean excessive capacity at peak periods, and a shortage at other times, as airlines acted on the basis of private, rather than social, costs and benefits. Although there is something in that argument, the restrictive ASAs meant that many airlines had no competition, and had few incentives towards efficiency.

While the ASAs regulated capacity, fares were generally set by the International Air Transport Association (IATA), the airlines' cartel. This met every six months to agree fares for every international route in the world, and agreement had to be unanimous. This gave every airline a power of veto, and produced a tendency to keep fares high, even if many airlines sought reductions. When airlines were unable to obtain lower fares through IATA, many of them simply sold tickets at a discount to 'bucket shops', which were technically outlawed, but convenient for airlines wishing to get round the IATA rules. Although IATA's procedures would have broken most countries' competition laws, airlines were generally granted exemptions which allowed them to take part in the conferences: even the Americans were allowed to attend as observers. In the UK, domestic fares were controlled, and route licences granted, by the CAA, which had to pay due regard to the interests of incumbent airlines.

This framework has been relaxed gradually over the last twenty years or so. In 1977, the UK and the USA signed a new ASA, known as 'Bermuda II', which allowed two airlines from each country to operate on the busier routes (dual designation), while the governments could only review the level of capacity offered by the airlines if there was evidence to suggest that the airlines had chosen an inappropriate level. This agreement opened the way for Laker Airways, and competition on the North Atlantic routes continued to increase, even after its demise. In 1978, domestic flights in the US were deregulated, and massive changes to the American airline industry ensued. We will not describe them in detail (see, for example, Bailey *et al.* 1985, for a fuller account); the main outcome that concerns us is that several 'mega-carriers' have emerged, with 'hub and spoke' route patterns radiating from their main bases. Although air travel was a very popular example of a contestable market, in which the fear of 'hit and run' entry would force incumbents to keep their prices low, their large networks have given the major airlines an advantage against most independent entrants.[13] When foreign passengers arrive at a 'gateway hub' and need a connecting flight, they are likely to choose the home airline because of the larger number of destinations offered. Since changing airlines in mid-journey can cause problems, they may then be predisposed to use the US carrier to get to the gateway, if it offers flights from their starting point. BA made marketing agreements with Delta and United Airways, and has now taken a stake in USAir, aiming to reduce the problems involved in changing airlines, so that the airlines able to offer a 'through service' from the interior of the USA to the UK have less of an advantage.

In the UK, the 1980 Civil Aviation Act instructed the CAA to 'have regard in particular to any benefits which may arise from enabling two or more airlines to provide the services in question' (s23 A (2)), and by 1985, the CAA was 'ready to license competing services by British Airlines even at the risk of some impairment of an existing British service . . .' (CAA 1985, para. 3). For domestic flights, this means that entry is now almost completely free, subject to safety licensing. Domestic fares must be filed with the CAA, which retains the right to disapprove them, but 'whenever possible the Authority will allow market forces to set or influence the levels of fares and rates for air transport' (ibid. para. 15).

During the 1980s the UK signed a number of 'liberal bilaterals' with other European countries, starting with the Netherlands in 1984. Any airline could fly between the two countries, subject to approval from its home government, and could offer any fare that was not vetoed by both governments (which became known as the 'double disapproval' rule). Over the next four years several airlines entered the London–Amsterdam market, frequencies nearly doubled, and prices fell by

---

[13] 'Get hit and run' would be a better description of the experience of many entrants, especially as incumbents can often respond with selective, short-lived, price cuts of a somewhat predatory nature (Kahn 1991).

between 7 and 20 per cent[14] (Abbot and Thompson 1991). An agreement with the Republic of Ireland had similar effects, while an agreement with West Germany allowed some American carriers which flew to Germany via Heathrow to offer 'fifth freedom'[15] tickets on the leg between Germany and the UK, and lower leisure prices. However, other routes which were liberalized saw no entry, although prices were probably above competitive levels, implying that contestability did not apply on these routes.[16]

The European Union has followed these bilateral moves with a policy of gradual multilateral liberalization (Vincent and Stasinopoulos 1990; Stasinopoulos 1992, 1993). When the transition period ends, in April 1997, any Union airline will be allowed to fly on any international route within the Union. Fares will be set freely, subject to the 'double disapproval' rule. Domestic flights will remain subject to national rules, and flights outside the EU will still be governed by bilateral treaties, although the European countries may attempt to act together in negotiating revisions to these treaties. An industry based upon free entry should gradually develop, provided that solutions can be found to the problems of airspace congestion and the shortage of slots at major airports.

At peak times some air routes over Europe are extremely congested, and the present air traffic control system cannot cope adequately with the volume of traffic wishing to use those routes. Aircraft must stay on the ground until it is known that their entire route will be free of other traffic, and the numerous air traffic control centres responsible for ensuring this have to do so verbally, by telephone. Some flights, especially charters with lower priority, are delayed for hours before a clear route can be confirmed. Many of the problems involved are technical, however, and increased investment in computer and communications systems should improve the situation over the next few years. Supra-national control centres, reducing the number of controllers who have to agree before each flight can take off, would increase capacity further, but most governments are likely to be reluctant to 'lose sovereignty' over their airspace.

---

[14] The greater reductions were in the prices of 'leisure' tickets, which offer lower fares, but are subject to restrictions (such as a minimum length of stay and non-transferability) which make them unsuitable for business travellers.

[15] International law defines five 'freedoms of the air'. The first is to fly over another country, the second to land there, the third to take passengers from your country to another, and the fourth is to take passengers from the other country to your own. The fifth freedom, to take passengers between two foreign countries, is much less frequently granted.

[16] Abbott and Thompson ascribed this to the low proportion of leisure travellers on these routes, since they might be willing to travel with an unknown, but cheap, entrant, while business travellers might require a familiar, reliable carrier. On routes where entry did occur, leisure fares fell by more than business fares, which fits this hypothesis.

The more serious problem is with access to hub airports. Many of the major airports in Europe are near their runway capacity, and cannot handle more flights than they do at present. A new airline wishing to operate a route to or from that airport can only do so if an incumbent gives up a landing and a take-off slot, at suitable times. The incumbents are naturally extremely reluctant to give up slots and face more competition, and the rules at most airports have no powers to force them. Slots are typically allocated each year by a committee of the airlines using the airport, and 'grandfather rights', which give first refusal to the airline which used the slot in the previous year, generally prevail.

For competition to develop fully, access to the main airports is crucial, especially if Europe follows the American pattern of 'hub and spoke' operations. Passengers wishing to travel between some city-pairs may face a range of possible routes via more than one hub airport, but many others will have no effective choice but to use a given hub airport. Furthermore, there may be competition on one or both legs of their journey, but if a shortage of slots means that only one airline can provide the pair of flights, the perceived benefits of not changing airlines will give it a great advantage. This is effectively the present position at most European hubs, and above all at Heathrow; BA is the only airline that could serve both halves of most of the routes through the airport. Heathrow serves more international destinations than any other airport, and 21 per cent of its passengers changed flights there in 1981; the large number of destinations gives it extra value to those passengers. It is plausible that Heathrow's international connections, and its proximity to London, might allow airlines to charge more than for a similar ticket from another airport. A 5 per cent mark-up, compared to other airports, was observed on European charter flights from Gatwick by Bishop and Thompson (1992). Since charter passengers are likely to be more price-sensitive than scheduled passengers, an average mark-up of this level seems plausible for services from Heathrow, even if the more expensive intercontinental flights have a lower percentage mark-up than European services. In 1989/90, BA earned 76 per cent of its revenue from scheduled flights from Heathrow services, and 5 per cent of that figure came to £165 million. This rough estimate of the value to BA of its Heathrow slots should be compared to its record shareholders' profit of £246 million in the same year.

The European Commission has suggested that incumbent airlines should be forced to give up a proportion of their slots at airports where demand exceeded supply. Other proposals include auctioning some or all of the slots at congested airports, which should ensure that they went to the flights with the greatest added value, while incumbents would rarely be able to afford the cost of blocking entrants by buying all of the available slots (McGowan and Seabright 1989). In the UK, the revenues from such an auction could prove controversial. If they went to the privatized British Airports Authority, it would gain windfall profits and an incentive not to loosen the capacity constraints, while if they were withheld by the Civil Aviation Authority, acting on behalf of the Treasury, the government might be attacked for its new 'tax' on air travel. One solution might be to place any revenues in an escrow account, to finance new capacity.[17]

BA's position at Heathrow had already been weakened, when additional airlines were allowed to use the airport for the first time since 1977. Under severe financial pressure, the US carriers Pan-Am and TWA had sought to sell their route licences to Heathrow to two of the stronger mega-carriers, United Air Lines and American Airlines, at the end of 1990. The existing traffic distribution rules at Heathrow, in force since 1977, had banned whole-plane charters and excluded airlines not already operating at the airport, in an attempt to reduce the excess demand for slots at the airport. The route sales would be useless if these rules remained in force, and their abolition was announced in March 1991. Since United and American have strong networks inside the USA, unlike Pan-Am and TWA, BA's market share on routes to the USA was threatened, as passengers going beyond a 'gateway' could choose a single airline for their whole journey, and members of 'frequent flier' programmes could use the airline that they normally fly with. These sales did not take any Heathrow slots from BA, but in the same week it was forced by the CAA to give up two slots a week at Tokyo, in order to allow Virgin Atlantic[18] to run a viable competing service. If this process continues, BA's position at Heathrow may become much less valuable.

4. THE OUTLOOK FOR BA

Predicting the future is rarely easy, but the interaction of several areas of uncertainty makes it even harder than usual to chart BA's likely course. If access to European airports is managed on the basis of auctions or some other non-discriminatory method once the industry is fully liberalized, then we should observe a period of intensive competition in European aviation. On the US model, this could then turn into a period of consolidation, with a few large carriers dominating the industry. Some airlines have already begun to position themselves for this, with

[17] Oum and Zhang (1990) provide examples in which such revenues would be more than adequate to finance the optimal expansion of capacity.

[18] BA's competition with Virgin had embarrassing consequences for the company when it was discovered that some BA employees had engaged in unauthorized 'dirty tricks' against the smaller airline. Virgin is suing BA in the US courts, having won a libel action over BA's initial response to the accusations, and the episode clouded Lord King's retirement from BA.

joint ventures including marketing agreements and cross-shareholdings. BA has taken substantial shareholdings in USAir, Quantas (which is being privatized by the Australian government), TAT, the largest 'independent' French airline, and Deutsche BA, a regional German airline. BA is one of the most profitable airlines in the world, and its operating costs are lower than many of its main European rivals, so it should be well placed to meet such competition. On the other hand, many European governments would be disinclined to see their 'national champion' airlines decline in importance, and so might be tempted to search for ways of supporting them.[19] If BA had to compete against airlines which continued to receive hidden subsidies, its present financial strength might be insufficient.

Another possible scenario would be that route licences are freely available, but that access to congested major airports continues to favour incumbents. This could be the result of inertia, or of governments deciding to solve the problem of congestion by managing access directly, and in such a way as to maintain present route patterns. If this situation arose, competition between congested airports might remain muted, but fiercer competition would be possible on routes to uncongested airports. Access would be completely open on routes between two uncongested airports, but since these tend to be the smaller airports, with fewer passengers, this openness might not lead to large-scale entry, and passengers would have to look to the faded champion of contestability to keep fares low. BA's main bases, Heathrow and Gatwick, are too congested to allow the full force of competition in this scenario, which would favour the airline, while it might be able to use the massive spare capacity at Stansted to develop more regional services. BA's alliances with other airlines may allow it to take over some of their slots at other airports for its own use. BA was also involved in an abortive attempt to 'sidestep' the problem of congestion at major hubs, when it tried to create Sabena World Airlines. This company, a joint venture between Sabena, KLM, and BA, would have operated two or three flights every day to or from a large number of destinations from a hub at Brussels, which is relatively uncongested. By creating a new hub, the airlines would have been able to escape any restrictions on competition that were 'required' at other, congested, airports. Even if there was no problem with access to other airports, the new hub would have allowed Sabena World Airlines to avoid the high prices that would probably be charged to ration demand at presently congested airports.

If the European Union does not agree a multilateral package to

[19] In September 1993, Belgium proposed that the European Union should finance 'restructuring' in the airline industry, and delay liberalization, while the chairman of Air France resigned the following month when the government refused to back his cost-cutting plans in the face of a strike.

increase access to routes and airports by a significant amount, BA's future will depend on bilateral agreements between the UK and other countries. There are some routes on which the UK carrier would have a significant comparative advantage, particularly those where there are far more connecting destinations at the UK end of the route than the foreign end, and so more passengers would wish to change aircraft (but not airlines, if they can avoid it) in the UK than abroad. Agreements to liberalize these routes (which would include many of BA's long-haul routes, apart from the North Atlantic) would probably benefit BA more than its competitors. On the other hand, BA may be at a comparative disadvantage on the North Atlantic routes, because there are more connecting destinations inside the USA than inside Europe (since many major European cities have direct flights from a limited number of US gateway airports). If the government liberalizes routes where BA has a comparative advantage, the airline will prosper; if it can only reach agreement to liberalize routes where British airlines have a comparative disadvantage, BA will suffer. Even in an era of liberalization, BA's fortunes depend crucially upon government actions.

To sum up, the 1980s were a good decade for BA. The airline abandoned a mistaken strategy of expansion at the wrong time, and after cutting its costs, was able to expand later when circumstances were more promising. Vigorous cost-cutting helped it to remain profitable in the difficult conditions of the early 1990s. The timing of the improvement in its fortunes was not necessarily closely related to privatization or to its announcement, although it is quite possible that the commitment to privatize provided the credibility that was needed to reduce the labour-force rapidly in 1981, without provoking industrial action. Productivity and profitability are clearly higher than they used to be, and higher than for many of BA's competitors, although the oft-quoted increase in labour productivity exaggerates the transformation. Over the next few years, as the EU's liberalization programme starts to bring dramatic changes to European civil aviation, BA's prospects are probably at least as good as those of any other airline in the region.

References

Abbot, K., and Thompson, D. (1991), 'De-regulating European aviation: the impact of bilateral liberalisation', *International Journal of Industrial Organisation*, 9/1 (Mar.), 125–40.

Ashworth, M., and Forsyth, P. (1984), *Civil Aviation Policy and the Privatisation of British Airways*, IFS Report 12, London: Institute for Fiscal Studies.

Bailey, E. E., Graham, D. R., and Kaplan, D. P. (1985), *Deregulating the Airlines*, Cambridge, Mass.: MIT Press.

Banks, H. (1982), *The Rise and Fall of Freddie Laker*, London: Faber & Faber.

Bishop, M., and Thompson, D. (1992), 'Peak-load pricing in aviation: the case of charter air fares', *Journal of Transport Economics and Policy*, **26/1** (Jan.), 71–82.

British Airways (1973), *Annual Report and Accounts, 1972/73*, Heathrow: British Airways.

—— (1989), *Annual Report and Accounts, 1988/89*, Heathrow: British Airways.

CAA (1984), *Airline Competition Policy*, CAP 500, London: Civil Aviation Authority.

—— (1985), *Statement of Policies on Air Transport Licensing*, CAP 501, London: Civil Aviation Authority.

Campbell-Smith, D. (1986), *The British Airways Story: Struggle for Take-Off*, London: Hodder & Stoughton.

Cronshaw, M., and Thompson, D. (1990), *Competitive Advantage in European Aviation, or, Whatever happened to BCal?*, Centre for Business Strategy, Working Paper 82, London Business School.

Department of Transport (1984), *Airline Competition Policy*, Cmnd 9366 London: HMSO.

Encaoua, D. (1991), 'Liberalizing European airlines: cost and factor productivity evidence', *International Journal of Industrial Organisation*, **9/1** (Mar.), 109–24.

Forsyth, P. J., Hill, R. D., and Trengrove, C. D. (1986), 'Measuring airline efficiency', *Fiscal Studies*, **7/1** (Feb.), 61–81.

HMSO (1969), *British Air Transport in the Seventies*, Report of the Committee of Inquiry into Civil Air Transport, London: HMSO.

Kahn, A. E. (1991), 'Thinking about predation: a personal diary', *Review of Industrial Organization*, **6/2**, 137–46.

McGowan, F., and Seabright, P. (1989), 'The deregulation of European airlines', *Economic Policy*, **9** (Oct.), 283–344.

Monopolies and Mergers Commission (1987), *British Airways Plc and British Caledonian Group plc: A Report on the Proposed Merger*, Cm 247, London: HMSO.

National Audit Office (1987), *Report by the Comptroller and Auditor-General on Sale of Government Shareholding in British Airways Plc*, London: HMSO.

Oum, T. H., and Zhang, Y. (1990), 'Airport pricing: congestion tolls, lumpy investment, and cost recovery', *Journal of Public Economics*, **43/3** (Dec.), 353–74.

Stasinopoulos, D. (1992), 'The second aviation package of the European Community', *Journal of Transport Economics and Policy*, **26/1** (Jan.), 83-7.

—— (1993), 'The third phase of liberalisation in community aviation and the need for supplementary measures', *Journal of Transport Economics and Policy*, **27/3** (Sept.), 323–8.

Vincent, D., and Stasinopoulos, D. (1990), 'The aviation policy of the European Community', *Journal of Transport Economics and Policy*, **24/1** (Jan.), 95-100.

Windle, R. J. (1991), 'The world's airlines: a cost and productivity comparison' *Journal of Transport Economics and Policy*, **25/1** (Jan.), 31–50.

Vogelsang, I., and Green, R. J., with Abdala, M. (1994), 'The divestiture of British Airways', in A. Galal, L. P. Jones, P. Tandon, and I. Vogelsang (eds.), *Welfare Consequences of Selling Public Enterprises*, OUP and World Bank Publications.

5

Privatization and Regulation of the Water Industry in England and Wales

SIMON COWAN*

1. INTRODUCTION

The ten water authorites in England and Wales were privatized in1989. This was the third privatization of network utilities following the sales of British Telecom in 1984 and British Gas in 1986. These three industries have many characteristics in common but there are some special features of the water industry which make the study of its regulatory regime of particular interest. These include the possibility of some form of yardstick competition, the importance of quality and environmental regulation, the danger of underinvestment, and the possible introduction of metering.

Section 2 discusses the economic characteristics of water supply and sewerage and describes the current structure of the industry. Section 3 describes the complex regulatory framework which was introduced at the time of the privatization of the water authorities, including the pricing and investment regimes, and the regulation of quality and externalities. Section 4 considers six key issues in the regulation of the industry; pricing, yardstick competition, investment, the setting of the price caps, metering, and the setting of environmental and quality standards. Section 5 concludes.

* Institute of Economics and Statistics, University of Oxford.

This chapter is part of the project on *The Regulation of Firms with Market Power*, and financial support from the ESRC and from the Office of Fair Trading is gratefully acknowledged. I would like to thank Chris Bolt, Colin Mayer, and John Vickers for very helpful comments on an earlier draft. The views expressed are my own and I am responsible for any errors.

2. THE ECONOMIC CHARACTERISTICS OF WATER SUPPLY AND SEWERAGE AND THE STRUCTURE OF THE INDUSTRY

The water supply and sewerage processes and their economic characteristics

The water supply process involves the abstraction of water from underground sources and surface sources such as rivers and reservoirs, the treating of this water to remove natural and man-made pollutants and the distribution of the water via a network of mains to the consumer. Once the consumer has used the water most of it returns in the form of sewage. This is collected in sewers (known collectively as sewerage) and must then be pumped to a nearby treament works. Solids are removed and are either incinerated, dumped at sea, or used as fertilizer on farm land. The liquid product of a treatment works is effluent and this must be treated before being placed back into the water cycle, e.g. by being put into rivers. Some raw sewage is not treated at all and is pumped straight into the sea.

Externalities can enter into this process at several stages. Rivers and lakes from which water is abstracted can be polluted by boats, factories, or sewage treatment works sited further upstream. Underground water sources can be polluted by farmers' use of artificial fertilizers or pesticides. The dumping of sewage sludge can cause harm to fish stocks and raw sewage which is pumped out to sea can lower the quality of nearby bathing beaches. The externality issue is closely related to the quality issue. The costs of maintaining the quality of both drinking-water and rivers will increase as the competing demands for water expand and as man-made pollutants affect water sources.

The demand for water is price-inelastic and is seasonal. Demand reaches its peak in the summer when raw water availability is at its lowest level. Many customers, including 98 per cent of domestic households, do not have metered supplies so their demand for water is completely price-inelastic. Charges for water and sewerage for these households are generally based on the rateable value of their properties rather than on the amount of water consumed.[1] On the cost side the industry is very capital-intensive and its fixed assets have very long lives. Many of the fixed assets have little or no alternative uses and so are largely sunk. Examples are reservoirs and the networks of water-mains and sewers. Quality and environmental improvements typically require new processes and thus new capital equipment.

The water industry is the classic case of a naturally monopolistic industry. An industry is said to be naturally monopolistic if supply by

[1] Most new customers are metered, although some companies charge them on a flat-rate basis.

one firm involves lower costs than supply by more than one firm (see Panzar (1989) for a discussion of natural monopoly concepts). Duplication of the fixed network of mains and sewers would generally be inefficient, although for some large customers some duplication might be cost-effective, especially if different qualities of water can be provided. Even though duplication of the network is generally inefficient there could in principle be scope for product market competition if there was a national grid (as in the case of electricity). The pumping of water long distances is at present too expensive to make such a grid economic. This means that there is little prospect of competing water-treatment works being able to supply their water through a common network of mains, although some companies are developing regional grids as security against localized water shortages. Common carriage would in any case face considerable quality problems since water from different suppliers would be mixed together. Raw sewage is even more expensive to pump than water and sewage-treatment works are often sited close to the source of the sewage. Large conurbations are the exception—they sometimes have only a handful of treatment works.

The water and sewerage industry thus is composed of a series of local natural monopolies. The fact that these monopolies are local means that there are several opportunities for indirect forms of competition. There can be competition between contiguous firms for the right to supply new houses and businesses which appear on the boundaries of the companies' supply areas. If the water companies face similar operating risks then a regulator can use yardstick competition to help determine prices. This is discussed in more detail in Section 4 and in Chapter 6 of this volume by Price. The existence of a considerable number of local natural monopolies means that there can be competition *for* the market. This is the franchise option, which is used extensively in France.

The industry in England and Wales

There are currently ten companies in England and Wales which supply both water and sewerage services. These are the former water authorities. Currently there are also twenty-five companies which supply only water. These are the former statutory water companies which supply about one quarter of the population with water and were privately owned before the privatization of the water authorities. The combined turnover of the core businesses of the ten water and sewerage companies (WSCs) in 1990/1 was £3.7 billion and their combined operating profit (in historical cost accounting terms) was £1.2 billion (source: OFWAT, *News Release*, no. 16/91). The water-only companies had a combined turnover of £516 million with a combined operating profit of £110 million. The companies range in size from Thames Water which had a turnover of £681 milllion, an operating profit of £207 million, and serves a population of 7.2 million, to Hartlepools Water Company[2] which had a turnover of £5 million and operating profit of £1 million, with a population served of 91,000. The number of water-only companies has been reduced from twenty-nine at the time of privatization by mergers. The industry currently has a large investment programme of £28 billion in 1990/1 prices up to the year 2000 (source: OFWAT, *Annual Report 1990*, p. 15) which is mainly driven by the need to comply with the various environmental and quality standards set by the EC and the UK government.

3. THE REGULATORY FRAMEWORK

The framework before privatization and the events leading up to privatization

The ten water authorities were created by the 1973 Water Act. Kinnersley (1988: chs. 5–9) provides an excellent description of the foundation and performance of the water authorities. The principle underlying this reorganization was known as 'integrated river-basin management'. The authorities' boundaries were determined by the desire to include the whole of a river's catchment area in one authority. The authorities had regulatory functions in addition to their utility functions of water supply and sewerage (see Vickers and Yarrow 1988: ch. 11). These regulatory functions included the planning and control of water resources, control of river quality and drinking-water quality, and other services such as flood protection and land and highway drainage. The reorganization was designed to achieve the benefits of economies of scale and scope, but the combination of the regulatory and utility functions in the same organizations meant that the authorities were both poachers (polluters of rivers via effluent discharges) and gamekeepers (regulators of river quality) and thus their objectives could conflict.

During the 1980s the water authorities were subject to three external disciplines relating to investment, borrowing, and operating costs. A useful description of these disciplines is contained in the MMC report (1986) on Southern Water Authority and the statutory water companies in its area. On investment they faced a two-part financial target, the first of which specified that new investment should earn the Treasury's required rate of return (5 per cent for most of the 1980s) while the second specified 'a low but increasing return on the current value of

---

[2] Strictly speaking the smallest company is Cholderton in Hampshire, which supplies 2,000 customers with a turnover of about £100,000. This company is generally excluded from water industry statistics.

existing assets' (MMC 1986: 7, para. 2.8). Thus there was a recognition
that existing returns for the water authorities were low and should be
increased. This principle was continued when the price controls for the
privatized authorities were set, as will be seen in Section 4. Borrowing
was controlled by an external financing limit which meant that any
investment above this limit had to be financed out of retained earnings.
Finally there was a 'performance aim' which specified a target figure for
operating costs. The progressive tightening of the investment and borrowing constraints throughout the 1980s meant that investment had to
be financed increasingly by internally generated funds and thus that
water charges regularly rose by more than the rate of inflation. Even so
there is a widespread perception that there was underinvestment during
this period.

The statutory water companies continued to supply water after the
1973 Act but they were subject to a very different regulatory regime to
that of the publicly owned water authorities. Dividends, transfers to
reserves and accumulated reserves continued to be controlled (for more
on these controls see MMC 1986: paras. 5.15–23). This was effectively a
form of rate-of-return regulation in which any reductions or increases in
costs were passed through very quickly to consumers.

The first steps to the privatization of the water authorities were taken
by the publication in 1986 of a White Paper and a report by Professor
Stephen Littlechild on the economic regulation of privatized water
authorities. The White Paper suggested that the ten water authorities
should be privatized in their existing form, i.e. including both utility and
regulatory functions. A system of price regulation was favoured over
direct controls on profits, the need for quality standards was acknowledged, and the option to use franchising was rejected because the competition for the market would be very infrequent and because of the
standard problem of underinvestment by the franchisee. Littlechild was
asked by the Department of the Environment to advise it on economic
regulation and especially to examine the applicability of the type of regulation known as RPI – X, which had first been applied (at his suggestion)
to the regulation of British Telecom's prices. He was to assume that the
authorities would be privatized in their existing form. He concluded that
regulation would need to be permanent and would need to cover quality
as well as price. The existence of ten authorities would enhance the scope
for competition by enabling capital markets to compare different authorities and the operation of a take-over mechanism unconstrained by
'golden shares' would force companies to be efficient. The regulator
would also be able to make comparisons between authorities of quality
and price performance. A price cap rather than rate-of-return regulation
was preferred because of its simplicity and cheapness and because it preserves efficiency incentives. Since the regulatory system would need to

be permanent there would be a need for periodic revisions of the price cap in order to avoid the allocative inefficiency losses caused by prices deviating from costs for long periods. Littlechild recommended that revisions of the X factor should be based on an industry yardstick to ensure that no authority could influence its own revised X factor. He also suggested that there should be a single X factor for each authority rather than separate ones for water and sewerage and that there were virtues of simplicity in having a uniform value of X across all authorities.[3]

The White Paper suggested that the existing structure of the authorities would be maintained after privatization. In 1987, however, the Department of the Environment decided to abandon the principle of integrated river-basin management and to set up the National Rivers Authority (NRA). This would be a public body which would be responsible for the control of water pollution, the general management of water resources including the licensing of abstractions, and which would also take from the water authorities the responsibility for land drainage, flood defence, and fisheries. The separation of the environmental and quality functions from the utility functions countered a major criticism of the original privatization proposals. Given that privatization was to occur it was clearly safer to make this separation, although the functions could have been separated without privatization of the authorities.

The current regulatory framework

The framework of current regulation for the water authorities and companies was formalized by the 1989 Water Act and by the Instruments of Appointment (known as the 'licences') issued to each undertaker under the terms of the Act. The 1989 Water Act has been succeeded by the 1991 Water Industry Act—hereafter 'the 1991 Act'—which deals with OFWAT and its powers, and the 1991 Water Resources Act, which deals with the NRA. The 1989 Water Act provided for the setting-up of the Office of Water Services (OFWAT) headed by a Director General (DGWS) on the model of OFTEL and OFGAS. The first Director General is Ian Byatt who was formerly the Deputy Chief Economic Adviser to the Treasury. Under Section 2 of the 1991 Act his primary duty is to secure that the functions of water and sewerage undertakers are properly carried out and 'to secure that companies . . . are able (in particular, by securing reasonable returns on their capital) to finance the proper carrying out of (their) functions'. Subject to this duty he also has the secondary duties of ensuring that the interests of all actual and potential

---

[3] Littlechild proposed a uniform X on the assumption that capital structures could be adjusted for the water authorities and that the statutory water companies would not be included in the same regulatory framework as the authorities.

customers are protected with respect to prices, ensuring that the interests of customers and potential customers in rural areas are protected, and that there is no undue preference or undue discrimination in the fixing of prices, promoting efficiency and economy, and facilitating competition. It is envisaged that, although competition for existing customers is unlikely, there could be competition at the boundaries of water undertakers' areas for the right to service new houses or businesses, and the Act gives the DGWS the right to make such 'inset appointments'. The DGWS can modify licence conditions, and can refer his proposed changes to the Monopolies and Mergers Commission (MMC) if the undertaker does not agree to them. Under Section 32 of the 1991 Act the Secretary of State for Trade and Industry has the duty to refer any proposed merger between water enterprises to the MMC provided the values of the assets of the acquiring company and the company being taken over each exceed £30 million and the merger was not in place before 11 January 1989. When considering such a reference the MMC has the duty under Section 34 to 'have regard to the desirability of giving effect to the principle that the number of water enterprises which are under independent control should not be reduced so as to prejudice the Director's ability ... to make comparisons between ... water enterprises'. Thus the potential value of yardstick competition is enshrined in the legislation. These sections were added to the Water Bill in January 1989 to prevent or deter further speculative purchases of statutory water companies by the three French water companies. Three references were made around the time of privatization under what is now Section 32 of the Act, and these will be discussed in Section 4. Under Section 145 of the Act undertakers will not be permitted to base any charge on the rateable value of a property after 31 March 2000, so by that date a new charging base will need to be determined. This issue will be taken up in the next section when metering is discussed. The statutory water companies were brought into the regulatory regime set up by the 1989 Water Act and were allowed to convert to public limited company status. The 1989 Water Act also contained provisions for the lifting of dividend controls for these companies.

One of the key advantages claimed in the Littlechild Report for privatizing the ten water authorities was that the capital markets could encourage productive efficiency because inefficient companies would be disciplined by the take-over threat. This conflicts with the need to maintain a sufficiently large number of comparators to enable the regulator to operate yardstick competition, since the most likely raider is another water company. The nine English water authorities were privatized with a 15 per cent limit on individual shareholdings until the end of 1994 (and the restrictions on ownership of Welsh Water are even stricter) so the idea of an active market for corporate control was downgraded.

The details of the regulation of water undertakers are to be found in the licences. The main conditions relate to charges and to the pass through of exogenous cost increases. Charges are controlled by a variant of the RPI – X formula known as RPI + K. There are five services whose charges are subject to the price cap, measured and unmeasured water, measured and unmeasured sewerage, and trade effluent (discharges into the sewerage network by industrial enterprises which are of different strength to ordinary sewage). The price cap is a variant of the 'tariff basket' type of cap (see Beesley and Littlechild 1989). A weighted average of the proportional price increases cannot exceed RPI + K (although there is provision for using up any K which was not used in the previous year). The weights are given by the share of that service in total regulated revenue in the previous year. A very useful description of the formula and its operation is given in Centre for the study of Regulated Industries (1991). Each company was given a specific K profile for ten years. The (unweighted) average K in 1990/1 for the water and sewerage companies was 5.4 (with a standard deviation of 1.1), while the average for the water-only companies was 11.6 per cent (with a standard deviation of 6.5). Six undertakers have a constant K for all years until 1999/2000, while all other undertakers have declining K values over the ten-year period, reflecting the need for more internal finance in the early years because of the early investment peak. The Littlechild report acknowledged that regulation would need to be permanent and the licence provides for a 'Periodic Review' of price limits after ten years, but with the option for the undertaker or the DGWS to ask unilaterally for a review after five years. In fact the DGWS announced in July 1991 that he would conduct a review of all K factors after five years.

One of the risks that investors face is that environmental and quality standards might be tightened and that this would not have been allowed for when the Ks were most recently set. This is covered in the licences by allowing 'Interim Determinations', or what is more generally known as cost pass-through. The cost pass-through mechanism seeks to ensure that cost changes which are genuinely exogenous and outside management control do not alter the wealth of shareholders. Thus the present value (at a cost of capital to be determined by the DGWS) of the incremental costs which will be incurred up until the next periodic review date is determined. If this present value passes a materiality threshold then the mechanism proceeds, otherwise the process is delayed until the next year (if a new application is made) or until the next periodic review. If the threshold is passed then the original K values in the years until the next periodic review are adjusted until the present value of the extra revenue earned equals the present value of the incremental costs. In general there will be a large number of different profiles of K values which achieve this (one simple way to do this is to allow full recovery of increased expenditures in the years in which they occur), and the DGWS is required to look at various financial and accounting ratios to help determine which of the K profiles is acceptable. Thus the cost pass-through mechanism is forward-looking and long-term,[4] and this is appropriate given the long-asset lives and the fact that increased environmental and quality standards typically require fixed investment.

There are further licence conditions which relate to 'infrastructure charges', the prohibition on undue discrimination and undue preference, the provision of accounting information to the regulator, and the determination of levels of service information and targets. Condition C allows undertakers to charge one-off fees known as 'infrastructure charges' when new properties join the water or sewerage networks (in addition to any connection charges). These are supposed to help the undertaker recover some of the additional costs it incurs by taking on an extra customer because of the marginal impact on the need for new capacity. They can be seen as a substitute for long-run marginal cost pricing in an industry where metering is not widespread. Infrastructure charges were fixed at the time of privatization and are subject to a separate price cap of RPI + 0. Levels of service are one aspect of quality and the water companies are required to provide information to the DGWS on their performance on matters such as pressure of mains-water, hosepipe restrictions, flooding incidents from sewers, and speed of response to billing enquiries. The DGWS has indicated that he will consider asking the Secretary of State to make regulations under the Water Act to lay down enforceable standards if performance relative to expectations is poor.

The companies face tough environmental and quality regulation in addition to the economic regulation by OFWAT. The European Community has issued Directives on Drinking-Water Quality and Bathing Beaches which all member countries must meet. The Drinking-Water Directive requires that companies supply wholesome water and this is specified in terms of chemical and aesthetic parameters. The companies must achieve compliance with this Directive by 1995. Progress on compliance with the Directive is monitored by the Drinking-Water Inspectorate (part of the Department of the Environment) which also monitors those quality regulations set by the UK government which are stricter than the EC's regulations. Similarly the Bathing Beaches Directive, which affects eight out of the ten water and sewerage companies, must be achieved by December 1995. On the environmental side

---

[4] The use of financial and accounting criteria in determining the appropriate K profile after a cost pass-through application, however, would tend to push K factors up in the early years. This issue is discussed further in the discussion in Section 4 on setting K factors.

the companies have to achieve compliance with the Control of Pollution Act, Part 2 (1976). This relates particularly to sewage treatment works which have recently failed to comply with their discharge consents or are at risk of failing to do so. Since privatization some of the environmental regulations have been tightened. The programme for achieving compliance with the Bathing Beaches Directive was accelerated and in 1990 the Secretary of State announced that the dumping of sewage sludge at sea would be phased out by 1998 and that the UK would adopt the EC's Municipal Waste-Water Directive which will require additional facilities at sewage treatment works which discharge into the sea and estuaries. This tightening of standards has already caused a successful cost pass-through application by South West Water, which will have its Ks for 1992/3 to 1994/5 raised by 5 points to pay for an estimated increase in costs of £309 million up to 1994/5.

The ten water and sewerage companies were privatized in December 1989, with sales proceeds of £5.3 billion. This represented a considerable underpricing of the shares, since there was excess demand at the sale prices for all ten companies and there were substantial first day premia.

4. REGULATORY ISSUES IN THE WATER INDUSTRY

Regulation of prices and diversification

The water industry has natural monopoly characteristics, is not remotely contestable because most of its assets are sunk (both literally and in the economists' sense that they have little or no alternative uses), and franchising of the local monopolies has not been used. This means that regulation of prices is necessary in order to prevent privately owned firms exploiting their monopoly power. The need for price regulation is increased by the fact that many consumers do not pay charges which are directly related to the quantity of water and sewerage services consumed (because they are not metered) and for them water charges are akin to property taxes.

The difference between price-cap and rate-of-return is a matter of degree. Rate-of-return regulation tends to be characterized by frequent (and possibly stochastic) regulatory hearings, where there is argument over the appropriate rate of return and rate base and where exogenous cost increases can be passed through. Typically tariffs on separate products are set separately so the regulator must allocate joint costs. Under rate-of-return regulation there can be incentives to over-expand the rate base, and quality can be over-provided if quality improvements are associated with capital investment. Incentives for the reduction of X-inefficiency or slack are small because the firm will lose any incremental profits earned at the next rate review (which will probably be soon). Price-cap regulation is characterized by a longer regulatory lag, by greater incentives for removing managerial slack (at least in the period immediately after a price review), an incentive to cut quality unless quality standards are separately regulated, and freedom to rebalance tariffs within an overall average price constraint.

The system of price regulation for water is an interesting mixture of these two stylized regulatory systems. Although prices are controlled over the medium term (five or ten years), they are set in accordance with the DGWS's primary duty of ensuring that the firms are able to finance their operations by earning reasonable returns on their capital. When the K factors were set a cost of capital and rate base were determined. There is also a cost pass-through mechanism which allows firms to pass through exogenous cost increases, and the regulator is also allowed to use this mechanism to seek reductions in charges when costs have decreased or are lower than expected. There is room for rebalancing of tariffs, although this must be done within the constraint that each firm must avoid undue preference or undue discrimination. The fact that the tariff-basket type of price cap is used makes it likely that any rebalancing will move the price structure closer towards a Ramsey price structure as long as this does not conflict with the undue discrimination provision.

The water companies are heavily constrained in their core businesses and since privatization they have diversified into areas such as as television, electricity distribution, and waste management. The possible effects of this on the operation of the core business have worried OFWAT. A recent model by Braeutigam and Panzar (1989) illustrates some of the problems that can be associated with the diversification of a regulated monopolist into a competitive market. In particular they argue (p. 390) that under rate-of-return regulation the firm has 'incentives to misreport cost allocations, choose an inefficient technology (in some cases), undertake cost-reducing innovation in an inefficient way, underproduce in the non-core market, price below marginal cost in a competitive market which happens to be included in the set of core markets regulated by an aggregate rate-of-return constraint, and view diversification decisions inefficiently'. These undesirable features vanish under price-cap regulation (as long as the regulator has complete information) because the regulator does not need to allocate joint costs.

In the water case the undertakers are required to provide detailed regulatory accounts but OFWAT does not need to allocate joint costs every year. When the time comes to reset K values, however, some allocation of joint costs will be necessary. The companies will have an incentive to allocate as much of the joint costs, such as management time, into the core business, where cost recovery is guaranteed. This would penalize water consumers and could lead to unfair competition in the non-core markets into which the company has diversified. Related to the problem of the allocation of joint costs is the possible over-pricing of inputs supplied by the non-core business to the core business. OFWAT announced licence amendments in September 1991 giving the directors of the core business the duty to ensure that they have adequate financial and managerial resources to run the core business, and that they re-certify that this remains true after a diversification. OFWAT also announced that it was working on a methodology to detect cross-subsidization and will consider whether guidelines on cost allocation are necessary. Determining such rules will be very difficult for the regulator given the asymmetry of information. A final problem of diversification is that it introduces noise into the process of estimating the cost of capital for the core business, since the share price is the market value of both businesses.

Yardstick competition

Since the industry is composed of geographically separate natural monopolies the regulator has the opportunity to make comparisons between firms. The chapter by Price in this volume deals with the issue of comparative competition in the water industry more fully. The idea of yardstick competition (see Shleifer 1985) is to relate each firm's allowed price to an average of the other firms' stated unit costs. This means that the firm cannot achieve a more favourable price at the next review date by strategic manipulation of its costs. In cases where the firms' cost levels differ because of different and exogenous operating environments Shleifer suggests that 'reduced-form' regulation is possible, in which the regulator regresses the unit-cost levels on a vector of explanatory factors, and a firm's allowed price is then the cost level predicted by the regression equation.

Implementing such a scheme is fraught with difficulty. First if some explanatory factors are not included in the regression and these are correlated with the included factors then there will be omitted variable bias in the coefficients. Second and probably even more serious there are considerable problems involved in the data. As discussed by Price there are problems involved in measuring costs in a highly capital-intensive industry, measures of output are difficult when many consumers are not metered and the product varies in quality (this is especially true for sewage) and explanatory factors are often imprecisely measured. Some factors are exogenous in the short run but become endogenous in the long run such as the inherited-asset condition. It is possible that the use of panel data techniques might overcome the latter problem.

In the original K setting process a comparative efficiency review was undertaken which took into account various exogenous factors such as regional wage rates and sparsity of population. For a more detailed description of the explanatory factors used see MMC 1990a: 125. As a result of the efficiency review undertakers were placed in four efficiency bands and the banding determined the assumed reduction in operating costs. In addition it was assumed that a benchmark saving of 1 per cent per annum was achievable by all undertakers 'to cover the spur to efficiency associated with privatisation and technological change in the future' (MMC 1990a: 125, para. 8). The MMC did not reveal the exact process by which the bandings and baseline-efficiency target were derived.

The 1989 Water Act enshrined the possible virtue of comparative competition by giving the Secretary of State for Trade and Industry the duty to refer almost all feasible mergers to the MMC. In the summer of 1990 the MMC reported on three cases. The first and most important case was that of the Three Valleys merger which involved three water-only companies to the north-west of London (Lee Valley, Colne Valley, and Rickmansworth) which served a population of about 2.3 million. These three companies shared an important water-treatment works at Iver and had co-operated on this since 1970. Lee Valley was owned by the French company CGE. The MMC found that the merger was against the public interest on the grounds that it would reduce the number of independent comparators that the DGWS would have, but that it could be allowed if all the claimed gains from the merger were passed back to consumers in the form of lower prices. The merger was allowed on the basis that efficiency savings of 10 per cent would be passed through to consumers after five years. In the Mid-Kent Water reference the MMC upheld the principle of maintaining the number of independent comparators by recommending that CGE did not have board representation at Mid-Kent Water (in which it had a minority shareholding of 29 per cent) and had no involvement with management. The Secretary of State for Trade and Industry then ordered CGE to reduce its stake to at most 19.5 per cent. In this case there would be very few efficiency gains from the merger, unlike in the Three Valleys case. In the third case Southern Water plc was allowed to maintain its minority shareholding in the Mid-Sussex Water Company because the company was already controlled by the French firm SAUR. Other mergers in the North-East and South-East which were in place before the legislation took effect have not been affected although the DGWS has agreed to integration of management in return for reductions in price limits.

It is important to maintain the number of independent comparators for three reasons. First, econometric analysis of the Shleifer type needs a large number of comparators to maintain degrees of freedom and to maintain the power of tests of the estimated coefficients. Second, as stressed by the DGWS in his evidence to the MMC inquiry on the Three Valleys case, losing data points is important not just for econometric reasons but also because the effectiveness of other methods (such as Data Envelope Analysis) which seek to identify efficiency frontiers depends crucially on the number of observations. Third, it is possible that the firms will collude against a regulator who is trying to operate yardstick competition and such collusion might be more difficult the greater the number of firms.

The methods that will be used at the next price review are still being discussed and it remains to be seen whether an implementable system of comparative competition can be set up. Over time as the industry becomes more stable the regulator's task will be eased by the availability of panel data and by improvements in the consistency of the accounting data provided to the regulator, but any workable system will require considerable information to be provided to the regulator. Of necessity the regulatory burden is not a light one.

Investment

In any regulatory relationship which involves sunk investment the firm's shareholders and debtholders face the risk that they will not be allowed to earn the returns that they were previously promised. The regulator, who might be assumed to have consumer welfare as an objective, will have an incentive to encourage sunk investment by promising adequate returns on this investment and then, once the assets have been sunk, to reduce prices so that they just cover variable costs. The firm, realizing that the regulator has these incentives, may be deterred from making investment *ex ante*. The problem of underinvestment is especially acute if the firm and regulator have finite horizons. A simple example of such a model is given by Vickers and Yarrow 1988: 88–91. More recent theoretical analysis has suggested that when the relationship between the firm and the regulator lasts indefinitely there can be efficient outcomes (see, for example, Gilbert and Newbery 1988; or Salant and Woroch 1992). The intuition is that the firm can punish the regulator for breach of promise by not investing, while the regulator can punish the firm for not investing according to its promised path by cutting the allowed price. If each side weights future payoffs highly enough neither side will want to 'cheat' and there will be an efficient outcome. If the price is restricted to be the same in every period then the likelihood of efficient investment will decline the longer the asset life is. Indeed if the assets have an infinite life then once the optimal capital stock is in place the firm cannot impose an effective punishment on the regulator because there is no need for further investment. There can, however, be an equilibrium even with infinitely durable capital if the firm promises a rising investment path which approaches the optimal capital stock and the regulator promises to reimburse the firm's investment costs each period.[5] In this case the firm does have a credible punishment since it can refuse further investment.

The water industry is required to meet increased environmental and quality standards and much of the extra expenditure needed to achieve this will be capital expenditure. The assets created will have very long lives by comparison with the average of British industry and will largely be sunk. In 1989/90 Thames Water made a depreciation charge in its historic cost accounts of £32.7 milllion while the net book value of its fixed assets (in historic cost terms) was £1420.5 million, indicating an average asset life of over 40 years. This is more than twice the estimated average asset life of 17 years for UK companies in general estimated by Mayer (1988: 8). OFWAT monitors investment programmes closely and has threatened price reductions if the programmes fall behind schedule. The evidence of sunk assets, long-asset lives, and OFWAT monitoring suggests that there might be a problem of underinvestment in the water industry. There are, however, three factors which alleviate the problem. First, the regulator has the primary duty to ensure that the firms earn reasonable returns on their capital. Greenwald (1984) presents a model in which rate-of-return regulation can induce the correct incentives to invest if regulators are restricted by 'an appropriate "fairness" criterion' (p. 86), and the regulator's legal requirement to secure reasonable returns on capital can be seen as such a criterion. There will always remain a residual risk for shareholders, however, as legislation can be changed, especially by incoming governments who might give higher weight to consumer interests in the short term. Second, many of the shares of the ten water and sewerage companies are held by a large number of small investors, who may serve as a political constraint on any future expropriation by the government or the regulator. Third, the undertakers were allowed large real-price increases in the first few years of the investment programme in order to help them finance a large part of the investment through retained earnings. Thus real charges are rising in advance of the quality and environmental improvements. This allows the firms to receive some of the returns on investment earlier than if prices had tracked the rise in quality.

The setting of the K factors

The process of setting the *K* factors for the ten water authorities and (then) twenty-nine water companies is described in the MMC report (1990*a*) on the Three Valleys merger and in OFWAT's cost of capital con-

[5] See Vickers 1991.

sultation paper (1991b). The process was related to the policy of the Treasury towards water prices before privatization. As discussed in Section 3 the water authorities were required to earn 'a 5 per cent return on new investment and a low but increasing return on the current value of existing assets' (see MMC 1986: 7, para. 2.8). Thus there was recognition that for new investment to be justifed it had to earn the (public-sector) cost of capital but that existing assets (because they were sunk) could continue to earn rates of return below the cost of capital.[6] Over time as the old assets wore out and were replaced by new assets earning the higher rate of return the average rate of return on all assets would have risen.

In setting Ks the Department of the Environment decided that the existing assets should continue to earn the low accounting rates of return which had been targeted by the Treasury (about 2 per cent on the current-cost value of assets). All new investment, however, was to earn a private-sector cost of capital. This was estimated on the basis of the capital asset pricing model to be 7 per cent for the water and sewerage companies rising to 8 or 8.5 per cent for the water-only companies (the higher figure being for those companies which did not have a large parent company and which therefore had relatively illiquid shares). The net present value of the cash flows attributable to the *new* investment should be zero if the new investment is to earn its required rate of return. The present value of all future cash flows would then be the value of the cash flows which were attributable to the existing assets.

The present value of future cash flows would of course depend on the assumed K level. The setting of the K factors was then reduced to the choice of K which gave an appropriate present value of future cash flows. The appropriate present value was called the 'indicative value' and was taken to be the value of the existing assets if the regulatory regime *had not changed*. This was thought to be appropriate because this implied that existing owners (the government in the case of the water and sewerage companies and the private sector in the case of the water-only companies) would neither gain nor lose from the change in regulatory regime. For the water and sewerage companies the indicative value was calculated by discounting the cash flows that the exisiting assets would have generated if they continued to earn the Treasury's low accounting rate of return (about 2 per cent in 1988/9). Thus if there was no depreciation the indicative value for a water and sewerage company would be the Current Cost Accounting (CCA) value of assets multiplied by the target rate of return (about 2 per cent) and divided by the cost of capital (7 per cent). In practice, of course, the existing assets would depreciate over time and the cash flow used in the indicative value

---

[6] The required rate of return in the public sector was raised from 5% to 8% in 1989.

calculation would be 2 per cent multiplied by the asset base for that year plus the CCA depreciation charge for that year. For the water companies a similar projection of the cash flows that the existing assets would have earned with no change in regulatory regime was made. MMC 1990*a*: 126) describes in more detail the basis of the calculation for the water-only companies. For the SWCs the discount rate used in the indicative value calculation was 5.5 per cent to allow for the lower level of risk under the previous regulatory regime.

For each company the K factor was initially set at the constant fifteen-year level which would set the present value of cash flows equal to the indicative value. This was known as the 'economic approach'. Various financial and accounting criteria were then used to determine what pro-file the K factors should have, since there is an infinite number of ways of choosing a K profile to achieve a given present value. In particular, minimum levels for the interest cover (profit before tax and interest divided by the interest charge) and the dividend cover (profit after inter-est and tax divided by the net dividend) were set as was a maximum level of gearing. The assumptions about the level and growth of divi-dends were crucial, since a higher initial dividend or higher dividend growth would make the achievement of particular interest and dividend covers in future years more difficult. The criteria for gearing, interest, and dividend covers, and the assumed level and growth rates of divi-dends, had the effect of pushing up K factors in the early years, so that Ks are decreasing over time. Any relaxation of these criteria would enable lower K factors to be set in the early years. In the summer of 1989 the government decided to give the ten water and sewerage companies a 'green dowry' which involved the writing-off of some debt—in effect converting it into equity—and the injection of just over £1 billion cash into their balance sheets. This served to relax the financial constraints and to lower or at least to flatten K factors. One beneficial effect of hav-ing higher Ks in the early years when the investment programme is at its peak is that the companies recover more of their capital early on, and this might help to ease the potential underinvestment problem.

The role of comparative competition in the original K setting process was limited. The OFWAT paper (1991) on the cost of capital does not even mention comparative competiton. The operating cost projections of each undertaker were adjusted by the assumed efficiency factor derived from the efficiency studies. This would have the effect of lowering the constant K value necessary to give a present value equal to the indicative value and would mean that the financial and accounting criteria would be more easily satisfied. The change in the regulatory regime can thus be seen to have two conflicting effects on water charges. To the extent that closer and more effective monitoring by the capital markets made the firms more efficient, and the regulator is able to acquire these benefits for consumers through yardstick competition, water charges would be lower than otherwise, while the effect of the introduction of a regime which increased the cost of capital would be higher charges than otherwise.

The process of setting K factors was thus driven by financial considerations. The required rate of return and the capital base (the indicative value) played key roles in determining the broad range of Ks but the main determinant of Ks in practice appears to be the financial criteria (which are known as the 'Key Indicators' for cost pass-through purposes). In its paper on the cost of capital OFWAT (1991*b*: 24) states: 'The assessment of minimum levels for particular key indicators was central to the process of determining initial K values. In the event, the impact that the economic approach had on K values for the first ten years was small.' The DGWS (op. cit. 26) has a preference for flat Ks because these ensure that customers 'did not pay for improved quality standards before they received the benefit of them . . . thus achieving a proper balance between charges paid by different generations'. He argues that the financial criteria should be relaxed in the next review and states (p. 24) that 'Subsequent evidence of market sentiment in a more settled position suggests that investors and creditors are prepared to take a somewhat longer perspective of the financial performance of water and sewerage companies.' The relaxation of the financial criteria and the reduction in the assumed rate of dividend growth which the paper argues for would allow lower K factors to be set. In addition OFWAT suggests that the cost of capital used in present-value calculations for K setting and for future cost pass-through applications should be lowered. The cost of equity was estimated to be in the range 5 to 7 per cent in real terms and the real cost of debt was estimated to be in the range 3 to 5 per cent. The assumed maximum level of gearing (debt/debt-plus-equity) was raised to 50 per cent or even 75 per cent in some cases. These figures suggest a weighted average cost of capital figure in the range 5 to 6 per cent, with a small increase to allow for Corporation Tax of 0.25 per cent. This is considerably lower than the figure of 7 per cent for the pre-tax real cost of capital which was used in the initial determination and will be the subject of considerable debate[7] over the period to the next review. It is clear that if lower numbers for the cost of capital and the financial ratios are used at the next review then the K factors will be reduced, though the extent of the reduction is unclear at present.

It is not clear, however, how the rate base will be determined at the periodic review. In the original K setting process the rate base was the

---

[7] The Water Services and Water Companies Association (1991) have issued a detailed three volume response to the OFWAT cost of capital paper arguing for a real cost of capital of 9.5% and questioning the OFWAT evidence on market sentiment over financial ratios and dividend growth.

indicative value but the OFWAT paper does not come to a conclusion about the appropriate rate base for use in 1995. One possible rate base could be formed by adding the current value (in 1995) of assets created since 1990 to an updated version of the indicative value. Thus if there was no depreciation the rate base in 1995 would be the original indicative value (about 2/7 times the CCA value of assets in 1989) plus the CCA value of assets created since 1990. Use of this asset base would allow continuation of the original policy of slowly increasing the overall rate of return by allowing all newly created assets to earn the market rate of return. The K-setting process was dominated by financial considerations but if widespread metering occurs then in future reviews the regulator will have to consider in more detail the long-run marginal costs of water and sewerage services, and will need to consider how two-part tariffs or more general non-linear pricing schemes could be used to encourage efficient pricing.

Metering

Whether all households should have meters is a key question for future policy. After 1 April 2000 the industry must find an alternative charging base to rateable values. OFWAT issued a consultation paper on alternative charging methods in November 1990. The economic benefits of installing meters include the reduction in operating costs as consumption decreases and the avoidance of extra capital costs as new reservoirs and other infrastructure investments can be cancelled or postponed. The costs are the costs of installation, the costs of reading and maintaining meters, and the loss of consumer surplus as consumption falls. In the Watts Report—Department of the Environment (1985)—it is implicitly assumed that the loss of consumer surplus is exactly 'balanced by the gain in equity among water consumers' (OECD 1987: 106). If the present value of all economic benefits and costs is positive then a decision needs to be made about the optimal time to introduce metering. It might be better to delay metering until metering technology improves. For more details on the economics of metering see Warford 1966, and OECD 1987.

Evidence from the metering trials recommended by the Watts Report suggests that for 95 per cent of properties the cost of meter installation would be below £200 but for the remaining 5 per cent of properties the cost might average £1000 (source: OFWAT 1990: 23). The total cost of a programme of general metering could be £3–4 billion at 1990 prices. The same post-Watts trials suggest that a 10 per cent reduction in water demand might occur with metering. Thus it appears that, while selective metering might be economic, a programme of general metering is not justified. This result might change as the real price of water increases and the costs of installation of meters falls. The DGWS announced in December 1991 (OFWAT 1991c) that he was recommending that metering is extended selectively in places where water resources are scarce, that more customers should be made aware of the right to opt for a meter at their own expense (which should be increasingly exercised as real water charges increase) and that all new properties should be metered.

Once meters are in place, even if only in some areas or for some types of property, many of the same issues of pricing policy which occur in other network utilities will occur in the water industry. Four issues are the balance between fixed and variable components in a two-part tariff, the question of short-run versus long-run marginal-cost pricing for the variable component of the tariff, the possibility of peak-load or seasonal pricing, and the possibility of non-linear tariff schedules. On the issue of the structure of the two-part tariff, the water industry asserts that up to 80 per cent of the costs of supplying water are fixed costs so there is a need for a relatively large standing charge. In Byatt (1991), OFWAT (1990), and OFWAT (1991c), the DGWS makes it clear that he would prefer one which had a relatively small standing charge and thus had a high marginal price of water. He draws a distinction between those costs which are related to the number of customers connected and those which relate to the volume of water supplied. Costs which in the short run are fixed, such as capital costs on a new reservoir, are related to the volume of water supplied and should, argues the DGWS, be recovered from the variable component of the tariff. On the issue of short-run versus long-run marginal-cost pricing the theory is clear that in the short run prices should be equal to short-run marginal costs but in the long run as the capital stock changes short-run and long-run marginal costs should converge—see Slater 1989. There are reasons of practicality for avoiding the swings in prices which such a policy would imply, however, and the DGWS, following the 1978 White Paper on nationalized industry pricing prefers long-run marginal-cost pricing (see Byatt 1991). Peak-pricing would be very desirable but is not feasible with current metering technology, although it is possible that this will change. One way to discourage peak consumption is to have a rising block tariff so that, as one consumes more, one pays more per unit—this is feasible since all it requires is total consumption over a period to be measured. For those who are not to be metered there remains a need to develop an alternative charging base by 2000. Two possibilities are a flat-rate fee or a banding system which might try to proxy household consumption by the number of rooms, total floor space, or property type. Several water companies are already investigating schemes of this type and the DGWS is encouraging further research. Tough decisions will also have to be made about whether unmeasured customers should contribute to the costs of installing meters in those households where metering is economically desirable.

The setting of environmental and quality standards

In Section 3 the current system of quality and environmental regulation was described. These regulations are exogenously imposed, mainly by the EC, and they are policed by public bodies. The current system of separation of environmental and quality regulation from economic regulation offers considerable scope for inefficiency. Baron (1985) presents a theoretical analysis of the regulation of a monopoly by separate environmental and economic regulators.[8] In his model the environmental regulator chooses the required pollution standard and fee first to minimize a weighted sum of expected environmental damages and expected abatement costs less expected pollution fees. The economic regulator then chooses the price and lump-sum transfer rules as functions of the firm's report about the parameter which characterizes its pollution-reduction technology. The economic regulator knows the pollution standard and fee that the environmental regulator has set but only knows the distribution of the pollution-reduction parameter. His objective is to maximize a weighted sum of consumer surplus and profits. The non-cooperative equilibrium is characterized by a higher pollution standard and a higher consumer price than the equilibrium achieved when the regulators cooperate. In addition the firm prefers the non-cooperative equilibrium because this enables it to exploit its privileged information about its pollution-reduction technology and earn an 'information rent'.

A very simple stylized model which captures some of the features of the regulation of quality in the water industry can be set up. Suppose that, as in the Baron model, the quality regulator chooses the required standard first to maximize its objective function, the direct utility that consumers receive which is increasing at a decreasing rate in the quality level. The economic regulator then chooses price to maximize consumer surplus. In the absence of asymmetric information the price is chosen so that the firm breaks even. The firm's unit-cost level is increasing and convex in the required quality standard. Demand is inelastic and fixed at one unit and consumer surplus is composed of direct utility less the price. The social optimum is where the marginal benefit to the consumer of increased quality is equal to the marginal social cost of quality improvement. The (subgame perfect) equilibrium of the non-cooperative game as specified is, however, for the quality regulator to set the standard at the maximum feasible level, which is where consumer surplus is

---

[8] See Bernheim and Whinston 1986 for a general analysis of the 'common agency' problem with moral hazard, and Stole 1991 for an analysis with adverse selection.

zero. The over-provision of quality arises because of the difference in the objective functions of the regulators. The quality regulator is assumed not to care about the costs of quality improvement (and hence the price that consumers face) but the over-provision of quality result holds more generally, as long as the quality regulator places a greater weight on the consumer's direct utility than on the costs of providing quality. In the water case those who set the standards do not directly consider the effects on prices and it is clear that there is no reason to expect the actual quality–price combination to be the optimal one. Byatt (1991) has argued that new environmental and quality obligations should be properly costed and should not simply be imposed without consultation with those who have to pay for them. Of course OFWAT does have a small role in quality regulation since it sets minimum standards for water pressure, interruptions of supply, and foul flooding, and on other aspects of service companies are required to provide the DGWS with information on their performance relative to their targets.

On the environmental side it is economically efficient to charge sewage-treatment works appropriately for discharges (although one alternative might be to issue tradeable permits) so that the firm internalizes the external costs, but it is not clear why it should be water consumers who should pay for the extra cleaning processes necessary to provide an adequate quality of water in so far as it is third parties such as farmers and industrial firms which cause the pollution of the water sources in the first place. There is a case for taxing the pollution of these third parties.

5. CONCLUSION

The water industry is still subject to very detailed regulation. The overall level of price increases is controlled, the regulator has statutory powers to prevent undue price discrimination, and investment plans and levels of quality and pollution are closely monitored. The prospects for direct product-market competition are tiny in spite of the government's announcement in October 1991 that it will relax the restrictions on competition at the boundaries so the companies have to look elsewhere for sources of growth, and their diversification decisions are subject to regulatory scrutiny.

The signs are that both the economic regulation of OFWAT and the environmental and quality regulation will become tougher still. OFWAT believes that the original price settlement was too generous to the industry and too harsh on consumers—the cost of capital paper quotes the Chairman of the Thames Customer Service Committee who said in 1991 of the financial and accounting criteria used in the original *K*-setting process that 'those assumptions looked simple enough at the time; but the success of the public issue, the strength of water shares in 1990, and comparisons with other utilities make them appear unduly generous today' (OFWAT 1991*b*: 8). OFWAT has revealed a tough bargaining position in its cost of capital calculations, has urged the companies not to take all the available price increases, and has criticized firms which have not maintained their investment programmes. A new government might further tighten the regime for the companies and might even consider taking the ten water and sewerage companies back into public owner- ship, although this would now be very expensive. Similarly environ- mental and quality standards are likely to continue to rise, especially since the price consequences of increased standards are not considered by those who set them.

Privatization of the ten water and sewerage companies inevitably required a substantial and detailed regulatory regime to be set up to safeguard the environment and quality standards and to control charges. An advantage of the new system is that the regulation of price and environmental and quality standards is now explicit and progress against targets can easily be checked, whereas the previous regime was opaque. The cost of this explicitness is the considerable complexity of the regulation. The future success of the regulatory system will depend largely on whether OFWAT can institute a workable system of compara- tive competition and can achieve the goals of both allocative efficiency and fairness between consumers and investors at the same time as ensuring that the firms are still willing to invest. In the absence of direct product market competition there is thus a very heavy burden on the economic regulator.

6. POSTSCRIPT

By late 1993 a number of these issues had been resolved. For *K*-setting the DGWS announced that he intends to keep to his original intention of having a cost of capital for new investment in the range 5–6 per cent. The idea of updating indicative values to use as asset bases was rejected, and instead OFWAT opted to use initial market values, averaged over the first 200 days of trading, and will adjust these figures for subsequent capital expenditure. The use of present values was downgraded as part of the *K*-setting process, and instead a revenue requirement for each year will be calculated as the sum of operating expenditure, the amount needed to maintain capital and the allowed return on capital. Some com- panies agreed to license changes that restrict the possible sources of cost- pass through, and the mechanism was changed to one based on a revenue requirement.

References

Baron, D. P. (1985), 'Noncooperative regulation of a nonlocalized externality', *RAND Journal of Economics*, **16**, 553–68.

Bernheim, B. D., and Whinston, M. D. (1986), 'Common agency', *Econometrica*, **54**, 923–42.

Beesley, M. E., and Littlechild, S. C. (1989), 'The regulation of privatized monopolies in the United Kingdom', *RAND Journal of Economics*, **20**, 454–72.

Braeutigam, R. R., and Panzar, J. C. (1989), 'Diversification incentives under "price-based" and "cost-based" regulation', *RAND Journal of Economics*, **20**, 373–91.

Byatt, I. C. R. (1991), 'Office of Water Services: regulation of water and sewerage', in C. Veljanovski (ed.), *Regulators and the Market*, London: Institute of Economic Affairs.

Centre for the Study of Regulated Industries (1991), *The UK Water Industry: Charges for Water Services 1991/2*, London: The Public Finance Foundation.

Department of the Environment (1985), *Joint Study of Water Metering: Report of the Steering Group*, London: HMSO.

—— (1986), *Privatisation of the Water Authorities in England and Wales*, Cmnd 9734, London: HMSO.

—— and the Welsh Office (1989), *Instrument of Appointment of the Water and Sewerage Undertakers*, London: HMSO.

Gilbert, R., and Newbery, D. (1988), 'Regulation games', Discussion Paper 267, London: Centre for Economic Policy Research.

Greenwald, B. C. (1984), 'Rate base selection and the structure of regulation', *RAND Journal of Economics*, **15**, 85–95.

Kinnersley, D. (1988), *Troubled Water*, London: Hilary Shipman.

Littlechild, S. C. (1986), *Economic Regulation of Privatised Water Authorities*, a report submitted to the Department of the Environment, Jan. 1986.

Mayer, C. (1988), 'The real value of company accounts', *Fiscal Studies*, **9/1**, 1–17.

Monopolies and Mergers Commission (1986), *Southern Water Authority: Eastbourne Waterworks Company, Folkestone and District Water Company, Mid-Kent Water Company, Mid-Sussex Water Company, Portsmouth Water Company and West Kent Water Company*, Cmnd 9765, London: HMSO.

—— (1990a), *General Utilities plc: Colne Valley Water Company and Rickmansworth Water Company*, Cm 1029, London: HMSO.

—— (1990b), *General Utilities plc and the Mid-Kent Water Company*, Cm 1125, London: HMSO.

—— (1990c), *Southern Water plc and Mid-Sussex Water Company*, Cm 1126, London: HMSO.

Office of Water Services (1990), *Paying for Water*, Consultation Paper (with 10 annexes), Birmingham: OFWAT.

—— (1991a), *Annual Report 1990*, Birmingham: OFWAT.

—— (1991b), *Cost of Capital: A Consultation Paper* (i and ii), Birmingham: OFWAT.

—— (1991c), *Paying for Water: The Way Ahead*, Birmingham: OFWAT.

Office of Water Services (1991*d*), *News Release*, no. 16/91, Birmingham: OFWAT.

Organization for Economic Co-operation and Development (1987), *Pricing of Water Services*, Paris: OECD.

Panzar, J. C. (1989), 'Technological determinants of firm and industry structure', in R. Schmalensee and R. D. Willig (eds.), *Handbook of Inudstrial Organization*, i: 3–56, Amsterdam: North Holland.

Salant, D. J. and G. A. Woroch (1992), 'Trigger price regulation', *RAND Journal of Economics*, **23**, 29–51.

Shleifer, A. (1985), 'A theory of yardstick competition', *RAND Journal of Economics*, **16**, 319–27.

Slater, M. (1989), 'The rationale for marginal cost pricing', in D. Helm, J. A. Kay, and D. Thompson (eds.), *The Market for Energy*, Oxford: Oxford University Press.

Stole, L. A. (1991), 'Mechanism design under common agency', mimeo, Massachusetts Institute of Technology.

Vickers, J. S. (1991), 'Privatization and the risk of expropriation', paper prepared for the Third Villa Mondragone International Economic Seminar, mimeo, Oxford University.

—— and Yarrow, G. (1988), *Privatization: An Economic Analysis*, London: MIT Press.

Warford, J. J. (1966), 'Water "Requirements": The investment decision in the water supply industry', *Manchester School of Economic and Social Studies*, **34**, 87–106.

Water Services Association and Water Companies Association (1991), *The cost of capital in the water industry*, i, ii and iii, London: Water Services Association.

6

Gas Regulation and Competition: Substitutes or Complements?

CATHERINE PRICE*

INTRODUCTION

The gas industry's privatization in 1986 was undertaken with what many regarded as indecent haste and on exceptionally favourable terms to the industry, even by the standards of other Conservative privatizations. Despite a number of criticisms (e.g. the Energy Committee 1985 and 1986; Price 1986; and Hammond, Helm, and Thompson 1986) the government sold the industry intact and with very light regulation. It was the second (and last) of the utilities to be sold as a single company and outlook for consumers was particularly bleak. However by early 1992 the industry was in turmoil as various regulators sought to curb its market power. This chapter examines the industry's progress from nationalized to private monolith, and compares its behaviour (particularly in pricing) in each setting. The main question addressed is how far regulation has developed and succeeded in redressing the ills caused by what is now widely regarded as an inappropriate privatization. The history of the industry is traced before and through privatization, and the nature of regulation imposed at flotation is described. This emerged not as the passive control which might have been imagined, but a dynamic relationship between the regulator (OFGAS) and British Gas (BG), developed in the context of intervention from bodies concerned with more general competition policy. Thus BG's reaction is traced in the context of a changing regulatory environment, which included the privatization of electricity and the subsequent 'dash for gas' by generators. The regulator's role in the industrial gas market is considered in more detail in Davis and Flanders' chapter in the companion volume.

The prospects in gas are not entirely clear, but it is certain that the industry is living in exciting times. So many agreements have been announced, denied, renegotiated in late 1991 and early 1992 that the situation may change again. This paper traces and projects some trends, and suggests that privatization of any industry is likely to be an interesting

* Department of Economics, University of Leicester.

beginning rather than an ending—happy or tragic—to an industry's development.

Gas was privatized in 1986, two years after the privatization of British Telecom. The industry had been nationalized in 1949 from a variety of municipally and privately owned companies and its original structure (twelve independent area boards) reflected its function as producer and distributor of gas within regional areas. In addition a Gas Council was incorporated with a co-ordinating role. Area boards were subject to the government(s)' various policies on nationalized industries between 1949 and 1972, including two White Papers (Treasury 1961 and 1967) which purported to give guidance on pricing, investment, and financial policies. In 1972 the area boards and the Gas Council were amalgamated into a single British Gas Corporation, largely to reflect the industry's new function as a national transmitter and distributor of North Sea gas. This source of supply required an integrated transmission system and rendered inappropriate the previous regional structure. It also created an unusually large and powerful nationalized corporation.

The finances of the industry improved dramatically with the advent of North Sea gas, although government policy to restrain nationalized industries' prices at times of high inflation occasionally disguised these. In the early days of nationalization, gas struggled to compete with cheaper coal and the 'modern image' of electricity. More cost-effective production methods were sought, and a major investment programme for oil gasification was overtaken by the discovery of commercial quantities of gas in the North Sea during the mid-1960s. Two factors contributed to the industry's early profitability after unification: the nature of gas supply as exploitation of a limited resource implied rising costs over time, so that the established supplies were generally cheaper than new supplies (this was especially true of southern-basin compared with newer more expensive northern-basin North Sea reserves). This was exacerbated by the sharp rise in oil (and therefore gas) prices in 1973 and 1978 which made fixed-price contracts signed before these increases particularly good value (for the purchaser).

Governments' general policies on nationalized industries suggested some form of marginal-cost pricing. Gas was among the most vociferous opponents of such pricing policies, pointing out special difficulties in implementing them where the definition of the margin is unclear. Marginal-cost pricing would suggest high profits in sectors of the industry subject to increasing costs, i.e. gas exploitation. This is counteracted by the decreasing costs inherent in any distribution system, the factor which defines the 'natural monopoly' element of utilities.

Ascertaining the objectives and policy of the gas industry when nationalized is not easy, partly because of unclear guidance from governments, and partly because of the industry's own secretive approach in discussing such matters. (It ruled the most general discussions of costs and pricing to be confidential for commercial reasons, and was much less forthcoming than most other nationalized industries.) However the industry's approach at this time is relevant both because tariffs are controlled relative to a given base (inherited from the nationalized structure) and because it may illuminate the privatized industry's management objectives since management personnel have changed little since privatization.

One of the most striking aspects of the industry's pricing policy was its definition of 'premium markets', i.e. consumers willing to pay more for gas than the value of its crude heat. In effect this meant the domestic market and industrialists who found the convenience or special qualities of gas heating particularly useful, and excluded the general industrial heat-raising market. Sometimes the industrial market was split according to whether the gas price was related to the 'gas oil' (higher price, higher quality fuel) or the fuel oil price used for basic energy needs. However the gas industry's next argument, that gas should be saved for premium users, and not wasted on non-premium users, had a strange implication. This was that premium users, who most valued the gas, should have access to it at lowest prices. Such an argument is not easily justified on economic grounds; the most likely explanation from the gas industry's viewpoint is that it protected and encouraged those markets with lowest long-term price elasticity of demand. Thus they could be wooed to gas through the lower premium price, and then would be faithful to the gas industry if prices rose later.

Such a scenario seemed likely in the 1970s, when the availability of future North Sea supplies was uncertain. The industry anticipated with unease a substantial decrease in reserves and rise in price by the end of the century, and the consequent shrinking of its market. Capturing a domestic and 'small industrial' market to prolong the industry's life and profitability was an attractive strategy. There is certainly evidence from the late 1970s that the margin between price and marginal cost was much lower for the domestic than for the industrial market. This is also the market with lowest elasticity of demand because the switching costs for consumers are much higher relative to their fuel consumption than in other markets, the very reason for its attractiveness to BG; the implication is that the divergence of price from marginal cost is least in the least price-elastic market (Price 1984), the exact opposite of either a short-run profit maximizing or a welfare maximizing Ramsey rule. Thus the gas industry's policy followed neither a marginal-cost pricing rule as recommended in some government White Papers (especially Treasury, 1967) nor the most generally accepted alternative, raising most those prices in least elastic markets. Perhaps the industry's reluctance to discuss pricing policy is not surprising.

The gas industry suffered repeatedly from the dichotomy between the government's principle of arm's-length management, and the practice of detailed intervention. Like all nationalized industries its prices were suppressed both under Labour governments in the 1960s and Conservative governments in the 1970s in the interests of general macroeconomic policy. In the 1980s, the same objectives (anti-inflation) led to *raised* prices and reduced Public Sector Borrowing Requirement, enforced by tighter external financing limits. But the gas industry suffered two particular actions pertinent to the current debate.

The first was the government imposition of a 30 per cent real rise in domestic prices during the three years from 1980. The pressure for such a change had come in one of the Price Commission's last reports (1979), whose publication was delayed by the general election. It is rumoured that on taking office Mrs Thatcher thought its recommendation of higher domestic gas prices (apparently fully justified by costs) were too politically sensitive to implement. However by the following January just such increases were announced in the House of Commons by the Secretary of State for Energy. Such overt fine tuning of an industry's price structure was unusual, and tilted the pricing balance of the markets supplied. In fact this represented an improvement in efficiency terms, reversing the domestic market's favourable treatment outlined above. However it does not lessen the impact of detailed fine-tuning by government on an industry's management morale.

The second intervention, though shared with other utilities, was less justifiable and even more politically motivated. The latter aspect was underlined by its announcement at the 1982 Conservative Party Conference, the last before the 1983 General Election. This scheme required both the gas and electricity industries to rebate standing charges for consumers using small amounts of fuel, and whose standing charges would otherwise have exceeded their fuel-related charges. This was seen as a response to the 'fuel poverty' lobby, who were particularly anxious about the deleterious effects of high fuel costs on the old and the poor. Analysis at the time and later (Gibson and Price 1986; and OFGAS, 1991) showed that such a scheme would miss many of the poor, and help some of the better-off—to paraphrase the words of the established Church such a scheme would have 'done those things it ought not to have done, and not done those things which it ought to have done'. But its political attributes were paramount. These were enhanced by the requirement that the scheme be subsidized from within the industries. OFGAS' recent publication (1991) highlights the problems that the consequent increase in commodity costs may create for poor large users of gas, but this was not acknowledged at the time. Ironically the rebate scheme gave beneficiaries (supposedly the poor and the elderly) a double incentive to reduce consumption; for each therm saved lowered the cost paid not only for that unit of fuel but also the standing charge, since this had to be lowered in line with total fuel charges.

Both these interventions are examples of the kind used by the government to justify its privatization programme—ironically both perpetuated by that same Conservative government, though Labour governments have also yielded to such temptations, as we have noted. However in the gas industry's case other forces inclined towards privatization. The most obvious was the industry's healthy financial position, which was an embarrassment so long as it was nationalized. Such awkwardness sprang from two sources. The first was susceptibility to charges of exploitative pricing. Governments and nationalized industries had never confronted the problems of losses (assumed to imply inefficiency) and profits (suggesting exploitation); this was one of the many difficulties of developing coherent pricing policies in the light of the nationalization acts' and general public assumptions that the industries should break even. Thus profits were 'difficult to explain', and the gas levy on some fields was introduced partly to conceal such profits; more justifiably it reflected the 'scarcity premium' arising from the exploitation of a non-renewable resource, and treated the southern-basin fields in a similar fiscal way to those northern-basin fields subject to petroleum revenue tax.

But what exercised the civil servants much more were the difficulties of managing an industry as profitable as gas. The traditional sanction of nationalized industry activity was through the annual review and request for Treasury funds needed for further investment. But the gas industry was clearly going to become entirely self-financing and independent of government funds during the 1980s. This posed control problems, especially given the independent and ebullient nature of the industry's chairman, Dennis Rooke.

The first proposal for privatization came in 1980, with the suggestion that British Gas showrooms should be sold. These occupied prime high street sites with the dual function of selling appliances (over which BGC had a virtual monopoly) and facilitating customer service. Both management and unions within the industry strongly opposed the proposal, which was eventually dropped with government muttering of grander designs to follow.

More ambitious plans gained credibility after the 1984 privatization of British Telecom, the first utility to be sold. However it is worth pausing to consider the differences between this sale and the proposal for gas. Telecom is subject to rapid technological developments, and was expected to sustain competition from other private companies after a very short time (though the hopes that regulation would no longer be required after five years proved unduly optimistic). Neither of these factors applied to gas, and even the extent of existing competition in the industrial market was a moot point, discussed at considerable length at the time of privatization by the Energy Committee (1986) and later by the Monopolies and Mergers Commission (1988). In this context we can identify access to gas pipelines to carry 'third party' gas, an essential prerequisite for gas to gas competition in an industry where the expensive network is owned by the incumbent monopolist. The development of competition in the industrial gas market is the subject of Davis and Flanders' chapter in the companion volume, but its role in the general privatization of the industry is crucial. This can be illuminated by pre-privatization legislation designed to encourage competition, and the reasons for its failure.

In 1982 the Oil and Gas (Enterprise) Act made available to potential competitors the use of BGC's pipelines. Where agreement on charges for their use could not be reached the Department of Energy was to act as arbiter (the system used for BGC's negotiations to buy gas from North Sea suppliers, which had achieved success for buyer and government in driving down prices). Like the standing charge rebate scheme this was implemented in a pre-election year, and considerable pressure was put on the government's friends to activate the conditions of the Act before the 1983 election (indeed so little success did the Act or its successors achieve that a similar scenario was necessary, with similar lack of result, before the 1987 election). The reasons for the Acts' failure lie in the power held by an incumbent monopolist, trying to protect the market from competition, and should have been a warning to the government about potential difficulties. BGC had immense market power, and could easily threaten to make life difficult through its nationwide hold on the market for any oil company attempting competition. The Act's powers were strengthened (and similar provisions extended to electricity, with familiar lack of response) in the 1983 Energy Act. No gas-to-gas competition had developed by the time the privatization bill came before Parliament at the end of 1985.

PRIVATIZATION

Gas privatization was announced in May 1985, and events then moved with enormous, and perhaps ominous, speed. The pace was determined by the government's temporary inability to sell British Airways pending litigation over the failed Laker airline. Since the proceeds from BA's sale were built into the government's financial estimates, they needed an alternative candidate for privatization. Speed and sales proceeds were of the essence, and here factors which had been an embarrassment for a nationalized industry became assets for the government. The most obvious was the industry's profitability, which could be 'cashed in' through the sales proceeds. Allied to this was the failure to engender competition in the industrial market, which clearly raised potential profits there. How far the government consciously took the cynical view that consumer exploitation in the interests of higher profits and selling price was desirable is not recorded. But the pre-privatization debate could certainly be interpreted in this way.

Discussion can be divided into two related parts—the structure of the privatized industry, and its regulation thereafter. The British Gas Corporation, formed in 1972 from twelve regional area boards and a central gas council, was an enormous monopoly supplier; it covered supply to the entire nation, but retained the regional structure for internal management purposes, so consumers continued to be billed by the relevant area board. Retention of these regional internal management structures made possible the sale of the industry in its constituent parts, selling each area board, and retaining the central supply and transmission function as either a public or a carefully regulated private firm. Indeed such a structure had been suggested to deal with the profitability problem under public ownership in the early 1980s. This would have had enormous advantages in providing incentives for gas sales by making common carriage available to all suppliers on the same financial basis, the very argument that has preoccupied regulators of BG since privatization. Such separation of the transmission system would enable the development of a market in gas sales and purchase between North Sea producers and independent companies. Moreover the regulator would have information from twelve regional companies with which to make yardstick comparisons. This is in stark contrast to the reluctance of BG to provide even basic pricing information to the regulator under the present régime. All these aspects would have operated in the consumers' interests, and was just the arrangement commended by Hammond, Helm, and Thompson (1985); Price (1986); and many others.

However they were certainly not in the interests of senior management, who were concerned to see their substantial empire retained intact. Dennis Rooke made it clear that he would co-operate with the privatization only if the Corporation were sold (and he retained control) as a whole. Given the effective opposition of management and unions to sale of the industry's retail outlets, this was not a combination the government wished to unite against the privatization and the government's haste to realize the profits resulted in the industry's sale to the private sector intact. The only exception was that certain onshore oilfields were sold separately, though this was part of an earlier decision about the industry's right to operate such fields.

The failure to divide the industry, either regionally or by market, raised considerable concerns about its market power. This can be considered both in its traditional sense, and in the newly significant sense of information available to the regulator, who would be required to moderate the industry's monopoly power. We have seen that the industry had monopoly in both the domestic and non-domestic sectors. In the former case gas supplied about 85 per cent of the domestic heat and cooking market where gas was available; and gas met 36 per cent of non-transport fuel demand in the industrial market. While a *regional* division of the industry would have been straightforward since regional administrative structures and identities had been maintained, the mutual use of pipelines by different end-users rendered division between *markets* impracticable in the time-scale envisaged. Thus the integrated industry would continue to supply both sectors, one in which it dominated supply and one in which it supplied over a third of the market.

The opportunities for restructuring the industry forfeited at privatization were compounded by the regulation applied after flotation. By the time gas was privatized the role of regulation as a (sometimes temporary) substitute for competition was established, and would be expected only where there was no actual or potential competition. The conflict between the regulator's task in constraining prices and encouraging competition is examined by Davis and Flanders in *The Regulatory Challenge* (Bishop, Kay, and Mayer (eds.) 1994), but here the context of the whole industry is considered. It was reasonable to expect some areas to be unregulated, e.g. the retail appliance outlets which were increasingly competitive. However the industry's monopoly power was evident in gas supply to both domestic and non-domestic markets. Against this background the decision to regulate only about 60 per cent of gas supply seemed naïve or exploitative, depending on the degree of cynicism possessed by the observer. The division was between *regulated tariff* supplies, to consumers using less than 25,000 therms per annum, and individually negotiated and confidential contracts for larger users. Thus the domestic and small industrial and commercial markets were regulated, and the larger consumers continued to have gas supplied with no public knowledge of its terms and no regulation. Since gas satisfied more than a third of the (non-transport) *fuel* market, it was difficult to argue that no monopoly power was present, despite BG's claim that it reacted only to oil prices. The failure of the Oil and Gas (Enterprise) and Energy Acts to generate any gas-to-gas competition left it with 100 per cent of the gas market in all sectors. This was a disturbing prospect, viewed with particular alarm by the House of Commons Energy Committee.

The Energy Committee was in process of producing a report on gas depletion when privatization was announced. This report was published in July 1985, addressed tangentially some issues of privatization and declared its intention to seek evidence on the proposed regulation. This subsequent report duly appeared the following January, although the details of the regulation were not published until December 1985. Several witnesses questioned the form of privatization, in particular the decision to maintain the Corporation intact, but the committee, while acknowledging these doubts, considered it too late in the legislative process to do more than debate the role of regulation within the given framework. However members were dubious about the development of gas-to-gas competition, and emphasized the importance of free access to the transmission system; to ensure this they identified the importance of clarity in the appeals procedure for use of the transmission system, of separate accounting for this system, and of the regulator's easy access to BG's accounts. It was not clear to the committee that effective gas-to-gas competition would develop without structural changes in the industry, a premonition confirmed by later developments.

In general, gas privatization seemed to be a hurried attempt by the government to 'plug a hole' in expected receipts from privatization. Some viewed it as an exercise in extraction of maximum consumer surplus, resulting in higher profits for the firm and therefore greater sale value. Certainly the lack of structural alteration and what was widely regarded as very light regulation was consistent with such a strategy. Moreover the size of the regulatory body (less than twenty when first instituted, and still below thirty employees in 1991) did not inspire confidence in the government's commitment to effective control of the industry. OFGAS excluded consumer representation, which was undertaken by a separate Gas Consumers Council. However the monolithic nature and monopoly power of the industry and its traditional secrecy contrasted with the apparently weak powers and limited jurisdiction of the regulatory body, and boded ill for gas consumers.

REGULATION

The regulation details were published in December 1985, and the formula for controlling tariff prices caused much pre-Christmas mirth when debated in the House of Commons, because of both its late release and its complexity. This arose from two factors which had not affected the (fundamentally similar) British Telecom regulation. One was that prices were aggregated differently in the two industries. In BT's case all the services to be controlled were averaged into a so-called tariff basket, where the weight for each price was the revenue which had been raised by that service in the previous time period. This meant that once the prices had been fixed for the forthcoming time period, the formula was already determined by the revenue weights inherited from the previous period. However since gas regulation was of a uniform tariff, division into separate markets (for example seasonally, regionally, or according to consumption level) would have been an artificial device, inappropriate in light of the industry's reluctance to differentiate the tariff either seasonally or regionally. Therefore the regulation applied to gas was of its average revenue, i.e. the total revenue divided by the gas sold in the year in question. Since the tariff consisted of a fixed standing charge and a uniform running rate, this could not be determined until after total sales were known. Gas demand varies considerably with winter temperature, so that sales and therefore average revenue are also variable. This meant that the average revenue had to be forecast for the coming year, and a correction factor included in the formula. This K correction factor, and its determination, did not simplify the presentation of the formula to MPs.

The uncertainty reflected by need for the K factor arose from the existence of a standing charge. Previous discussion about the standing charge rebate scheme illustrates the public sensitivity on this matter, and it was the cause of much discussion in the privatization debate. The government had suggested that the standing charge rise no faster than the rate of inflation, i.e. it wished to have a separate non-binding advisory constraint on this element of the tariff. The only change which the opposition managed to introduce to the legislation was to make this restriction mandatory. This in effect determined the commodity rate of the tariff also, since the aggregate was regulated and the only other element was subject to a separate constraint, though of course it left the industry some discretion if both constraints did not bind. In reviewing the initial quinquennium of legislation we shall see that they have not always raised both elements of the tariff by the maximum permissible amount.

There was another special factor which affected gas. This arose from the industry's role as purchaser and distributor, and the necessity to buy supplies from the North Sea under existing contracts containing various price-escalation clauses. Since such gas purchase costs were largely outside the control of British Gas, at least in the short term, regulation permitted such price increases (or decreases) to be passed directly through to the consumer—the so-called Y element. However this exemption created its own difficulties. When new contracts were negotiated the Y element reduced the pressure on British Gas to achieve the best bargain, since high costs could be passed on to consumers in the regulated market. Moreover the suppliers would also know of this pass-through, and be able to take advantage of BG's reduced bargaining incentives. The counter argument was that in the non-regulated market (about 40 per cent of BG's business) BG would have an incentive to reduce purchase costs because these markets were supplied under competitive conditions—the justification for not regulating them. But we have already seen that such competition was very limited, and this weakened the incentives to reduce costs leaving monopoly power to enable substantial pass-through for all markets.

A related disincentive effect arose from the distinction between gas purchase costs and others, in that these so-called gas costs could be passed on, while prices for other services were subject to a steady reduction under the formula. Thus where there was a choice of providing services via the gas and non-gas costs, there was a distortion in favour of the industry choosing the 'gas cost' route. One example of this is the provision of gas at winter peak. The seasonal nature of gas demand poses considerable costs for the industry; gas taken unevenly from the North Sea, to fit the demand pattern, is more expensive, so the industry meets at least some of this seasonal demand from storage. In constraining the recovery of storage costs in the tariff but not the gas purchase price, the regulatory formula encourages the industry to abandon storage in favour of more expensive and more seasonal gas supplies. The intermittent and confidential nature of gas supply contracts makes this effect difficult to measure, but its difficulty was acknowledged and amended at regulatory review. The original gas regulation was to remain in place for at least five years, after which time either BG or OFGAS could ask for a review by the Monopolies and Mergers Commission (MMC). In fact OFGAS undertook its own review, to which BG agreed, so it did not need to to be referred to the Monopolies and Mergers Commission for arbitration. In due course we shall consider this review and the light it has thrown retrospectively on the original regulatory process.

The regulator's duties were not concerned only with the price-cap formula; he also has a duty to encourage competition. This duty is shared with other competition regulators who have a more general remit, notably the Office of Fair Trading and the Monopolies and Mergers Commission; for gas the strong monopoly powers preserved by privatization and the weak regulation imposed gave these bodies a more prominent role than in other utilities. Ironically it was the allegation of price discrimination in the *unregulated* sector which first attracted the MMC's attention, and this is an important factor in the development of competition in the industrial market discussed by Davis and Flanders. For present purposes we need only note that the MMC established the presence and abuse of monopoly power. Remedies included publication of non-negotiable price schedules in the contract market and more detailed charges for gas transport, and the reservation of 10 per cent of new fields for other suppliers. Most sinister for BG was the recommended review of these arrangements after five years in the light of achieved competition.

The troika of regulators which emerged proved a powerful force in somewhat unpromising circumstances and threw an interesting light on some aspects of the regulatory process. Although OFGAS is charged with controlling prices only in the tariff sector, it is intervention in the non-regulated sector which has been most significant. Moreover the price discrimination which was the subject of the 1988 MMC report had been practised for years by the nationalized industry, with the knowledge of government departments which felt unable to intervene. Thus subjecting the industry to general competition policy in the private sector permitted intervention in practices which had not been accessible when BG was nationalized; privatization introduced a new transparency into regulation. The fact that the MMC report, drastically changing the industry's competitive conditions, could be produced only two years after the shares were sold also suggests that the purchase of such shares may have been more risky than many had assumed at the time. It was believed that competitive conditions were defined for shareholders at flotation, and that significant changes (at least unfavourable) would be unfair. However the government accepted and implemented the MMC report, despite the adverse effect on BG's profits. A further change is now likely following the joint OFGAS/Office of Fair Trading report. This might have implications for other privatization issues if competitive conditions were subject to later alteration and the investment appeared less assured.

Another lesson from the MMC report is in the powerful incentive for an industry to change its behaviour. The anxiety of BG to return to confidential contracts in the industrial market (presumably to continue the price discrimination which triggered the reference) has led the industry to make considerable concessions on allowing third-party use of its pipelines—one of the pre-conditions of such confidentiality; we should normally expect an industry in BG's position to raise access charges above costs to restrict entry (Laffont and Tirole 1990). However analysis of the gas carriage schedules shows that the industry has moved from a position of reluctantly producing inadequate information (the subject of an early dispute between the industry and its regulator) to one where the transport charges seem so low that it is difficult to understand why anyone should choose to buy gas from BG, rather than from another source and transport it through BG's system (Price 1992). The only explanation for this change which is not otherwise in the industry's interests is a rapid return to confidential contracts.

RELATIONS BETWEEN BG AND OFGAS

Relations between the industry and its chief regulator have often been stormy. BG was a potentially difficult industry because of its secretive history. It was unlikely to welcome the attentions of a regulator, particularly since it had traditionally believed, with supreme confidence, that BG's interests and the national interest coincided. The regulator's job was not helped by the monolithic nature of the industry, so that comparative-performance indicators were not readily available, and the small size of the regulator's office was in marked contrast to the vast number of employees at BG's disposal. Moreover the chairman, Dennis Rooke, had already caused difficulties for more than one Energy Minister. Given the disparate sizes of the two groups and the immense market power inherited by the privatized industry the outlook for effective regulation was not bright in 1986.

However in arguments over information the regulator called BG's bluff, and generally obtained what was required. Consultants were employed on a regular basis to strengthen the office staff, and the separation of the Gas Consumers Council from the regulator's office (if only by one hundred yards) helped to provide a stronger check on the industry. The intervention of the MMC, and the request for OFGAS to implement the decision, was also crucial in strengthening OFGAS' hand. However the most significant factor was probably the personality of the Director General, James MacKinnon, who proved to be as obstinate as Dennis Rooke and his successor in pursuing his ends. At the very least he made it clear that BG would not be able to flout the rules with impunity, and has reacted to BG actions with threats of litigation on several occasions. Usually the altercation has resulted in a partial or total back-down by BG.

But in whose interests should the regulator be operating? The separation of the GCC makes it clear that he is not merely representing consumers. The regulator himself has pictured his role as that of surrogate competition, making regulation even more like the beer which can reach those parts which competition cannot reach. And of course the conflict between regulation and competition is a very real one, shown by Davis and Flanders in their analysis of potential competition in the industrial sector. There is certainly a concern that gas shareholders should receive an adequate reward for their investment, and this raises a number of issues about appropriate return in such industries, both in whole and in their different parts. It also calls into question how far structural (rather than regulatory) changes in the industry which affect profits can be implemented after shares are sold to private buyers. Rate of return became increasingly relevant as the time for review of the regulation drew near, and led to one of the most important joint exercises between the industry and its regulator, to allocate costs of production to different activities, and hence markets.

The incentives for BG to use cost allocations strategically are intimately bound up with the regulatory régime under which it operates.

The great advantage of price-cap regulation is that it removes the obvious 'cost-plus' regulation associated with the rate-of-return restraint which had been practised in the USA. Unfortunately many of these problems reappeared when the regulation was to be reviewed, for it was difficult to judge its appropriate level other than in terms of the industry's (or the regulated sector's) rate of return. The initial price-cap regulation on British Telecom was seen as a temporary measure, so review of regulation was not anticipated, though events have proved this view to be unduly optimistic. By the time gas was privatized the semi-permanence of regulation in areas where competition seemed unlikely was recognized. However initial regulation emerges from a variety of political and financial considerations, and is privately determined by the government and interested parties. Revision of regulation is different: the issue is less politically fraught; there is no incentive to ensure a good return to investment, though the Director General of Gas Supply must 'secure that . . . [BG] are able to finance the provision of gas supply services' (Gas Act 1986); and there is at least a degree of public consultation. Rate of return is an inevitable factor in this review process.

Whether it should be the rate of return to the industry as a whole or just to its regulated sector is unclear, but has important consequences for the industry's incentives. If the costs of supplying the regulated sector are clearly distinct from those of the industry's unregulated activities then only the regulated return would be relevant. Even here there are problems of identifying equivalent investments to determine an appropriate rate of return, but at least the task can be undertaken separately for the regulated part of the industry. However since the essence of network industries is that assets and costs are shared between markets such separation is not feasible. The Director General of Telecommunications focused on return for the whole industry, which removes the need for disaggregation of costs. However the Director General of Gas Supply has concentrated on return in the regulated sector, requiring the costs attributable to the regulated sector to be identified. Hence the habit which BG developed of allocating costs differently for different purposes and the need to undertake the joint-cost exercise.

This was to allocate the costs of production and assets to the different activities and markets. The difficulties of cost allocation had arisen in an number of contexts. For example the two early cases of carriage charges eventually produced by BG in autumn 1986, suggested that costs of transport were very high (to deter potential users); they were in marked contrast to the industry's answer to the Energy Committee the previous year claiming that costs varied regionally so little that regional price variations were not worth considering. The problem of inconsistent cost allocations became more severe when evidence was given to the MMC which showed quite different attributions for different purposes. BG's explanation for the discrepancy convinced neither the MMC nor the regulator, and so a joint-cost allocation exercise was initiated.

When the regulated sector is reviewed the industry wants to emphasize the cost of supplying this sector, implying a low return and justifying a laxer constraint in the next time period. This is a clear incentive, but was complicated for BG by investigation of the non-regulated contract market. In order to argue here that discriminatory practices did not result in excessive profits, the industry wanted to allocate a large proportion of costs to the non-regulated sector. At the same time it was attempting to limit competition, and so also wished to justify deterrent rates for use of the network—which the Gas Act makes clear must be charged to other users at the same rate as BG charges it for its own use. To some extent high carriage charges could raise costs in both regulated and unregulated markets, but even so the industry could not allocate more than 100 per cent of its costs to these sectors.

However a third market did provide some room for manœuvre, namely the interruptible gas market. This was available only to consumers buying very large amounts of gas, and BG could prevent significant movement from the firm to the interruptible industrial markets through restrictive conditions and information about the firms concerned. One way of increasing costs in the tariff and firm contract market was to use the device of attributing negative 'onshore' costs to the interruptible market. BG argued that interruptible gas enabled more firm supplies to be sold because load balancing was helped by the lack of commitment to peak supply. However while cost of delivering interruptible gas may be close to zero it is difficult to believe it is negative as BG claim. Clearly such a mechanism enabled BG to 'balance its books' while keeping costs high to justify discriminatory pricing and lax regulation.

The use of rate-of-return also revives other incentives associated with this type of regulation, since the regulatory regime becomes one of periodic rate-of-return review, with price cap in the interim. The industry's reaction to this combination depends on how myopic it is between reviews: if it behaves on a year-to-year basis then the cost-reducing incentive effects of the price cap will dominate; immediately before a review, and earlier if the industry is far-sighted, its behaviour will reflect that of a rate-of-return regulated institution. This is familiar from the US experience, and includes not only the way costs are allocated, but more importantly from a real-resource allocation point of view, the level and type of costs likely to be incurred. British Telecom and British Gas are single industries with no counterpart in the private sector. The existence of several firms in the electricity and water industries at least allows some basis for comparison, and the Director General of Water Supply expects to use 'yardsticks' in assessing costs of the firms. However there is little such opportunity in gas.

We should therefore expect that BG will wish to raise its capital base in order to justify a higher absolute level of profits, and a laxer constraint in the next period. This will mean a concentration on markets with a high capital base—i.e. a continued protection (through low prices) of the domestic market, and other sectors which have a high proportion of peak demand, which is very capital-intensive to supply. We would also expect it to try to disguise profits, especially in the period immediately before a review. This was evident when British Telecom ceased a regular annual series of price-restructuring exercises in the year before its regulation was to be reviewed. Such behaviour is not obvious in the case of gas, perhaps because the timing of review was less determinate. This uncertainty may alleviate some of the jerkiness of transition from price-cap regulated to rate-of-return regulated behaviour; on the other hand it may merely perpetuate the worst features of both.

In the event OFGAS undertook the review in 1991, and BG has agreed to the implementation of the recommendations from April 1992, the earliest date at which alterations were possible, despite some wavering in the light of major reform in the contract market. There has been some consultation in the process of the review, and a short consultative process after its publication, but the most significant factor is the cost allocation exercise. Even though its results are not published it provides an opportunity to examine both BG's behaviour during the first quinquennium as a regulated private industry, and the way in which the industry and its regulation may change. Though detailed discussion of the MMC report on the unregulated sector is left to Davis and Flanders, developments in the two sectors are closely related. This is particularly true of the 1991 regulation review and the 1992 agreement on BG's share of the contract market.

BG'S RETURN TO PRIVATIZATION AND REGULATION, 1986 TO 1991

A review of the nationalized industry's behaviour before privatization is appropriate here, especially its pricing policies, since these will be the main focus of BG's reaction to later events. We have noted that the British Gas Corporation had protected its so-called premium markets, by charging less to the domestic and firm industrial consumers whom it felt valued gas most (and would be the most loyal longer-term consumers, especially where their fuel-burning appliances locked them into the gas system for a long period). Thus the pattern of prices was rather a strange one. The government's official policy seemed to be some form of marginal-cost pricing, without resolving the problems which such a policy causes in decreasing-cost industries. Efficiency and profit maximization both suggest that where marginal costs do not produce sufficient revenue, prices should be raised most above costs in markets with lowest price elasticity of demand. This would be the 'premium' markets, by definition, while the BGC did exactly the reverse, protecting these markets through low prices. Therefore we would expect BG to reverse these policies to achieve maximum short-run profits under privatization. At privatization we should expect to observe the effects of two factors—the change in objectives and the change in regulation. However the former may be mitigated by the continuation of the same senior management. The effect of regulation depends on the relative dominance of short-term (partial price-cap) and long-term (rate-of-return) factors.

Analysing the role of regulation in the structure of tariffs is complicated by the nature of that regulation. It applies to only one market sector—the tariff market—and a single uniform tariff. There is thus little room for manœuvre, and the possibility of rebalancing with the standing charge is circumscribed by a separate constraint on this element. However some movements are discernible. One is that lower commodity rates have been offered to larger consumers within the tariff market. This will not affect domestic consumers, but does make the transition between the tariff and the contract schedules smoother, and reduces the incentive to flare gas in order to qualify for lower prices at higher quantities (an incentive exotically described as the 'flame of shame'). Incidentally, it also starts to tilt the balance in the direction which both profit and efficiency maximization would suggest, reducing prices to consumers with more elastic demand within the tariff sector. This is to be welcomed on efficiency grounds. The new band introduces some scope for 'abuse' of the original tariff constraint, in that the smaller consumers can now be charged a higher rate which is counterbalanced by the lower cost to high consumption tariff users, while still satisfying the *average* revenue constraint. However the small number of consumers at the top end of the tariff range probably makes this insignificant, and OFGAS have not shown particular concern at this stage.

Within the tariff constraint we would also expect to see heavier price increases on the least price-elastic element. The problem is that it is unclear whether this is the commodity charge or the standing charge and attempts to discover this have not resulted in definitive results. We may observe that the constraint has not been binding on the standing charge, which has risen less than the maximum permitted amount. The separate regulation of the standing charge reflects concern about the distributional effects of such large increases; the fact that BG have not raised this element as much as they might suggests that they are sensitive to the political pressures which lie behind the constraint.

Since regulation applies to a tariff with no regional or seasonal differentiation, a policy stoutly defended by the BGC, we might expect privatization to induce the introduction of such distinctions. This would

almost certainly increase both profit and efficiency, though the appropriate tariff structure would depend on the costs of introducing the necessary measurement and billing devices. So far there is no move to change
the tariff structure, but we see seasonal elements in carriage charges and
contract schedules. These are of a rather different kind (much more
marked in the carriage charges, which is probably appropriate given the
lack of dilution of BG costs by the gas purchase element present in the
contract schedules). There is also a long-standing discount for interruptible supplies which reduce the demand on the gas system at peak.
Carriage charges in themselves define a regional pattern of prices, and it
is hard to see how BG can obey the requirement that it charge itself on
the same basis as potential competitors while delivered BG gas is not
distinguished by region or season. This point formed a significant part
of the OFT/OFGAS report in the autumn of 1991.

It is impossible to compare either carriage charges or contract schedules with pre-privatization behaviour, since the former did not exist and
the latter were confidential (and discriminatory). Nevertheless it seems
that BG is increasing the formal differentiation of its prices (though of
course the price discrimination may itself have included very fine-tuned
differences). In the gas delivery market it is practising price absorption
of the kind anticipated by spatial monopoly theory (Phlips 1983). The
increase in transparency and differentiation has been marked over the
past five years, and is likely to have implications for other markets.
However the report of the Office of Fair Trading and changes in early
1992 suggest that even during the review of regulation the government
remained dissatisfied with the degree of competition. Such a view seems
rather naïve from the government which privatized an industry with
strong monopoly powers and very light regulation, and defended the
industry's view at the time that there was substantial inter-fuel competition in the non-tariff market. This may be genuine change of heart, but
investors might feel that they had been subject to some sleight of hand in
having additional restrictions imposed after the shares had been sold.
Such actions are likely to be good news for consumers however, and will
probably increase overall efficiency. This is discussed further in considering future prospects for regulation and competition.

In balancing the level of charges between markets, we have noted that
prior to privatization the industry raised prices above marginal costs
least in those markets which were most price-elastic. Study of BGC's
policies in the 1970s and early 1980s showed that this was disturbed by
the government's intervention to raise domestic prices from 1980 to
1983. However it is not only prices which BG can influence, but also
costs, as the joint-cost allocation exercise indicates. Thus we should also
expect to see BG increasing the costs allocated to the tariff market, and
this is indeed evident. Since the joint OFGAS cost allocation is not avail-

able to the public we cannot check the validity of such a change, but we can note that in evidence to the MMC, BG made it clear that the proportion of costs attributable to the tariff market was higher than they had previously claimed. This was needed, of course, to ensure a laxer regulatory constraint at review. Whether without this device the constraint would have been tightened even more is a moot point.

Unconstrained efficiency maximization requires marginal-cost pricing in each market, but profit requirements are likely to preclude this outcome. A revenue-constrained industry maximizing efficiency or profits will raise price above marginal costs most in markets with lowest price-elasticity of demand (though by different amounts in each case). Although we do not know how demand responds to separate changes in standing charge and running rate the Department of Energy (in Helm, Kay, and Thompson 1989) has produced estimates of elasticity with respect to total charge, and these are shown in Table 6.1.

TABLE 6.1. Gas price elasticity of demand with respect to own price

Market	Short run	Long run
Domestic	−0.2	−1.1
Other industry	−0.3	−1.5

Source: Department of Energy.

These estimates confirm the anticipated outcome that demand is more elastic in the long run and for the non-domestic sector. It suggests the ratios in the relevant markets with different objectives shown in Table 6.2.

Cost analyses show the allocations of costs, and observations of average revenue set out in Table 6.3.

TABLE 6.2. Gas prices: ratios of $pj - MCj : pj$ with different objectives

Market	Unconstrained efficiency maximization	Profit maximization	
		Short run	Long run
Domestic	0	5	0.9
Other industry	0	3.3	0.7

They yield the figures for Table 6.4.

These ratios demonstrate a remarkable switch from protection of the domestic market in 1980, before the government forced domestic price increases, to a situation where the proportional mark-up in the domestic

TABLE 6.3. Gas prices: costs and average revenue

Market	1980		1983		1991	
	Cost	AR	Cost	AR	Cost	AR
Domestic	27	21	39	38	34	49
Firm industrial	18	28	30	25	26	28
Interruptible industrial	16	20	21	21	23	17

Source: Price 1991.

TABLE 6.4. Gas prices: ratios of $Arj - Cj : Arj$

Market	1980	1983	1991
Domestic	−0.3	0	0.3
Firm industrial	0.4	−0.2	0.07
Interruptible industrial	0.2	0	−0.4

market is much closer to that implied by both profit and efficiency maximization. The most efficient ratio of prices with budget constraint lies between the (unconstrained) efficiency-maximizing and profit-maximizing positions, depending on the tightness of the budget constraint. For this purpose it is the long-run price elasticity which seems most relevant. What is striking both before and after privatization is the presence of a (different) market which is supplied *below* cost (i.e. with a negative ratio of $Arj - Cj$ to Arj). Both welfare and profit considerations indicate positive mark-ups in all markets, albeit at a differential rate. These types of distortion are consistent with revenue maximization subject to budget constraint before privatization and profit maximization subject to rate-of-return regulation afterwards, though their magnitude remains surprising. They illustrate the effects of ownership and regulatory régime on the relation between price and cost. Presumably this arises from pursuing maximum profits after privatization, but achieves the happy coincidence of improving efficiency. The distortions from budget-constrained welfare maximization seem to be less (and are at least in the appropriate directions) than for the nationalized industry.

The non-gas costs can be separated from the foregoing tables to yield the figures shown in Table 6.5 which suggest increased managerial efficiency under privatization (particularly since these figures are in money terms), though this is complicated by the non-allocation of some costs in the 1991 exercise. Nevertheless there seems to be a prima-facie case for suggesting there have been efficiency gains.

TABLE 6.5. Non-gas costs of gas supply (pence per therm)

Market	1980	1983	1991
Domestic	14	21	14
Firm industrial	4	12	4–9
Interruptible industrial	2	3	2–3

REVIEW OF REGULATION

In late 1990 OFGAS announced its intention of reviewing the regulatory formula, using the joint-cost allocation exercise conducted with BG, and invited submissions from interested parties. These were received and processed, and in spring 1991 OFGAS published its proposals, again followed by a short consultation period. The essence of the proposed changes was to tighten considerably the level of regulation—increasing the X factor from 2 to 5 per cent, and introducing a requirement to achieve some efficiency gains in gas purchase also (of 1 per cent a year). A new energy efficiency element was introduced. This permitted 100 per cent pass-through of BG's costs incurred under the energy efficiency heading. The next review was set for five years after 1992, making the period determinate.

The tightening was expected in light of the influence of political and financial factors present at flotation but not at subsequent reviews. It also follows the pattern of British Telecom and the British Airports Authority, the other reviews so far completed. BG agreed to the new formula in the autumn of 1991.

However much more fundamental changes have occurred (almost simultaneously) in the non-regulated market. In October 1991 the Office of Fair Trading reported that competition was not developing in the contract market, despite the 'dash for gas' by several independent electricity generators. They identified the remedy as the separation of the transmission and storage operation into a separate subsidiary, and the divestiture of 60 per cent of the existing gas contract-market to competitors. Several months of negotiation followed, during which the parties made various announcements about their agreement, though these were often mutually inconsistent. In March 1992 it appeared that BG had agreed to these conditions, while expecting some further review of the tariff constraint to compensate for lost profits. The Director General of OFGAS had not agreed to such a review, so the industry faced simultaneous tightening of constraints in both the regulated and non-regulated sectors.

Views on the efficacy of these arrangements vary, but the Director General of Fair Trading is satisfied that the new subsidiary and the divested supplies will be operative by 1994. The Gas Consumers Council is concerned at the possibility of increased exploitation in the remaining markets; the manner in which BG auctions existing supplies, and its choice of which suppliers and customers to retain are crucial. What is striking is the refusal of either regulator to modify his own actions in light of the effect that the other has on the industry. In particular, the requirement for 5 per cent per annum efficiency gains in non-gas costs changes considerably when the transmission and supply activities must be separated, presumably at extra cost.

PROSPECTS

Regulation of gas has been both more eventful and more effective than was predicted during the short time for discussion prior to privatization. The degree of transparency, and the introduction of possibilities for competition show the importance of government will in implementing such policies, a will apparently present only since privatization. In so far as this results from privatization it is a real bonus. However the development of effective competition is very embryonic, and recent conditions imposed by the Office of Fair Trading (under threat of referral to the MMC) indicate that actual rather than potential competition must be demonstrated. The industry's own role in creating such competition has become vital, and much of the regulatory process became a spirited dialogue between industry and regulator(s). This is a long way from the static model envisaged in 1986.

However the nature and degree of such competition, though no doubt deeply affected by the industry, depends also on extraneous circumstances. One of the greatest stimuli to gas competition has been the privatization of the electricity industry, which has created enormous interest, and some contracts, for gas purchases for generation. Some of this is BG-supplied gas, and some is competitors' gas carried by BG. OFT and OFGAS have made it clear that it requires competition to develop in existing markets and not just in new supplies of this kind. The government's suggestion that competition may be extended to the tariff market raises the issue of whether regulation and competition can co-exist, unless the incumbent firm remains unfairly handicapped by regulation applied more leniently to entrants. Experience in the United States shows that gas-to-gas competition is possible in the contract market; for the time being local monopolies for domestic supply will have to remain, and so will their regulation.

One solution to this dilemma is to move in the direction of the electricity industry's organization, one which was suggested for gas but which fell on ears deafened by the required speed of privatization. Indeed much of the discussion and structure of the electricity industry was a result of the opportunities patently missed for gas. What becomes clear as regulation proceeds is that the original structure is not sacrosanct, and that investors' interests are not necessarily protected at the cost of consumers. Changes have affected not only the environment within which the industry operates, but the structure of the industry itself as it separates gas transport into a separate subsidiary and sells gas supplies to its competitors. This has been agreed under a Conservative Government, and since the Labour Party no longer intends to renationalize gas, the parties' policies seem very close. If the 1991/2 arrangement achieves satisfactory results a separated private industry might yield greater efficiency than did the unified and secretive nationalized BGC.

The most appropriate structure would be that widely advocated at the time of privatization—a central purchasing and national transmission body, which would then sell gas to local distribution companies. This would separate out the carrier element, and meet concerns about the effectiveness of 'Chinese walls' within BG. It would also enable the increasing costs of gas purchase (and exploitation) to be separated from the decreasing cost element of local distribution. The process could be extended by distinguishing purchasing from national transmission and developing a market in the purchase and sale of gas at the beach-head. This divided structure would provide the regulator with information from a variety of sources and would enable some internal competition while reducing the monolithic nature of the present industry. The shares in such an industry would be tricky to allocate, but some mechanism could allot existing shareholders an appropriate stake in the new companies. The need for regulation would not disappear (it never can while elements of natural monopoly remain) but its process would be clearer, and this might be preferable, even for the industry, to the 'creeping regulation' which it presently experiences. The 1991 OFT/OFGAS report clearly sets the stage for such a scene and the changes agreed in early 1992 represent a first move in this direction. It is intriguing to note that the much-feared regulatory capture of regulators by their industries, experienced in the USA and widely feared for BG, shows no signs of emerging. This is largely attributable to the part played by general competition policy and its regulators, working alongside OFGAS.

Substantive reform depends crucially on the political will of the government. We have seen that this has been much more effective since privatization than when the industry was nationalized, and than many predicted at privatization. Indeed the government's own objectives are demonstrably different after than they were during the privatization process. The criticisms then made of the the industry's structure have been borne out by the problems of implementing regulation. But the determined intervention of both OFGAS and general competition bodies like the MMC and OFT, their support from the government and the response of the industry is encouraging for consumers, and for economic efficiency. Given potential competition from other European markets in buying North Sea gas supplies, competitiveness within UK purchase and supply should prove beneficial. A new government of whatever hue may feel the limited success of these policies justifies their logical extension to further reorganization of the gas industry.

POSTSCRIPT

The exciting times for gas have continued since this chapter was written. The pressures and tensions it describes resulted in a second referral of the entire industry to the Monopolies and Mergers Commission in summer 1992 and a report in August 1993. It recommended legal divestiture of the gas transportation business from gas supply (further to the accounting changes described above) and a slow introduction of competition into all markets over the subsequent ten years. In December 1993 the government rejected these recommendations, leaving the industry intact as at privatization (with internal-accounting separation) but introducing competition into the whole market much more quickly. The competitive timetable thus mirrors that in electricity, with abolition of monopoly even in the domestic market, well before the end of the millennium. In the meantime there is a new gas regulator and a new chairman of British Gas, as well as increasingly vocal competitors.

These events have changed the focus on issues for the immediate future. As in all network industries it is access to the transportation system which determines the competitive conditions, and discussion continues on the most appropriate charging structure and level. The responsibilities as well as rights of potential competitors in the domestic market need definition, particularly with respect to the obligation to supply less profitable customers. OFGAS is being strengthened to supervise more closely the changes which will be necessary. While these changes to encourage economic efficiency continue, there is evidence that privatization caused a significant improvement in the industry's productivity (Price and Weyman-Jones 1993). It is an appropriate time to review the changes and tensions in UK gas regulation and to look forward to the development of this market within a more settled regulatory structure in the immediate future. The government's decision to advance competition without restructuring the industry strengthens the regulator's role and indicates that regulation and competition are indeed substitutes rather than complements.

References

Bishop, M., Kay, J. A., and Mayer, C. (1994) (eds.), *The Regulatory Challenge*, Oxford: Oxford University Press.

Department of Energy (1989), 'The demand for energy', in D. R. Helm, J. A. Kay, and D. J. Thompson (eds.), *The Market for Energy*.

Energy Committee (1985), *Gas Depletion*, House of Commons Paper 76, London: HMSO.

—— (1986), *Regulation of the Gas Industry*, House of Commons Paper 15, London: HMSO.

Gibson, M. and Price, C. (1986), 'Standing charge rebates: costs and benefits', *Energy Policy*, **14/3**, 262–271.

HM Government (1982), *Oil and Gas (Enterprise) Act*, London: HMSO.

—— (1986), *Gas Act*, London: HMSO.

HM Treasury (1961), *Financial and Economic Obligations of the Nationalised Industries*, Cmnd 1337, London: HMSO.

—— (1967), *Nationalised Industries: A Review of Economic and Financial Obligations*, Cmnd paper 3437, London: HMSO.

Hammond, E., Helm, D., and Thompson, D. (1985), 'British Gas: options for privatisation', *Fiscal Studies*, **6/4**, 1–20.

Helm, D R., Kay, J. A., and Thompson, D. J. (1989) (eds.), *The Market for Energy*, Oxford: Clarendon Press.

Laffont, J.-J., and Tirole, J. (1990), 'The regulation of multi-product firms—II', *Journal of Public Economics*, **43**, 37–66.

Monopolies and Mergers Commission (1988), *Gas*, Cm 500, London: HMSO.

—— (1993), *Gas and British Gas plc*, Cm 2314, 3215, 2316 and 2317.

Office of Fair Trading (1991), *The Gas Competition Review* (summary report), London: HMSO.

OFGAS (1991), *New Gas Tariff Formula Tariff Structures*, London: HMSO.

Phlips, L. (1983), *The Economics of Price Discrimination*, Cambridge: Cambridge University Press.

Price, C. (1984), 'Distribution costs in the U.K. gas industry', *Leicester University Economics Discussion Papers*, no. 31.

—— (1986), 'Privatising British Gas: is the regulatory framework adequate?', *Public Money*, **6/1**.

—— (1991), 'Privatisation and Regulation: the effect on the U.K. Gas Industry', *Leicester University Economics Discussion Papers*, no. 165.

—— (1992), 'Regulation of the U.K. gas industry', *Annals of Public and Cooperative Economics*, 2/1992.

Price, C. M., and Weyman-Jones, T. J. (1993), *Malmquist Indices of Productivity Change in the U.K. Gas Industry*, Economics Research Paper no. 93/12, Loughborough University of Technology.

Price Commission (1979), *Gas Prices*, London: HMSO.

7

Privatization of British Steel

JONATHAN AYLEN*

INTRODUCTION

British Steel was privatized in December 1988 with the government retaining a 'golden share' as a barrier to take-over until the end of 1993. Since then, British Steel plc has maintained its profitability in boom and recession and held its position as one of the world's lowest-cost steel producers.

This paper was written as part of the privatization debate during 1988. By then, the British Steel Corporation had made a remarkable turn-round from record-breaking losses to being highly cost efficient and profitable. The paper develops two themes. The first is the importance of a competitive product market as a source of efficiency. The second theme is the significance of a market for corporate control—take-overs and mergers—as an element in the restructuring of European steel. Privatization exposes British Steel to the market for corporate control.

At the time of writing, the European Community retained controls on steel output. Sections 3 and 5, for example, argue political intervention slowed the rate of restructuring across European steel. Section 6 concludes a competitive product market and free trade are more important goals than privatization *per se*. Problems of intervention and national ownership are reinforced by the absence of a market for corporate control of steelmaking assets. The next three sections ask what an efficient European steel industry should look like and discuss how a more efficient industry structure might be established through collaboration or merger. The paper finishes with a new conclusion highlighting the return of a competitive European steel market, but suggesting restrictions on the market for corporate control are more intractable.

* Senior Lecturer in Economics, University of Salford, and economics columnist for *Steel Times International*.

The advice of Ian Walker and Peter Mottershead is much appreciated, but their helpful comments do not imply their approval. This paper was written before the European Community's decision to end all controls on steel production from 1 July 1988; the Community will continue to monitor the market, and external trade restrictions remain in place. It was first published as 'Privatisation of the British Steel Corporation', *Fiscal Studies*, 9/3 (Aug. 1988), 1–25.

1. BRITISH STEEL: THE BARE FACTS

British Steel is now one of the world's two lowest-cost bulk steel producers, alongside POSCO of South Korea (Figure 7.1). The Corporation has a cost advantage over its leading rivals in West Germany, France, Italy, and Japan. By comparison, major integrated steel firms in the USA have costs over 20 per cent higher for similar, but lower quality, products (Marcus 1987).

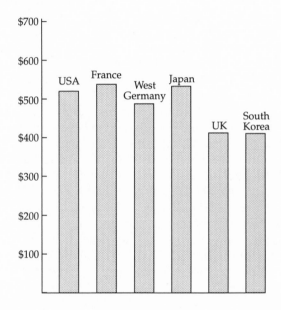

FIG. 7.1. Costs per tonne of steel shipped, 1987.
Note: US dollars per tonne of carbon steel shipped by integrated works at actual operating rates.
Source: Marcus 1987.

The turn-round of the British Steel Corporation (BSC) is one of the most remarkable in business history, and without parallel in the steel industry itself. As recently as 1980/1 the Corporation made a total loss of £1 billion on a turnover of just under £3 billion, earning a place for a while in the *Guinness Book of Records*. BSC had seen its market halve in volume terms compared with the peak years of the early 1970s. By 1980 British Steel was fundamentally uncompetitive, with a cost per tonne almost a third above those of West German producers, and by rights should not have survived. The Corporation is now forecast to make

£0.4 billion profit before tax, on a likely turnover of £3.8 billion in the financial year 1987/8.

The see-saw from chronic losses to profitable operation was largely achieved by a leap in total-factor productivity and a corresponding fall in costs per tonne. Labour productivity more than doubled between 1980/1 and 1986/7 as the number of employees almost halved and out-put recovered. Productivity gains alone cut annual costs by £880 million between 1980/1 and 1986/7 (in current prices). In world terms, UK labour productivity stood at 40 per cent of US levels in 1980 (Aylen 1982). Yet by 1986 productivity had exceeded US levels, and almost matched West German and Japanese performance (International Labour Organization 1986; Scholey 1987). Conservation measures reduced energy consumption by 16 per cent between 1980 and 1983, with further slight gains since, amounting in all to a cut in annual costs of £140 million by 1986/7 (Fitzgerald 1988). Rationalization of production facilities during the early 1980s against a background of rapidly falling steel consumption enabled British Steel to retrench back to five major integrated works. Even so, capacity remains underutilized. Economic recovery in the UK stabilized the domestic market for steel while European prices began to recover after 1985. Low costs, rising prices and a chance to expand output through profitable exports brought a marked improve-ment in performance. By 1986, British Steel had become the strong firm in a weak industry. British Steel's operating profit in dollars per tonne exceeded those found elsewhere in the European Community, were ahead of the deteriorating Japanese average for this sector, and markedly superior to the protected but loss-making US steel industry. Among the major players, its only real rivals in terms of profit margin are state-owned POSCO in South Korea, China Steel of Taiwan, and pri-vately owned Dofasco of Canada (Marcus 1988: 8). Although there is scope for further cost reduction, notably through better use of working capital and through retrenchment to fewer sites, there is every prospect of sustained future profitable operation.

2. A CASE FOR PRIVATE ENTERPRISE?

At first sight there seems to be no case, on efficiency grounds at least, for privatizing British Steel. After all, the dramatic turn-round in perfor-mance since 1980 has been achieved under public ownership. In many respects a more important transition has already taken place, from what we have termed a 'bureaucratic' model of public enterprise to a 'market' model (Aylen 1987*a*). That is to say, before 1980 there was an overlap between government and BSC finances with losses accepted for social reasons. There was confusion about objectives and political interference in decisions. In particular there was close political scrutiny over input decisions, such as investment, plant closure, employment levels, and domestic coal consumption, and attention to politically sensitive outputs, such as steel prices during periods of inflation (Cockerill 1980). Overall enterprise efficiency was subordinated to immediate, short-term political concerns. After 1980 there was a growing shift towards financial autonomy through emphasis on restoring profitability and introduction of overall cash limits. Clear commercial objectives were set, and social objectives were subordinated to the need for lower costs and financial viability. Performance was monitored by outcomes with less concern for 'second-guessing' input choices. BSC was required to publish a set of performance ratios at the end of each year, demonstrating progress made on labour productivity, energy efficiency, and capital utilization. Within the Corporation there was a switch to plant-level wage bargaining tied to local productivity achievements. By the end of the decade quarterly productivity bonuses were approaching 20 per cent of workers' earnings. It is hard to escape the conclusion that changes in the structure of incentives facing the management and work-force were largely responsible for the dramatic turn-round in British Steel's fortunes.

Nor is there systematic evidence from other industries to suggest that British Steel would achieve lower costs or higher total factor productivity under private ownership. Any study assessing the relative performance of public versus private ownership must fulfil three conditions. It must compare like with like. It should control for differences in input prices which might favour one form of ownership or another. And any comparison should take account of all aspects of efficiency by comparing total costs or total factor productivity across the two sectors. In general, surveys of efficiency and cost comparisons which meet these criteria suggest there is no difference in performance between state-owned enterprises or privately owned firms where they operate side by side in a similar market (Millward 1982; Millward and Parker 1983; Vickers and YArrow 1985). Admittedly, many of the sectors which permit such comparisons are subject to some form of government regulation which may limit the general validity of their conclusions. Broadly speaking, electricity generation and distribution in the United States are better served by public ownership; there is little to choose between Canadian railways or Australian airlines, whether public or private; while rubbish collection in most countries is perhaps best left to the private sector. The only reliable comparison for steel worldwide (Tyler 1979) compares publicly owned, privately owned, and multinational subsidiaries in Brazil. A thorough comparison finds no statistically significant difference between the technical efficiency of public, private, or foreign firms. Instead, Tyler ruefully concludes that performance overall in this developing country is generally low across all sectors compared with what might be achieved in ideal, best-practice circumstances. In the UK, Rowley and Yarrow (1981) compared the weak performance of cartelized private steel under central price regulation between 1957 and 1967 with the poor performance of the British Steel Corporation following nationalization between 1967 and 1975, with ambiguous results. Hindsight shows this particular private–public comparison straddles a long period of overall competitive failure. While, as Marxists have recognized, it is an ironic paradox to accuse public enterprise of poor performance relative to private industry when the very failure of private industry motivated nationalization (Fine and O'Donnell 1985).

Historical comparisons for the UK also suggest that utilities such as nineteenth-century town gas (Millward and Ward 1987) and inter-war power-stations selected to supply the grid (Foreman-Peck and Waterson 1985) were equally well provided by the public or private sector. However, the private sector was swifter to close down obsolete, high-cost power-stations. Private companies not selected to supply the Central Electricity Board grid included a smaller 'tail' of inefficient firms than the comparable group of unselected publicly owned generating stations. We highlight the faster speed of exit among private firms in this study because of the persistence of excess capacity in European steel where public ownership is widespread.

What we conclude from all these studies is that a competitive environment in the product market, and the right set of management incentives rather than a particular form of ownership, make for cost efficiency. A comparative market structure with ease of entry and exit, and monitoring of management on the basis of outputs rather than inputs, make for good performance. Ownership may well be incidental. Indeed, Kay and Thompson (1986: 25) go so far as to suggest that private firms in a regulated environment— of the sort, say, currently found in European steel—may actually have higher costs than directly controlled public enterprises. They conclude that privatization will only improve performance if supported by liberalization, and if the two conflict, liberalization is to be preferred. The issue for steel is whether there is a case for privatization which combines a worthwhile transfer to private ownership with more competition.

3. COMPETITION IN EUROPEAN STEEL

Steel is a highly politicized industry. In democratic societies, steelworkers have considerable lobbying powers, owing to their strong geographical concentration as voters and income-earners in parliamentary constituencies surrounding large plants. Appeal to the median voter helps explain why the steel industry is characterized by an extraordinary degree of local control, state ownership, and government intervention across the world (Franko 1981). In the UK there are strong regional implications, since all BSC's large works are located in areas of relatively high unemployment. A Conservative government refused to sanction British Steel's proposed closure of Ravenscraig steelworks in Scotland.

The steel industry is also characterized by the absence of multinational companies. Multinational firms have the advantage that they can compare costs at a wide range of locations and transfer skills and production to places which offer the lowest costs of production. High exit costs discourage multinational entry. The enormous sunk costs in this capital-intensive industry make it very difficult to get out of foreign operations if things go wrong (Aylen 1987b). The initial, irretrievable commitment for the first stage of an integrated work is 2 to 3 billion US dollars. This is too large an outlay for even the world's biggest companies to contemplate losing with equanimity. Nor do steel firms have any peculiar, proprietary knowledge to use as a bargaining counter with local governments. Knowledge of current technology is readily available world-wide, at a price. The absence of multinationals, and a high degree of national ownership and intervention, mean that reallocation of steel production in accordance with shifts in comparative advantage is slow to take place. Instead, substantial cost differences persist between major producers world-wide.

A high degree of national ownership and political commitment resulted in the European crisis cartel for steel (the 'Davingnon Plan' founded in 1980). If anything, this intervention has slowed down the rate of adjustment in the Community. One of the avowed aims of the crisis cartel is to reduce surplus steelmaking capacity in Europe (Figure 7.2). This is a contradiction in terms, since its very existence discourages exit (Aylen 1984). It has allowed marked cost differences between major producers to continue, whereas a market would have eliminated the less efficient steelmakers, at least in the absence of subsidies. Output quotas artificially support steel prices, thereby giving firms a profit incentive to delay exit from the industry. In effect, the marginal revenue enjoyed by any European steelmaker has been sustained above the marginal cost of the least efficient capacity, thereby encouraging firms to keep obsolete capacity in operation. However, nature imitates economic analysis. Some firms now find it even more profitable to keep plant idle and sell their quotas to more efficient steel producers instead, just as theory predicts. British Steel is said to have been buying quotas on this basis throughout 1987 and making a profit over and above the premium paid, even when selling a semi-finished commodity product such as slabs on the world market.

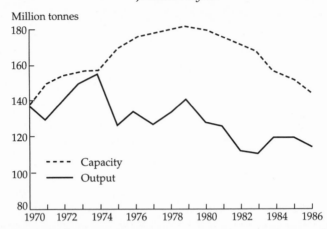

Fig. 7.2. Steel capacity and output in the European Community. (Nine countries. Capacity is effective rather than nominal capacity.)

Source: Derived from OECD statistics.

In addition, the bargaining mechanism by which quotas are allocated delays closures. The crisis regime is maintained by direct government-to-government negotiations. Ministerial gatherings are shadowed by Eurofer—a powerful lobby composed of the major steelmakers in Europe. The quota bargain is renegotiated annually. This repeated game inevitably raises acute national sensitivities. The European steel cartel is based on an implicit bargain whereby output quotas effectively depend upon existing capacity. Firms which maintain surplus plant are in a position to claim more production rights. Each year the Community threatens to end the quota regime if it does not achieve an appropriate level of closures. Each year a game of bluff and counter-bluff is repeated. In the end, the Commission has lost credibility as its bluff has always been called. As a result, a combination of rational self-interest and national pride has delayed adjustment. When closures have been agreed, plants have been selected on the basis of equiproportional sharing of misery across countries rather than considerations of industrial efficiency. The diplomatic consensus is evident in Table 7.1. Cut-backs have been strikingly uniform across Europe with almost all countries, apart from West Germany, reducing rolling-mill capacity by a fifth between 1980 and 1986.[1]

---

[1] Like steel, synthetic fibres in western Europe were characterized by persistent excess capacity and losses in the late 1970s. A similar pattern of nationalization of loss-making firms and government intervention to prevent closure of obsolete plants was to be observed. Again, the EEC set up a crisis cartel to reduce capacity and, temporarily, to share the European market. Shaw and Shaw (1983) argue that the Davingnon cartel for man-made fibres preserved the weak competitors and uneconomic plants, while rationalization

TABLE 7.1. Reductions in capacity within the European crisis cartel, 1980–1986

	Rolling-mill capacity		
	Change, 1980–6 (million product-tonnes)	Remaining capacity, 1986 (million product-tonnes)	Percentage change
Major producers			
West Germany	–6.73	42.2	–14
Italy	–7.20	30.4	–19
France	–6.14	21.4	–22
UK	–5.43	17.4	–24
Belgium	–3.43	13.1	–21
Netherlands	–1.73	5.5	–24
Luxemburg	–1.04	3.9	–21
Minor producers			
Denmark	–0.07	0.9	–7
Ireland	+0.28	0.3	New supplier
New member of cartel			
Greece	+0.39	5.0	+8
TOTALS	–31.10	140.1	–18

Source: Derived from Bruce *et al.* 1987.

Adjustment of capacity to likely demand is further delayed, because the European crisis regime is bound up with attempts to 'manage' the whole system of world trade in steel. The USA has voluntary trade restraint agreements with twenty major steel-exporting countries. There is a similar system of secret European-wide external trade restraints. The two protection arrangements are feeding off one another (OECD 1985). Market shares among third countries are becoming frozen by both US and EEC measures alike. Voluntary restraint measures confer rents upon outside suppliers as compensation for lower export volumes. Foreign suppliers who do well out of the existing US and EEC trade measures have an interest in seeing administered trade flows continue and even extended to any new producers who threaten the stability of the system. EFTA (European Free Trade Association) members in Scandinavia, who have free access to the European Community through reciprocal trade agreements, have tacitly colluded in maintaining the EEC crisis cartel (Brown 1984). Austria—also an EFTA member—has been disciplined by anti-dumping inquiries and Yugoslavia is the latest

was strongly influenced by the international location of plants. As with the steel cartel, both market shares and market structure were frozen by European intervention. Since the cartel has ended, extensive restructuring has taken place through diversification, merger and take-over (Marsh and Rawsthorn 1988).

focus for complaints of 'underpriced' steel. Consumers not only suffer from higher prices and lower choice. The most restricted sources (with the exception of Canada which enjoys privileged access to the USA) also tend to be lowest cost/highest quality sources.[2]

4. PRIVATIZATION AND THE MARKET FOR CORPORATE CONTROL

Privatization now offers one way of restructuring the steel industry across Europe during the 1990s with the end of the European crisis cartel. The main case for private ownership of steel rests on the opportunities if affords for mergers and take-overs which are open to private companies. Private ownership implies a market for corporate control which is absent when firms are state-owned. In effect, a newly privatized British Steel plc could take over other steelmaking assets, or be taken over itself. The existence of a market for corporate control of newly privatized firms provides perhaps the only strong economic argument for moving steel back into the private sector. Seen in this context, privatization of British Steel is just one step in a move towards European-wide liberalization of steel.

The issue of privatization as a way of freeing-up share ownership is analysed by Mayer (1987). From his point of view, public ownership is a highly artificial constraint on the pattern of shareholdings. State ownership is equivalent to strict equality of shareholdings across the population at large, echoing a point of Brittan and Riley (1978). Such a restriction effectively prevents individuals from disposing of their shareholdings and so precludes bids by rival companies and makes it difficult for management to agree freely to merger.

Public enterprise—a constraint on share disposal—may be justified if private ownership is characterized by market failure. Mayer focuses on the time-consistency problem. Before nationalization in 1967, private-sector steel firms might reasonably have anticipated bankruptcy midway through the substantial lumpy investment then needed to modernize the UK bulk-steel industry. Their pattern of cash flows could readily have been exploited by customers able to turn to competing sources of supply, such as imports. In the absence of a complete set of contracts, the private sector might have expected the quasi-rents on the completed projects to be driven down to zero. In such circumstances it is

[2] Similar phenomena are observed in other widely contested industries. World clothing-trade flows have been organized by a succession of Multi-Fibre Arrangements (Silberston 1984). As a result, importers are locked into traditional sources of supply by restrictive quotas. Despite shifts in comparative advantage which favour new lower-cost producers, Hong Kong still supplies half of the UK's clothing imports. Sutton (1988) points out that operation of the Common Agricultural Policy has similarly fixed the European sugar-refining industry.

not wise to invest in the first place. Public ownership—a constraint on the disposal of shares and elimination of the chance of bankruptcy or take-over—may well have been justified in these circumstances to see the industry over the 'hump' of modernization.[3]

In British Steel's case, the transitional phase back to international competitiveness is complete. Any artificial restriction on share ownership is no longer justified. A private company is subject to the sanction of take-over and bankruptcy in a way that public enterprises are not, at least in usual circumstances. The existence of a market for corporate control of British Steel's assets has two clear advantages. First, threat of take-over is the most effective mechanism available for keeping managers on the path of profit-making righteousness. Second, actual take-overs are one route to restructuring European steel. In the absence of a market for corporate control, administrative rationalization of steelmaking assets across Europe is likely to be slow, costly, and subject to extensive political negotiation. We explore these arguments in turn.

It is easy to overstate the case for a private-capital market as a disciplinary device. The property-rights tradition (Alchian 1965; Demsetz 1966) claims that self-interested owners of capital have an incentive to ensure profit attributable to them is maximized. Private owners will monitor their firm to ensure that it seizes profitable opportunities and minimizes costs in order to increase the residual profit. However, as long ago as 1848 John Stuart Mill appreciated managers were little more than agents for owners, whether they were in the private sector or the public sector. The divorce between ownership and control gave managers freedom to act in their own interests (Mill quoted in Harris 1959):

Individuals acting for their own pecuniary interests are likely to be in general more careful and economical than a public board; but the directors of a Joint Stock Company are not acting for their own pecuniary interests, but for those of their constituents. The management of a company is representative management, as much as that of an elected public board, and experience shows that it is quite as liable to be corrupt or negligent.

In British Steel's case the government took an especially close interest in monitoring a 'public board' in circumstances in which isolated private owners of a company might well have sold their small share stake and shrugged off the capital losses. The government appointed Ian MacGregor and then exercised tight control through cash limits and agreed performance indicators (Aylen 1984; Abromeit 1986). In this instance the political costs associated with huge public-sector losses

---

[3] The same argument was used to justify initially US government support for the American steel industry through trade protection, first granted in 1969. The industry was offered a 'breathing-space' to restructure. Rent-seeking behaviour soon ensured the temporary protection became permanent.

gave an incentive for government to monitor the Corporation more closely than any set of self-interested, but isolated, shareholders. Yet, at other times, politicians, civil servants, and pressure groups have diverted resources of British Steel towards goals other than profit. Employment has been artificially maintained to reward voters. Pricing policy has been modified to meet macro-economic objectives. Clearly it has not always been the case that political capital was earned from efficient operation of public owned firms. In this respect, there is a case for 'fixing' ownership of British Steel in the private sector—not because it will be better controlled at the moment, but because it reduces the scope for future intervention. By privatizing British Steel, the Government is putting itself on the side of virtue, saying it is literally 'no longer our business'. But reducing scope for government intervention is a negative argument for privatization. It would be wrong to expect undue pressures for efficiency from private shareholders. As Grout (1987) has emphasized, if capital markets are to be efficient at pooling risk and if individual shareholders are to spread their exposure to risk, it is desirable that any given shareholder has only a slender interest in the conduct of a particular firm in his or her portfolio.

The threat of a hostile take-over bid may, however, prevent managers pursuing goals of their own. 'Corrupt or negligent' managers who pursue unprofitable courses of action are likely to see their share price fall. A low valuation makes a company easy meat for predators anxious to do a better job. The mere presence of the threat of an unwelcome bid should spur managers on to watch the interests of their shareholders and restrain their own tastes for growth, capital spending, a quiet life, or anything not consistent with maximizing the value of the firm. There is a particular risk of overinvestment in a declining industry (Shleifer and Vishny 1988). Executives familiar with running steel firms may well continue investing in steel, even though it is a declining business for the firm concerned, and not a particularly profitable thing to do. After all, managers with specific skills in steelmaking accumulated over a working lifetime have a vested interest in keeping themselves employed as steelmakers, even if profits beckon the firm into diversification. In the absence of information about alternative courses of action, it is difficult for shareholders to monitor the executives who are, at least nominally, under their control. It is striking that US integrated steel firms, which are potential victims of corporate raiders, have resisted the temptation to reinvest in steel capacity, having been constrained by its poor earnings potential and consequent implications for their stock price. Instead, these managers have run down their capital stock, lobbied for trade protection to help preserve the stability of their oligopoly, and set prices in such a way as to maximize return on their existing assets (OECD 1985). They are now wresting wage concessions from the work-force and resorting to Chapter 11 bankruptcy proceedings to maintain profits. The presence of a market for corporate control has promoted efficiency in the US integrated steel sector at a time when European firms have pursued other goals such as output maximization at a cost to Community tax-payers.[4]

5. EUROPEAN STEEL: A MARKET SOLUTION

Threat of a hostile take-over is a useful disciplinary device. *Actual* take-overs are one mechanism for restructuring European steel. The argument for privatizing British Steel is part of the argument for restructuring the European steel industry within a competitive framework. The main aim of any regrouping should be to realize a more efficient industry structure while keeping any newly formed companies open to contest from world competition.

Given that government intervention has virtually halted restructuring of European steel for eight years, there is a case for trying market forces. There are potential gains to consumers and producers alike from restructuring the European steel industry. Many of the gains to consumers could be realized by simply abandoning the quota regime and its rampart of external import controls. Freeing up the product market in this way has only incidental implications for ownership of British Steel. The gains to producers (and ultimately consumers too) arise from the profit opportunities inherent in restructuring. These gains do have implications for ownership, unless corporate restructuring is to be confined to capacity swaps rather than merger, diversification, and exit. In turn this implies freeing-up the market for control of steelmaking assets, not just in the UK but also across Europe where a series of bid-blocking devices have built up to prevent any contests for corporate control of steel firms. Ideally, a market solution should reward those with the most efficient level and type of capacity and should enable the more efficient steelmakers to win out against the less efficient, either through direct competition or take-over.

In principle, operation of the European crisis cartel is like a sales tax on steel, borne by consumers for the benefit of (most) producers. Immediate benefits would arise for consumers if the cartel were abandoned, and this now looks set to take place in June of this year, although the French and West Germans want a modified cartel arrangement to

---

[4] Not all commentators are convinced that the presence of a market for corporate control is promoting efficiency across the economy. Scherer (1988) argues that take-overs do little to improve corporations' operating efficiency, either in theory or in practice. He sees corporate restructuring as a costly and disruptive process. Instead, the discretionary powers of managers should be limited by greater shareholder representation on more active corporate boards.

continue (Dawkins and Goodhart 1988). At present, the cheapest steel made in the best plants is rationed by quotas in order to maintain prices. Costs are higher than need be because the most efficient mills are under-utilized to divert orders to the worst. In addition, external controls further reduce price competition and reduce choice within the Community. Admittedly it would be wrong to exaggerate the welfare gains to consumers from a move to a free market. Briefly, until 1987 the quota constraints on output were not binding on many individual producers. Secondly, development of a secondary market in quotas helps lower the resource costs of production.[5] In effect, a market in quotas begins to replicate the plant-loading decisions a single owner of a multi-plant system would make, with European plants employed in merit order of marginal cost. So, at the moment, UK output has increased while higher-cost producers such as West Germany are retrenching. The flaw in this system is the subsidies which keep Italian state producers in high-cost operation. But then at least consumers do not suffer welfare losses so long as the Italian taxpayer is reducing the market clearing price of steel across the Community. Again, the secret external import restrictions have not always been binding. Throughout the early 1980s, European prices were among the lowest in the world and so the EEC was an unattractive destination for even low-cost exports from Brazil or Japan. Unlike the US market, there were few quota rents to be earned by successful importers. Only during the mid-1980s have prices surged to make sales worthwhile. Yet, at this time, the main producer with surplus export capacity—Japan—suffered a severe loss of competitiveness with the appreciation of the yen. However, if the tightness of the market persists, low-cost producers such as British Steel will be able to align their prices up to world levels. It is a characteristic of markets such as steel with price-inelastic demand curves that transfers of revenue from consumers to producers can be either negligible or dramatic. So far, they have been negligible. In the absence of increased price competition from world producers selling into Europe, transfers from consumers could well become dramatic.

6. A FREE MARKET AND PRIVATIZATION

A free product market for steel within Europe has incidental implications for privatization of British Steel. First, opening British Steel completely to the competitive world market for steel will reduce the

---

[5] Rigidity of market shares was one failing of the cartel when first introduced. An 'efficient' cartel would reward the lowest-cost firms with larger shares and profits and we would expect output to shift around the Community in line with firm efficiency, as it is now beginning to do (McGee 1988: ch. 6).

Corporation's value when it is floated, as compared with a situation where it has privileged access to a protected and cartelized European market. Success in abolishing European Community output quotas and moves towards freer trade in steel could jeopardize the privatization altogether. An end to quotas and a possible price war would not only lower expected earnings but also increase the uncertainty surrounding the future stream of dividend payments. Greater variance in earnings tends to be associated with lower share valuation for a given level of profitability. But, in the longer run, removal of rents associated with the European cartel should discourage new entry to the industry, and prompt ageing, obsolete, or inefficient capacity to exit. A free market for steel may thereby make the world steel industry a potentially more profitable place for efficient producers, such as British Steel, which have a genuine comparative advantage. Nevertheless, the paradox remains that abandonment of the European crisis cartel and trade controls may be incompatible with the timetabled privatization of British Steel in 1989. Seen in this light, announcement of privatization in December 1987 may be regarded as an attempt to influence impending quota negotiations rather than a hard and fast statement of immediate intent.

As we have argued, the second impact of moving to a free market on privatization of British Steel is the demonstration effect of having a once-subsidized company under private ownership and control. In such a politicized environment, privatization of British Steel is a statement of government withdrawal from the industry. Transfer of the Corporation to the private sector signals the Corporation is operating autonomously and in a commercial manner. Decisions on pricing, output, and capacity will not be distorted by subsidy. Such detachment places the UK in a strong position to bargain for similar behaviour from its European partners. In other words, privatization is part of the political case for an end to output controls in Europe and for a freer world-trading regime in steel products.

Free trade, abandonment of EEC controls, and privatization go together.

Fiscal Studies

Sale of British Steel should not take place unless regulation of trade and output is set to disappear. There is a danger that a private steel firm would have a profit incentive to indulge in rent-seeking behaviour, such as lobbying for continued trade protection and cartelization. It is easier to weigh the balance of social welfare and pursue policies of reform while companies are still in public ownership, since loss of profit and privilege is borne by the state itself. Governments can trade-off lower profits from a state enterprise against gains to steel consumers. Owners of a newly privatized steel company have no such incentive to trade-off social gains against their own private losses. Anxious to maintain their advantaged position, they would lobby government in an attempt to protect profits. As US experience shows, the returns to private lobbying in steel are high. Crandall (1981: ch. 7) estimates the US steel industry received between over one-third to nearly two-thirds of a billion US dollars in rents from the operation of the Trigger Price Mechanism for trade protection in 1979 alone. This was equivalent to between a fifth and a third of the operating profits earned by the industry in that year. These rents were distributed between the two main lobbyists—the owners of capital and unionized labour.

An end to output controls is also necessary to protect domestic consumers against the local monopoly power of a newly privatized steel corporation. Binding restrictions on output encourage European producers to supply their local markets first, where consumer loyalty is highest and transport costs lowest. Output restrictions would prevent other continental producers entering the UK market, even if the newly privatized producer were earning monopoly profits. Absence of production quotas and external import controls would make the UK market freely contestable by direct exports. Open entry to the British market is the best protection a steel consumer might have. So we have a paradox familiar from other privatizations. A free market in steel jeopardizes privatization. Yet privatization should not take place unless the EEC crisis regime of output controls and external trade protection is abandoned. If there is any doubt, the benefits of a free market regime should be placed ahead of any incidental gains from privatization.

7. AN EFFICIENT INDUSTRY STRUCTURE

A move towards a more efficient industry structure across European steel is a potential source of welfare gain on the supply side of the industry. A more efficient industry structure can be defined as one which minimizes the total for a given level of demand, regardless of the location of production or the number of firms required to supply it (Baumol 1982). Provided the European market is open to outside competition, existing steel firms should be forced by market pressures to regroup into an efficient structure of production—eventually. But there are many barriers to exit and constraints on restructuring, so it is important to consider policy measures which might hasten the evolution of market structure.

Restructuring of European steel does not necessarily imply changes in ownership. After all, one can foresee a complicated sequence of bargains which might bring about profitable co-operation towards lower-cost production. Cost reductions could be achieved by buying, swapping, and selling production capacity within the existing corporate framework. However, freeing-up the market for corporate control through a switch to private ownership gives one more mechanism by which restructuring may take place. Successful management teams, such as the British and the Dutch, could achieve greater overall efficiency in European steel production if they had a chance to take over the badly managed steel firms. In many cases, the less successful operators have individual modern items of plant that could be utilized more efficiently by other managements. It is potentially cheaper in present circumstances to buy up and use existing equipment in Europe rather than invest in new capacity, especially at the rolling and finishing end.

What constitutes an efficient industry structure is an empirical question. Certainly the ideal structure is likely to differ from industry to industry according to cost conditions peculiar to that industry. Logic suggests scale economies in an industry such as steel ought to result in greater concentration of production. That is to say, the outlook for European steel is mergers, fewer firms in each product line, or even monopoly. In this way, production can be concentrated in a few, well-located, giant plants.

Steel production is dominated by economies of scale. The initial capital outlay for entry into bulk steelmaking is larger than that found in any other industry. There are substantial technical economies of scale with respect to capital cost and operating cost (Table 7.2). This is especially true of flat-product manufacture, hot strip, and plate, but also true to a lesser extent for heavier long products such as medium and heavy sections and rails. Mini-steelworks based on electric-arc melting are competitive for rod and bar products derived from billets, provided input costs are favourable. Mini-steel plants are the low capital-cost, high marginal-cost technology in this industry. But here again there are economies of scale and the size of efficient US works is increasing to reflect the unit cost advantage of ultra-high-power transformers. It is evident that two minimum efficient scale plants (rather than five) would be ideal for supplying all the UK's heavier products coupled with, perhaps, two mini-steelworks (there are two at present). Comparable restructuring could be anticipated in Western Europe, where an obvious solution is for heavy-product manufacture to gravitate towards a few well-placed coastal sites, with finishing facilities—which exhibit fewer economies of scale—located closer to mid-European markets. This implies that large swathes of the French, Belgian, Luxemburg, and West German steel industries would close, as coastal sites in Holland, the UK, and perhaps France and Italy are rounded out nearer to their optimum capacity. How is the transition to a more efficient industry structure to be achieved in practice? In the face of growing competition, not just within Europe but from Korea, Taiwan, Brazil, and even Mexico, leading producers face two choices, exit or loyalty.

TABLE 7.2. Plant size and industry structure in steelmaking

Process stage[a]	Minimum-efficient scale (m.e.s.)[b]	Capital cost of m.e.s. plant[c]	Scale coefficient[d]	Operating cost penalty per tonne for a plant 50% of m.e.s. size	Number of plants in UK now in operation[e]	Number of plants if of m.e.s.
Plant items within works						
Sinter plant	4 million tonnes p.a. (380 m² grate area)	£120m	0.66	+60%	6	3
Blast furnace	3 million tonnes p.a. (13 m hearth)	£110m	0.60	+75%	11	3
Oxygen steelmaking	3.5 million tonnes p.a. (2 × 340 t)	£200m	0.66	+13 to +25%[f]	5	3
Hot-strip rolling mill	3.75 million tonnes p.a. (3/4 continuous, 1700 mm wide)	£270m	0.30	+50%	4	2
Complete steelworks						
Integrated flat-product works making slabs and rolling strip and plate	5 million tonnes p.a.	£3bn			4	2
Mini-steelworks making rod and bar for wire and construction	0.5 million tonnes p.a.	£0.1bn			2	2

[a] Each works incorporates a number of process stages. These major processes have been selected for illustrative purposes but the other production stages exhibit similar economies of scale.

[b] Minimum-efficient scale is defined where overall costs per tonne fall to within 10% of the lowest attainable cost. In all cases, economies of scale continue up to the largest technically feasible plant size constructed so far world-wide.

[c] Capital costs based on perimeter cost of plant erected at UK location at mid-1987 prices.

[d] Scale coefficient is equivalent to n in the relationship:

$$C = aX^n$$

where C is total capital cost, X is plant capacity, a is a coefficient, and n is the scale exponent.

[e] Aylen (1982) finds the UK had plant items of similar size to those found in West Germany—a situation which has now shifted in favour of the UK.

[f] Operating-cost savings are based on West German experience. The figure for oxygen steelmaking relates to UK experience during the 1970s and so understates the available savings due to overmanning prevalent at the time.

Sources: Industry estimates. These figures incorporate assumptions regarding plant design, scope of supply, location of works, plant availability, and efficiency of operation, and should be treated as broad estimates of magnitude.

Diversification and eventual exit is one response already seen in the private-sector steel industries of Japan and West Germany. The big five Japanese producers have chosen to diversify. Nippon Steel aims to reduce its dependence on steelmaking from 80 per cent of turnover in 1987 to half of turnover by 1990, while steelmaking capacity is being cut back from 34 million to 24 million tonnes. The remaining four large steelmakers have similar, if more modest, plans for diversification. Kawasaki, for example, anticipates 60 per cent of its business will remain in steel by the year 2000. Similar patterns are to be seen in West Germany, where some leading producers are merging their steelmaking activities. All are in a position to jettison bulk steelmaking eventually and survive. Klöckner shows 44 per cent of turnover is non-steel-related; Mannesmann and Thyssen 66 per cent; and Hoesch 70 per cent; while publicly owned Salzgitter is heading towards 50 per cent and looking for acquisitions to help diversify further.

In marked contrast, British Steel has become more strongly focused on a narrow range of steelmaking activities, having sold off virtually all its non-steel subsidiaries and hived off rod, bar, and engineering steel companies through collaborative deals with the private sector. Apart from activities in aluminium, Hoogovens of the Netherlands has concentrated on steelmaking too. There is a clear implication that those keen to remain loyal to iron and steel would have a profit-seeking interest in buying up steelmaking assets from those anxious to diversify. British Steel, having been forced by political imperative to stick to a narrow range of commercial activity, may now be able to make the most of its increasingly specialized managerial skills.

We do have the precedent of other industries to suggest how steel might evolve in these circumstances. One obvious parallel is the rationalization of European petrochemicals (Jackson 1985). Petrochemicals has many similarities to steel in terms of capital and skill intensity and manufacture of a basic range of standardized 'commodity' products. The real difference is in terms of initial capital commitment. A typical minimum-efficient size works making a basic 'building block' chemical, such as an ethylene cracker, costs $0.5 billion in a European location. A complete integrated steelworks making strip products on a minimum-efficient scale would cost ten times as much: $5 billion.

In the early 1980s European petrochemicals shared many of the same problems now facing steel. These included excess capacity and imminent competition from newly active producers with potential cost advantages over European producers. The solution was swift rationalization, whereby individual companies swapped and closed bulk chemical and plastics capacity. Some European firms left bulk petrochemicals altogether. Others bought or exchanged capacity to become as big as possible in their chosen product line. Hoechst sold its polystyrene interests in Shell. ICI and Enichem got together to make PVC. Monsanto sold out its acrylonitrile interests to BASF. Esso shut down its ethylene capacity in Cologne and sold off other plant in order to operate jointly an optimum size plant built jointly with Shell at Mossmorran. The motive for swapping capacity was to close down the less efficient plants, to load the more efficient and to exploit market power in specialized product lines.

There are muted signs that capacity swaps or agreed mergers of this sort are already under discussion for steel. Vallourec, a French tube steelmaker, is said to be negotiating with British Steel over an alliance in the tube market, while Mannesmann of West Germany is reported to be holding similar talks over co-operation in tube manufacture with Finsider of Italy. Usinor-Sacilor of France and Cockerill Sambre of Belgium are to combine their merchant bar production. At the same time, the French company will take over Cockerill's electrical steels business, an area of existing strength at Usinor-Sacilor. The French group also collaborates with Arbed on sheet piling and rails and with Riva of Italy on reinforcing bars. In some respects, product swaps or collaborative production are to be preferred to outright take-overs, because they do not have such a deleterious effect on producer concentration. Although output within each particular product line becomes heavily concentrated in the hands of just one or two firms, rivals in adjacent product areas at least have the skills to skip back into their old market area if excess profits beckon. In steelmaking, capacity swaps are more likely to accord with acute national sensitivities in an industry with considerable political power. After all, swapping implies some form of reciprocity. Exchange of assets implies equivalent bargaining power on the part of both participants, typically access to each other's national markets. Equal sharing of the misery of closure seems to command universal agreement within the existing European crisis cartel. Difficulties arise if comparative advantage means the capacity selected for closure is always in the same country.

9. CONCENTRATION, CORPORATE CONTROL, AND CONTESTABILITY

There is an argument for supposing that contests for corporate control are likely to replace capacity swaps as a mechanism for rationalizing steel. This implication derives from the work of Sutton (1986, 1988) and Shaked and Sutton (1987) on vertical product differentiation within oligopolies. Certain steelmakers are positioning themselves in the world market through research and development (R&D) and marketing in such a way as to accumulate a competitive lead over smaller rivals (Scholey 1987: 262; Aylen 1987*b*). Ultimately their rivals either have to match their effort or have to give up. A few firms may be able to find market niches (e.g. Rautaruuki Oy of Finland in Arctic steels). Eventually steel is likely to become concentrated in the hands of a limited number of leading OECD producers. Vertical product differentiation means that successful managerial teams have a market power advantage over potential partners, and will prefer take-over as a mechanism to realize profits instead of sharing. Capacity swaps enable participants to secure many of the gains of merger, such as economies of scale, rationalizing complementary spare capacity, or even securing monopoly power, without actually consummating marriage. But existence of product leadership introduces a 'valuation discrepancy'. A product leader has an edge over a potential take-over victim in the same sector. The acquiring firm will place a greater value on the profits of a target firm once it is under its control than the market ascribes to the firm under its current management. Take-over is one of the ways that a leading firm can realize a return on the fixed costs of product development, while at the same time securing scale advantages from reorganization.

But there is a tension here between product leadership and economies of scale which result in enhanced concentration and the likelihood of higher profits inducing new entry into steelmaking. The more firms merge or co-operate to reduce costs and exploit higher-quality products, the more likely it is that new firms will sneak into the industry to compete away some of the returns realized by moves to oligopolistic price-fixing and capacity reduction. So it is not sufficient to provide a better product which raises your market share if developments can be readily duplicated by rivals. Vertical product differentiation involves raising the fixed costs of competition. The essence of this form of competition is to provide customers with a new steel product exhibiting premium characteristics, but costing little extra to make, yet which is expensive for your rivals to research and develop. British Steel's technical leadership in steel sheet continuously coated with plastic or paint is a case in point. The initial development outlay and subsequent 'learning' needed to duplicate this product range are high and probably growing.[6] Yet the unit costs for those who make the product badly are higher (due to reject rates and smaller-scale production) than the unit costs for those who can make it well.

The strongest evidence for vertical product differentiation in steel is to be found in the realm of R&D effort (Aylen 1987c; International Iron and Steel Institute 1987). The ten biggest companies now account for a third

[6] In the past, products with high R&D costs such as electrical steels have often been made under licence with fees paid to the initial developer for 'know-how'. Lower transport costs, more open markets, and the potential for multinational operation swing the balance away from sale of licences towards direct supply of the world market by the developer.

of the western world's total R&D effort in steel (Figure 7.3). Five are
Japanese and diversifying away from steel production. Five are
European, including British Steel, which ranks fourth in the world steel
R&D league. Other new features of differentiation include the growing
trend towards branding and marketing of a hitherto standard product—
again initiated in Europe by British Steel—and vertical integration forward into stockholder networks, which also raises the absolute cost of
entry. The aim is not so much to deter new entrants to steelmaking: they
will be put off anyway by the huge initial outlay required. Rather, the
aim of vertical product differentiation is to exclude from the market
existing weaker rivals who are unable to support the outlay of fixed
costs needed to enhance the value of their particular products in the eyes
of the steel customer. Those who have incurred the high fixed costs can,
of course, spread the outlay over a greater and greater volume of sales
by winning larger markets or, at the limit, by taking over other producers. It remains to be seen whether 'British Steel' has the distinctive brand
image of Pepsi-Cola, or Coca-Cola, although there are signs of this in
specialized markets such as sections for the construction industry in the
USA. The process is likely to be cumulative as profitable steelmakers

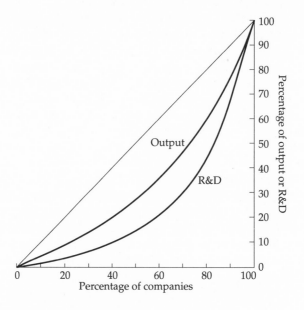

FIG. 7.3. Concentration of steel output and R&D, 1986/7.

Note: Concentration of steel output (tonnes) and R&D (personnel) among the
western world's 40 largest steelmakers.

Source: International Iron and Steel Institute 1988, and Aylen 1987*c*.

push forward with product development and branding in an attempt to prevent less profitable firms or late comers from the newly industrializing countries from ever catching up.

Vertical product differentiation does not imply a particularly desirable market structure. After all, the aim is to acquire market power in order to enjoy monopoly profits from a distinctive, high-quality product made at much the same unit cost as your rivals. In the long run, oligopolistic competition of this sort threatens the contestability of the European steel market. Evidently there is a trade-off between lower resource costs of production brought by a more efficient industry structure and departures from marginal-cost pricing due to product differentiation.

For the time being at least, the world steel market is potentially highly competitive in the absence of trade controls. In 1986, 26 per cent of world steel was traded across international boundaries despite restrictions. Growth in world steel trade reflects falling tariffs, lower transport costs and widespread entry by new producers in newly industrializing countries. More fragmented supply has made the world steel industry more competitive, and long-established oligopolies—for instance within the USA, West Germany, and Japan—less stable. Admittedly, sunk costs are higher than in any other industry world-wide and the high social costs of closure add to the barriers to exit. But at the same time there has been considerable, often subsidized, entry and there is substantial excess capacity in existence at a time of stagnant world demand. Even if demand were to rise, there is scope for reviving underutilized assets in developing countries through new management. New technology has lowered the barriers to entry into rod, bar, and light products in circumstances where electric power is cheap, steel scrap plentiful and markets widely dispersed. In the USA, the 60 or so mini-mills now account for 20 per cent of steel production, up from less than 3 per cent some twenty years ago. The growing contestability of a world market of fairly fixed size goes a long way to explain the lobbying for government intervention such as trade protection and cartelization in the USA and the EEC. So, for the moment, increased concentration does not pose an undue threat, given the potential discipline exerted by surplus capacity.

We do not foresee a rapid upsurge in concentration within Europe as soon as the cartel is abandoned. Shifts towards a more efficient industry structure will take time not only because of barriers to exit, but also because of barriers in the market for corporate control. Arbed of Luxemburg plans to establish a majority group of local shareholders in its firm, which holds the key to rationalization in Belgium as well as Luxemburg. The British government is taking steps to prevent anyone building up more than a 15 per cent stake in British Steel for five years following privatization. The Dutch government has reduced its stake in Hoogovens from 28.4 per cent to 15 per cent, but at the request of

Hoogovens this measure of public ownership has been maintained. State ownership makes French, Austrian, and Italian bulk steel producers immune to take-over threats. In West Germany, the leading banks have effective control over the five main private steel firms through direct ownership, through proxy voting rights on holdings under their custody, and through representation in supervisory boards. The sixth firm, Peine-Salzgitter, is state-owned. In short, European steel is protected against hostile take-over bids.

Ultimately the case for a free international market in corporate control is a selfish case. In the last analysis, a take-over bid is a voluntary exchange of assets. It is beneficial to have foreign investors willing to fund the substantial sums required for development in this industry, if they can do so more cheaply or with more skill than domestic owners. Admittedly, there is a case for restrictions to avoid predatory bids whereby a high-cost, subsidized overseas producer buys up and closes plants in order to load its own capacity preferentially, for instance to forestall local employment losses. Such a move would reduce European welfare by transferring output from a low-resource cost to a high-resource cost location. But, taken overall, these bid-blocking devices are likely to slow down the rate of restructuring across the European steel industry and allow cost and quality differences to persist longer than necessary. There is scope for international agreement to free-up the capital market for steelmaking assets in the same way that controls are now being removed from the product market. An obvious solution—albeit very much a second-best one—would be to permit hostile bids by other non-subsidized European steel producers. This is at least politically feasible—even if it excludes third parties for the time being, and so attenuates the threat of take-over which we have argued is conducive to efficiency and lowers the value of steel firms as other, cash-rich companies are prevented from bidding.

10. CONCLUSION: THE ROUTE FROM PRIVATIZATION

The first precondition for successful privatization of British Steel is free competition and free trade in the European steel market. Flotation of British Steel in 1988 coincided with the end of production quotas in the European steel market. British Steel and its leading rivals, such as Usinor-Sacilor, responded by vertical integration forward into stock-holding and distribution to help secure market shares. The European Community is taking steps to prosecute cartels among steel producers. Following success in flat stainless steel, the Commission have moved on to investigate the market for sections and some strip products. Although the product market has been liberalized within Western Europe, it is not yet clear how the Community will respond to export thrusts from the new market economies of Eastern Europe.

Restrictions on the market for corporate control have proved more intractable. Restructuring has taken place in some products but not others. British Steel purchased capacity to make sections in Germany from Klöckner and is currently negotiating with Aristrain, a leading sections producer in Spain. In this fashion, an efficient industry structure is beginning to emerge in one subsector of the European industry through voluntary sale and agreed merger.

But the German steel industry has prevented foreign take-over with the support of government and the banks. Publicly owned Peine-Salzgitter was quietly privatized through sale to the German group Preussag, while foreign purchase of both Klöckner-trading and Hoesch Stahl was prevented by local interests. The German steel industry remains fragmented and continues to lose competitiveness. Privatization of British Steel helps foster a market-based system of corporate control in the UK. The response in Germany has been to reinforce the bank-based nature of corporate control in steel.

At the same time, the French state steel group Usinor-Sacilor which has undertaken most acquisitions is being investigated by the Commission for receiving covert subsidy from a state-owned bank. French experience highlights the assymetry between private ownership and public ownership. There is a likelihood that Usinor-Sacilor can acquire assets at higher prices or operate with lower efficiency than an organization subject to sanction of bankruptcy or take-over. In this fashion, restructuring without privatization may take place through the transfer of assets to *less* efficient managerial teams.

Evidently, privatization is just one component in a transition to a more efficient industry structure within European steel. Free trade in steel products within an open world market coupled with a vigorous competition policy represents the best discipline on the emerging dominant and monopolistic European steel producers. A more liberal capital market among non-subsidized companies would help promote the necessary production agreements, capacity exchanges, and outright take-overs required to restructure European steel. Interference to preserve domestic ownership of steel production seems to be hastening the eclipse of German steel.

References

Abromeit, H. (1986), *British Steel: An Industry between the State and the Private Sector*, Leamington Spa: Berg.

Alchian, A. A. (1965), 'Some economics of property rights', *Il Politico*, **30**, 816–29.

Aylen, J. (1982), 'Plant size and efficiency in the steel industry: an international comparison', *National Institute Economic Review*, **100** (May), 65–76.

—— (1984), 'Prospects for steel', *Lloyds Bank Review*, **152** (Apr.), 13–30.

—— (1987*a*), 'Privatization in developing countries', *Lloyds Bank Review*, **163** (Jan.), 15–30.

—— (1987*b*), 'The destination of species', *Steel Times International*, **11** (Oct.), 47–8.

—— (1987*c*), 'Research and development: diversification and revival', *Steel Times International*, **11/5** (Dec.), 46–8.

Baumol, W. J. (1982), 'Contestable markets: an uprising in the theory of industry structure', *American Economic Review*, **72/1**, 1–15.

Brittan, S., and Riley, B. (1978), 'A people's stake in North Sea oil', *Lloyds Bank Review*, **128** (Apr.), 1–18.

Brown, D. (1984), 'Success brings problems for Swedish steel: booming exports have raised the spectre of foreign restrictions', *Financial Times*, 21 Aug.

Bruce, P., Dawkins, W., Garnett, N., and Wyles, J. (1987), 'Europe's steel industry: another crisis, another plan', *Financial Times*, 17 Mar.

Cockerill, A. (1980), 'Steel and the State in Great Britain', *Annals of Public and Cooperative Economy*, **51/4**, 439–57.

Crandall, R. W. (1981), *The U.S. Steel Industry in Recurrent Crisis: Policy Options in a Competitive World*, Washington, DC: Brookings Institution.

Dawkins, W., and Goodhart, D. (1988), 'EC ministers agree to end steel output controls', *Financial Times*, 28 May.

Demsetz, H. (1966), 'Some aspects of property rights', *Journal of Law and Economics*, **9**, 61–70.

Fine, B., and O'Donnell, K. (1985), 'The nationalised industries', in B. Fine and L. Harris (ẹds.), *The Peculiarities of the British Economy*, London: Lawrence and Wishart.

Fitzgerald, F. (1988), 'Energy, high technology and economics in modern steel-making', mimeo, Institute of Energy, 54th Melchett Lecture, 8 Mar.

Foreman-Peck, J., and Waterson, M. (1985), 'The comparative efficiency of public and private enterprise in Britain: electricity generation between the world wars', *Economic Journal*, **95**, suppl. 83–95.

Franko, L. G. (1981), 'Adjusting to export thrusts of newly industrialising countries', *Economic Journal*, **91**, 486–505.

Grout, P. (1987), 'The wider share ownership programme', *Fiscal Studies*, **8/3**, 59–74.

Harris, A. L. (1959), 'J. S. Mill on monopoly and socialism: a note', *Journal of Political Economy*, **67**, 604–11.

International Iron and Steel Institute, Committee on Technology (1987), *Research in the Steel Industry: Technical Exchange Session*, Brussels: IISI.

—— (1988), *World Steel in Figures 1988*, Brussels: IISI.

International Labour Organization (1986), *Iron and Steel Committee, Eleventh Session Report III, Productivity Improvement and its Effects on the Level of Employment and Working Conditions in the Iron and Steel Industry*, Geneva: ILO.

Jackson, T. (1985), 'European petrochemicals: suddenly the only option is to become bigger', *Financial Times*, 19 Sept.

Kay, J. A., and Thompson, D. J. (1986), 'Privatisation: a policy in search of a rationale', *Economic Journal*, **96**, 18–32.

McGee, J. S. (1988), *Industrial Organization*, Englewood Cliffs: Prentice-Hall.

Marcus, P. F. (1987), 'Steel price warfare', presentation to Institute of Purchasing and Supply, pub. as *World Steel Dynamics*, 7 Apr., New York: Paine Webber.

—— (1988), 'Perspectives on the domestic steel business', presentation to American Iron and Steel Institute Annual Meeting, pub. as *World Steel Dynamics*, 19 May, New York: Paine Webber.

Marsh, P., and Rawsthorn, A. (1988), 'European man-made fibres: a long, hard road ahead', *Financial Times*, 8 June.

Mayer, C. (1987), 'Public ownership: concepts and applications', Centre for Economic Policy Research Discussion Paper no. 182.

Millward, R. (1982), 'The comparative performance of public and private ownership', in Lord Roll (ed.), *The Mixed Economy*, London: Macmillan.

—— and Parker, D. (1983), 'Public and private enterprise: comparative behaviour and relative efficiency', in R. Millward (ed.), *Public Sector Economics*, London: Longmans.

—— and Ward, R. (1987), 'The costs of public and private gas enterprises in late 19th-century Britain', *Oxford Economic Papers*, **39**, 719–37.

Organization for Economic Co-operation and Development (1985), 'Steel', in *Costs and Benefits of Protection*, Paris: OECD.

Rowley, C. K., and Yarrow, G. K. (1981), 'Property rights, regulation and public enterprise: the case of the British steel industry 1957–1975', *International Review of Law and Economics*, **1/1**, 63–96.

Scherer, F. M. (1988), 'Corporate take-overs: the efficiency arguments', *Journal of Economics Perspectives*, **2/1**, 69–82.

Scholey, R. (1987), 'European steel: what future?' *Ironmaking and Steelmaking*, **14/6**, 257–65.

Shaked, A., and Sutton, J. (1987), 'Product differentiation and industrial structure', *Journal of Industrial Economics*, **36/2**, 131–46.

Shaw, R. W., and Shaw, S. A. (1983), 'Excess capacity and rationalisation in the West European synthetic fibres industry', *Journal of Industrial Economics*, **32/2**, 149–66.

Shleifer, A., and Vishny, R. W. (1988), 'Value maximisation and the acquisition process', *Journal of Economic Perspectives*, **2/1**, 7–20.

Silberston, Z. A. (1984), *The Multi-Fibre Arrangement and the UK Economy*, London: HMSO.

Sutton, J. (1986), 'Vertical product differentiation: some basic themes', *American Economic Review, Papers and Proceedings*, **76/2**, 393–8.

—— (1988), 'How industrial structure differs: some preliminary results from a six-country study of the food and drink sector', paper to ESRC Industrial Economics Study Group, London Business School, 7 Jan.

Tyler, W. G. (1979), 'Technical efficiency in production in a developing country: an empirical examination of the Brazilian plastics and steel industries', *Oxford Economic Papers*, **31/3**, 477–95.

Vickers, J., and Yarrow, G. K. (1985), *Privatization and the Natural Monopolies*, London: Public Policy Centre.

8

Competitive Tendering and Efficiency: The Case of Refuse Collection

S. DOMBERGER,* S. A. MEADOWCROFT,** AND D. J. THOMPSON†

1. INTRODUCTION

Attempts to promote efficiency in the provision of local authority services through competitive tendering are viewed as a significant element of the Government's privatization policy. Not surprisingly, those who are opposed to the principle of privatization have been vociferous in their criticisms of the policy, claiming to have uncovered evidence of widespread failure and falling standards among private contractors (TUC 1984).

The importance of reliable evidence on the impact of competitive tendering cannot be overstated in view of the highly politicized nature of the debate. Yet it is fair to say that much of the evidence that has emerged in recent years has tended to be of the anecdotal kind reflecting the strong desire of opponents and supporters alike to undermine each other's case. The use of examples and counter-examples of 'successes' and 'failures' by both sides amounts to casual empiricism which only serves to maintain the 'not proven' verdict on the impact of the policy.

In recent years a number of local authorities in England and Wales have issued formal tenders for their refuse collection services and many of these have led to contracts being awarded to private contractors. As a consequence, statistical information is now becoming available on the cost of privately contracted refuse collection services and it is now possi-

* Professor at the Graduate School of Business, University of Sydney.

** Economist, Office of Telecommunications. At the time the paper was written, was a Research Officer at the Institute for Fiscal Studies.

† Department of Education. At the time the paper was written, was a Senior Research Fellow at the Centre for Business Strategy, London Business School.

This paper was first published in *Fiscal Studies* in 1986. The authors are grateful for financial support from the Economic and Social Research Council in carrying out the research upon which this paper is based. Helpful suggestions on an earlier draft were made by Dieter Helm, Ian Walker, officials at the Department of Environment, and participants at the Esmee Fairbairn Local Government Study Group. Thanks are due to the Chartered Institute of Public Finance and Accountancy for providing data. The usual disclaimer applies.

ble to provide more reliable evidence on this debate than has generally been available hitherto.

The objective of our paper is to compare the costs of those refuse collection services that have been subjected to the tendering process with those that have not. The paper examines whether significant cost reductions have been associated with the use of private contractors and provides an assessment of the potential benefits of the tendering process. We shall also examine the thorny issue of quality of service. Opponents of competitive tendering have often claimed that in those cases where costs appear to have fallen, the same has been true of the quality of service provided. If this were true then the value of any reported cost reductions would clearly be overstated.

The paper is organized as follows. Section 2 considers the recent history of competitive tendering, and Section 3 the major theoretical arguments that have been put forward on its effects together with a summary of previous evidence. Section 4 goes on to outline the empirical methodology that we adopted, including a description of the data used and the statistical techniques employed. The results are reported in Section 5, and their robustness is considered in Section 6, along with the issue of quality of service. Finally, Section 7 contains some concluding remarks and an evaluation of competitive tendering policy.

2. POLICY BACKGROUND

In February 1985 a consultation paper (Department of Environment 1985) set out the Government's intention to introduce legislation to extend competitive tendering to a wide range of local authority services and activities. The proposed legislation would place authorities under a duty to initiate competitive tendering (and make public the comparative costs of in-house and out-house provision) for a number of activities or services to be designated by the Secretary of State. In particular the paper identified refuse collection, street cleaning, cleaning of buildings, vehicle maintenance, grounds maintenance, and catering services. With respect to refuse collection it was proposed to subject all of such work to competition in all authorities unless there was evidence that some authorities carry out the activity on too small a scale for the statutory requirements to be worth applying.

In the consultation paper the government argued that 'far too many authorities appear to have been unwilling to open services to competition'. This certainly appears to be true in the case of refuse collection, even though this was one of the first local authority services to be privately contracted and remains, to date, the service in which most private contracts have been awarded. In 1981 there were only two local authorities (Maldon and Mid-Bedfordshire) that had private contracts for the refuse collection service. In that year Southend contracted out its refuse collection service and since then there have been 55 formal tenders issued for refuse collection, street cleaning, or associated services (see Table 8.1). In 29 cases the contract was awarded to the private sector and in 26 cases the contract was retained by the DLO (direct labour organization).

TABLE 8.1. Tenders issued and contracts awarded, 1981–1986

	Tenders	Contracts
April 1981–March 1982	6	4
April 1982–March 1983	23	13
April 1983–March 1984	9	6
April 1984–March 1985	14	4
April 1985–March 1986	3	2
TOTALS	55	29

Note: The figures in this table refer to tenders/contracts for refuse, street sweeping, and associated services. The number of contracts awarded includes 8 for all services, 16 for refuse collection only, and 5 for cleansing only.

Source: BFI-Wastecare Ltd 1986.

3. THE IMPACT OF COMPETITIVE TENDERING: THEORY AND EVIDENCE

Refuse services are provided free (to domestic customers) and are usually supplied by the relevant local authority in each area. This does not of course require that the actual operation of the service is carried out by the local authority. There is no a priori reason why the authority could not contract a private company to provide this service to consumers. Whether refuse services should be provided free, and by a single body, are not issues we propose to discuss further in this paper. Rather we shall focus on the crucial issue of why differences in performance might be expected between services that are tendered and those that are non-competitive.

It could be argued that in-house (public) provision affords a greater measure of control over a number of input and output characteristics associated with the service. This applies to employment policies, equipment procurement, and the like. At the same time it is clear that public provision removes, to a significant extent, the incentives and constraints that apply to firms operating under competitive market conditions. This

would not matter much if it could be assumed, as it has been traditionally, that public enterprises would seek to act efficiently and minimize
costs. Increasingly, however, such an assumption has been called into
question and the absence of a profitability objective means that there is
no strong incentive to maximize 'productive efficiency'.[1] Given that the
financial requirements of the enterprise are met through local taxes, the
incentives to minimize costs are limited.

In the absence of a profit incentive a local authority intent on pursuing
efficiency must regulate performance directly. However, it will face
asymmetries in the information available to itself and to the operators of
the service. This could make it difficult for it to determine the extent of
inefficiency and thus to implement corrective measures. In other words,
the public servants who control the resources that are allocated to the
service in question cannot easily determine whether the service is being
provided at a higher cost than necessary because the relevant information about efficiency is not readily available to them.

Advocates of competitive tendering argue that it largely overcomes
the problems both of incentives and of information. The tendering
process itself generates information about the relative efficiency of the
operators who bid for the contract, provided of course that the level of
service is specified correctly and with precision. As regards incentives,
once a fixed-price contract for refuse collection has been granted it is
clearly in the operator's interest to minimize costs since only in this way
can profits be maximized. There are, however, potential problems with
this apparently straightforward process. First, effective competition in
the tendering process may not emerge. Sunk costs incurred in bidding
or asymmetries in information between incumbents and entrants may
discourage bidding. Second, once a contract is awarded the operator
may act opportunistically to increase profits by failing to fulfil his obligations. For example, the contractor may try to renegotiate the contract
terms in his favour. The operator also has an incentive to reduce costs by
reducing service standards if he can do so without being detected. Such
opportunistic behaviour can be held in check by having tightly specified
contracts that leave little ambiguity in the standards of service required
and, coupled with this, monitoring and enforcement of the contract during its lifetime.

The characteristics of refuse collection indicate that neither of these
potential problems is likely to be significant. The sunk costs of entering
the tendering process are likely to be low whilst asymmetries in information between incumbent and entrant are unlikely to be large. A contract can be specified for refuse collection in which the expected outputs
are measurable and in which monitoring of compliance is comparatively

---

[1] For a strict definition of productive efficiency and further discussion of this issue, see
Domberger and Piggott 1986.

straightforward. The scope for unconstrained opportunistic behaviour by contractors is thus not large, provided that sanctions can be applied if there is a failure to comply, as is the case when contracts are subject to periodic re-tendering. Both these factors suggest a priori that refuse collection is a service where tendering is particularly likely to be effective.

These are issues to which we shall return in interpreting our findings. First, we briefly outline previous empirical work. Only three studies consider the effect of the private contracting of refuse collection services and only two of these relate to UK data. McDavid (1985) used two approaches in looking at the experience of Canadian municipalities in privately contracting residential waste-collection services. First, case studies of two cities that had switched from public to private contracts revealed cost savings and productivity improvements. For example, in Richmond public collection was 66 per cent more expensive than private collection and private crews were 65 per cent more productive than public crews. Second, a cross-sectional analysis, with data from a survey of 126 Canadian municipalities conducted in 1981 and 1982, showed public collection was 50 per cent more expensive than private collection. This substantial cost difference was confirmed when a regression analysis was used to allow for service level, scale of output, collection method, and environmental conditions. Public collection was still 41 per cent more costly than private collection.

The Audit Commission (1984) looked at refuse collection in England and Wales using a computer model developed by the Local Authorities Management Services Advisory Committee (LAMSAC) called the 'ROSS Model'. It concluded that although privatized services produce on average better results than the average local authority direct labour organization (DLO), privatization was not necessary to secure efficient performance; a quarter of DLOs had costs as low as or lower than the average privatized service.

Hartley and Huby (1985) looked at a range of cases where local authority or health authority services have been privately contracted in the UK. Their analysis, which was based on a detailed questionnaire survey to the authorities, showed that private contracting had generally been associated with substantial reductions in costs.

4. ESTIMATING THE COSTS OF REFUSE COLLECTION

The aim of our analysis is twofold. First, we seek to determine whether there are significant cost savings in cases where the refuse collection service has been privately contracted. Second, we wish to establish whether authorities that have undertaken competitive tendering but retained the service in-house have been able to achieve similar cost savings.

The approach we use is to specify and estimate, by means of regression analysis, the determinants of the costs of refuse collection. The basic 'cost function' takes the following form:

$$C = f(Q,P,X) \tag{1}$$

where C represents total costs. These are determined by the level of output Q, the price of inputs P, and various output characteristics X which will be described in detail below. A more precise description of the relationship that we estimated is given by:

$$\begin{aligned}
\log C = {} & a_1 + a_2 \log UNITS + a_3 \log WAGE + a_4 FREQ1 + a_5 \\
& FREQ2 + a_6 METH1 + a_7 METH2 + a_8 METH3 + a_9 \\
& METH4 + a_{10} \log DEN + a_{11} \log DISP + a_{12} \log HOUS + a_{13} \\
& RECLAIM1 + a_{14} RECLAIM2 + a_{15} RECLAIM3 + a_{16} CON\text{-} \\
& TRACT + a_{17} TEND + \epsilon
\end{aligned} \tag{2}$$

This is the familiar Cobb–Douglas formulation (after taking logarithms) which facilitates empirical estimation and aids interpretation of the results. However, this formulation incorporates a number of assumptions which need to be briefly considered. First it is assumed that the dependence of cost on output (Q) is constant over the relevant output range. Previous research (Hirsch 1965; Collins and Downes 1977) generally suggests that the production function of refuse collection exhibits constant returns to scale, which is consistent with this assumption.

Equation (2) also implies that output (Q) and its various characteristics have an independent influence on costs (C) and do not interact. In other words, although the variables defining the various output characteristics affect the absolute-cost level of disposing of a given quantity of refuse, there is no reason to believe that they affect the relationship between costs and output. Thus, although it is more costly to collect refuse twice rather than once a week, in both cases costs are expected to increase by the same proportional amount if the quantity collected doubles.

The dependent variable in our cost function—total cost C—was measured by gross expenditure on refuse collection. The independent variables to be included are, following equation (1), measures of output, output characteristics, and the price of inputs. In addition, our estimated-cost function includes variables indicating those local authorities that have tendered the refuse collection service. A brief description of each variable is outlined below; a more detailed definition is given in Appendix 8.1.

We have measured the level of output by the number of units (*UNITS*) served (i.e. the number of pick-up points). We also considered using the quantity of waste collected but this variable is subject to significant measurement error. A third possibility—population served—

appeared less appropriate on a priori grounds (the number of pick-up points is likely to be a more important determinant of costs than the number of people served by the collection service) and this was confirmed by our analysis.

Our cost function includes two types of output characteristics—service quality and local conditions. The two most important dimensions of service quality are frequency and method of collection. Frequency of collection is measured by the percentages of waste where there is more than one collection a week, one collection a week or less than one collection a week. The percentage of waste where there is one collection a week was used as a benchmark for the frequency of collection variables and the other possibilities are measured by FREQ1 and FREQ2. Method of collection is measured by the percentage of waste collected by each of five different collection methods. The essential difference between the various methods lies in whether the customer has to carry his dustbin to and from the kerbside or whether this is done by the operative. (A precise definition of the different methods is given in Appendix 8.1.) The back-door method was used as a benchmark in our regression equation and the other four methods are measured by the variables METH1 etc.

Apart from service quality there are a number of local factors that are likely to affect the cost of the refuse collection service. These are the density of units, averaged distance to disposal, the percentage of household units, and the extent of reclaimed waste. The density of units (DEN) is likely to have a negative effect on total cost; the proximity of pick-up points and shorter walking distances in areas of high density would suggest that costs should be lower in these areas. Similarly, the greater is the distance to the disposal point where the collection vehicle is emptied (DISP), the greater is the cost. The percentage of household units (HOUS) was included as an explanatory variable because the output measure we used (the total number of units) includes domestic, commercial, industrial, and other units. Commercial and industrial units produce a greater amount of waste per unit than domestic units. This means that for a given number of units the cost of collection will be lower the greater the percentage of domestic units. Finally, many authorities undertake a range of waste-reclamation activities. Three of these were chosen as being likely to be particularly important in affecting total cost: the amount of waste paper reclaimed (RECLAIM1), the number of abandoned vehicles collected (RECLAIM2), and the number of bottle-banks owned and operated by the local authority (RECLAIM3).

The two main inputs in the refuse collection process are labour and vehicles (see Table 8.2). The price of vehicles was not included in the analysis since this price is unlikely to vary systematically between local authorities. However, local labour-market conditions, and hence the supply-price of labour, will vary. We have included the average earn-

TABLE 8.2. Estimated breakdown of refuse
collection costs, 1984

	Percentage
Drivers and loaders	53
Vehicle standing costs	18
Vehicle running and maintenance	11
Other costs	29
Income	(11)
TOTAL	100

Source: Audit Commission 1984.

ings of manual workers in each local authority area (*WAGE*), taken from the New Earnings Survey, as a measure of the supply-price of labour.

The cost function that we estimated included a variable indicating those authorities that have awarded private contracts after tendering (*CONTRACT*) and a variable indicating those authorities that have tendered but have awarded the contract to the 'in-house' unit (*TEND*). The estimated coefficients on these variables capture the magnitude of cost difference between authorities where all the other determinants of costs are controlled for. They show the proportional difference in costs between authorities that have tendered, or awarded private contracts, and those that have not.

The private-contracting variable is a dummy variable which takes the value 1 where more than 10 per cent of waste is collected by private contractors and 0 otherwise. We have adopted this specification because there are some authorities in which particular types of waste (e.g. bulky household waste, trade refuse, or abandoned vehicles) are collected by contractors but in which the main refuse service is not tendered. The tendering variable is a dummy which takes the value 1 if the local authority has issued a formal tender document (between April 1981 and the end of the financial years 1983/4 or 1984/5) and the result of the tendering exercise has been to retain an 'in-house' collection service. Otherwise it takes the value 0.

The main source of data for these variables was the *Waste Collection Statistics* published by CIPFA (Chartered Institute of Public Finance and Accountancy). Data were available in a suitable form for two years (1983/4 and 1984/5) and for local authorities in England and Wales. There are a total of 403 authorities. However, some authorities did not provide a return for either one or both years, or the return did not include information on all the relevant variables. In addition, our final regressions excluded one authority in 1983/4 (which privately contracted part of the refuse collection service) that appeared to be an outlier as a result of data errors. As a result the sample was restricted to 610 observations. Within this sample there were 11 authorities that privately contracted the refuse collection service in 1983/4 and 19 in 1984/5. In addition the sample included 10 authorities that had tendered but retained the service in-house by the end of the year 1983/4 and 10 by the end of the year 1984/5. Table 8.3 shows the number of authorities that had awarded private contracts and the percentage of waste collected by contractors. There are a number of local authorities that have tendered but are not in our sample. In 1984/5 there were seven authorities that had tendered but that were excluded on the basis of incomplete information on either frequency or method of collection.

TABLE 8.3. Authorities in our sample and numbers with private contracts in 1983/4 and 1984/5

Percentage of waste collected by contractors	Number of authorities	
	1984/85	1983/84
0	267	283
1–9	19	11
10–79	6	5
80–100	13	6
TOTAL	305	305

5. RESULTS

The basic-cost equation produces a good fit to the data; the adjusted R^2 statistic is 0.925 indicating that most of the variation in costs between authorities is determined by the factors that we have included in our analysis.[2] The estimates of the coefficients are shown in Table 8.4. Most of the coefficients are of the expected sign and are statistically significant.

The results that are of most interest are the effect of different methods of collection on total cost and the impact of tendering and private contracting. We now look at these in more detail.

Method of Collection

The coefficients on the variables *METH1* to *METH3* are all negative, showing that the back-door method of collection is the most expensive.

---

[2] Much of the variation in total cost can be explained by differences in the size of the refuse collection service. When the number of units is included as the only explanatory variable the adjusted R^2 statistic is 0.857. However, the other explanatory variables explain 49 per cent of the variation in total cost not explained by differences in size.

TABLE 8.4. Regression results

Variable	Description	OLS results Coefficient[a,b]	OLS results t-statistic[c]	White estimate t-statistic[c,d]
CONSTANT		-2.76	-3.97	-3.87
UNITS	Number of units	1.04	54.94	52.87
WAGE	Average earnings	0.90	7.51	7.32
FREQ1	More than once a week	0.65×10^{-2}	10.62	10.40
FREQ2	Less than once a week	-0.36×10^{-2}	-2.78	-3.66
METH1	Kerbside	-0.26×10^{-2}	-10.88	-9.95
METH2	Other collect and return	-0.12×10^{-2}	-2.45	-2.40
METH3	Skep or other normal method	-0.71×10^{-3}	-2.68	-3.05
METH4	Special collections	0.30×10^{-3}	0.16	0.15
DEN	Density of units	-0.15×10^{-1}	-1.88	-1.82
DISP	Average distance to disposal	0.28×10^{-1}	1.87	1.98
HOUS	Percentage of units that are domestic households	-0.43	-5.28	-3.65
RECLAIM1	Reclaimed paper	0.73×10^{-4}	4.27	5.14
RECLAIM2	Abandoned vehicles	0.87×10^{-4}	1.44	1.68
RECLAIM3	Bottle-banks	-0.37×10^{-3}	-0.31	-0.35
CONTRACT	Privately contracted	-0.25	-7.66	-4.58
TEND	Tendered but retained in-house	-0.19	-4.52	-4.58
	Number in sample	610		
	R^2	.927		
	$\bar{R}^2$	.925		

[a] Coefficients expressed as, e.g., 0.8×10^{-2} are interpreted as, e.g. 0.008.
[b] Some of the variables are entered in logs and some in levels and this, together with the units in which the variable is measured, affects the interpretation of the coefficient estimates.
[c] Significance levels for the t-statistics (one-tailed test) are 1.65 (5%) and 1.29 (10%).
[d] The White estimates of the t-statistics make adjustment for the presence of heteroskedasticity.

TABLE 8.5. Percentage of waste collected by
different methods of collection

Method	Percentage
Back door	52
Kerbside	21
Other collect and return	5
Skep and other normal	19
Special collections	3
TOTAL	100

Note: Based on 372 authorities in 1984/5.

Many local authorities use this method both for household and commercial collections. Table 8.5 shows that over half of all waste is collected from the backdoor.

The estimated coefficient on METH1 implies that the effect of a change from back-door collection to kerbside collection is to reduce total cost by 23 per cent. The savings from switching from back-door to 'other collect and return' method of 'skep or other normal' method are smaller but still significant; they are 11 per cent and 7 per cent respectively. The relative sizes of these coefficients are in line with a priori expectations based on the walking distance that each method implies. The Audit Commission (1984) also found that large savings can be made by changing the method of collection. Its findings indicated a total potential saving of some 25 per cent (similar to our own result) if every authority made the change to kerbside collection.

The Effect of Tendering and Private Contracting

The coefficient on the dummy variable for private contracting is highly significant and shows that costs are lower (by about 22 per cent) where private contracting is taking place.[3] This result suggests that the introduction of private contracting has yielded substantial cost savings—a conclusion confirmed by analysis of the trend in costs in authorities where private contracting has been introduced. Real costs have fallen in

---

[3] The coefficient in Table 8.4 indicates that private contractors' costs are a proportion, given by $e^{-0.25}$, of the costs of other authorities. This proportion equals 78%. This interpretation is based on the assumption that the private contracting dummy variable is exogenous. Authorities with high costs are the most likely to consider tendering. If our equation omits some variables that are relevant to determining authorities' costs then the contracting and tendering variables will be endogenous and our estimated coefficients may be biased. The implication is that our results will underestimate the cost differences associated with private contracting and with tendering.

these authorities. The coefficient on the dummy variable for services that have been tendered but awarded 'in-house' is also highly significant and shows that costs are lower for these services by about 17 per cent. This result suggests that tendering has yielded substantial cost savings even where the service has continued to be provided by the public sector. In fact the coefficients on the two dummy variables are not significantly different from one another. This indicates that it is the introduction of competition, rather than awarding contracts to private firms, which is the critical factor in achieving lower costs (see Kay and Thompson (1986) for a more general discussion of competition and ownership). This finding can be compared with the conclusion reached by the Audit Commission (1984) which suggested that private contracting is not necessary to achieve efficient performance. It concluded from its analysis that there are many DLOs that perform as well as or better than privately contracted services. Our own results (like those of the Audit Commission) show that whilst some in-house services are provided with the same level of efficiency as privately contracted services, the vast majority are less efficient.

Moreover many of the more efficient DLOs are those that have been subjected to competitive tendering. Figure 8.1 shows the distribution of measured efficiency for authorities where tendering has taken place (including both services awarded to private contractors and those awarded to in-house units) and where it has not. The efficiency measures are calculated from the residuals of the regression equation, estimated with the two dummy variables related to competitive tendering omitted. The residuals measure how much higher (+) or lower (−) actual costs are compared with the predictions of our cost function.

The results show that only a small number of authorities where competition is absent match the efficiency of authorities where tendering has been introduced. The majority do not. This pattern of results is similar to that found by Foreman-Peck and Waterson (1985) in their analysis of electricity generation by the public and private sectors in Great Britain in the 1930s.

6. ROBUSTNESS OF RESULTS

The objective of this section is to examine further the reliability of our empirical results. First, we look at the statistical robustness of our results. Second, we examine two issues—service quality and 'loss-leading'—that might suggest that our estimated cost savings are overstated.

The empirical results presented in the previous section are for a pooled time-series cross-section sample, using data for the two years

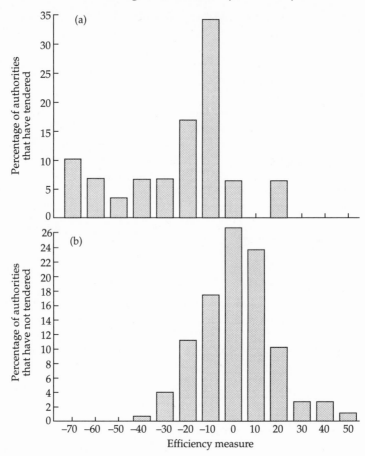

FIG. 8.1. Distribution of efficiency measures, 1984/5. (a) tendered services; (b) non-tendered services.

Note: Authorities with efficiency measures below zero are more efficient than average, and vice versa.

1983/4 and 1984/5. However, we also estimated the cost function separately for each year. The coefficients proved to be stable between the two years except for the coefficient on the tendering variables which are lower in the 1983/4 equation. Many authorities were tendering for the first time in 1983/4 and this suggests that there are one-off costs (e.g. redundancy payments, costs of tendering process) that occur in the first year of tendering. To test this hypothesis we estimated our basic regression again with the pooled time-series cross-section sample but included two variables which distinguish the first year of a tendered service (DUMMY2) from subsequent years (DUMMY1). (See Appendix 8.1 for precise definitions.) The results, shown in the table in Appendix 8.2, support the hypothesis that there are one-off costs. Savings in the first year (12 per cent) are lower than those in later years (25 per cent).

The regression results presented so far are for a sample of 610 observations. The sample size is restricted because some of the observations have missing variables. We re-estimated the cost function omitting variables that were less important and were missing for some observations. These variables were *DISP*, *RECLAIM1*, *RECLAIM2*, and *RECLAIM3*. By doing this we were able to increase the sample size to 679 observations and increase the number of authorities in our sample that had privately contracted more than 10 per cent to 20 in 1984/5 and 12 in 1983/4. Again our results do not change: the estimated coefficients, also shown in the table in Appendix 8.2, are not very different.

It has been suggested that the cost of refuse collection may vary between urban and rural areas for reasons that may not be captured by the other explanatory variables included in our estimated cost function. We re-estimated our equation including an urban/rural dummy variable taking the value 0 where the local authority is either a London borough or a Metropolitan district, and 1 otherwise. The coefficient on this dummy variable was negative and significant, suggesting that refuse collection is cheaper in non-metropolitan areas. However, the results on the size of savings from private contracting and tendering are unaffected: the coefficients on these variables remain unchanged when the urban/rural dummy variable is included.

Our cost-function analysis has shown that there are significant savings from tendering refuse collection services and that this finding is statistically robust. However, as discussed in Section 3, these savings may only be short-term if the contract has been underpriced. This may occur, first, because contractors have underestimated the costs of refuse collection and as a result have subsequently failed to meet the contract. However, we are not aware of any refuse collection contracts that have been terminated on these grounds.

Second, the savings may have been achieved as a result of 'loss-leading' in which the contractors have deliberately underpriced the contract. It is not obvious, on a priori grounds, that such loss-leading would be a worthwhile strategy. The circumstances in which it may pay (for example, where there are significant advantages of incumbency in the tendering process as a consequence of information asymmetries or the transaction costs associated with switching suppliers) are unlikely to apply to refuse collection. Nor is 'loss-leading' likely to deter competitors from entering the tendering process when the sunk costs of doing so are, in the case of a service like refuse collection, not very great. Loss-leading, therefore, does not appear a likely strategy. Empirical evidence will only become available, however, when a significant number of contracts come up for renewal, and so far this has happened to only three contracts in our sample. Nevertheless, an analysis of the change in the cost of the refuse collection service over the period 1980/1 to 1984/5 for these three authorities provided no evidence of an increase in the real cost of these services.

It has often been suggested that the cost savings resulting from private contracting have been achieved at the expense of a deterioration in the standard of service provided. Our cost analysis has accounted for the two most important aspects of service quality—method and frequency of collection. However, there are other dimensions of service for which no information was available. These include missed collections, spillage of refuse and the non-closure of gates. For example, the TUC report (1984) suggests a number of cases where service quality has declined as a result of private contracting.

Meadows (1985) provides some evidence on this issue from detailed case studies of five local authorities that have gone out to competitive tender for the refuse collection service. He concluded that 'those authorities which have [awarded private contracts] have considered that they have continued to receive the same standard of service required at a lower cost than they were facing before'. He also found that 'the penalty clauses for non-performance built into the contract were considered sufficient to ensure the required standard of service'. There is some evidence from small-scale market research studies to support this view (for example, see Gears 1984).

7. CONCLUSIONS

The objective we set ourselves at the beginning of this article was to identify whether competitive tendering has reduced the costs of refuse collection. Our findings show that where services have been tendered, costs are significantly lower (by broadly 20 per cent) than where they have not been. Our method of analysis makes allowance for differences between areas both in the characteristics of output and in various geographical factors. Our findings are not, therefore, a result of any systematic difference in the nature of the service provided between authorities where tendering has been introduced and those where it has not been. We are also satisfied that there is no evidence to suggest that these cost savings have been achieved at the expense of a deterioration in the quality of service provided to householders. Neither does the evidence suggest that the lower costs of tendered services result from 'loss-leading' behaviour (by either private contractors or in-house units) to establish (or reinforce) incumbency in a particular market. It is not obvious, in any case, that there would be any gain from such activity.

We therefore conclude that where tendering has been introduced this has resulted in a significant improvement in the efficiency with which refuse services are provided. Our results also show that the cost savings achieved where tendering results in the contract being awarded to the in-house unit are similar to those achieved where the contract is awarded to a private company. This finding is of course consistent with the growing literature that points to the importance of competition in inducing enterprises to act efficiently (see, for example, Bailey 1986; Millward 1982; Yarrow 1986).

Our findings indicate that the more widespread introduction of tendering could significantly reduce local authorities' costs. For example, if all authorities (rather than only 38 out of 403) had tendered their refuse services in 1984/5 then costs would have been cut by £80 million. This has obvious implications for the forthcoming legislation which will widen the scope of competitive tendering more generally.

APPENDIX 8.1

TABLE 8.6. Definitions of variables

Variable	Units	Log or level	Description
C	Pounds	Log	Gross expenditure. This includes expenditure on employees, premises/depots, provision of disposable sacks, dustbins, and sack-holders, and expenditure on transport and movable plant, agency services, establishment expenses, and other running expenses. Establishment expenses include an apportionment of central and departmental administration where such apportionments are made. Expenditure on premises and transport and movable plant includes all capital-financing charges and contributions to Repairs and Renewals Funds in respect of vehicles and movable plant.
UNITS	Number	Log	Number of domestic, commercial, industrial, and other units.
WAGE	Index	Log	Average earnings of adult male workers from the New Earnings Survey.
FREQ1	Percentage	Level	Percentage of waste collected more than once a week.
FREQ2	Percentage	Level	Percentage of waste collected less than once a week.
METH1	Percentage	Level	Percentage of waste collected kerbside. This includes cases where the householder moves the dustbin close to or onto the street for collection.
METH2	Percentage	Level	Percentage of waste collected by other collect-and-return method. This refers to the situation where either the operative collects from the front of the house or a dustbin is collected from the back-door but is returned to the front of the house by the operative, and the householder is then responsible for its subsequent removal to the back.
METH3	Percentage	Level	Percentage of waste collected by skep or other normal methods. A skep is an individual dustbin-sized container carried by the operative; the contents of the dustbin are first emptied into the skep and then carried to the collection vehicle.

Variable	Unit	Type	Description
METH4	Percentage	Level	Percentage of waste collected by special collections.
METH5	Percentage	Level	Percentage of waste collected by back-door collect or return. This method refers to a situation where the operative has to collect the sack or collect and return the dust-bin which has not been placed on the kerbside or in front of the house.
DEN	Units per hectare	Log	Density of units.
DISP	Kilometres	Log	Average distance to disposal.
HOUS	Percentage	Log	Percentage of units that are domestic.
RECLAIM1	Tonnes	Level	Tonnes of paper reclaimed.
RECLAIM2	Number	Level	Number of abandoned vehicles.
RECLAIM3	Number	Level	Number of bottle-banks.
CONTRACT	(0,1) dummy	Level	Dummy variable: = 1 if privately contracted more than 10%; = 0 otherwise.
DUMMY1	(0,1) dummy	Level	Dummy variable: = 1 if privately contracted more than 10% and not first year con-tracted out; = 1 if tendered and awarded in-house and not first year; = 0 otherwise.
DUMMY2	(0,1) dummy	Level	Dummy variable: = 1 if privately contracted more than 10% and first year con-tracted out; = 1 if tendered and awarded in-house and first year; = 0 otherwise.
TEND	(0,1) dummy	Level	Dummy variable: = 1 if a formal tender has been issued but the service has been retained in-house; = 0 otherwise.

APPENDIX 8.2

TABLE 8.7. Regression results for alternative specifications of tendering and private contracting variables and for a larger sample

Variable	Description	OLS results using DUMMY1 and DUMMY2		OLS results for larger sample	
		Coefficient[a]	t-statistic[b]	Coefficient[a]	t-statistic[b]
CONSTANT		-2.75	-3.97	-2.15	-3.17
UNITS	Number of units	1.03	54.66	1.03	64.29
WAGE	Average earnings	0.90	7.54	0.81	6.94
FREQ1	More than once a week	0.64×10^{-2}	10.63	0.65×10^{-2}	10.89
FREQ2	Less than once a week	-0.36×10^{-2}	-2.73	-0.39×10^{-2}	-2.91
METH1	Kerbside	-0.27×10^{-2}	-10.95	-0.25×10^{-2}	-10.76
METH2	Other collect-and-return	-0.12×10^{-2}	-2.64	-1.00×10^{-3}	-2.17
METH3	Skep or other normal method	-0.77×10^{-3}	-2.92	-0.69×10^{-3}	-2.65
METH4	Special collections	0.54×10^{-3}	0.29	0.58×10^{-3}	0.31
DEN	Density of units	-0.12×10^{-1}	-1.50	-0.12×10^{-1}	-1.65
DISP	Average distance to disposal	0.32×10^{-1}	2.14	—	—
HOUS	Percentage of household units	-0.45	-5.55	-0.42	-5.09
RECLAIM1	Reclaimed paper	0.70×10^{-4}	4.14	—	—
RECLAIM2	Abandoned vehicles	0.11×10^{-3}	1.83	—	—
RECLAIM3	Bottle-banks	-0.46×10^{-3}	-0.40	—	—
CONTRACT	Privately contracted	—	—	-0.27	-8.06
TEND	Tendered but retained in-house	—	—	-0.19	-4.51
DUMMY1	Tendered, not first year	-0.28	-7.97	—	—
DUMMY2	Tendered, first year	-0.13	-3.21	—	—
	Number in sample	585		679	
	R^2	.930		.924	
	$\bar{R}^2$	.928		.923	

[a] Coefficients expressed as, e.g., 0.8×10^{-2} are interpreted as, e.g., 0.008.
[b] Significance levels for t-statistics (one-tailed test) are 1.65 (5%) and 1.29 (10%).

References

Audit Commission (1984), *Securing Further Improvements in Refuse Collection: A Review by the Audit Commission*, London: HMSO.

Bailey, E. E. (1986), 'Price and productivity changes following deregulation: the US experience', *Economic Journal*, Mar.

BFI-Wastecare (1986), *Analysis of Contract Awards, 1981–1986*, Apr.

Collins, J. N., and Downes, B. T. (1977), 'The effects of size on the provision of public services: the case of solid waste collection in smaller cities', *Urban Affairs Quarterly*, Mar.

Department of Environment (1985), *Competition in the Provision of Local Authority Services*, London: HMSO.

Domberger, S., and Piggott, J. (1986), 'Privatisation policies and public enterprise: a survey', *Economic Record*, June.

Foreman-Peck, J., and Waterson, M. (1985), 'The comparative efficiency of public and private enterprise in Britain: electricity generation between the World Wars', *Economic Journal*, **95**, suppl. 83–95.

Gears, M. (1984), 'Efficient refuse collection: an approach to the problem of the efficient collection of household waste', *Contract Services*, Nov./Dec.

Hartley, K., and Huby, M. (1985), 'Contracting-out in health and local authorities: prospects, progress and pitfalls', *Public Money*, Sept.

Hirsch, W. Z. (1965), 'Cost functions of an urban government service: refuse collection', *Review of Economics and Statistics*, Feb.

Kay, J. A., and Thompson, D. J. (1986), 'Privatisation: a policy in search of a rationale', *Economic Journal*, Mar.

McDavid, J. C. (1985), 'The Canadian experience with privatising residential solid waste collection services', *Public Administration Review*, Sept./Oct.

Meadows, W. J. (1985), *UK Case Studies on Urban Services: Contracting Out of Refuse Collection Services*, Organization for Economic Co-operation and Development, Group on Urban Affairs: Project Group on Urban Studies, Mar.

Millward, R. (1982), 'The comparative performance of public and private ownership', in Lord Roll (ed.), *The Mixed Economy*, London: Macmillan.

TUC (1984), *Contractors' Failures: The Privatisation Experience*, Nov.

Yarrow, G. (1986), 'Privatisation', *Economic Policy*.

9

Delivering Letters:
Should it be Decriminalized?

SAUL ESTRIN* AND DAVID DE MEZA†

1. INTRODUCTION

Throughout the world it is illegal to compete with the state post office in the collection and delivery of letters.[1] Is this an instance of the madness of crowds (of bureaucrats) or is there a good economic or other justification for outlawing competition? As background to discussing the substantive issues we first provide a brief historical account of the evolution of the monopoly in Britain.

In the Middle Ages private mail services co-existed with those of the Crown. Until the sixteenth century the state did not claim privileged rights over the conveyancing of post. The original motive seems to have been 'national security' as Queen Elizabeth sought to suppress treasonable correspondence. In the seventeenth century the raising of revenue became an influential justification for the postal monopoly but the emphasis had shifted towards the maxim of public service by the end of the nineteenth century. These new arguments for the monopoly were epitomized by an article in the *Pall Mall Gazette* in 1892:

The sole reason why the Post Office has a remunerative monopoly is to enable it to include services which are unremunerative. Free competition in London or other large towns would make short work of the present Post Office rates. And if these rates are forcibly maintained, the country ought to get some compensation in the shape of a reasonably good service to every corner of the Kingdom. (Daunton 1985: 49)

* Associate Professor of Economics, London Business School.
† University of Guelph, Guelph, Ontario, Canada.

The authors would like to thank Polly Vizard and Miguel Delgado for their research assistance and acknowledge helpful advice and comments from Robert Albon, Jane Black, Paul Richards, and Hugh Wills, and participants at the Conference on Competition and Innovation in Postal Services in July 1990. Any errors remain the responsibility of the authors.

[1] New Zealand is unique in having recently privatized its post office but at the time of writing has retained its statutory monopoly.

Of course, the case for the monopoly did not go unchallenged. One of the most eloquent and surprising critics was Rowland Hill himself. He advocated repeal of the legislation on the grounds that:

It implies the removal of an offence from our statute book and the probable rise of a wholesome competition wherever the service is performed with less than the greatest efficiency and cheapness: a competition which more perhaps than any other external circumstance, would tend to compel the department to have due regard to simple merit in its offices and economic efficiency in all its arrangements. (Coase 1939: 430)

Alfred Marshall took a similar view. In two letters to *The Times* in 1891 (Coase 1961) he was concerned with the Post Office's 'lethargy' and 'slothful' behaviour and with the 'vivifying' effect of competition causing its 'stiff joints (to) become more supple'.

The letter monopoly has been maintained to the present day, except that the Secretary for State for Trade and Industry now has power to suspend it, as indeed occurred temporarily during the 1971 strike when postal services were 'licensed out' to private operators. Moreover, the 1981 British Telecommunications Act also enables the Minister to grant licences which render legal specific activities otherwise covered by the Post Office's exclusive privilege. This power has been invoked by the government to introduce some competition with Post Office letter services. In 1981 the statutory monopoly was weakened in two respects. First, licences were granted to charities to deliver Christmas cards. Second, the market for time-sensitive valuable mail with a minimum charge of £1 was opened up to competition providing a legal basis for the *de facto* operations of many private courier services. In 1982 the monopoly was further relaxed when private document exchanges were given the legal power to operate (so that firms can rent a box into which correspondents can deliver letters by hand). Recently (June 1989) the Prime Minister said '. . . greater competition would be good and we may have to consider ending the monopoly on the postal letter service . . .'.

2. THE NATURAL MONOPOLY DEFENCE OF STATUTORY MONOPOLY

The case for allowing competition in letter delivery is that to succeed, new entrants to the industry must offer at least some consumers a better deal. This may not be difficult since a post office protected against the rigours of competition has limited incentives to introduce new products or keep down the costs of existing services. The potential drawback of permitting new entry is that postal delivery is probably a natural monopoly. If the market is divided between several competing firms, economies of scale and scope may be lost and overall costs increased.

A standard criticism of this defence of the statutory monopoly is well expressed by Milton Friedman (1962: 29):

It may be argued that the carrying of mail is a technical monopoly and that a government monopoly is the least of all evils. Along these lines, one could perhaps justify a government post office but not the present law, which makes it illegal for anybody else to carry mail. If the delivery of mail is a technical monopoly, no one will be able to succeed in competition with the government. If it is not, there is no reason why the government should be engaged in it. The only way to find out is to leave other people free to enter.

This position is strongest if the postal market is contestable. A contestable market is one in which there are no sunk costs, so that a firm can realize the full value of its assets any time—this effectively means that a firm considering entry into a contestable market does not face a risk of losing its assets if entry is unsuccessful or only short-lived. Moreover, the incumbent is assumed to be unable to change price at short notice. In such a market, if the existing firm is inefficient, a new and more efficient firm will enter and take the whole market—so retaining the benefits of the economies of scale. In a contestable market there is only one firm in the market at any given time, but there is a constant threat of entry which ensures that the established firm does not exploit its market position by pricing high.

Even if the assumptions of contestability hold, Panzar and Willig's (1977) classic paper shows there are some circumstances under which a natural monopoly is vulnerable to entry (is 'unsustainable', in their terminology). The conclusion that natural monopoly does not justify a statutory monopoly is further weakened for, if the assumptions of contestability fail even slightly, the conclusions may be radically different (Schwartz 1986). Moreover, the strict assumptions of the contestable market model are not particularly plausible in the case of postal services. Sunk costs are almost certainly important in practice. At first sight it may seem that all that is needed for a local letter-delivery business is a van (that can be resold easily) and a few employees (who can be hired on weekly contracts). However, when the costs of planning (especially of collection and delivery routes) as well as advertising the service are considered, it is clear that these sunk costs are important and that any potential rival to the Post Office must be prepared to stay in the business on a long-term basis before committing itself to entry.

If economies of scale are important and the market is not contestable, the case for allowing competition is no longer clear-cut. Suppose, as shown in the left-hand diagram of Figure 9.1, that the monopoly Post Office faces the demand curve DD and the average cost curve AC which, being downward sloping, implies increasing returns to scale. As a nationalized industry, the Post Office does not set out to maximize profit,

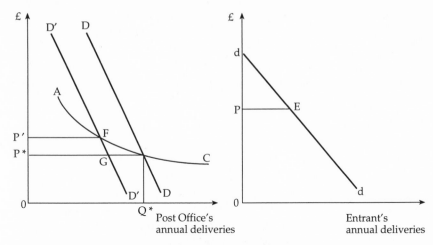

FIG. 9.1. Effect on demand of abolishing statutory monopoly

but can instead be assumed to seek to cover all costs including normal profits. The Post Office therefore sets price *P** delivering *Q** letters, determined by the intersection of the average cost and demand curves.

Now suppose that the statutory monopoly is abolished. Granted the Post Office remains in the market and continues to price at average cost; a commercial rival calculates that if it offers a superior service at price *P*, it can earn profits. When the new service is introduced some of the Post Office's customers switch to it and this means that the Post Office's demand curve shifts to the left, *D'D'* in Figure 9.1, so that its price increases to *P'*.

The bad news associated with the entry of the new firm is that the price of the existing service has risen because some of the economies of scale are lost. The good news is that a new product has appeared—in effect the price of the new firm's product has fallen from infinity to *P*. The overall change in consumer surplus can be measured in the usual way. In the right-hand graph, *dd* is the demand curve for the entrant's product given that the Post Office charges *P**. Were that the end of the story the consumer surplus generated by the new product would be the area *dEB*. But the left-hand graph shows the price rise from *P** to *P'* on the demand curve *D'D'* which involves a loss of consumer surplus measured by the area *P'FGP**. So, consumers are harmed by entry if *P'FGP** > *dEP*. And this is more likely to be the case if economies of scale are strong, for then *P'* will exceed *P** by a lot; or if the new product is a good substitute for the existing service, for then *D'D'* will be far to the left of *DD* and *dd* will be relatively elastic, making *dEP* small. If entry stimulates the Post Office to increase efficiency however, its average cost curve will shift down in the left-hand panel of Figure 9.1, bringing P' closer to $P*$ and so making the case for competition stronger.

What this analysis demonstrates is that entry cannot be guaranteed to benefit consumers. To make further progress a more explicit treatment of the factors governing entry and the nature of post-entry competition is required.

3. A THEORETICAL FRAMEWORK

There has been little discussion of sustainability outside the contestable market setting, despite its policy relevance. The question of whether in the presence of economies of scale there can be entry when all firms are profit maximizers, and of whether the equilibrium involves too much or too little entry, has been addressed. (Mankiw and Whinston (1986) provide a neat interpretation and extension of this literature.) However, the analysis has not been adapted to the case when the incumbent is an average-cost pricer, or is set a target profit below the maximum attainable. As we show, this makes a considerable difference to the results. This is important in the present context for there can be little doubt that, despite the recent improvement in its returns, the British Post Office, like others around the world, does not seek to maximize profit. This follows indirectly from the form of regulation and directly from the fact that all estimates of demand elasticity put it well below unity. Hence, price is certainly below the profit-maximizing level.

Our basic model supposes an incumbent monopoly (call it the Post Office (PO)) producing a single good. Average costs are declining at all outputs and the incumbent sells the highest output consistent with covering costs. There is one potential entrant (the rival, R) who can offer a product which may be a close or distant substitute to that offered by the PO. The production costs incurred by R may be either higher or lower than those of the PO. However, in contrast to PO, the rival seeks to maximize profits. In deciding whether to enter, R correctly anticipates the market share he will obtain and the equilibrium post-entry price. In order to make these predictions, the entrant must know the nature of post-entry competition. The two common models are Bertrand competition and Cournot competition, though both must be somewhat modified to take into account the fact that the PO is an average-cost pricer. Under Bertrand competition, each firm maximizes its objective function given the price of the other. This is rational if firms must decide on their strategy without knowing what their rival has chosen and if output can be adjusted at shorter notice than price. Bertrand competition is very aggressive. If the firms are selling close substitutes and there are economies of scale, it is typically the case that it is impossible for both firms to survive. Cournot competition is rather less cut-throat, but is still far from being collusive pricing. Here, the firms make simultaneous output choices and prices are then set to clear the market. Implicitly, output must be chosen ahead of price. Neither model is fully satisfactory, but together they serve to indicate the range of outcomes. It is possible to analyse models in which one firm's choice is observed by the other firm prior to its own decision. However, it is generally difficult to explain what it is in the environment which gives one firm the advantage (or sometimes disadvantage) of being the first mover. More interesting than imposing an exogenous order of play would be to analyse markets in which the firms interact on a repeated basis and perhaps in which capacity can only be slowly adjusted. There is not yet a fully satisfactory theory to deal with such a case.

Returning to the static game, consider first the case of Cournot competition. Given that entry occurs, curve RR in Figure 9.2 shows the profit-maximizing output of the rival, Q_R for various outputs of the Post Office Q_P. Similarly the curve PO shows how PO's profit-maximizing output varies with the production chosen by R. The case drawn is for the two firms having the same cost function. If both firms were profit-maximizers, the equilibrium outputs would be Q_P^* and Q_R^* at least if both firms are covering costs at these production levels. The relative slopes of the lines PO and RR follow from standard and plausible assumptions concerning demand and costs.

Our purpose is to investigate entry possibilities if PO is an average-cost pricer. The implication of this is that at any Q_R at which the Post Office could make positive profits by restricting its own output, it will actually produce more than shown by PO, expanding until its profits are eliminated. In Figure 9.2, AB shows the reaction curve of the average-cost pricing Post Office. $\hat{Q}_R$ is the maximum output of R at which PO is actually able to cover its costs. Unless point A lies above the intersection of RR and PO, entry is not feasible. Equilibrium occurs at $\bar{Q}_R$, $\bar{Q}_P$ supposing that R is able to cover its costs when PO chooses $\bar{Q}_P$. That is, in the symmetric case the question is whether $\bar{Q}_P > \hat{Q}_R$. If this condition holds, the rival will not enter. If $\hat{Q}_R > \bar{Q}_P$, entry occurs and the question is then whether consumers gain. In Figure 9.2, $\hat{Q}_R = \bar{Q}_P$ so entry is just possible.

We have argued elsewhere (see Estrin and de Meza 1988) that in the Cournot case, with a homogeneous product and economies of scale throughout, entry is impossible if the Post Office is at least as efficient as any potential entrant, and that if entry does occur, because the potential entrant is more efficient than the Post Office, the loss of economies of scale ensures that customer welfare will be reduced. This implies that repeal of the statutory monopoly would in all likelihood have no effect but, if it did, post users would suffer. Even if the Post Office is grossly inefficient, this conclusion applies.

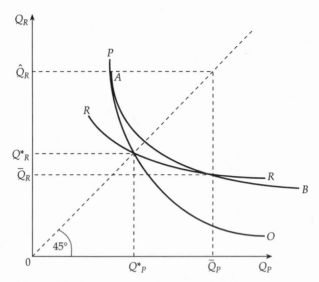

Fɪɢ. 9.2. Reaction curve of average-cost pricing Post Office

The assumption that both firms sell an identical good is crucial to these results. If instead they offer imperfect substitutes, post-entry competition is less severe, making entry easier and, because a new product is created, the benefits to the consumer if entry does occur greater. Were the Post Office monopoly repealed it is indeed unlikely that entrants actually would offer the same service as the Post Office. A further route by which entry could lead to gains is if the Post Office is thereby stimulated to become more efficient causing its cost curves to shift down. This effect could more than offset the loss of economies of scale, even in the homogeneous product case.

To investigate further we simulate the effects of entry into the postal business. Before doing so we outline the model if the post-entry game is Bertrand.

Under Bertrand competition prices are the strategic variables. Hence, the reaction curve diagram now appears in price space and is shown in Figure 9.3 where P_P is the Post Office's price and P_R that of the potential entrant. Thus, RR shows how the profit-maximizing rival's price varies with P_P and line PO shows how the profit-maximizing Post Office price varies with P_R. It is not inevitable that these reaction curves be upward sloping. If they are, it implies that if the price charged by your competitor rises then it is profitable to take the opportunity to increase your own price. Two goods for which this is true are termed strategic complements. This is a fairly plausible assumption and is built into our

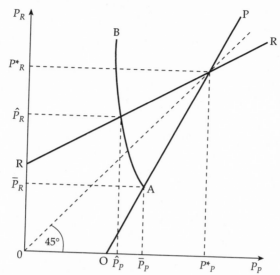

FIG. 9.3. Dual profit-maximizing equilibrium

subsequent simulations. However, the theory is a little changed if the goods are strategic substitutes.

Granted that both firms are profit-maximizers, equilibrium prices in the symmetric case of Figure 9.3 are P_R*P_P*, at least as long as each firm covers its costs at these prices. If the goods are close substitutes and there are economies of scale it is typically the case that there are losses where the reaction curves intersect. If so, it follows that no entry will occur. However, we now assume that profit-maximizing Bertrand duopolists can at least cover their costs.

We are interested in the case in which PO is an average-cost pricer. The implications of this switch in behavioural assumption is that at any R at which the Post Office could make positive profits, it will actually choose a lower price than shown by PO. For average-cost pricing, the PO's reaction curve is thus given by AB where $\bar{P}_R$ is the lowest rival price at which PO can cover costs. Curve AB is downward sloping reflecting the fact that the higher is P_R the further to the right is the demand curve faced by PO causing an average cost pricer with economies of scale to lower its price.

If entry does occur with average-cost pricing, the equilibrium is $\hat{P}_P$, $\hat{P}_R$. The PO charges less than in the profit-maximizing duopoly equilibrium and so profitable entry is even less likely. However, it could be the case that if the goods are sufficiently differentiated then at $\hat{P}_P$, $\hat{P}_R$ the rival does cover costs. If so, it will enter if allowed to do so. The Post

Office will end up charging more as a result of entry, but since a new product is available in the market there is no a priori way of determining whether consumers are better off overall. In contrast to the Cournot model, if the two firms sell identical goods it is easy to see that in the presence of economies of scale there is never a pure-strategy equilibrium and so this case is not pursued.

4. A SUMMARY OF SIMULATIONS

The analysis so far suggests that statutory protection for the Post Office is never harmful and may actually benefit consumers because entry, while profitable for the new firm, could dissipate economies of scale, increase prices, and reduce consumer welfare. But these unambiguous results depend on the entrant offering an identical product to the Post Office. To investigate the trade-offs when the Post Office and the entrant are offering heterogeneous goods, we undertake a simulation exercise.

$$C_i = F_i + a_iQ_i - b_iQ_i^2, \quad i = N, M \tag{1}$$

when Q_i is the firm output. Inverse demand functions are

$$P_i = a_i - BQ_i - \gamma Q_j, \quad i \neq j, i, j = N, M \tag{2}$$

The model was calibrated to own price elasticities of demand in the region of 0.2–0.5 and elasticities of returns to scale from 1.2 to 1.5. Under Cournot assumptions the only instances of disadvantageous entry involve very close substitutes and unrealistically high cost advantages for the entrant. With differentiated products cases of profitable and advantageous entry were possible under seemingly reasonable configurations. A representative case is of fairly modest scale economies with a 10 per cent increase in volume raising costs by 7.5 per cent. The entrant sells a fairly distinct product for in equilibrium it charges 60 per cent more than the Post Office and yet still captures 20 per cent of the market, earning in the process a 3.5 per cent return on turnover. The loss of volume causes the Post Office price to rise by 4.5 per cent but the opportunity to buy a new good means consumers are better-off in aggregate by some 3.5 per cent of their initial spending. Taken together, the simulations suggest no real case for a statutory monopoly, a conclusion which is reinforced if entry eliminates x-efficiency.

We undertook a similar exercise for the case of Bertrand competition, using the same functional forms, with price rather than quantity as the strategic variable. Entry is quite rare. If a sufficient quality or cost advantage enables the entrant to make positive profits, there is a tendency for the Post Office to be able to survive. But when the Post Office and the entrant share the same structure of costs and economies of scale are not 'too great', there is profitable entry which raises social welfare.

However, it should be noted that there are some cases of welfare-reducing profitable entry with Bertrand competition. In particular, the entrant can survive with a low elasticity of demand (0.3 in the monopoly equilibrium), and modest economies of scale (1.25) but with its cost similar to the Post Office's at low levels of output but much higher as output increases. This might typify an entrant which is labour-intensive and employs a bespoke delivery system rather than a systematic delivery round. Entry strategies along these lines can be profitable but reduce consumer welfare.

Looking across all the cases, the general conclusion suggested by these single-product simulations is that in the presence of an average-cost pricing Post Office, permitting entry is rather unlikely to result in aggregate losses to the consumers and could well yield gains.

5. THE 'CREAM SKIMMING' DEFENCE OF STATUTORY MONOPOLY

Should the Post Office Set Uniform Prices?

The most common defence of the statutory monopoly is that in its absence entry would be predominantly attracted to the high-profit relatively low-cost routes and services. It would be left to the Post Office to reach those inaccessible locations with low volumes of mail that commercial operators spurn. Left with this costly rump, the Post Office would have to increase its charges substantially. If this is truly what happens, the question is, why would it be a bad thing?

The way the story is often told, it appears as though the commercial entrants would actually reap the high surplus that the Post Office currently earns on a subset of its services. It is implied that this involves a mere transfer from the presumably deserving public sector to an undeserving capitalist and so is undesirable on distributional grounds. In fact there is no very good reason for thinking that the commercial operators would earn high profits. Even if the Post Office does not respond to entry by cutting its own prices on formerly high-surplus services, the lure of such allegedly high profits would surely attract multiple entry and the profits would be competed away. So the real issue is whether bringing prices more closely into line with costs is desirable.

Economists are prone to think that if prices reflect costs, efficiency will be served. Consumers will then only buy goods and services which are valued more highly than the alternative outputs which could have been produced with the resources used up in their production. However, it needs some thought as to the correct cost to relate prices. Suppose first that when deregulated, letter delivery were really a contestable market. The price of each service would then fall to the average cost of providing it. Deliveries to inaccessible rural locations would cost more than to towns. But what is actually required for an efficient allocation of resources is that prices are proportional to marginal, not average cost. A uniform tariff may get closer to achieving this than the average-cost pricing emerging in a contestable market. The main difference between regions is in delivery costs (Tabor 1987) and these are also the primary source of economies of scale in the system. Suppose in the extreme, that delivery costs are fixed with respect to the volume of mail delivered but higher in rural areas than in urban areas. Sorting and collection costs are the same everywhere. The marginal cost of mail posted to rural areas would thus be the same as mail posted to urban areas. A uniform tariff would thus be economically efficient (they would constitute Ramsey prices). But in a contestable market with freedom of entry, rural mail would be more expensive. Even ignoring any administrative costs, breaking the uniform tariff would be inefficient.

To investigate these matters more formally, let the average cost of each letter posted to the cheap region be

$$ AC_L = a + bQ + \frac{F}{Q} \tag{3} $$

and to the expensive region

$$ AC_H = \hat{a} + \lambda bQ + \frac{\lambda F}{Q} \tag{4} $$

where Q is letters per address. The proportion of addresses in the cheap region is α. The number of postings to each address is $Q = A - BP$ where P is the uniform price. It is straightforward to compute the change in consumer surplus from moving from a break-even uniform price to a multiple-price scheme that breaks-even for each region, as would arise in a deregulated contestable market.

Our model fails to take into account possible cost complementarities between the volume of deliveries in the two areas. However, these are not likely to be great and in view of the very small values for welfare changes generated by the model, even when costs are very different between regions, further sophistication will not alter the qualitative conclusions.

Table 9.1 reports the results. The first case uses Tabor's (1987) data that rural mail is 14 per cent of the total mail (i.e., $\alpha = 0.86$), and costs some 48 per cent more in total to process than does urban mail. Sorting costs are much the same in both areas ($a = \hat{a}$). The elasticity of returns to scale is 1.49, and demand elasticity is 0.3. Rural prices are 52 per cent higher and urban prices fall by some 6.5 per cent as a result of breaking the uniform tariff. Urban prices fall by so much because of scale

TABLE 9.1. Uniform pricing, postal services

	(1)	(2)	(3)	(4)	(5)	(6)	(7)	(8)	(9)	(10)	(11)
$\hat{\alpha}$	0.67000	0.60000	0.96000	0.60000	0.60000	0.60000	1.60000	0.60000	0.25000	1.60000	0.90000
α	0.67000	0.60000	0.48000	0.60000	0.60000	0.60000	0.80000	0.60000	0.25000	0.80000	0.50000
F	0.27000	0.32000	0.32000	0.376000	0.37600	0.37600	0.00000	0.32000	0.40000	0.00000	0.32000
b	0.00000	0.00000	0.00000	0.0000	0.00000	0.00000	0.20000	0.00000	0.10000	0.00000	0.00000
λ	2.66000	2.00000	2.00000	1.25000	1.25000	1.25000	2.00000	2.00000	2.00000	1.50000	2.00000
a	0.86000	0.75000	0.75000	0.75000	0.75000	0.75000	0.75000	0.75000	0.75000	0.75000	0.75000
β	0.30000	0.50000	0.30000	0.30000	0.50000	1.00000	0.50000	0.30000	0.30000	0.30000	0.20000
A	1.30000	1.50000	1.30000	1.30000	1.50000	2.00000	1.50000	1.30000	1.30000	1.30000	1.20000
Results											
Q_l	1.019553	1.04721	1.06594	1.00811	1.01473	1.03764	1.00000	1.02648	1.08161	1.06000	1.03836
Q_h	0.843592	0.80000	0.75905	0.97545	0.95355	0.84142	0.58333	0.90871	0.90566	0.82000	0.87346
P_l	0.934821	0.90557	0.78020	0.97298	0.97054	0.96236	1.00000	0.91175	0.72798	0.80000	0.80818
P_h	1.521359	1.40000	1.80316	1.08183	1.09289	1.15858	1.83333	1.30429	1.31447	1.60000	1.63272
Δ Surplus	-1.06809	-0.01751	-0.00632	0.00014	-0.00043	-0.00774	-0.16493	-0.00553	-0.00826	0.01800	-0.00155

economies. Although these price changes are large, the overall change in consumer surplus is small (1 per cent) and negative for reasons discussed above. Various combinations of parameters are reported in Table 9.1, but in all cases indicate that at best efficiency gains from setting prices at average cost for each region are small and may be negative.

These are maximal measures of gain from breaking the uniform tariff because it is plausible that if the Post Office were to maintain its comprehensive service, charging a differential between rural and urban mail would involve significant administrative costs. High-cost areas or addresses would first have to be designated which would doubtless involve considerable controversy. An identifier could then be added to the post code. A system of monitoring whether the right identifier and correct postage paid for any particular address would have to be introduced. Finally, a procedure would have to be established to handle cases where the wrong postage had been paid. Confusion on the part of the public would probably result in a considerable volume of wrongly stamped mail, let alone intentional fraud. Moreover the extra costs incurred by users in determining correct rates and the time taken by counter staff in answering enquiries would be sufficient to outweigh what would anyway be small efficiency gains. The first class/second class tariff discrimination is much easier to police, understand, and administer.

Rowland Hill himself favoured a two tier tariff structure, arguing that secondary distribution letters to places of inferior importance could be surcharged. He was only persuaded to drop this proposal to facilitate the passage of his other proposals. However the present analysis suggests that there is no justification for the Post Office to move from a uniform to a two tier tariff based on a differential delivery costs. This is true whether the Post Office retains its monopoly and were to unilaterally introduce the new scheme or whether it were forced on the Post Office as a result of deregulation in a contestable market.[2]

If the Post Office is committed to maintain its uniform tariff, the possibility of more serious losses from deregulation arise than those which occur in contestable markets. Assuming entry and exit are costly, as in our earlier modelling exercises, there is the possibility that entrants could profitably enter low-cost services even though they are less efficient than the Post Office, because the uniform tariff means that on these services the Post Office maintains prices considerably above costs. Even if the rival is equally as efficient or more efficient than the Post Office, the encouragement to entry provided by uniform pricing may result in

---

[2] It is sometimes suggested that transaction costs will only be incurred in a deregulated competitive market if it is efficient that they should be. This is easily seen to be false. The market test of whether to stream customers is whether there is a group for whom supply costs are sufficiently below the average to cover the costs of identifying them. This test ignores the higher prices paid by the high-cost users. Real resources are used up to what may be wholly or partly a redistributive role.

losses from the dissipation of economies of scale. We now extend our earlier models so as to address these issues (see Estrin and de Meza 1988 for a fuller account).

In our simulations of this model we find, as might be expected, that cream skimming increases the likelihood of profitable entry under both Cournot and Bertrand competition. None the less, in most cases of successful entry, the Post Office and the entrant are offering products sufficiently heterogeneous that the total size of the market is expanded, the loss of economies of scale is more than matched by the gains for the new customers and overall welfare is increased. But disadvantageous entry is more likely in the case of cream skimming, particularly for Cournot competition. Typical patterns for disadvantageous entry are when economies of scale are assumed to be relatively low and the rival offers a similar product to the Post Office but has significant cost advantages. Cases of disadvantageous entry also arise with Bertrand competition.

To this point, we have argued that uniform tariffs have attractions, but if the Post Office does maintain them deregulation in a non-contestable market may well have significant welfare costs. But there is an important qualification to this argument in favour of the *status quo*. If the Post Office were allowed to break the uniform tariff should a competitor appear in a particular sub-market, then our earlier simulations suggest that it would be impossible to enter profitably by offering a similar product even if the entrant has large cost advantages. So it is possible that knowing the Post Office is allowed to break the uniform tariff would be an effective deterrent to disadvantageous cream-skimming entry. In practice the uniform tariff will never or seldom be broken and so the policy of permitting flexible pricing by the Post Office may be the best approach.

6. POLICY IMPLICATIONS

The theoretical modelling and the simulations based upon it suggest that allowing one or more private firms to compete with the Post Office could be harmful even though it is perhaps more likely that benefits will accrue. That entry could lead to efficiency losses is, as always, the consequence of an externality; that is a cost imposed by the entrant's actions but borne by other parties. The externality in question is that in diverting traffic from the Post Office economies of scale are lost and, the prices paid by the Post Office's remaining users must rise.[3] The loss involved is made more precise by the following equation:

[3] This may appear to be a pecuniary rather than a technological externality and therefore not a source of efficiency loss. However as the Post Office sets price above marginal cost the initial equilibrium is not first best and prices are not good measures of opportunity cost.

$$E = \frac{A\eta^A}{1 + \epsilon\eta^A} \tag{5}$$

where E is the external cost if the entrant attracts an extra letter from the Post Office as a result of a perceived quality or price advantage; A is the Post Office's average cost per letter; η^A is the elasticity of the Post Office's average cost and ϵ is the elasticity of demand.

At first sight diverting a letter from the Post Office entails an externality equal to the difference between average and marginal cost, for this represents the extra amount which must be raised from the remaining users if the Post Office is to continue to break-even. However, the consequent price rise will cause a further loss of volume and therefore a second round of efficiency losses and so on. The more elastic is demand the larger will these repercussions be, as the equation shows. As an illustration, suppose elasticity of demand is 1.0, η^A is –0.2 and A equals 20, implying a marginal cost of 16. While the gap between average and marginal cost is only 4, equation (5) reveals that E is 5.

The three policies which will now be proposed are based on this externality perspective:

(a) Where externalities are present the standard economic remedy is to tax them, at least if the tax itself is not too costly to administer and not subject to excessive manipulation by special interest groups. The application here is to allow letters to be conveyed by any operator for whatever price they choose, provided that the proceeds of a tax on each letter is paid to the Post Office to compensate for cream-skimming losses and reduced economies of scale. Thus, if the Post Office loses business it would be compensated financially and so able to maintain its current tariff structure. The competition would provide a spur to Post Office managers and workers to increase efficiency but would not harm them or the public. Giving the proceeds of the tax to the Post Office is not actually efficiency enhancing. Desirable entry is potentially precluded by the refund. But the distributional effects of entry will be tempered by the refund and the adverse consequences of miscalculating the tax will be minimized. Compensating the Post Office is a safety-first approach.

At first sight such a scheme may seem vulnerable to administrative problems. Private firms have an obvious incentive to under record volume and public resources would therefore have to be devoted to policing activities. Such difficulties may be overstated for, after all, it has not proved infeasible to collect VAT. However, there is an alternative means of implementing the tax proposal which may avoid some of these difficulties. Commercial carriers are prohibited from charging directly for a letter. Rather, the carrier sets the tariff he wishes and Post Office stamps to that value must be affixed to the letter. The carrier then feeds the letters through an electronic reader which registers their value and cancels the stamps to prevent them being re-recorded. At the end of each month the Post Office reads the machines and pays the firm the difference between the value of the stamps and the tax.

(b) A reduction in the minimum legal charge available to private delivery services from the present £1 to, say, 50p. Even at this price there is unlikely to be competition for the bulk-mail services, so there would be little loss of Post Office economies of scale or problem with cream-skimming. Where externalities are low there is no case for suppressing competition.

(c) Allowing post clubs to operate provided each member pays a significant annual levy to the Post Office. A post club involves setting up a network between members who contract to join for a minimum period. The point of the levy is twofold. First, it would restrict membership to high volume users. Delivery and collection from such users is normally by means of a dedicated service, rather than as part of a general round. Economies of scale are thus unlikely to be very important. Secondly, the Post Office receives the levy to compensate for cream-skimming losses and so to keep prices down.

There is a sense in which schemes (a) and (c) involve compulsory franchising. Commercial firms do the Post Office's work for it but only when they can do so at less than the Post Office's marginal (not average) cost. Yet these schemes involve considerable decentralization: were an explicit franchising scheme to be introduced with the Post Office choosing whether or not to contract-out services, it would likely be biased against hiring outsiders. An independent agency would be unlikely to be sufficiently knowledgeable about what needs doing, nor to have much incentive to encourage innovative services which might prove to be failures.

That the revenues from schemes (a) and (c) is returned to the Post Office might seem to give management little incentive to improve performance. If the Post Office loses business it is compensated financially. But it is difficult to see that there would be fewer incentives to efficiency than under a statutory monopoly. There could be no more effective indictment of management than that competitors are taking all the business. Moreover, if that does happen there will ultimately be fewer managers and those let go will hardly come on to the labour market with the best of recommendations. But, if stronger incentives for efficiency are required, part of the revenue could be directed to a separate body responsible for the provision of socially desirable, but unprofitable, postal services. The Post Office could compete with other companies in tendering to provide an even more direct spur to Post Office effort and, as many of the loss-making burdens would no longer be the direct responsibility of the Post Office, it would enable them to keep their average charges down. But whether it is worth the cost of setting-up and controlling a new bureaucracy is debatable. Channelling the money straight to the Post Office may be simpler.

References

Coase, R. H. (1939), 'Rowland Hill and the Penny Post', *Economica*, **6** (Nov.), 423–35.

—— (1961), 'The British Post Office and the Messenger Companies', *Journal of Law and Economics*, **4**, 12–65.

Daunton, M. J. (1985), *Royal Mail*, London: Athlone.

Estrin, S., and de Meza, D. (1988), 'Should the Post Office's Statutory Monopoly be Lifted?', London School of Economics, mimeo.

Friedman, M. (1962), *Capital and Freedom*, Chicago: University of Chicago Press.

Hunt, L. C., and Lynk, E. L. (1990), 'An Empirical Examination of the Case for Post Office Divestiture in the UK', mimeo.

Mankiw, N. G., and Whinston, M. (1986), 'Free Entry and Social Efficiency', *Rand Journal* **17** (Spring), 48–58.

Panzar, J. C., and Willig, R. D. (1977), 'Free Entry and the Sustainability of Natural Monopoly', *Bell Journal* **8** (Spring), 1–22.

Pryke, R. (1981), *The Nationalised Industries*, Oxford: Martin Robertson.

Schwartz, M. (1986), 'The Nature and Scope of Contestability Theory', *Oxford Economic Papers* **38** (suppl.), 37–57.

Tabor, R. (1987a), 'Can Competition Pass "Go" with a Natural Monopoly?', *Public Finance and Accountancy* (8 May).

—— (1987b), 'Who Benefits from "One Price for Everyone"?', *Public Finance and Accountancy* (12 June).

10

British Rail:
Competition on the Network

DAVID STARKIE[*]

During the early part of the 1980s a number of the non-core assets of British Rail (BR) were sold to the private sector. There were proposals, too, to dispose of specific railway lines such as that between Fenchurch Street and Southend in south Essex. However, it is arguable whether the simple transfer of assets to the private sector serves the objective most strongly canvassed by those promoting privatization. This objective is increased efficiency in the supply of services.

Professors Beesley and Littlechild[1] have argued that privatization of assets alone will procure such benefits. Private firms are able to respond more easily to demand by having better access to capital, and they have a stronger incentive to produce goods and services in the quantity and variety that consumers prefer, especially where monopoly power is limited by the existence (even when only potential) of close substitutes. But privatization which also enhances competition is more likely to secure a wider range of benefits.

A major barrier to competition in the railway industry is its large, unavoidable fixed costs of production, which arise because many inputs into the industry are 'lumpy'. To run one train service between two cities, for example, requires a minimum outlay on track, formation, motive power, rolling-stock, and administration. As these inputs are used more intensively, i.e. as more services are run, their cost is spread over more units of output so that average costs fall until the point when the railway is used so intensively that the track becomes congested and management overstretched. But railways frequently operate on the falling segment of their cost curves. Either market demand will have decreased, leaving spare capacity in the system, or new technologies such as moving-block signalling will have enabled higher capacities to be achieved from existing track. Railways therefore are referred to as 'natural' monopolies in the sense that a single firm can fulfil market demand more cheaply than two.

[*] Director of Putnam, Hayes and Bartlett Ltd.

[1] 'Privatization: principles, problems and priorities', *Lloyds Bank Review*, July 1983.

Although railways are natural monopolies in this sense, their true monopoly power as means of *transport* has now been all but eliminated by competition from aviation and road transport. But despite this competition BR is not as efficient as it might be.

When inefficiency is substantial, falling average costs are not enough to maintain the railway monopolist's inherent advantage. The opportunity exists for a more efficient firm to set up in competition but producing at a lower cost. What prevents this happening is a second important characteristic of many railway assets. Embankments and cuttings, the rail formation, and the platforms, etc. are fixed *in situ*—they are sunk, committed irreversibly to a specified market. Consequently, potential competitors are faced with substantial risks if they enter a particular market in this way. They face BR with equivalent infrastructure written-down or written-off and with the potential to eliminate its inefficiencies that provide the opportunity for entry by a private enterprise company. Once entry is accomplished the inefficiencies of BR might quickly disappear leaving competitors with unamortized assets they are unable to transfer.

It is thus not feasible for the private sector to build new permanent way and terminals in competition with BR. There may be special cases which provide exceptions; for instance, where existing track and terminal capacity is saturated and the particular market still has considerable growth potential. But even in these circumstances, it is most likely that BR will be able to add to its existing infrastructure at a lower cost than a potential rival could build new rights-of-way or terminal facilities.

If competition from new rail infrastructure is out of the question, private enterprise could take over existing permanent way (at book value) in competition with BR (or other private companies). But BR have eliminated some of the obvious spare capacity in the system established by competing rail companies in the nineteenth century to achieve economies of use. Consequently, the opportunities for competing rail services using alternative, existing infrastructure between common centres are few.

Similar, but again limited, opportunities for increased competition exist where the permanent way carries multiple tracks so that track ownership can be divided. Although modern signalling makes it feasible to divide double tracks into lengths of single track with two-way operations,[2] more flexibility can be achieved where there are four running tracks with competing companies handling two each (and each having restricted running rights over competitors' lines). However, there is a limited length of quadruple track and the train-control, rail formation and stations would have to remain in single ownership. Although wor-

---

[2] Some of the world's busiest lines in terms of tonnages handled are single track (but highly specialized) railways.

thy of further investigation (especially where there is not too much fixing of freight, slow passenger and fast passenger traffic), it is probable that in many instances the additional complexities of operation would negate the increased efficiency achieved by competition.

A more logical way to proceed would be to work with and not against, the constraints to competition inherent in the technology of railway systems. This approach would recognize that most scale effects are inherent in the permanent way, train-control, and stations—precisely the assets irretrievably committed to a particular rail market once installed. In contrast the rail vehicles—locomotives, wagons, carriages—are mobile between markets and economies in their use are well encompassed by the market opportunities available. This distinction begs for wider recognition within the institutional framework.

By distinguishing the ownership of the permanent way from the ownership of the vehicles an opportunity presents itself for having competing trains running on shared track. In other words, one would emulate a practice which is common in road and air transport. Private coach companies compete against each other on the state-owned motorway system and rival airlines (some in the private sector) utilize airports in separate and often state ownership. The last analogy is the more useful because of the scheduling and safety implications. Airlines arrange for access times to the terminal and runways and immediate air space; in effect, they rent this access. Translated into rail terms, access to lines and terminals would be rented by competing train companies who would then sell services directly to the public.

Such a policy may sound distinctly different from that which we associate with railways in modern Britain but its strength lies in the fact that it represents a further development of what is now happening and what used to happen on a large scale until 1948.

Before nationalization in 1948, railways in Britain had developed quite complex structures reflecting in some cases a distinction between ownership of track and ownership of rolling-stock. In the early 1930s there were something like 700,000 private rail wagons. In 1948, much of this huge private wagon fleet was incorporated within the nationalized railway. But private wagons never disappeared entirely from the network (some specialist wagons were retained by private companies in 1948) and in recent years their role has grown very rapidly. They now form a substantial component within the rail freight system.[3] In terms of tonne-miles, private wagons carried 40 per cent of BR's freight traffic in 1982. If coal and coke tonnage, carried mostly in 'merry-go-round' fleets running between collieries and power-stations, was excluded, the private wagon proportion accounted for as much as two-thirds of tonne-miles.

[3] For further information see *The Future of Rail Freight: An End to Uncertainty*, a submission to government by the Private Wagon Federation, London, July 1983.

Within this total, individual companies generate large flows of ore, cement, aggregates, and oil, as well as general freight, and their investment in private wagons is substantial.

Thus there already exists in the operational freight railway a large private-sector component and one that is based on a distinction between mobile and sunk assets. The next logical step would be for the private sector to extend into the motive-power sector, purchase locomotives, employ or lease crews, and offer train services directly in competition with each other and with British Railways. Companies generating large volumes of traffic, might consider it worthwhile to operate their own freight trains, just as many now operate 'own-account' lorries carrying road freight. But this would depend on their ability to utilize adequately the locomotives. The majority would probably prefer to hire the locomotive and train services (just as in effect they now do) but with the option of buying services from private 'hire and reward' train companies.

The Venice Simplon Orient Express Company Ltd, operating private coach stock between Victoria and the channel ports is an example, albeit rather special, of the principle extended into the rail passenger market. The company agrees with BR the 'train path' in the busy south-east network and hires the locomotive and crew. With a more flexible approach the locomotives and crew could be hired from a private-sector company quoting a rate for the job in competition with the state sector.

This extension of the private sector in the operation of railways would be facilitated if the assets of BR were divided into two groups. The permanent way, train control, maintenance depots, and termini could be vested in one company (the name British Railways remains appropriate),[4] which would also handle overhead functions like general administration. Rolling-stock could be vested in a separate, public sector company or companies (which I shall refer to collectively as British Trains—'BT'). BR's charges to BT and private sector competitors would be based on direct train-control cost, track wear and tear, and directly attributable terminal costs, supplemented by additional charges, broadly reflecting judgements of what the market will bear, to assist with covering common costs (see Figure 10.1). But there is a large 'social' railway—services considered necessary for social reasons—which fail to cover their direct costs. These would exist alongside competitive services. But there is the danger that the grant, paid to maintain social services, might be used to cross-subsidize BT's competitive use of BR's system. This could happen, for example, where social and competitive services offered by BT used common rolling-stock. To eliminate this possibility, one approach would be to fence in the competitive market to prevent misuse of the grant.

---

[4] There would be some divestment of administration and marketing to train companies.

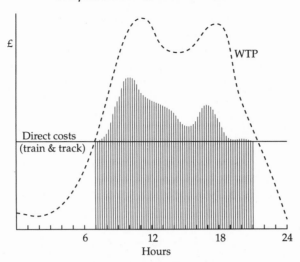

Fɪɢ. 10.1. Bidding for the use of the rail right-of-way

The dashed line in Figure 10.1 illustrates the aggregate willingness to pay (WTP) for a journey between two towns (at a specified quality of service) at different times of the day. Train operators are not able to expropriate the whole of this because of an inability to perfectly discriminate when charging. The yield to the train company from each service operated is shown by the vertical lines. The amount exceeding direct costs (the latter shown as constant per service) represents the maximum that the permanent way company can expect to extract as a contribution towards the joint and common costs of the right-of-way.

For the large proportion of present services not susceptible to provision by direct competition, competitive franchising would provide a means of improving efficiency; services would be open for tender to be operated in a specified manner for a particular period. A distinction between 'track' and 'trains' might be appropriate also when franchising the social railway. The expertise required to operate train services *per se* is different from that required for maintaining the permanent way— recognized in BR's existing corporate structure which distinguishes between operations and engineering.

With an extended role for the private sector, it will be important to ensure that the economies of an integrated railway system are maintained. These economies are realized through new technologies like the computerized information system. Private train companies too will need to have access to the information system. An integrated passenger timetable is another example; the present one includes more than a score of private, seasonal railways aimed at the tourist market (and for the most part run by volunteers). Professional, private-sector services as they develop, will need to be incorporated in the system-wide timetable.

The suggested approach begs the question of the extent to which a more efficient railway system would be achieved by purchasing cheaper equipment (buying low-cost locomotives overseas was suggested by the Serpell Committee in 1983);[5] by the better utilization of both equipment and labour; and by savings in locomotive and rolling-stock maintenance. One would expect private-sector train companies to avail themselves of these opportunities and to force the pace of adoption by the state-sector railway.

The benefits of competition extend beyond cost savings. Competition in services would have the effect of optimizing the price and quality of services offered. For the passenger railway, BR display a tendency to market a standard service with increasing emphasis on quality—speed, on-board catering, air-conditioning—manifest in the High Speed Train Services. It may have judged the market accurately. But it is possible also that the market could support a wider variety of price/quality packages.[6] For example, the private sector may wish to test-market a lower standard of inter-city service based on simpler rail technology. Lower fuel consumption, reduced vehicle depreciation and less wear and tear on the track could produce a lower ticket price acceptable, despite the slower, less comfortable ride,[7] to a number sufficient to support the service—the young, pensioners, and so on.

A further benefit of the suggested competitive model would be the provision of better guidance for investment in rail infrastructure and the elimination of the arbitrary allocation of overhead and joint costs. Under the proposed framework for competitive services, the contribution towards costs not attributable to the direct provision of a train service would come from track 'rents'. If these rents fail to cover renewal of infrastructure specific to a competitive sector, the market will have signalled an eventual withdrawal of these services. Conversely, where competition for train paths pushes up rents, expansion of track and terminus capacity will be called for.

Finally, one can speculate on the long-term structure of a competitive railway industry. We might expect an initial increase in the overall size of the freight and inter-city sectors. A wider variety of services and/or lower fares and charges should produce an increase in demand for rail

---

[5] *Railway Finances* (1983), London: HMSO.

[6] More freedom of entry into airline markets has produced this effect. See Peter Forsyth (1983), 'Airline deregulation in the United States: the lessons for Europe', *Fiscal Studies*, **4** (Nov.); and David Starkie and Margaret Starrs (1984), 'Contestability and sustainability in regional airline markets', *Economic Record* (Sept.).

[7] There might be a beneficial effect of smaller trains operating at more frequent intervals. See Alan Walters (1982), 'Externalities in Urban Buses', *Journal of Urban Economics*, **2**, for a discussion of trade-offs between vehicle size and service frequency.

travel. In the longer term, the character of the industry will depend also on the government's view of the size of the social railway and thus on the amount of infrastructure that the government is willing to support.

It is difficult to judge whether the public sector's involvement in freight and inter-city services would continue as at present. This depends upon whether there are economies or diseconomies of scale and scope in the provision of train services.[8] Large companies may be able to balance and match rolling-stock to different market demands rather better but at the expense of managerial diseconomies.[9] The most plausible outcome is that the state sector will maintain a substantial presence alongside a range of private-sector firms.

[8] Economies of scale are to be distinguished from economies of utilization (sometimes referred to as economies of traffic density). Economies of scope refers to the advantages of jointly producing multiple outputs, i.e. different types of services.

[9] Recent studies of US railroads have suggested only limited economies of scale. R. H. Spady (*Econometric Estimation for the Regulated Transportation Industries* (1979), New York: Garland), for example, concludes that there are managerial diseconomies of scale in rail transport.

11

Railway Privatization

JOHN DODGSON*

1. RAILWAY PERFORMANCE AND RAIL PRIVATIZATION OPTIONS

This chapter considers the difficulties involved in privatizing Britain's railways by reviewing the alternative options that were available. Throughout the 1980s British Rail was low in government priorities for privatization. Eventually a White Paper on rail privatization was published in 1992[1], and the resulting Railways Act came into effect on 1 April 1994. A new public-sector company, Railtrack, took over the existing railway infrastructure, and was to charge for access to the network. All passenger services will eventually be franchised through the new Office of Passenger Rail Franchising, though the process is expected to take a number of years. BR's freight business will be sold to the private sector. A Railway Regulator will ensure fair access to the network. British Rail will gradually disappear, even though a House of Lords amendment means it will be allowed to bid for passenger franchises in competition with the private sector.

A major difficulty in privatizing the railways has been that the industry as a whole has been unprofitable. In 1990/1 British Rail earned £2923 million from its passenger, freight, and parcels businesses, but in addition received £700 million in subsidies for operating unprofitable passenger services. The bulk of these losses were made by non-InterCity services outside the South-East, and elimination of the losses would require massive, and politically unacceptable, route closures. Policies involving such closures have either not been implemented in full (Beeching, in the 1960s), or rejected altogether (Serpell, in the early 1980s). Privatization or liberalization therefore needed to be accompanied by methods to secure continuing financial support from the public sector.

* Senior Lecturer, Department of Economics and Accounting, University of Liverpool.

I am grateful to Bill Bradshaw, Chris Nash, and Peter White for comments on an earlier draft of this chapter. However, I alone am responsible for the contents. The chapter was largely written in 1992 before publication of the White Paper on railway privatization, though it has been amended slightly subsequently.

[1] See Department of Transport 1992.

In addition, the government's search for a workable solution appears to have been dominated by rejection of privatization of British Rail as a single monopoly organization, and a desire to find an alternative that would create competition *within* the railway industry. As we shall show in this chapter, that search has been made extremely difficult by the nature of the cost structures in the industry.

Since 1982 British Rail has been divided up into business sectors. Table 11.1 shows the financial performance of the sectors in 1990/1.[2] (The consistently unprofitable parcels sector was split between the passenger businesses in 1991, while the European Passenger Services sector created in 1990 will not be in a position to earn revenue until after the opening of the Channel Tunnel in 1994.) In 1990/1 Network South-East had a revenue/cost ratio of 0.87, and was required under then-current government objectives to be self-supporting by 1993, while Regional Railways (formerly Provincial) had a revenue/cost ratio of 0.38. InterCity had a revenue/cost ratio before interest of 1.06. Demand for the rail-passenger businesses has been generally buoyant, with traffic growing from 18,350 million passenger-miles in 1983 to 21,327 million in 1988/9, before dropping back to 20,624 million in 1990/1.

The freight businesses have faced a more hostile environment. The Trainload Freight sector deals with bulk coal, metals, construction, and petroleum traffic, and handled 123 million tonnes of British Rail's total of 138 million in 1990/1. The sector is profitable, but its fortunes are closely tied up with the future prospects for the coal, electricity generation, construction, and steel industries. Railfreight Distribution handles automotive, chemicals, intermodal (including Freightliner), and international traffic, and is much more vulnerable to competition from road hauliers. Its heavy losses in 1990/1 partly reflect the very unprofitable Speedlink network of wagonload services which it abandoned in summer 1991.

The £700 million of financial support for the subsidized railway shown in Table 11.1 came in the form of central government block grant under the Public Service Obligation (PSO), together with £101 million of support for local services operated by Regional Railways in the former Metropolitan County conurbations and provided under Section 20 of the 1968 Transport Act. During the 1980s the Conservative governments imposed tough financial obligations on British Rail through a three-year cycle of targets. The PSO was to be reduced by 25 per cent in real terms between 1983 and 1986/7, and then by a further 25 per cent between 1986/7 and 1989/90. InterCity was ineligible for PSO after March 1988. The targets set in December 1989 to reduce PSO for Regional Railways to £350 million by March 1993, and to eliminate PSO for Network

---

[2] These financial performance figures are partly dependent on cost-allocation techniques which are discussed in Section 2.2 below.

TABLE 11.1. British Rail, sector results, 1990/1

	The subsidized railway		The commercial railway			
	(1)[a] Network South-East	(2)[a] Regional Railways	(3)[a] InterCity	(4)[b] Trainload Freight	(5)[b] Railfreight Distribution	(6)[b] Parcels
Revenue[c] (£m.)	998.3	303.7	851.2	509.5	172.8	115.8
Costs[d] (£m.)	1153.2	807.1	801.5	410.8	325.1	141.6
Revenue/Cost ratio	0.87	0.38	1.06	1.24	0.53	0.82
Surplus (loss) before subsidy (£m.)	(154.9)	(503.4)	49.7	98.7	(152.3)	(25.8)
Subsidy (£m.)	142.7[e]	528.8[e]				

(1) Commuter services in a wide area around the London conurbation.
(2) Rail passenger services not in the Network South-East or InterCity sectors (formerly known as the Provincial sector).
(4) Bulk haulage of coal, metals, oil, and construction industry traffic.
(5) Automotive, chemicals, intermodal, and international rail-freight traffic.
(6) Includes letter traffic for the Post Office, and British Rail's own parcels services.

[a] The passenger railway.
[b] The freight railway.
[c] Turnover excluding subsidy.
[d] Exclude interest.
[e] A further £28.4 million of support was provided within the PSO for policing costs on the subsidized railway. Because this figure is not broken down between NSE and Regional Railways, it is included in the revenue totals for the two subsidized sectors shown in the table.

Source: British Railways Board Annual Report and Accounts 1990/91, 38.

South-East, looked unlikely to be met because of the recession. Nevertheless, total PSO and Section 20 support to British Rail fell by around fifty per cent in real terms between 1983 and 1990/1.

The rail privatization that did take place in the 1980s took the form of the sale of subsidiaries. British Rail Hovercraft Ltd was sold in 1981, British Transport Hotels from 1982 through to 1984, the Sealink UK ferry company in 1984, Travellers Fare station catering in 1988, BREL (British Rail Engineering Ltd) in 1989, and the Horwich Foundry and the Vale of Rheidol narrow-gauge railway in 1988/9. There was also increased private-sector involvement in on-train catering, train cleaning, and station maintenance, and in property redevelopment.

Despite the substantial progress under public ownership in improving productivity and reducing government subsidy requirement in the main railway businesses, the government did still see full privatization as a policy objective. Four main proposals for privatizing British Rail were set out in 1988 by the then-Secretary of State for Transport, Paul Channon (Redwood 1988):

(1) The 'regional option', a division on a regional basis, with a number of companies serving different parts of the country (Gritten 1988). These would be likely to be based on routes radiating from London, just as did the 'Big Four' private companies before nationalization, and some of the constituent pre-grouping companies before 1923.

(2) The 'sector option', with companies based on the existing business sectors. The profitable Trainload Freight and InterCity sectors would be likely to be disposed of first.

(3) The 'track authority' option, with a separate track authority which would own the infrastructure and charge private companies for the right to run trains on the network (Irvine, 1987). The track authority might remain under public ownership.

(4) The 'British Rail plc' option, privatization as a whole, the only option which seemed to have been firmly ruled out.

A further option would involve some form of franchising. Companies could bid for the right to operate particular rail routes or services. This might involve competition for subsidy for operating unprofitable services (rather in the way that local authorities seek competitive tenders for unprofitable bus services), or it might involve the franchising of profitable long-distance routes where companies would bid for the exclusive right to operate a particular service. The successful bidders might be required to maintain track and other infrastructure, or these costs might remain the responsibility of the tendering authority.

2. THE STRUCTURE OF COSTS IN THE RAILWAY INDUSTRY

Optimal industry organization, and hence feasible options for privatization, are constrained by cost structures. Thus if an industry is a pure natural monopoly, unit costs will increase if the industry is broken up into a number of separate firms. Furthermore, cost interdependencies between parts of a business will impose constraints on the way the business might be divided up into individual companies. In this section we review evidence on cost structures and interdependencies in the railway industry.

2.1 Returns to scale, returns to density, and returns to scope

The railway industry (like other transport industries) is one which appears to be characterized by more-or-less constant returns to firm size (i.e. scale), economies of density, and some economies of scope. Evidence for the first two comes primarily from statistical cost studies of the railway industry. There is a long tradition of these studies in the United States, where there is a sizeable number of (private) railroads to provide data. Earlier US cost studies used *ad hoc* cost functions and were not based on the underlying theory of production (Griliches 1972; Harris 1977), or were based on the restrictive Cobb-Douglas model (Keeler 1974). Later analysis (Brown *et al.* 1979; Caves *et al.* 1981) used the more general multi-product translog cost model. Despite differences in method, there is fairly consistent post-war evidence from the various American studies of broadly constant returns to scale with respect to firm size for all but the smallest companies. In addition, both Harris and Keeler found evidence of economies of traffic density, with lower average costs per traffic unit for companies with high traffic volumes per mile of track or route.

Statistical cost analysis of European railways is more difficult because of differences in accounting conventions between railways, but Vigouroux-Steck (1989) pooled annual data for thirteen Western European companies, including British Rail, to estimate a translog variable cost function over the period from 1971 to 1987. Although the data need to be treated with caution (Nash 1990: 4), this study also showed roughly constant returns with respect to firm size (though with lower average costs for medium-sized firms), and economies of density with increases in train-miles per route mile (except for the two highest density systems, the Dutch and the Swiss). Finally, my own historical study of 14 British companies in the period 1900 to 1912 also used the translog model, and showed constant returns to scale with respect to firm size. There was also some, less clear-cut, evidence of economies of density (Dodgson 1992).

There are economies of scope when it is cheaper to provide two (or more) types of output jointly rather than separately. Some such economies are related to economies of density. Thus it is generally cheaper to provide freight and passenger services on one route than on two separate routes. On very busy routes with both express passenger trains and slower freights and/or local passenger trains, it may be necessary to segregate slow and fast trains by having two separate pairs of running lines, but it will still generally be cheaper to have one four track route than two separate two-track routes. There are also economies of scope in carrying different types of passenger on the same train, rather than in providing different trains for different classes of passenger (such as those who prefer a low-fare/low-quality combination, and those who prefer a higher-fare/higher-quality option). Low-cost entrants to the deregulated US airline industry, like People Express, who tried to cater exclusively for low-fare travellers with a 'no frills' service were ultimately unable to compete with established carriers who retained a mix of fare/quality options, and who were therefore able to earn higher revenues per passenger by the use of sophisticated fare discrimination ('yield management') techniques.

Not all possible economies of scope may be effective in practice. Before sectorization it was thought to be advantageous to have locomotive fleets that could be used for different parts of the business. For example, locomotives might be used for passenger services during the day and freight or parcels at night, or locos might be available for different types of freight trains. However, the allocation of particular fleets to particular sectors or subsectors has considerably improved locomotive utilization, since the sector managers are responsible for the costs of those assets and so are determined to maximize the net revenue they generate for their business.

The impact of economies of traffic density on railway economies was illustrated indirectly by maps of rail-traffic density published in the Supplementary Volume to the Serpell Report (Department of Transport 1983). These maps showed passenger and freight volumes in terms of total annual gross train weights (in thousands of tonnes) over each section of the network. That for freight and passenger traffic combined is reproduced as Figure 11.1. The data relate to 1982 (though the freight data were actually BR's 1982 forecasts for 1986), but the overall pattern of traffic flows will not have changed enormously over the 10 years from 1982 to 1992. The map illustrates the considerable disparity in volumes across the network, with greatest densities in the South-East, on the West Coast Main Line (WCML) from London through the West Midlands and the North-West to Glasgow, the East Coast Main Line (ECML) from London through York and Newcastle to Edinburgh, the Midland Main Line through Leicester and Nottingham to Sheffield, the

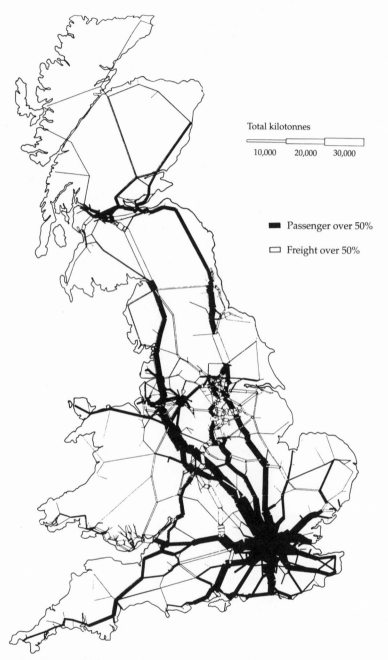

Total kilotonnes

10,000   20,000   30,000

■ Passenger over 50%

□ Freight over 50%

FIG. 11.1. British Rail: traffic densities in terms of gross train weights on each section of route. Passenger-train tonnages are for 1982, and freight-train weights were BR forecasts for 1986.

Source: Department of Transport (1983), *Railway Finances: Report of a Committee chaired by Sir David Serpell, KCB, CMG, OBE*. suppl. vol., London: HMSO. Crown copyright reproduced with the permission of the Controller of HMSO.

Great Western main line to Bristol and South Wales, and the NE–SW route from Sheffield to Birmingham, Bristol, and the West Country. It is no accident that those passenger sectors with the best financial results (namely InterCity and Network South-East) cover those routes with the high-traffic densities.

2.2 Allocating infrastructure costs

The problem which has bedevilled the determination of the profitability of the parts of the rail business in the past has been the allocation of the common and joint elements of infrastructure and general administration costs to the different parts of the business. The joint nature of some of the costs means that cost-allocation procedures must involve some arbitrary element. In turn, this means that the sector-profitability results shown in Table 11.1 are partly dependent on such procedures.

The methods used by BR to determine profitability at the sector level are the prime-user and sole-user costing methods. Under both methods, a hierarchy of users is determined for each asset or section of route. The 'prime user' is the sector which is the most important user of the asset, and then other sectors are ranked in declining importance. Under the prime-user method, used for terminals, carriage cleaning, and shunting and marshalling (Allen 1989: 107), the costs of the asset are allocated by determining which costs could be avoided if the marginal user no longer requires to use the asset. These avoidable costs are then allocated to this marginal user. Remaining costs are allocated to the next user up the hierarchy on the same principle, and all remaining costs are allocated to the prime user.

The sole-user method, used for track and signalling infrastructure, differs in that the prime user of the section of route decides what capacity would be optimal for its trains. The cost of this is then calculated and allocated to this sector. The second user then decides what additional capacity would be needed, and the cost of this is allocated to it, and so on. Since the sole-user method is concerned with optimal capacity rather than the capacity actually in existence, it may leave some existing costs, namely those of surplus capacity, uncovered. The costs of such surplus capacity are allocated to the sectors using the route 'in a structured way, identifying responsibility for its longer-term removal' (Allen 1989: 104), so that the sector best able to secure the removal of the excess capacity has an incentive to do so.

From April 1992, in a reorganization known as Organizing for Quality (OfQ), almost all assets were to be assigned to one of the businesses. Hence, all signalling control centres and equipment, stations, and depots would be 'owned' by one of the businesses, and there would be significant internal trading between businesses. British Rail HQ was to establish a regulatory framework for contracts and charges between sectors (Welsby 1991: 217–19).

3. PRIVATIZATION: THE SEARCH FOR A COMPETITIVE SOLUTION

The nationalized railway industry has in the past been subject to detailed criticism of its productivity record (see in particular Pryke and Dodgson 1975; Select Committee on Nationalised Industries 1977; Department of Transport 1983). However, as noted in Section 1, British Rail in the 1980s met a succession of tough government targets for the reduction of real levels of PSO subsidy. In 1989 the Monopolies and Mergers Commission pointed out the 'impressive achievement of Provincial in significantly reducing its costs while increasing its revenue' and thought this was 'a clear endorsement of the Board's policy of sectoral management of the railway' (Monopolies and Mergers Commission 1989: 5).

This is not to say, however, that privatization would not produce further benefits. British Rail was hampered by the need to negotiate national wage rates, rather than ones which reflect local labour-market conditions. In consequence, there may be no problems in recruiting staff in some areas, and serious shortages in others. The Monopolies and Mergers Commission interviewed a number of Area Managers

all of whom emphasized the progress made in recent years in improving manpower efficiency. They also expressed the view that there was scope for further significant improvement, which they considered could best be achieved through local productivity initiatives, some entailing acceptance of changes in working practices that cut across the traditional demarcations between different grade groups. . . . standard working practices agreed on a national basis did not always meet the widely varying needs of the different sectors. However, they felt they were constrained by the terms of national agreements from negotiating variations to suit local circumstances. (Monopolies and Mergers Commission 1989: 60)

Privatization in the railways, as elsewhere, would be likely to reduce the extent of such inflexibilities.

It is a presumption of this chapter (and no doubt of much of the rest of this volume) that competition will also have desirable effects on costs and quality of service if it can be achieved. In the rest of this chapter we therefore look at the possibilities of achieving competition in either a privatized or regulated railway industry.

3.1 Route competition

One possibility for competition is to have competing routes. Before nationalization in 1948, and particularly before the Grouping into the

'Big Four' railway companies in 1923, there were many competing rail routes in Great Britain. However, as indicated in Section 2.1, the existence of economies of density means that it is sensible to concentrate traffic on as few routes as possible, and most competing routes have been closed. This was in particular the main theme of the 'second Beeching Report' of 1965, *The Development of the Main Trunk Routes*:

It is evident that railway economics are such that the cost per unit carried falls rapidly as the traffic density over a route increases. In addition to the resulting reduction in route cost per unit carried, economies also arise from more effective utilization of lineside facilities such as yards, maintenance depots, stations, etc., and from more intensive use of motive power and rolling stock. Therefore, if an available flow of traffic, which could be carried by one route, is spread over two or more alternative and under-loaded ones, the costs per unit carried are bound to be inflated. (British Railways Board 1965: 8).

Consequently, many of the competing routes were closed. Where two routes remain, the second has generally been downgraded with lower line speeds and track capacity than the main routes (e.g. London, Waterloo–Exeter; London, Paddington–Birmingham; Glasgow Central–Edinburgh) though there are a few routes where competition is possible (e.g. London–Glasgow via Carlisle or Edinburgh; London–Southend; London–Cambridge; Liverpool–Manchester).[3]

Construction of new competing rail lines is unlikely to be a viable proposition. The controversy over the route for construction of a new line from London to the Channel Tunnel has shown how much opposition there is to new rail lines both on environmental and on self-interest grounds. The existence of economies of density militates against new construction unless there are capacity and/or speed restriction problems on existing routes. Finally, in a competitive framework, a new entrant would be at a considerable disadvantage *vis-à-vis* an incumbent because of the very high element of sunk costs. Existing railways' construction costs are sunk, and so faced with entry they can reduce their prices below the level that the entrant needs to charge in order to recover its construction costs. A potential entrant, knowing this, would not enter.[4]

[3] Adamson *et al.* (1991: 68) note that there are only seven InterCity routes where this type of competition is possible, and they account for less than 10 per cent of InterCity revenue.

[4] An incorrectly informed entrant might however make a mistake. In the latter half of the nineteenth century the North Eastern Railway had a complete territorial monopoly of the North-East of England. It charged the same freight rates from the West Riding of Yorkshire to Hull and to ports much further north, despite much shorter distances. Hence there appeared to be a profitable entry opportunity, and in 1885 the newly constructed Hull and Barnsley Railway breached the NER's monopoly in the southern part of its territory. However, the resulting price competition forced the Hull and Barnsley into receivership in 1887 (though services continued to operate), and the NER retained the rest of its regional monopoly until the 1923 Grouping (see Irving 1976).

While the contestable markets hypothesis has been applied to both airlines and buses,[5] where the main elements of capital are mobile and so can be moved to other routes if entry on one particular route proves unsuccessful, the existing, vertically integrated, rail industry is certainly not contestable. There are, however, much greater prospects for competition and contestability when train operators have access to a commonly provided infrastructure of routes. Next we consider in turn competition under present circumstances, competition with a liberalized regime of access, and competition in the case of a rail track infrastructure authority which is not involved at all in the operation of train services.

3.2 Competition on the network under the present regime

Until April 1994 BR owned their infrastructure. They could *choose* to let other companies use the network for a fee which was subject to negotiations but not subject to any regulations as to its level. BR insisted that all trains be driven by BR traincrew, although there were both private locomotives and private rolling stock on the system. All such private locomotives, passenger coaches, and freight wagons had to be approved by BR as suitable and safe for use.

There is a long tradition of use of private-sector freight wagons. In March 1991 BR owned 20,763 freight wagons, and there were 13,640 private freight vehicles licensed to use the network. In 1986 BR permitted a major West Country aggregates producer, Foster Yeomans, to operate its trains using its own locomotives. Four (later five) diesel locomotives were constructed by General Motors in North America and four similar locomotives were built for another aggregates company, Amey Roadstone, in 1990. These locomotives were driven and maintained by BR staff, but have achieved very much higher performance standards, mileages, and availability than the BR locomotives available for the traffic. It seems that the demonstration effect of these machines also had a major impact on the performance requirements of the latest generation of BR freight diesels.

The private sector also became involved with the operation of freight services. Tiger Rail, a private company, took over responsibility for some former Speedlink routes when BR abandoned them in 1991, while Charterail, a bi-modal company in which BR had a 22 per cent stake, was also involved in developing freight-rail services. However, both companies were unsuccessful financially.

---

[5] Though neither of these industries appear to be perfectly contestable they might be said to be 'imperfectly contestable'. See in particular Morrison and Winston (1987) on airlines; Dodgson and Katsoulacos (1991) on local buses; and Jaffer and Thompson (1986) on express buses.

Private-sector involvement in passenger-train operation has been more limited. The luxury train market, illustrated by the Venice Simplon Orient Express (VSOE) and the Royal Scotsman, provides services in privately owned coaches hauled by BR-owned and crewed locomotives. There are some other privately owned sets of coaches which are used for excursions and tours. In 1992 Stagecoach, the largest British bus operator, reached agreement with InterCity to take over responsibility for marketing of seated coaches on some overnight trains between Scotland and London, while Virgin expressed an interest in leasing some trainsets on the East Coast Main Line.

In July 1991 the Council of the European Community passed a Directive (91/440/EEC) to be implemented by the beginning of 1993. This requires separate accounts for rail infrastructure and operations. Article 8 requires fees for use of infrastructure. These are to be determined by member states, but should avoid discrimination between railway undertakings and 'may in particular take into account the mileage, the composition of the train and any specific requirements in terms of such factors as speed, and load and the degree or period of utilization of the infrastructure'. Article 10 requires that access to member states' rail networks on a non-discriminatory basis be granted to international groupings (railways in at least two member states involved in providing services between them) for international traffic, including transit traffic, between the member states involved in the groupings, and for international combined-transport services operated by individual railway undertakings.

The effects of liberalization of access for international traffic might themselves be relatively limited, but in October 1991 the Secretary of State for Transport also requested BR to liberalize access for domestic services in advance of legislation. BR were asked to respond positively to private sector proposals for new freight or passenger services, to charge fairly for track and other facilities, and to allow private operators to use their own locomotives (as we have seen, already possible) and (not previously permitted by BR) their own drivers and other traincrew. The government appointed consultants to advise them on fair ways of charging for, and securing access to, rail infrastructure.

3.3 *Competition with more liberalized access?*

So far the increased private involvement in train service operation has not created direct competition. Private companies have been involved in services which are clearly differentiated from existing BR services (VSOE offer a significantly different price/quality combination to Network South-East services), or they have taken over services which BR planned to withdraw as uneconomic (some Speedlink routes or

Anglo-Scottish overnight seating services). BR's existing monopoly powers meant that it was very unlikely to permit access to its network to services that would abstract from existing sector revenues. Effective liberalization would therefore have to permit access to the network that might not be in BR's financial interest. This meant that an independent regulator would be needed to ensure fair access to railway infrastructure.

Systems of both pricing and access needed to be devised. One approach to pricing would be to have a published scale of infrastructure charges. Track maintenance costs vary with train and axle weights and train speeds, and signalling costs vary (*ex ante*, but not *ex post*) with speeds, so a scale based on the type of matrix of tonnages and speeds used by BR civil engineers to assess track maintenance costs[6] might form the basis for a train-mileage-based system of charges. Capital charges would also need to be levied, while additional charges would be needed for the use of stations. Such a system would have the benefits of simplicity and transparency, but suffers from a number of defects. If a new operator's trains are not competing directly with existing sector services, then sectors can gain by selling spare capacity. If, however, the new operator is abstracting revenue from existing services, the competition will not be fair if track charges for the newcomer differ from the remaining track costs that must be borne by the BR sectors. Alternatively, charging all the sectors the same train-mile costs as entrants might mean that not all infrastructure costs are covered. Alternatively, to ensure both this and a fairer basis for infrastructure use, track costs might be shared among operators on some basis related to the use made of the infrastructure.

Track capacity might not be spare at the time the newcomer wishes to operate, or the capacity which is spare might have a lower commercial value (for example, because it is off-peak or because it does not permit intensive use of the entrant's rolling stock). In these circumstances some form of bidding or auctioning system may be necessary. This is obviously more complex, and the regulator would need to be sure that the sectors were not unfairly withholding capacity in order to prevent competitive access.

3.4 Competition with a rail infrastructure authority

A bidding system had also been proposed with the rail infrastructure privatization option. Under the situation envisaged by Starkie, 'access to lines and terminals would be rented by competing train companies who

---

6 See Monopolies and Mergers Commission 1989: 79.

would then sell their services direct to the public'. (Starkie, this volume, p. 227)

Under a bidding system, what is being offered for sale is a level of railway capacity to be shared between a number of railway operators, some of whom will be offering non-competing (e.g. freight and passenger) services, and some of whom might be offering competing services. There is likely to be an enormous number of ways a given amount of capacity could be divided up (see also Nash 1990: 6). If the potential operators were all to bid secretly simultaneously, the bids are likely to be mutually inconsistent. Does the track authority accept the highest bid, and then offer the remaining capacity for rebidding, and continue this process until no more offers are forthcoming? If it did, use of capacity might not be optimal because there might be other combinations of bids which would be mutually compatible and would yield more revenue. Moreover, the process of recalculating what capacity remained at each stage would be a complex one. Initial bidders might also wish to reconsider their initial bids if later succesful bids involved competitive services which would reduce the expected return from their own bid. As Adamson *et al.* point out:

If a tenderer were not successful in its initial bid, it would have to re-optimise iteratively its need for paths through the network to arrive at a second choice, in the light of the fact that some paths were already committed to a competitor. The interdependence inherent in train planning would make timetabling with competitive bidding a tortuous process, with the likelihood of unclear product differentiation and unstable prices. (Adamson *et al.* 1991: 69)

Nash has suggested that the 'theoretical simplicity of the "bidding" model is an illusion' (Nash 1990: 6). I believe that a necessary (but not sufficient) requirement for its advocates would be to demonstrate the existence of auctioning models which determine the existence of efficient equilibria in auctions where what is being offered are sections of a total which could be divided up into parts in an extremely large (possibly infinite) number of ways.

There are also capacity-level problems with a separate track authority. Private infrastructure authorities might have an incentive to underinvest. Helm and Thompson (1991: 238) argue that existing privatized utility regulation in the UK (particularly the (RPI-X) control of prices) may result in underinvestment by firms with high sunk infrastructure costs. As an example, the BAA appeared to become much less concerned about shortages of runway capacity in the South-East once it had been privatized. Conversely, if the track authority remained in public hands, it might have insufficient incentive to match capacity to demand, whereas a major advantage of sector management has been the incentives managers have to take a careful look at the levels and costs of the capacity for which they are responsible (Nash 1990: 5). Investment in new track capacity might also be constrained by government-imposed public spending limits. Finally, whatever the form of infrastructure ownership, there are interdependencies between track capacity and train-service improvements: for instance, many increases in train speeds as a result of investment in new rolling-stock also require associated infrastructure investment, and it is difficult to see individual train operators being willing to fund such infrastructure improvements when they might then be liable to competition from new entrants taking advantage of the better infrastructure facilities.

While there may be benefits to be had from 'on the rail' competition, I really doubt that a satisfactory market mechanism could be devised to replace the existing system of co-ordination by planning. Physical co-ordination between services on a section of rail capacity is so important that an attempt to rely primarily on market systems would likely lead to a chaotic outcome. As a distinguished former railwayman has noted in this regard 'foisting upon the railway a structure of ownership and management which offends every professional principle of railway operation is likely to result in an outcome which will be expensive, unsuitable and unsafe' (Bradshaw 1991: 25).

3.5 Sectors and regions

The sector option for privatization had the major advantage that it coincided with the existing division of the railway business, while cost-allocation techniques had been devised to allocate all the costs of railway operation to particular sectors. Sector privatization could also proceed in stages, with the commercial Trainload Freight and InterCity businesses being privatized first. A difficulty in assessing their market value is in appraising the effects on their profitability of whatever form of liberalized access to the network was chosen. The major problem with the sector option is that the existing administrative system of deciding which sector is responsible for which costs, with an internal regulator of disputes, would be replaced by commercial relationships. Since allocation of joint and common costs very often involves the application of judgement rather than clear economic principles, it is difficult to believe that the present arrangements would not be replaced by continual bickering and litigation between the parties.

The regional option would avoid most (but not all) of these problems. Regional companies could be based on existing mainlines out of London. Given the evidence on constant returns to scale in railway operation, there should not be major cost disadvantages of such a split-up. There may however be marketing disadvantages in fragmenting the InterCity business, while some of the main developments in new train services, such as the inter-regional Express network created by Regional Railways, and the existing and prospective cross-London services, might be inhibited once they were the responsibility of separate companies.

Regional companies would have to compete for funds in capital markets, and so there would be some 'yardstick' competition. However, all of the regional companies would need some government financial support for unprofitable services, and their commercial success would partly depend on how succesful they were in getting this. There is also a danger that support for the regional option harks back to a 'golden age' that never existed. Economic historians have shown that the pre-grouping companies at the turn of the century were generally much more interested in collusion than in competition (see in particular, Cain 1980). With regard to yardstick competition, cross-company Total Factor Productivity comparisons between 1900 and 1912 show big differences between companies, with a refusal of all but the TFP growth-leader, the North-Eastern Railway, even to compile basic operational statistics in the form of ton-miles and passenger-miles (see Dodgson 1993).

3.5 Competition for subsidy: franchising unprofitable services

As Table 11.1 showed, the bulk of railway losses were made by Regional Railways services. Some of these services use parts of the InterCity network, but many are relatively self-contained. There has now been over seven years experience with the process of tendering for the operation of unprofitable local bus services, and the system appears to have been very succesful. Costs have been reduced, and there have been relatively few complaints by bidders about the fairness of the system.

Though there are some important differences between bus and rail services, there seemed to be no reason why the system should not be instituted for many unprofitable rail services. Not all suitable services need to be put out to tender at once, so experience can be built up. Government would need to specify minimum standards of service, and may wish to specify maximum-fare levels. While local authorities might be better able to determine local transport needs, many services cross existing boundaries, while subsidy of services would place an additional financial burden on local government, so the system might best be administered centrally. One problem with rail services not present with buses is the supply of rolling-stock. The option being adopted to deal with this is the establishment of competing rolling-stock leasing companies within British Rail (see also Rickard 1991: 80).

Operation of services by companies with a direct financial interest in their success should make them more responsive to passenger needs, and encourage efficient utilization of assets. In Sweden operators tender with county transport boards for fixed-term contracts to operate local rail services. Although the national rail company won all the contracts in the first year of the scheme, in the next year, 1990, three of the counties awarded a four year contract to an independent company (BK Tag) to operate five secondary routes. BK Tag was awarded a further rail contract, to operate stopping services on a mainline, in August 1991 (Fogelmark 1992).

4. CONCLUSIONS

Economists have rightly argued (see in particular Kay and Thompson 1986) that competition might be more important in securing efficiency than private ownership *per se*. After a shaky start, government appears to have got this message, and later privatizations seem to have been driven by a search to secure competition. This seems to be particularly the case with the search for a way of privatizing British Rail. Although very little has been published about the studies that the government has conducted on the way to privatize the railways, it is clear that the search proved to be a very difficult one. It is the contention of the present chapter that some of the ways suggested to privatize BR would have been so complicated that the benefits of competition would be submerged by adverse consequences. Competition might best be secured by competition for franchises to operate unprofitable services, and by allowing regulated access to the network, where the aim of the regulator would primarily be to ensure fair access for entrants.

I believe that there should still be benefits of privatization. A privatized railway system would have proper access to the capital market for investment and leasing, while the opportunity for government to interfere with railway management would be reduced, though not eliminated. In particular, the private sector might have the will to break up the system of national wage bargaining and reform the industry's tortuous industrial relations.

I am however sceptical about the practicality of the complete split between infrastructure and operations which will occur when Railtrack takes over responsibility for all railway infrastructure in April 1994. This may prove to be unwieldy from the point of day-to-day operations, while I am sceptical whether an effective system of access charges can be devised to secure efficient short- and long-run use of infrastructure. Perhaps a form of British Rail plc with considerably greater freedom of access, and competitive tendering for subsidies, might not have been such a bad idea after all.

References

Adamson, M., Jones, W., and Pratt, R. (1991), 'Competition issues in privatisation: lessons for the railways', in D. Banister, and K. Button (eds.), *Transport in a Free Market Economy*, London: Macmillan.

Allen, D. (1989), 'Management accounting developments in British Rail', in M. W. Pendlebury (ed.), *Management Accounting in the Public Sector*, Oxford: Heinemann.

Bradshaw, W. (1991), 'A review of policies for the future of Britain's railways', paper presented to the Railway Study Association, London, 13 Nov.

British Railways Board (1965), *The Development of the Main Trunk Routes*, London: BRB.

Brown, R. S., Caves, D. W., and Christensen, L. R. (1979), 'Modelling the structure of cost for multi-product firms', *Southern Economic Journal*, **16**, 256–73.

Cain, P. (1980), 'Private enterprise or public utility? Capital, output and pricing on English and Welsh railways, 1870–1914', *Journal of Transport History*, **1**, 9–28.

Caves, D. W., Christensen, L. R., and Swanson, J. A. (1981), 'Productivity growth, scale economies, and capacity utilization in US railroads, 1955–1974', *American Economic Review*, **71**, 994–1002.

Department of Transport (1983), *Railway Finances*: *Report of a Committee chaired by Sir David Serpell*, (2 vols.), London: HMSO.

—— (1992), *New Opportunities for the Railways*: *The Privatisation of British Rail*, London: HMSO.

Dodgson, J. S. (1993), 'British railway cost functions and productivity growth, 1900–1912', *Explorations in Economic History*, **30**, 158–81.

—— Katsoulacos, Y. (1991), 'Competition, contestability and predation: the economics of competition in deregulated bus markets', *Transportation Planning and Technology*, **15**, 263–75.

Fogelmark, L. (1992), 'Private operator meets local needs', *Developing Railways*, *1992*, 48–9.

Griliches, Z. (1972), 'Cost allocation in railroad regulation', *Bell Journal of Economics*, **3**, 26–46.

Gritten, A. (1988), *Reviving the Railways*: *A Victorian Future?*, London: Centre for Policy Studies.

Harris, R. G. (1977), 'Economies of traffic density in the rail freight industry', *Bell Journal of Economics*, **8**, 556–64.

Helm, D., and Thompson, D. (1991), 'Privatised transport infrastructure and incentives to invest', *Journal of Transport Economics and Policy*, **25**, 231–46.

Irvine, K. (1987), *The Right Lines*, London: Adam Smith Institute.

Irving, R. (1976), *The North Eastern Railway Company, 1870-1914*: *An Economic History*, Leicester: Leicester University Press.

Jaffer, S. M., and Thompson, D. J. (1986), 'Deregulated express coaches: a reassessment', *Fiscal Studies*, **7**, 45–68.

Kay, J. A., and Thompson, D. J. (1986), 'Privatisation: a policy in search of a rationale', *Economic Journal*, **96**, 18–32.

Keeler, T. (1974), 'Railroad costs, returns to scale and excess capacity', *Review of Economics and Statistics*, **56**, 201–08.

Monopolies and Mergers Commission (1989), *British Railways Board: Provincial*, Cm 584, London: HMSO.

Morrison, S. A., and Winston, C. (1987), 'Empirical implications and tests of the contestability hypothesis', *Journal of Law and Economics*, **30**, 53–66.

Nash, C. A. (1990), *Role of Rail in Future Transport Policy*, Rees Jeffreys Road Fund, Transport and Society Discussion Paper no. 12, Oxford.

Pryke, R. W. S., and Dodgson, J. S. (1985), *The Rail Problem*, London: Martin Robertson.

Redwood, J. (1988), *Signals from a Railway Conference*, London: Centre for Policy Studies.

Rickard, J. (1991), 'Discussion' [of Adamson *et al.*], in D. Banister, and K. Button (eds.) *Transport in a Free Market Economy*, London: Macmillan.

Select Committee on Nationalised Industries (1977), *The Role of British Rail in Public Transport*, London: HMSO.

Starkie, D. N. M. (1994), 'British Rail: competition on the network', this volume.

Vigouroux-Steck, C. (1989), 'Exploratory analysis in the estimation of transport cost functions for European railways', unpub. MA thesis, University of Leeds.

Welsby, J. (1991), 'Regions give way to businesses' *Railway Gazette International*, Apr., 217–19.

12

Privatization and Domestic Consumers

JOHN WINWARD*

On first inspection, discussion of privatization from the point of view of domestic consumers appears an unrewarding prospect; consumer organizations have generally viewed ownership as one of the less interesting aspects of industrial organization. In practice, however, the privatization programme has been about much more than ownership, raising questions about the potential for liberalization of markets, industrial restructuring, and the extended regulation (or re-regulation) of particular sectors. It is these aspects that have been of most significance for domestic consumers, and the organizations that represent them.

It follows that some privatizations (or types of privatization) are much more significant to consumers than others. The group of industries that were in public ownership at the beginning of the 1980s was diverse. Not all the public industries produced (or produce) goods or services consumed by private households. This does not mean that their activities have no effect on consumers; several were (and are) producers of primary or intermediate goods whose efficiency—and therefore the prices which they charge—directly influence the final prices paid by individual consumers. For example, the price of primary fuels is a major factor in the final cost of electricity. Given the dominance of coal stations in the UK generation mix, the disparity between the price of British coal and world market prices has been of great significance to electricity consumers. Nevertheless, the direct consumer interest in these industries is limited. Consumer organizations would not normally expect to involve themselves, for example, in the quality of the output of primary industries; they would expect managers in the intermediate industries to tackle issues of this sort.

A second very important criterion is the degree of competition which a particular industry faces, or to which it could efficiently be exposed. The simple change of ownership of a single car manufacturer, for example, is unlikely to raise major consumer issues. By contrast, very significant issues have been raised by the privatization of the utility industries. The utilities exhibit two characteristics which make them significant:

* Director of Research, the Association of Consumer Research.

first, their core businesses have natural monopoly characteristics; secondly, the services they supply are merit goods.

In practice, the industries had developed structures which blurred any neat divisions between different aspects of their businesses. Industries with a core utility network (i.e. one which exhibits some degree of natural monopoly) have tended to beget monopolies in parts of their structure which do not themselves exhibit subadditivity of costs. In the case of the telephone industry, for example, the supply of handsets was until comparatively recently a *de jure* monopoly, while British Gas' network of showrooms established a scale monopoly in the sale of gas appliances (and—for a time at least—an almost complete monopoly over the sale of certain types of gas appliance).

PRICE CONTROL

In the presence of monopoly, consumers are at risk of exploitation, most obviously by the capture of excessive profits. The post-war nationalization programme was, among other things, one in a series of attempts to regulate the capacity of the natural monopoly industries to generate excessive profits. Being charged merely with breaking even, the nationalized utilities had no apparent incentive to profit-maximize. By the early 1980s, however, the non-profit-making status of the industries had become compromised. Concern about low-return public-sector investments pre-empting scarce capital and 'crowding out' better investments elsewhere in the economy had led to a series of government interventions, the net outcome of which was a complex web of pricing principles and financial controls.

A 1967 White Paper established the principle that prices should be set by reference to long-run marginal costs. In practice, LRMC rules seem to have been viewed by industry management as too imprecise to use as the main tariff-setting tool, though they were acknowledged to provide an 'outer envelope' for pricing decisions. In any case, the LRMC principle was 'supplemented' in the later White Papers by other, more concrete government targets. These sought to control the rate of return on assets employed, and the year-by-year capital flows between the industries and government (External Financing Limits).

The levels at which targets were set were 'agreed' between government and the industries in a bargaining process which was secretive and confused. It was never entirely clear that such targets could legally be imposed on the industries—indeed such an imposition appeared to breach both the statutory duties of the industries and the 'Morrisonian principle' of an arm's-length relationship between the industry and the government. Nominally, the industries continued to set their own tariffs

after taking account of a range of factors, including the views of consumer organizations. Yet the Nationalized Industry Consumer Councils
(NICCs) had almost no access to information on pricing matters and
very few resources. A Department of Trade review of the NICCs recognized that it was a part of their role to 'ensure that consumers' views are
clearly heard on costs and prices' but went on to argue that their views
'could not be decisive'.

In practice, the decisive voice was that of the Treasury. Financial targets and External Financing Limits became the major influences on
tariff-setting. Mechanisms were developed which allowed the Treasury
to extract surpluses from the industries (for example the Gas Levy and
the 'negative EFL'). The effect was to create a perverse environment in
which government was simultaneously the economic regulator of
monopoly undertakings, banker to the same undertakings, and the principal beneficiary of any monopoly profits which they could accrue.
Unsurprisingly, this created significant internal conflicts in the
agent–principal relationship between the industries and the government.

Matching this confusion of roles, the pricing mechanisms themselves
were neither theoretically compatible, nor actually applied in an inter-
nally-consistent way. LRMC pricing is a forward-looking tool; depending on the specific circumstances of an industry it could produce prices
either significantly higher or significantly lower than prevailing average
costs. Rate of return targets, on the other hand, are retrospective in
application and reflect the belief that 'shareholders' (in this case either
taxpayers or the Treasury itself) are entitled to dividend payments on
past investments. Moreover, financial targets and EFLs sometimes
appeared to be set inconsistently, so prices set to achieve the financial
targets could prove inadequate to meet the EFL. The electricity-supply
industry, for example, consistently overshot its financial targets in the
early 1980s. This appeared to be necessary in order for it to achieve sufficient surplus to meet the negative EFLs it was set over the same period.

The lack of clarity in the aims, principles and procedures of tariff-
setting made it particularly difficult for consumer organizations to
mount effective cases against tariff increases. Even outright opposition
was ineffectual, as the economic regulator—the government—was very
often the originator of the increase in its other roles as principal shareholder or banker. A report from the Post Office Users National Council
as late as December 1991 reported that 'Council argued that
Government, as sole shareholder, should not at a time of severe recession be requiring a doubling of the return on capital employed.'
Government declined to respond.

The absence of any clear mechanism for deciding pricing strategy, or
determining, for example, what constitutes a 'reasonable' rate of return,

also exposed consumers to the risk of sudden price discontinuities (which LRMC pricing was specifically designed to avoid). Gas prices were held down in the 1970s (in pursuit of anti-inflationary policies), only to be rapidly increased in the 1980s; domestic gas tariffs doubled between 1980 and 1984. Nationalized utility tariffs have also been used to pursue more specialized social objectives (as an alternative to expenditure on social security measures), for example the introduction of a 'standing charge rebate scheme' for households using very small amounts of electricity and gas. This scheme, announced by the Secretary of State for Energy at a Conservative Party conference, was primarily intended to benefit poorer pensioner households. It was opposed by both the Gas and Electricity Consumers' Councils on the grounds that it indiscriminately channelled benefits towards those who used small amounts of fuel (including second-home owners) and distributed extra costs amongst the balance of the industries' consumers (who were not necessarily better-off).

By comparison, the rules on price setting that emerged from the privatization process were almost certain to be an improvement, if only because they separated the regulators (OFTEL and its successors) from the beneficiaries of price increases. As almost all the 'X factors' set at the time of privatization have been negative (the major exception being those in the water industry), privatization appeared to offer the more immediate benefit to residential consumers of falling prices. This, however, is not straightforward.

In the pre-privatization period, governments must weigh the long-term advantages of rigorous regulation against the short-term goal of maximizing flotation proceeds. A priori, this suggests that the immediately post-privatization regime will be less rigorous than would be optimal, and quite possibly less rigorous than might be expected under continued public ownership. Post-privatization revisions in the price formulae suggest that this has indeed been the case; in the period following their flotation, more rigorous price controls were imposed on both gas and telecommunications by their regulators, without either industry seeking a formal review by the Monopolies and Mergers Commission. British Gas' regulator concluded that 'a considerable tightening of the formula was possible' (from 2 per cent to 5 per cent) while ensuring that '. . . the resulting price was enough to give a fair return to British Gas and its shareholders'.

The price caps set at flotation, of course, reflected the tariffs then in force, and government's control of financial targets (and by extension prices) allowed those tariffs to be increased ahead of flotation. The explicit reason for this was to make the industries more profitable. The rate-of-return targets for the electricity-supply industry rose from 2.27 per cent in 1987/8, to 3.75 per cent for 1988/9, and to 4.75 per cent for

1989/90. At the time of British Gas' flotation, analysts Hoare Govett noted that '. . . in the last five years it increased . . . profits after tax by nearly 50%'. Increases in profitability were financed by increases in prices, particularly in the tariff market. It was these increased tariffs to which the post-privatization caps were applied.

LIBERALIZATION AND COMPETITION

Although privatization created regulatory bodies with considerable power to impose direct price control, the strategy behind privatization was closely linked to optimism about opening up the utility industries to direct competition. The Littlechild Report of 1983, for example, saw regulation only as a way of 'holding the fort' until competition emerged (and specifically suggested five years as the period after which '. . . the extent and strength of competition should have become more apparent').

In some cases, the potential for additional competition appeared fairly straightforward. As noted above the utility industries had, over time, accrued highly integrated structures in areas of their operations that are not natural monopolies. Electricity generation, for example, had (in England and Wales) been concentrated in the hands of the Central Electricity Generating Board (CEGB). This went well beyond anything suggested by economies of scope or scale, and generation seemed an area into which competition could quickly be introduced by reconstruction of the industry. In the event, while the electricity-supply industry was restructured during its privatization, only a limited break-up of the CEGB (into two large generating companies) was undertaken. This decision, based on an eventually futile desire to include the uneconomical nuclear sector in the flotation, has been widely viewed as a policy failure.

Nearer to the true utility services, the prospects for competition must be of a different sort as the fundamental networks remain natural monopolies. If competition is to be introduced, it must be through new technologies bypassing these networks (for example local telecommunications distribution by wireless rather than cable), by converging technologies which can replicate the utility service as an incremental activity (for example the provision of voice telephony alongside cable television), or by technology that can turn the networks into 'common carrier' facilities (for example better metering allowing several gas companies to share a distribution pipeline).

In practice competition of this sort has, as yet, made very little impact on the residential sector; the overwhelming majority of individual consumers remain dependent on their traditional service providers. Even in telecommunications, where new technology seemed most promising, competition has been slow to develop. Cellular mobile telephone technologies have entered the market, but have remained many times more expensive than conventional telephony and constitute a new product rather than a close competitor to PSTN services. The 'telepoint' services launched in the late 1980s very quickly failed. Although Mercury has been available to both residential and business subscribers, it has targeted the latter group and remains a marginal player in the residential market. A consultation document published in 1992 by OFTEL repeats the sentiment expressed by Professor Littlechild in 1983, in practically identical language: 'once competition is well established, regulation should decrease'. However, the OFTEL document recognizes that '. . . the position at the moment is that in most areas of the country BT has an effective monopoly . . . for local network access and local telephone calls.' In gas, water, and electricity, widespread competition for residential customers appears even further away.

It is, of course, too early to conclude that competition cannot or will not emerge. However, the continuing absence of competition in the domestic sector is not simply a matter of disappointment: it creates a specific set of problems for a regulatory structure which is based, in large part, on the promotion of competition. The combination of privatization and market liberalization had two principal goals. First, it was hoped that the utility industries would become more efficient and that those efficiencies would be shared by consumers and shareholders. Secondly, it was believed that the scope for 'political interference' in the setting of prices would be reduced, and that more 'rational' pricing would emerge.

The structure of the competition that has emerged so far certainly does not ensure (or even facilitate) the accomplishment of either of those goals. While the residential sector has remained dependent on the local network supplier, larger industrial consumers have gained access to alternative suppliers, creating considerable imbalances in the bargaining power of different classes of consumer. Such partial competition might help to drive managerial inefficiencies out of the system but does not guarantee that any of the economies will flow to domestic consumers. Rather than transferring power and resources from producers to consumers, it sets the interests of one group of consumers against those of other groups, compromising the role of the regulator.

The desire to bring prices more closely into line with costs had also, of course, underlain the principle of long-run marginal-cost pricing. As noted above, however, this had failed to provide more than general guidance on the precise level of prices. It continues to appear overoptimistic to believe that pricing decisions can be reduced to a technical exercise. In utility services, cross-subsidization arguments are not simple. A degree of cross-subsidization is unavoidable if tariffs are to be kept manageably simple, and the existence of common or joint costs makes cost allocation between different services or classes of customer imprecise.

Value-based arguments are equally ambiguous. Theoretical considerations of social equity and social efficiency pull in opposite directions, the latter tending to encourage the channelling of benefits towards those customers whose purchasing decisions are most price sensitive, the former tending to direct them towards customers who have least freedom of choice.[1] On top of this, though, a partially competitive market creates an incentive to rebalance charges against those groups of consumers who remain captive purchasers. While it might prove possible to justify this on grounds of social efficiency (Ramsey-pricing arguments), in terms both of its outcome and its motivation such rebalancing is uncomfortably difficult to distinguish from price discrimination.

In the case of British Telecom, it was clear at the time of privatization that some rebalancing—favouring those services of most significance to business users—would take place. The UK was not alone in its starting point; telecommunication network suppliers seem universally to have encouraged widespread take-up of telephone services, and to have set prices to different classes of customer accordingly. This is not necessarily for reasons of social policy; the value of networks increases as more consumers are connected. Nevertheless, the effect had been to distribute price benefits to residential consumers.

The rebalancing of UK telephone charges since privatization has reflected a wider international trend towards cost-based tariffs (an OECD study notes a 'general trend away from value-based tariffing towards a closer cost-orientation').[2] However, the UK (in the period covered by the study) moved more quickly than most other countries. This seems mainly attributable to the declared UK policy of liberalizing telecom markets, which makes cross-subsidies more difficult to sustain. Of the eleven countries examined in the OECD study, the UK was one of

---

[1] While *primarily* redistributive motives have rarely been acknowledged in the tariff-setting of the nationalized industries, society has been willing to accept (or encourage) cross-subsidies to ensure that, for example, rural consumers are not prevented from having a supply of electricity. Sometimes these aims were made explicit, as in the 'social clause' in the North of Scotland Hydro-Electric Board's 1943 statute which required it 'to collaborate in the carrying out of any measures for the economic development and social improvement of the North of Scotland District'. The Board could therefore declare that it was '. . . justly proud of its record in this area . . . Virtually all potential consumers have been connected despite the obvious uneconomic circumstances'. Less dramatically, residential gas tariffs have been adjusted over time so that consumers in the South-West pay the same as those much nearer to the North Sea fields from which UK gas supplies are sourced.

[2] It also reflect changes in technology which have caused long-distance transmission costs to fall more quickly than local distribution costs.

only two in which the 'residential tariff basket' rose in real terms between 1979 and 1988.

Such comparisons are, of course, highly dependent on the period over which they are measured. The OECD report covers the period preceding and immediately following BT's privatization. In subsequent interventions by the regulator, the original freedom to rebalance tariffs has been limited (the Director General explicitly citing equity considerations as a constraint on the speed with which rebalancing can take place). There is now, for example, an 'informal understanding between the Director General and BT that the Median Residential Bill should not rise by an amount greater than the rate of inflation'. OFTEL appear minded to accept further rebalancing of charges, but it is clear that, in doing so, the regulator will need to make delicate distinctions between legitimate competitive behaviour, and illegitimate price discrimination.

In the immediate future it appears that liberalization can only benefit the majority of residential consumers indirectly, by forcing efficiency gains on the incumbent supplier which the regulatory regimes must then ensure are passed through. There is evidence that efficiency gains have been achieved in these industries since privatization, though the so-called 'Thatcher effect' seems also to have improved those industries that have remained in public ownership. It is difficult to partial out the effects of liberalization and privatization from other factors. OECD concluded that '. . . there is little evidence that the processes of rebalancing have speeded up the rate of tariff reductions in real terms. Rather, the main pressure for downward prices is coming from technological change and is common to most of the OECD countries.'

REGULATING QUALITY

Price is, of course, only one dimension of value for money. In competitive markets, consumers can choose between a range of goods and services at different price/quality levels. Although utility industries can be categorized economically as multi-output industries, domestic consumers have been offered a very restricted range of service levels: limited time-of-use tariffs in telephony and electricity supply, a two-tier letter post, no choice at all in gas and water supplies. In the absence of competition, consumers face two further problems. First, it is not clear what level of service it is reasonable to expect at any particular price level. Secondly, there is no direct power to influence the industry's level of quality by changing supplier, or to gain personal redress when things go wrong.

Consumer organizations have long argued that the quality of service of the utilities should be monitored and regulated. At least three stages are needed. First, the standards to which an industry is working need to be set and made public. Secondly, performance needs to be measured and monitored. Thirdly, there should be penalties on industry management for non-performance, and redress for individual consumers who receive less than adequate service.

Such issues were, of course, raised by the NICCs in discussion with the industries long before the privatization programme was introduced. In the absence of powers to require action on the part of the industries, however, the attention given to quality monitoring varied considerably from industry to industry. The need for service-quality indicators was recognized as long ago as the 1978 White Paper on the nationalized industries. While the industries did begin to produce a wide range of financial indicators, however, quality indicators developed much more patchily, even within a single industry. Of 23 national indicators published by the Electricity Council at the time of the industry's privatization, for example, only 4 were primarily concerned with service quality. At the same time the London Electricity Board, in collaboration with its Consultative Council, had begun to report a wide range of service indicators.

It should be noted that the absence of monitoring does not necessarily indicate low quality standards. British Gas, for example, has always tended to perform well in comparative studies of consumer satisfaction, yet it has been one of the most reticent of the industries in publicly stating the standards to which it is working, or achievement against them. The 1982/3 British Gas Annual Report has eight pages of 'performance ratios' and 'key statistics'; none deal with quality of service. A single reference in the text reports that 'Surveys of customers' opinions on work done by British Gas have again confirmed improvement in customer satisfaction.'

Different regulatory structures will have different implications for quality levels. When privatization was being discussed, much attention was given to the Averch Johnson thesis that rate-of-return regulation would create an incentive to overinvest (and, by implication at least, set quality levels too high). Price-cap regulation, on the other hand, creates incentives for industry management to improve profitability by reducing service levels. Although the Littlechild Report makes passing reference to this problem, little attention was given to quality regulation at the time of BT's privatization. Consumer organizations argued strongly for quality regulation during the privatization debates, but this did not appear to be viewed at the time as a significant issue. It quickly became one.

Before privatization, British Telecom had published a comparatively wide range of quality indicators. In 1984–5, following privatization, the company announced that it now considered these to be commercially confidential, and declined to publish them. This forced the Director General of Telecommunications to open the question of quality monitoring. In 1986 OFTEL issued a consultation document on Quality of Service and, later the same year, its own report on service quality. In October 1987, BT resumed publication of quality measures. In the same year, research carried out independently by both the Consumers' Association and the National Consumer Council showed that both service levels and consumer perception of BT had declined. In turn, this raised the issue of quality of service regulation to significance, and led the DG to warn that declines in service quality would be viewed as the equivalent to price increases, and would be taken into account in the revision of the price-control formula.

The Competition and Service (Utilities) Bill, published in 1991, finally recognizes the significance of quality regulation, and retrospectively confers on the various utility regulators specific powers to set, monitor, and enforce quality standards. In fact, all the regulatory bodies have followed OFTEL's lead in concentrating on quality issues. This, in itself, is a demonstration of the wide discretion and the negotiating strength of the regulatory offices.

Monitoring is mainly based on industry-generated data, and progress has been mixed. The Office of Gas Supply noted that 'British Gas did not possess an information base which would have allowed OFGAS to pursue an appropriate analysis'. The Office of Water Services described the systems of monitoring in place in 1989 as 'for some companies . . . woefully inadequate', leading it to publish data which is qualified both by a reliability measure (a reflection of the quality of the data collection), and by accuracy (including a band which is only accurate to within plus or minus one hundred per cent). It should be noted that, while progress in these industries has certainly reflected the strength and determination of the regulatory bodies, comprehensive quality data is also produced by utility industries that have remained in the public sector, for example the Post Office.

GUARANTEED STANDARDS

Even when an industry is achieving high standards of service overall, individual consumers will inevitably experience lapses. During the privatization programme, there has been rapid development of 'Guaranteed Standards' schemes. Under such schemes, consumers receive a fixed-level rebate if they suffer a loss of some specific service. The first post-privatization scheme was negotiated between OFTEL and BT, and announced in March 1988. Similar schemes have since been introduced for water and electricity supplies. Although the post-privatization regulators have been instrumental in spreading and refining these schemes, they are not an invention of the privatization programme itself. Guaranteed standards were first introduced by East Midlands Electricity Board, and by 1989 were in place in eight electricity boards, covering a range of services. Specific details of the existing schemes have been criticized by consumer organizations for their limited scope, for their often sweeping exclusion clauses, for the fact that not all the schemes are automatic (consumers have to make a claim, often within a set period and in writing), and for the restrictive nature of the compensation (often in the form of rebates on future bills, rather than cash). Nevertheless, it seems likely that further development of such schemes will form an important strand in future quality regulation.

COMPLEXITIES OF REGULATING QUALITY

Quality regulation presents some interesting challenges to regulators and consumer organizations; 'quality' is clearly an elusive thing to define and measure (certainly in contrast to a price). Attempting to capture fully the concept of quality in a regulatory system stretches the idea of regulation as a 'market proxy'. The supply of telephone handsets, in which a *de jure* restraint was lifted and the market transformed from monopoly to full-scale competition, provides a contrast.

Until 1981, three private manufacturers produced a standardized range of telephone handsets to strict specifications laid down by the network supplier. These handsets were not of low technical quality, indeed the mechanical construction (i.e. the integrity of the telephone's body) was specified to a high standard, likely to give long life under normal use. A wide range of handsets was already available on international markets and, following deregulation, a large selection quickly became available (by 1985 over one hundred different models). Many of the new phones offered specific benefits from a user's point of view, for example by improved ergonomic design or because they were smaller and lighter than the models previously available (offering specific benefits to some categories of consumer). New technologies allowed new features to be added (re-dial, programmable memories, etc.). At the same time, purely hedonistic choices became available (a much wider range of colour and appearance, for example).

As well as being dramatic in its effects, the deregulation of this sector perhaps illustrates the complexity of *ex post* quality measurement. The wide diversity of choices which emerged is to be expected in a properly active market. Undoubtedly, the overall effect has been to increase consumer welfare—new choices and options became available while the option of renting from BT remained. Many good handsets at good prices have become available. However, not all of the telephones now on sale will be of a higher quality than the limited range formerly provided by the network company. And while it is relatively easy to agree formal measures for the quality of handset construction, it is less easy to devise a measure which accurately captures the added welfare that flows from access to telephones sculpted in the form of Mickey Mouse. It does not follow that consumers will value construction quality more highly than aesthetic features, nor indeed that the majority of consumers would demand handsets made to the high standards of construction demanded by the network provider (and which are therefore heavy and large).

In fully competitive markets, managers have a direct incentive to capture that complexity. Regulated monopolies, by contrast, are likely to take a much more restricted view of quality measurement. Indeed, 'quality information' has sometimes been produced which is of little use as a consumer performance indicator. Both the Post Office and the independent Consumers' Association have for many years produced statistics on letter-delivery performance. Whereas the Consumers' Association measured delivery times as they would be experienced by service users (from time of posting to time of delivery), until 1989 the Post Office timed its letter samples from sorting office to sorting office. As this failed to capture delays between the post-box and the sorting office, or between the delivery office and the home, there could be significant differences between the quality of service reported, and the service actually experienced by consumers.

The method by which data is captured can also be a matter of controversy. Utilities themselves often rely on reports made by their own staff, while consumer organizations normally collect data from users of the service. In some cases, the gap between the two accounts can be considerable. This is particularly true of, for example, broken appointments in home visits. In 1987/8, statistics published by the London Electricity Board suggested that only 2 per cent of home visits were broken by the Board. In a national survey carried out by the Consumers' Association in the same year, 15 per cent of domestic customers who had arranged a home visit from the electricity industry claimed that their appointments had been broken.

Regulatory systems will tend towards measures that are easily quantifiable and can be made statistically reliable, yet these may fail to measure what consumers are mainly interested in. Standards relating to home visits tend to concentrate on the keeping of appointments, rather than the satisfaction with the quality of workmanship, yet survey work suggests that the latter is a significant area of concern to consumers. The Guaranteed Standards Schemes introduced for the water industry cover measurable dimensions of quality such as response times to written complaints. Survey work carried out by the Consumers' Association before privatization showed that more than one in five consumers were dissatisfied with the perceived quality of drinking water; the most common complaints were about poor taste or smell. It seems likely that a competitive company wishing to increase its market share would be more concerned to improve the taste of its product than the time taken to reply to letters, yet issues of this sort are clearly fitted uneasily into a formal regulatory system. OFTEL, for example, has begun to collect its own figures on subscribers' satisfaction with BT service overall, but notes that 'subjective measures need to be treated with caution'. It remains unclear how such measures can be used in the regulatory framework, other than as part of the informal bargaining process.

A further issue arises from the distinction between utility and non-utility services. As noted above, the utilities have often enjoyed *de jure* or *de facto* monopolies in services related to their core business but which do not themselves display natural monopoly characteristics. It is not entirely clear where the boundaries of utility operations should be drawn. The electricity and gas industries, for example, have traditionally conducted their own metering and billing systems. Such activities are very closely bound to the core utility business, but could in principle be separated out. Utility regulatory theory quite correctly concentrates on the pure utility functions. Yet consumer research tends to show that the main problems arise in the quasi-utility services (like metering and billing) or in services that have no utility characteristics (home-wiring, gas-appliance servicing). Further restructuring of the industries might take the most problematic of the services outside the boundaries of utility regulation. It would be optimistic to think that this alone will stop them being problematic.

CONCLUSIONS

To date, the most significant benefit to domestic consumers of privatization has been—ironically perhaps—the establishment of a more powerful, open and logical regulatory regime. By making the profit motive explicit, it has become easier to address than was the case under nationalized ownership.

Competition, by contrast, has so far failed to emerge as a significant force in the domestic sector. Although direct competition continues to be promised, it is still far from clear that the natural monopoly aspects of the utilities can be significantly circumvented. That competitive supply is rapidly becoming available to large industrial users makes regulation more complex, rather than less—the creation of two markets, one competitive, one monopolistic, with significant common costs raises considerable risks of undue discrimination.

Privatization was presented as a policy that would make all consumers better off. The logic of liberalization, though, is that some groups of consumers will do better than others, and indeed some are likely to end up absolutely worse off than they would otherwise have been. If regulatory interventions to promote competition directly disadvantage large groups of consumers, the job of 'selling' such policies will not be easy. Privatization has failed to transform tariff-setting into a purely technical exercise. Under these circumstances, it is easier to remove the politicians from the regulatory process than to remove the politics. Perhaps because of this, in many respects the post-privatization regime has exhibited more continuity with the past than might have been expected. While the nature of the debate has shifted, there is little evidence of a decisive termination of the 'post-war consensus'. Issues of social policy have continued to be debated in the regulatory process, and regulators have been able to use their powers to intervene in the behaviour of the utilities towards problems as diverse as disconnection policy, low-user tariffs, and energy efficiency.

The regulation of service quality, alongside price, has emerged as a major issue (at least compared to the attention it was given when the regulatory regimes were being established). While progress has been made, it has been made at a time when companies in competitive markets have been giving increasing attention to the 'total quality' of their goods and services—the aim being to satisfy consumer requirements rather than to achieve internally generated quality measures. By contrast, quality regulation in the utility field continues to be heavily bounded and narrowly 'rational', concentrating on what can easily be quantified and measured. It remains to be seen how true consumer quality—as perceived by consumers themselves—can be integrated into a regulatory system. It seems likely that this will happen through a process of negotiation, rather than—for example—modification of licence conditions.

Quality regulation itself provides an example of how the newly formed regulatory bodies have succeeded in establishing a locus in areas over which they have no clear statutory powers. This appears, on the whole, to have worked to the advantage of consumers and it is arguable that a certain amount of regulatory vagueness is a good thing. However, regulation is a bargaining process in which the regulated industries still have the greatest interest, and the greatest power. The process of decision-making—for example over price-formula revisions—has been more open than that which it replaced, but the extent and nature of consultation also seems to be largely at the whim of the individual regulator. It is notable, and perhaps regrettable, that there is in the emerging UK system no equivalent to the open hearings of the US regulatory system. These at least ensure that the complex and uncertain business of regulation takes place under the public gaze.

13

What is the Alternative?
Ownership Regulation and the Labour Party

FRANCIS MCGOWAN*

Probably one of the most profound 'achievements' of the UK government's privatization programme has been its impact on the policies of the political opposition, and particularly those of the Labour Party, the subject of this paper.[1] For much of its existence public ownership has been one of the pillars of Labour Party rhetoric and to, some extent, policy (though the latter has been a subject of vigorous internal debate). Over the 1980s, however, in the face of privatization, the Party's commitment to recapturing the public sector (let alone extending its frontiers) has steadily diminished. What was for so many years a contentious issue within the Party as a whole has become a relatively minor issue of principle and an even smaller component of the Party's programme.

Ironically, the ratchet effect which Mrs Thatcher and others associated with Labour in power (that the policies of successive governments would embed socialism ever more deeply in British society) has proved rather easy to reverse. Indeed the ratchet has been rather more effective in the opposite direction: privatization appears to be a much more difficult policy to undo than nationalization, financially, logistically, and politically. Yet, whatever the problems of reversing the programme, the way in which the Labour Party has effectively accepted the new regime is surprising. There have, it is true, been striking revisions in a number

* Lecturer in the School of European Studies, University of Sussex.

The author is grateful for comments on earlier drafts by John Chesshire, Martin Chick, Michael Waterson, and the editors, and to Arne Kaijser for an informed view of Swedish developments. The usual disclaimers apply.

[1] The reason for focusing on Labour is twofold: they are the party most likely to form the core of an alternative government in the UK; and they have had the greater stake in the issue of public ownership, and correspondingly the greatest adjustment in policy to make. The Liberal Democrats have for the most part adopted policies much closer to those of the government (albeit with a much stronger emphasis on competition). Although the article was conceived, researched, and largely written before the result of the 1992 election was known, the issue of how new policies on ownership regulation and competition are dealt with remains important.

of policies (regarding the European Community and nuclear deterrence) and the degree of pragmatism exercised by the leadership and accepted by the membership has astonished supporters and opponents alike. Yet, public ownership has traditionally been a core Party principle. Why has this change taken place and what policies have emerged as substitutes? What are the limitations and the limits of the new policies? This paper seeks to answer these questions. After noting the theory and practice of nationalization in the UK, the paper follows the changes in Labour policy over the 1980s in Party statements and the theoretical debate concerning this decision. It then analyses the remaining commitments in this area and assesses the Party's policies for controlling and regulating privatized industries (particularly the utility industries which have been the core of the Conservative privatization programme).

In considering current policies, it briefly examines how public ownership and privatization have been addressed in countries which have been governed by socialist or social democratic parties over recent years. These include: Germany (where the Social Democratic Party had to reverse a similar commitment in the 1950s); Sweden (where, despite the dominance of the Social Democrats in government over much of the last forty years, a relatively non-interventionist policy on public ownership has prevailed); France (where there was a post-war consensus in favour of public ownership, until the 1980s), and Austral(as)ia (where Labour governments have pursued privatization and deregulation as a matter of policy since the mid-1980s).

On the basis of these reviews of the policy debate in the UK and international experience, the paper identifies some of the issues which have not yet been fully resolved by Labour. In particular it reviews the Party's approach to questions of ownership and control, and regulation and competition. The paper also considers some of the broader constraints on policies towards privately and publicly owned companies (such as the institutional 'legacy' of privatization and emerging European Community policies which impinge upon publicly owned firms) in the 1990s.

THE LABOUR PARTY AND PUBLIC OWNERSHIP

The question of property ownership and the rights and claims of various individuals and collectivities to particular goods and services is not a new one; numerous and diverse forms of ownership have emerged over time, as have the philosophies underpinning them (Katzarov 1964). The debate over public ownership developed in response to the experience of private ownership and the system it supported. Economists, philosophers, and politicians viewed it as a means of correcting market failures either within a specific sector or in the economy as a whole and/or as a means for achieving fundamental economic and social change (Rees 1984).[2] While these objectives implied distinct approaches and priorities for public ownership, they did overlap, particularly regarding the use of public ownership of industries for the pursuit of goals other than the efficient operation of the enterprise in question. Such views have been primarily but not exclusively associated with social democratic or socialist movements. [3]

The relationship of these various perspectives on public ownership to the policies implemented varies widely. In most Western societies, the role of more Utopian strategies for public ownership has been limited in practice, aside from rhetorical invocation. When in power, governments of the Left have adopted rather less ambitious approaches in terms of the scale of public ownership, the nature of management, and the purposes of the policy. A pragmatic approach to public ownership in terms of both its extent and its character has prevailed: for the most part (and barring exceptional cases such as the coal industry) nationalization was used as an instrument of micro- or macro-economic policy rather than for fundamental social change.

The British Labour Party's commitment to public ownership is rooted in just such a mixture of idealism and pragmatism. In the early days of the Party there was considerable interest in extending the principle of social ownership, for both idealistic and efficiency reasons. Even then, however, the idea presented problems for the movement: attempts to push for what was then called socialization of the whole economy were opposed by the Party's leadership. None the less the idea was widely enough accepted to be incorporated into the new Party's constitution. Clause Four, paragraph four stated:

To secure for the producers by hand or brain the full fruits of their industry, and the most equitable distribution thereof that may be possible upon the basis of the common ownership of the means of production and the best obtainable system of popular administration and control of each industry and service.

In the inter-war period, there was considerable debate on the interpretation of that provision. However, such Labour governments as there

---

[2] In the light of the critique of public ownership over recent years, it is interesting to note that a major argument for nationalization was to combat the deterioration of competitive capitalism into monopoly. For some economists of socialism (notably Oskar Lange), where competition was replaced by monopoly, the only guarantee of efficiency and justice was public ownership. See Persky (1991). Such ideas were at work in a less ideological sense in the UK, see Hannah (1990).

[3] Corporatist ideas prevalent in the inter-war period envisaged a strong role for the state as a participant in economic affairs. Equally, less extreme right-wing governments have engaged in programmes of nationalization in many European countries. See King (1973).

were in that period were either too short-lived or too weak to pursue the policy very closely. The main exception in terms of a policy was electricity (where the 1923 Labour government began the process of reform which resulted in the creation of the state-owned National Grid in 1926) and the London Passenger Transport Board proposed by Herbert Morrison in 1931 (the legislation was not passed until 1935). He set out the basis for the subsequent application of nationalization in the Party's policy: while nationalized industries were to be accountable to the public and run in the public interest, organizationally they were constituted as public corporations, mirroring in most respects commercial companies with boards of directors and a conventional management structure (Sloman 1978).

In this period, nationalization became associated with two ideas, improving the efficiency of the sectors in question and to some extent tackling monopoly abuse on the one hand and rather less concretely, using the firms to promote economic development and incorporating them into the planning process on the other. In both senses, therefore, the policy was underpinned by an essentially pragmatic vision, one which was distinct from that implied by the rhetoric. This distinction persisted into the post-war period.

The 1945 victory of the Labour Party was accompanied by a substantial nationalization programme with most of the basic utility industries brought into public ownership, directed to these very goals. The bulk of the programme was uncontroversial. While there was some token resistance from the Conservatives, for the most part the programme was accepted. Many of the industries (such as those in the energy sector) had been the subject of inquiries in the 1930s which called for reorganization and a greater public role. When the Conservatives were re-elected in the 1950s, the only major sectors to be returned to the private sector were the road haulage and steel industries (Pryke 1971; Cairncross 1985).

There was considerable debate within the Labour Party on the extension of nationalization over the 1950s and 1960s. There had been plans to extend public ownership to a number of distribution and processing industries and to establish public competitor companies in sectors where it was felt that private industry was inefficient or inflexible (Lewis 1952). Surprisingly, some of the leadership on the right of the Party such as Gaitskell and Crosland were in favour of greater public participation in this way and through nationalized industry diversification, rather than a major expansion of nationalization *per se* (Crosland 1956). Indeed Gaitskell was active in promoting ideas of competition and market mechanisms in the public and private sectors (Chick 1991). The attempt by the leadership to limit the commitment to a new programme of widespread nationalization provoked a furious debate within the Party at the end of the 1950s. Gaitskell tried to have Clause 4 paragraph 4 removed from the constitution of the Party but failed, outvoted at the Party's annual conference.

Despite this, once re-elected, Labour government policy on ownership actually fell short of what even Gaitskell had argued for: there was no extension of nationalization (beyond renationalizing steel); there was no real attempt to permit diversification; attempts to integrate nationalized industries into the Economic Plan were little more than gestures (though they were used in the elaboration of energy and transport policy). Instead considerable effort was made to improve the efficiency of nationalized industries, while reorganization of economic sectors was promoted by the consolidation of private companies through the Industrial Reorganization Corporation (Hague and Wilkinson 1983).

To some extent, the inaction of the government rekindled moves within the Party to debate how public ownership should be organized. From the late 1960s on there was increasing interest in the idea of a State Holding Corporation building on the IRC, along the lines of the major Italian holding company, the Istituto per la Ricostruzione Industriale.[4] After Labour's defeat in 1970, the problems of the Heath Government[5] and the apparent leftward shift of policy of the Party in opposition, such ideas coincided neatly with the moves to adopt a more 'socialist' economic policy. The Party's 1973 programme included plans for nationalization of 20–25 of the largest UK companies, planning agreements, and the establishment of a National Enterprise Board (NEB) (Hatfield 1978).

In the 1970s, Labour embarked on a modest programme of nationalization largely aimed at reorganizing companies for strategic or social reasons (the former illustrated by the aerospace industry and the latter by the shipbuilding industry) and creating a greater presence in other industries (most notably oil). The programme—which encountered severe difficulties and faced considerable criticism—was, however, seen as falling short of commitments made in the manifesto (a persistent criticism of the time). Other measures focusing on public ownership—such as worker participation and the development of the NEB—were also pursued at a relatively modest pace (Hare 1985). Possibly the most telling example of the lacklustre commitment to public ownership occurred in the wake of the 'IMF crisis' of 1976, when, faced with severe economic difficulties and having to implement a variety of policy reversals, the government had to sell part of the public stake in BP (Dell 1991).

[4] The ideas were developed by Stuart Holland and Richard Pryke. Both authors later shifted their positions. Holland, whose support for holding companies was best expressed in Holland (1972), moved to the left while Pryke reassessed the public sector in the early 1980s (Pryke 1981).

[5] After attempting a radical strategy which had many of the characteristics of the government of 1979, the Conservatives performed a U-turn on economic policy, most vividly illustrated by the nationalization of Rolls Royce.

The economic crisis of 1976 confirmed the gap between the policies sought by the Left of the Party and those which the government was prepared to implement. The previous year, the Left had rallied round the so-called 'Alternative Economic Strategy', a radical blueprint for restructuring the British economy. This envisaged further nationalization as one mechanism for managing a much more planned and inwardly orientated UK economy.[6] Such efforts became less and less relevant to the government, however, and the then domination of Labour by the Right was reflected in the 1979 manifesto which made relatively few commitments on public ownership. It envisaged principally an expansion of 'the work and finance of the National Enterprise Board, using public ownership to sustain and create new jobs' (Labour Party 1979) as well as developing the public banking sector, and increasing the public share of North Sea Oil. On competition issues the manifesto also committed Labour to a strengthening of the Price Commission, merging it with the MMC.

Labour Party policy prior to Thatcher therefore moved in a series of overlapping phases, each of them aligned to a particular aspect of the ideal of public enterprise. Initially, policy was designed to reorganize key infrastructural industries and render them more efficient, fulfilling a remedial role for market failures and protecting the public. A second phase concentrated on competitive public enterprise, mainly as the spur to guiding economic development and the competitiveness of particular sectors. A third phase developed this idea into a preference for state holding companies, with a clear emphasis on using such companies for fostering industrial development with a regional and technological focus. At each stage, the public-sector's development was supposedly co-ordinated with planning, at least in principle, and also with sectoral policies (using large public participation in the fuel and transport sectors to develop energy and transport policies).

However, this rather abstract characterization of policy does not capture the problems which accompanied each aspect of the policy. The actual experience of public ownership and the way in which it was implemented diverged from the ideal. True, the first objective was largely met in the nationalization of the industries containing the natural monopolies and other key industries. However, rarely were they effectively integrated into the planning process (itself a rather weakly applied policy). Instead such initiatives were used for a variety of policy objectives which often contradicted commitments to managerial autonomy and the improvement of the public sector's performance (most of

---

[6] See CSE (1975). While this document admits that 'widespread nationalization is simply not popular' (p. 74), it still called for much deeper commitment to public ownership. More generally there was undoubtedly in the rank and file what the deputy leader later called an 'unthinking attachment of socialists to public ownership' (Hattersley 1987).

the measures to improve the conduct of the nationalized industries were made by Labour governments) (HM Treasury 1967 and 1978).

The second was even less vigorously pursued. The ideal of competitive public enterprises spurring the UK economy into action was never very successful: the IRC experience of using the state to reorganize existing private companies came to be the preferred option. Indeed what appeared to be the norm in the 1970s was the acquisition of uncompetitve private enterprises with the objective of rationalizing them. In practice, however, such companies were generally used to pursue other economic objectives (as in the advance ordering of power plant to maintain employment in the manufacturing industries concerned) (Surrey, Buckley, and Robson 1980). The final objective was only met rather weakly through the NEB's activities in the latter years of the Callaghan government, and its effectiveness is still debated. Some components of the holding company were successful but in many cases they were not.

This mixed record reflected the wide gap between the demands of the Party in opposition (when the more radical ideas had more influence) on the one hand and the actions of the Party when in government on the other. It also reflected a failure to identify objectives for public enterprise to follow, thereby allowing a much broader and *ad hoc* range of special interests to prevail and contributing to the poor performance of the industries in question. The nature of the way in which industries were used reflected a failure of 'planning' not only in the narrow sense of co-ordinating the activities of public enterprise but also in the broader approach to managing the economy.

LABOUR POLICY SINCE 1979

The relatively modest commitments made by the Party during the 1970s, in both manifestos and in government (as distinct from the debate on policy when in opposition), particularly the absence of commitment to using nationalization as a key policy lever, were widely criticized by the Left of the Party. When it was able to dominate decision-making in the immediate period after the election defeat, it sought to incorporate many of these ideas more rigidly into policy. The shift in the balance of power within the Party was reflected in a much more radical economic policy, not least towards the public sector: just as in the early 1970s, major commitments to the transformation of the public sector were adopted.

As the Conservatives' programme of privatization began, the Party initially committed itself to renationalization without compensation and the creation of a Statutory Power which would enable the government to take companies into public ownership (Hodgson 1981). Existing public companies would be permitted to diversify their activities. Many of these commitments found their way into the 1983 manifesto, though some of the more drastic were moderated. Although renationalization was still a commitment, compensation on the basis of purchase prices was now the official line. A number of industrial sectors (including the chemical and pharmaceutical industries) were targeted as ones where the government would take a public stake. In an echo of a previous long standing commitment, the manifesto also indicated that state-owned companies would be able to expand and gain access to private capital markets (Labour Party 1983).

The 1983 defeat was not due to such policies though there are many who have argued that the policies were symptomatic of the broader policy approach rejected by the electorate. Correspondingly they were identified as part of a policy programme which had to be revised. There was an acceptance within a growing section of the Party that the policies were not only becoming less relevant as strategies but were positively harmful electorally. Over the next few years the Party engaged in the first part of a process of reassessment of economic and other policies, with public ownership one issue. Coupled with moves to recover the initiative from the Left in internal policy-making, there was an internal debate over the Party's attitude to the market and the role of the state within it.

In the wider debate on the problems of the Party's economic policy there was an increased emphasis on ideas of consumer power. Though generally directed there was a clear recognition that consumer interests had to be better protected in the public sector. Linked to this was an acceptance that the way in which public industries were organized did little to endear them to the public: 'The largely passive public response to the Conservatives' privatization programme between 1979–85 was a measure of a long-term failure to make socially run institutions sufficiently responsive to public needs' (Smith 1986: 15). How well a more 'user friendly' attitude would have succeeded in protecting public enterprise is debatable: the Conservatives were keen to privatize almost regardless of the relative performance of the industry. Moreover, throughout most of the privatization process there was generally a majority of opinion opposed to privatization but that did not prevent privatizations from taking place or from being oversubscribed. Privatization may have been opposed but the depth of feeling on the matter was never such as to render it a serious obstacle to Conservative policy or a serious source of additional support for Labour. However, regardless of the merits of the argument, the fact that the argument was being made is symptomatic of larger changes in attitude.

The most important of those changes concerned perceptions of the relative balance between state and market in economic management and the interdependence of the British economy with its trading partners (particularly in Europe). In both cases, the most important recognition was that such factors imposed constraints on the scope of policy. Such a view impinged upon the question of ownership, along with the acceptance that previous models of public ownership were deficient (a view which was incidentally probably more prevalent on the left of the Party and in left-wing proposals on public ownership) (Murray 1987). As a result, the case for nationalization weakened and a new attitude to the ownership question began to emerge.

The first publicly promulgated variation of the new policy emerged in the idea of 'social ownership' (an unconscious echo of the debate at the beginning of the century). This policy set out, on the one hand, to redefine the character of industries taken out of public ownership, and on the other, to take public ownership away from its associations with monopolies and 'lame duck' industries. In this latter respect it paralleled interventions of the sort pioneered by some local authorities (the best known being the Greater London Enterprise Board).

On the issue of renationalizing privatized companies, the opposition sought to adopt what it considered to be a less threatening policy. Announced at the 1986 Party conference the aim of this policy ('social ownership') involved a redefinition of what was regarded as a publicly owned company and created a special category of companies from those industries which had been privatized. A key part of the policy was that private shares in the privatized industries such as BG and BT would be converted into non-voting securities which could be sold. The proposal mirrored other Labour policies of the time which sought to redefine historically controversial policy proposals in a less controversial form (for example proposals for a National Investment Bank marked a major shift away from the Party's previous commitment to exchange controls). The idea of extending the public sector into other areas of the economy was not completely dead but it did not merit much attention. Instead, as the progress of privatization continued, the policy on ownership became an increasingly reactive one. In the 1987 manifesto, the principal commitments were in the area of social ownership, for utilities and, echoing the role of the NEB, high-tech industries. (Labour Party 1987).

The defeat in 1987 prompted a more formal and wide-ranging policy review during which the Party's approach to ownership was further diluted. Arguably, the period immediately following the election was the time when Labour policy appeared to move closest to embracing the market. Initially, members of the Shadow Cabinet came close to accepting the logic of popular capitalism (primarily over the issue of share ownership). However, as the formal Policy Review Process began, it was clear that the acceptance of the market was still hesitant. In the lead report initiating the debate, a rather critical view of competition policy and regulation emerged:

Consumers expect economic efficiency to mean that they should be well served. But just as market competition can enhance service to the consumer, so the control of monopolies over their market can diminish the quality of goods and range of services available. (Labour Party 1988)

The implication of the report was that consumers should not be subject to the whims of monopolies abusing their market power. To what extent this goal was to be met by regulating monopolies or enhancing competition was not clear, however. On the privatized companies/utilities the report indicated continued interest in the idea of redefining them as 'public interest' companies which would be set targets of performance to be enforced and monitored by the regulatory agencies. More evidence of the consumer orientation came in the document's treatment of ownership *per se*: 'We must be ready to recognize and remedy deficiencies such as inadequate attention to consumer interest and to workforce participation that in the past have characterized the Morrisonian form of public ownership' (Labour Party 1988: 5). It also noted that the commitment implied by Clause Four had been defined too narrowly in the past, citing Sweden as a place where public ownership did not extend very far. However, while there was a recognition of the problem of monopoly there was no clear indication of how tackling that problem would be integrated into overall policy, and certainly no attempt to criticize the Conservatives for being insufficiently pro-competitive.

The thrust of the review began the move away from wholesale renationalization as well as from any major intervention in the nature of the privatized firms. This was probably because of the political and financial costs of renationalization rather than because of any great acceptance of the superiority of private ownership. Certainly, over those years the task of renationalization grew with every privatization and, while Labour spokesmen opposed each measure, they became increasingly reluctant to commit themselves to reversing them.

These views were if anything reinforced by the consultation process. In drawing together opinion the Party came to the view that while market failures existed and needed government to rectify them, elsewhere markets and private ownership should prevail (Labour Party 1990). In terms of the privatized industries, the Party's main objective was to establish a Consumers' Protection Commission (CPC) to cover all utilities (public and private), apparently bringing together and strengthening existing regulatory bodies (Labour Party 1990: 17). The CPC would be responsible for protecting consumer rights and monitoring utility performance with powers to institute enquiries into pricing, service quality, and other issues of public interest. There would also be a strengthened Select Committee to look at these issues.

This apparent emphasis on regulation was mirrored by reduced commitments to renationalization. On water, the document noted that 'in the light of the experience of the more effective regulation of the industry we shall determine the best way of restoring public ownership', indicating that responsibility might be returned to local government. A fair price would be paid in compensation. On electricity, the document argued that the new system was incoherent and expensive: 'there is neither effective competition nor any organization responsible for security of supply. In order that government can play the necessary strategic role in the industry we will take control of the National Grid and give it responsibility for maintaining security of supply and the powers to do so.' There would also be a return to public ownership of BT through a purchase of shares to 51 per cent (though this was premissed on the then public stake of 49 per cent being maintained).

In areas related to privatization, the Party made a clear commitment in some areas, less clear in others. The policy of compulsory tendering for local authority services would be abandoned and be replaced with a looser contractual framework for maintaining service quality within the public sector. On home ownership, there would be no attempt to reverse (or even prevent) the council house sales programme but there would be an extension of the right to buy for private tenants (and presumably local authorities would be given the freedom to use the proceeds from such sales to build new houses).

The Labour Party has to some extent gone along with the milder rhetoric of the 1980s on the need to promote consumer interests. In the field of education and health, Labour spokesmen at least initially were keen to argue that the government was stealing their ideas, though subsequently they have been quite happy to let the government take the credit for the consequences of those policies. A similar development has accompanied the Citizens' Charter where the opposition was apparently developing ideas of a contract between public services and the public long before the Conservatives put forward their proposals in 1991 (Labour Party 1991). In all of these cases, the importance of the consumer aspect has not been reflected in the embracing of market solutions to those problems, however. Indeed, more recently, it has positively opposed the application of such solutions in these sectors.

Similarly the Party has rejected (though with less vehemence) the use of such mechanisms as the dominant strand of policies in critical sectors. Clearly, overall industrial policy diverges strongly from current policies, but in specific industries the differences from the Conservatives are also marked. The reliance on market mechanisms in areas such as energy and transport would be reversed. While the focus of policy would not be the companies themselves, the types of sectoral policies pursued would inevitably act as a constraint on their conduct. The document emphasized the need to develop policies in the infrastructure industries of transport, telecommunications, and energy and justified these on the grounds of regional development, industrial innovation, and environmental protection (such as in the areas of energy efficiency, increased rail transport, and a national fibre optic network).

Labour's programme as outlined in the recent manifesto (Labour 1992) reflected many of these ideas, although the document's overall vagueness indicated even more equivocation about commitments. Its main concrete proposals were to renationalize the National Grid Company which would then be given new duties and powers (which would be used to encourage domestic coal supplies). On water, the only other target for renationalization, the manifesto identifies it as a 'priority for return to public control'. Regulation would be overseen by a CPC to cover all utilities (implying that the existing regulatory agencies would be maintained). There would also be a Consumers' Charter (covering all goods and services) and a Quality Commission (replacing and building on the Audit Commission) to monitor local authority services. There is however no mention of competition policy, though during the campaign it was clear that the Party's main concern was with mergers policy.

The manifesto marked a near total abandonment of the ideas espoused in the early 1980s (though even at the height of the Left's power the programme was never as radical as the Party's opponents claimed). A rather ambiguous but broadly accepting attitude towards the market had been adopted. As it has reined in its preparedness not only to expand the public sector but also to recapture it, the emphasis in policy has shifted from ownership to control, using a mixture of partial ownership and sectoral policies to achieve the goals of nationalization (Waterson 1990). Since the election the Party's policy has if anything weakened further, with many in the party leadership calling for the abandonment of the Clause Four commitment.

Other Countries

How far is the new Labour policy in line with its equivalents in other countries? How have other socialist or social democratic governments addressed the ownership issue? Because of the relative novelty of privatization, only a couple of governments have had to address that issue directly. Instead, the questions facing left-of-centre governments has been how far to extend the scope of the public sector and what sort of relationship would exist between the government and public enterprises? On these issues, the approaches of these governments are instructive in so far as they give a flavour of the diversity of responses which governments are able to make to the ownership issue. In this section we note some of those approaches.

Germany

In some ways the German experience offers the closest historical parallel to the process which the Labour Party has had to undergo. The Social Democrats had a record of commitment to social ownership dating back probably as far back as, if not further than, the Labour Party.

After the Second World War, both the Social Democrats (and the Christian Democrats) were committed to a large programme of nationalization (Maunder 1979; Hardach 1980). However, over time this commitment was undermined by the success of the Christian Democrats' actual policy of building the Social Market Economy (a policy which even involved a limited privatization programme). In response, the Social Democrats abandoned their commitment to nationalization at the party congress in 1959. When the SPD re-entered government, extending the scope of the public sector was not a priority.

Since then the Social Democrats have been able to ignore the issue of ownership at the Federal or for the most part at the *Land* level (though here they have pursued active industrial policies). They have held to the consensus on issues of ownership and of regulation. Overall they have been hostile to any idea of dismantling the regulatory structure which protects German industry. In large part their hostility is shared by the Christian Democrats who pursued a rather limp programme of regulatory reform and privatization prior to unification and have scarcely exploited the sea change of integrating the East as an opportunity for radical reform of German industrial organization.[7]

Sweden

The Swedish case is probably the best known example of a 'socialist' country. Ruled by a Social Democrat government for most of the last fifty years, the country has developed a wide-ranging public sector (Verney 1959). However, state ownership has not been a major component of that system, and where it exists, it is generally at one remove from government. Many services are owned at the local level and often take the form of private companies as well as public agencies. One novel aspect of the Swedish experience is that some of the natural monopoly industries have been structured in a more competitive way than elsewhere in Europe (there is a form of a competitive spot market for bulk electricity supplies while track and train authorities have been introduced in the railway sector).

[7] This was despite the opinion of the German *Kartellamt* in a number of industries. On the contrast between different aspects of German policy towards regulation, see Cowling and Tomann (1990).

Why did Social Democrat-led governments not pursue public owner-ship during their time in power? Mainly because the Socialists have regarded public ownership as a rather bureaucratic manifestation of socialism, one which could prove inefficient and wasteful. They have also had to operate within coalition governments and have seen nation-alization is an unpopular programme (Milner 1989). How far the former served as a rationale for the constraints imposed by the latter is difficult to say. What was interesting was that the only non-Socialist government in the period took a number of heavy industries into public ownership and that the successor Social Democrat government engaged in a much more rigorous restructuring of them. A form of indirect public owner-ship was proposed in the 1970s in the plans for wage-earner funds. These were a mixture of corporate taxation paid into special funds whose proceeds were allocated to the work-force of the company. When the proposals were first made it was intended that over time, this mech-anism would ultimately lead to worker ownership of Swedish industry. In practice the programme proved rather unpopular and was applied rather half-heartedly (Linton 1985).

As in Germany, the support of the Social Democrats for competition policies has been rather lukewarm (even though, in some respects, many sectors are already organized quasi-competitively). Concern over the efficiency of the major public industries appeared to prompt a review of policy, involving partial privatizations and some deregulation of indus-tries by the Social Democrats (a policy extended by the subsequent centre-right government). This looks even more likely to happen follow-ing their defeat in the recent election.

France

There has been a widely held perception in the UK that public owner-ship in France has always been closely associated with planning. For many in the Labour Party it has been a model for the integration of these two policies. However, while it is arguable that the two elements were closely integrated in the years following the war, subsequent experience suggests that they have not been closely co-ordinated. Indeed the Nora Report and the establishment of *Contrats de Programmes* were partly designed to allow greater autonomy to the state enterprises at the same time as bringing them together strategically (Estrin and Holmes 1983).

By comparison with the UK, the policy of public ownership was arguably more closely linked into the system of economic planning (Shonfield 1965; Hall 1986); though the great nationalizations of the UK and France were introduced after the war as part of a wider programme of reconstruction, that programme was more coherent in France than in the UK and was in any case sustained more consistently in the years that followed (though with what success is debatable). One reason for this may be the framework of the *Contrats de Programme*, which has allowed greater autonomy at the same time as some control on the operations of firms has meant that performance of the nationalized industries has been less of an issue in France than in the UK (Parris, Pestieau, and Saynor 1987).

Over the 1980s the relatively bipartisan character of French policy towards nationalization crumbled, first in the wake of the Socialist election victory of 1981 (when a major expansion of public ownership was carried out (Hayward 1986)) and then in the Chirac government of 1986 when a privatization programme was introduced. When returned to power in 1988, the Socialists elaborated what was known as the 'ni-ni' policy (neither nationalization nor privatization) and public ownership is unlikely to rank very high in future policy, even though the current right-wing government has embarked on another programme of privatization.

The outcome of this most recent policy switch is unlikely to undermine the determination of the Socialists (and other mainstream French political parties) to use public-sector companies as the leading edges in economic development. It appears unlikely that competition policy will play any significant role in policy.

Australia/New Zealand

Perhaps the most surprising developments on public ownership under socialist parties have come about in Australasia. Over the 1980s, the Labour governments of both countries developed tough supply-side economic policies, including a commitment to reforming publicly owned enterprises and regulated sectors. In both cases, the policies appeared motivated by an attempt to recover national competitiveness in the context of the rapid development of the Pacific region.

In New Zealand, the government of David Lange was considerably more in favour of free market than that of its predecessor, the ostensibly conservative National Party. In the field of public ownership it implemented policies of 'corporatization' (a means of putting relations between state enterprises and government on a more contractual and arm's-length basis), privatization, and deregulation. In the electricity industry, the government separated out the various elements of the industry and opened the sector to competition. In air transport and telecommunications, services were liberalized and the state companies were sold off (Bollard and Buckle 1987; Easton 1989).

In Australia, a similar policy has been adopted, though the pace has been rather different. Under the former chancellor Paul Keating, the primary focus was on macro-economic policies at first, with trade liberalization and micro-economic reform following. The latter has seen the proposed privatization of the domestic and international airlines and the deregulation of inter-state services, the proposed liberalization of telecommunications (with the sell-off of the second carrier) and attempts to open up markets between states of the Commonwealth (the degree of autonomy at this level and the limits of Commonwealth government authority have been a severe constraint on how far and how fast reform can go).

In both countries, the policies were justified as part of a much wider programme whose rationale turned on increasing the competitiveness of the country though they also appeared designed to wrong foot opposition parties. In both countries the policy shifts have created severe problems for the parties themselves: in the case of Australia, the influence of the party platform on actual policies has been a constraint on the pace of change. To balance this, there has been a coincidence of interest between the Labour reformists and branches of the civil service. In the case of Australia, the most important elements of the latter were the Treasury and the Industry Commission, an agency which historically was an anti-protectionist sounding board for policy and more recently has reviewed regulatory systems within the country (Mauldon 1988; Pusey 1991).

Although each of these examples illustrates very divergent approaches to the issue of public ownership, two factors stand out. The first is the relative unimportance attached to expanding the scope of ownership; if anything, interest appears to be moving in the other direction. The second factor is the much less clear record on regulatory reform: some countries have pursued this objective quite enthusiastically, some have begun to consider it, and others appear to reject any role for it.

LABOUR, OWNERSHIP, AND REGULATION IN THE 1990S

It is clear that Labour is not alone in reassessing its policy on public ownership: in a number of countries, parties of the Left are either in the throes of revising their own policies in the area or have made their decisions many years ago. For most of those countries, however, their approach appears to have been more coherently constructed than in the UK: even if there remain unresolved issues, the boundaries of policy are clearer than in the case of Labour. Indeed, there appear to be many factors insufficiently developed or considered in the Labour Party's approach, even if it is viewed in isolation from international comparisons (though on the issue of regulatory policy, the Labour Party's lack of focus is not unusual). In this section we note some of those shortcomings: in particular the unresolved tension between sectoral policies involving privatized industries and competition policy and, by extension, the possible tension between these policies and the approach adopted by the Commission of the European Community in many of these sectors.

One of the most interesting and potentially conflictual aspects of the Labour Party's programme is the commitment to sectoral policies (though these have been turned down in the manifesto). The rationale for such policies is curious. It might be regarded as a recognition of the failure of past efforts at generalized planning. When in government, the formal planning process (both macro and micro) was rather weak and the co-ordination of nationalized industries within it even weaker. Perhaps, armed with a less ambitious 'planning' agenda and a more arm's-length relationship with privatized firms, there is a hope that sectoral strategies will work better than in the past. Yet it is worth recalling that possibly the most important element of policy in the past has been the way in which specific industries were used to pursue more general policy objectives, either as a means of controlling inflation or for protecting employment. Formal policies often existed, but they were normally secondary to much broader objectives and more immediate expedients.

It will be a challenge to develop sectoral policies which are able to resist the pressures of day-to-day government. Even more difficult will be negotiating with the privatized industries themselves, for a Labour government would effectively be reinventing such policies after a long hiatus of non-policy under the Conservatives. Of course, the Conservatives were not unwilling to lean on public-sector companies for similar reasons to those of previous regimes. They retained the informal *de facto* policy towards such industries at the same time as they espoused the rejection of policy in favour of market mechanisms. Yet, while there were a number of expedient decisions which arguably compromised the Conservatives' stated objectives of competition, in the wake of privatization, competition is being promoted by the regulatory authorities.

Now the Labour Party seeks to revive policies at the sectoral level, using the industries—whether public or private—to those ends. Given the Party's criticisms of industries such as the ESI, the implication is that these new policies will replace the existing emphasis on market forces. Just how far the Party will be able to take issues such as environmental protection, regional development, or innovation support remains to be seen. In certain cases they appear to be confident that a mixture of reinstating a strategic share in these industries and developing a well defined agenda for policy will be enough to ensure the compliance of privatized companies.

In energy, for example, the Party intended that consolidating regulatory responsibilities, creating new agencies for renewables and energy efficiency, and directly intervening in key energy markets, would be

enough to secure the agreement of the privatized energy industries to
their energy policy. However, it is not at all clear that such policies
would have been effective in dealing with the problems which emerged
at the end of 1992. The Conservative government's effective continuation of the existing market-based approach different solution would not
have been an option for a Labour government, but it is difficult to see
what a different government could have done without risking legal
action. Similarly, attempts to use privatized industries for industrial policy purposes (as the plan for a national fibre optic grid implied) may be
difficult to pursue.[8] Privatized industries operating within a competitive
market framework are likely to be difficult to control in the same ways
as nationalized industries operating in protected markets.

   Yet it is not at all clear that the Party has considered these issues in
any great depth. Indeed, the whole issue of how economic policies and
competition policy are reconciled has not received much attention. This
is unfortunate since, for a number of reasons, the competitive regimes
which have emerged in a number of sectors may not be so easily incorporated into current Party policy as the *fait accompli* of privatization itself
has been. While there are precedents for Labour adopting competition-
orientated policies (notably in the 1950s) such considerations, for all the
rhetoric concerning the promotion of consumer interests, have not been
very high in discussions of privatized sectors.

   The issue of regulation raises similar questions about Labour's policy.
The main thrust of Labour's regulatory policy appears to be to create an
overarching institution, underpinned by greater Parliamentary scrutiny.
The emphasis of the modest proposals made so far is that the delibera-
tions of these agencies will focus on questions of price and quality (and
so far they seem prepared to permit those institutions to remain independent).[9] These could potentially involve the development of a sophisticated system of incentive regulation, though it is not clear whether
such a possibility is part of Labour's strategy. The consequences of cen-
tralizing all regulatory responsibility in a single agency is difficult to
assess: on the one hand it may provide some additional resources and
may counter risks of capture; on the other it could make capture more
likely. However, the experience of the smaller separate agencies has
been relatively positive: it may be that small size and the separate identities of the regulators may be a good guard against capture (Waterson
1990 and 1991).

   However the way in which the issue of regulation has been developed

   [8] This is in any case a policy which many Labour supporters have criticized: Garnham
(1990).
   [9] Much will however depend on the remit of the CPC. There may be a risk that the regulatory agency will be expected to pursue other aspects of policy beyond those of price and
quality monitoring. If so, there may be difficult conflicts of objectives. See Schmalansee
(1980) on the US experience of this.

does not take into account questions of competition policy. Clearly questions of price and quality are a very large part of the competition issue. However, the thrust of Labour Party analysis has been to treat these issues rather narrowly, effectively ignoring their role in regulating competition though clearly the former are one part of that. It would be wrong to argue that the British utility sector is now characterized by highly competitive and decentralized structures. The expediency with which all privatizations were carried out has meant the process of introducing competition would always be a struggle to achieve. Even so, some surprising achievements have taken place. In the telecoms, gas, and electricity sectors (and to a lesser extent transportation) there are now semi-competitive structures in place. However, we have not heard how these are to be tackled by a Labour government.

In the last Labour administration, there were occasional disputes between the government and challengers to specific regulatory policies (notably the case of Laker and air transport policy). How will a Labour government cope with a cluster of such industries and the difficult issues raised by, for example, the incursion of privatized regional electricity companies into the regional gas-supply market?

Much will depend on how deep the Party's acceptance of the marketplace goes. There have been some attempts to interest Labour in a more pro-competitive strategy. Some argued that in the wake of monopolistic privatizations in the case of BG, and to a lesser extent BT and BA, the Labour Party should take the initiative and propose a more competitive structure for the industries in question (e.g. greater regional decentralization and competition in telecoms), perhaps using public ownership as the framework for a variety of competitive experiments (Leadbeater 1986). However, such views have scarcely found favour with the leadership or the rank and file of the Party: in many ways, and despite the debates of recent years about consumer interests, the Party remains too closely identified with 'producer' interests. It is likely that, as sectoral policies develop and conflict with competition considerations, the former will prevail (at least until challenged in the courts).

Moreover, there is another factor which may also militate against such conduct. Even if through a mixture of bribes and threats, a Labour government were able to impose its own policy agenda on these industries, the extent to which that agenda would be compatible with broader obligations is debatable. It is clear that in a number of sectors where the UK has been to the fore of reforming (primarily through privatization and subsequently through regulation), the EC Commission has also been developing policies which may have similar consequences to those currently in operation in the UK.

The Community's emerging programme for the utility industries is one which emphasizes competition, involving the separating-out of the competitive from the monopolistic aspects of the industry, the establishment of transparent accounting procedures, limits on government intervention, etc. The scope for intervention in sectoral matters through other mechanisms such as procurement would also be constrained by EC commitments: EC rules on the purchasing of equipment for the major utilities, or even services for local authorities may be difficult to reconcile with any attempt by Labour to use procurement for 'pro-active' industrial or social policy objectives (Geroski 1989). More specifically, how would a Labour government be able to discourage the use of gas in power generation now that EC Policies have rescinded any restrictions in this area? It would be wrong to suggest that the thrust of Community policies is incompatible with all Labour's plans (the recent positive attitude of the Commission to further subsidizing of the coal industry would sit quite comfortably with Labour attempts to support the UK coal industry).

Curiously enough, policy towards the Community has been an area where the Party has taken as great a step as in the case of ownership. The most recent policy statements identify interdependence and the need to work within Community rules. Moreover in some respects (such as mergers) Labour's policy on competition appears to be relatively limited and does appear to recognize that a deciding role will be played by the Commission.[10] Whether this acquiescence will extend to its approach towards competition in privatized utility industries is not clear, particularly if as seems likely those policies will limit the extent to which publicly or privately owned firms could be used to support aspects of domestic policy.

If a Labour government were to take power, these rules would still exist. Indeed if anything they would be becoming tougher. Such policies imply an arm's-length relationship with the industries, with clear rules on regulation and transparency. They would entail governments denying themselves the option of intervention.

Indeed it may be that what has happened in the UK in terms of the pursuit of deregulation and ownership changes may be a sign of things to come elsewhere in the Community. Although strictly speaking forbidden from ruling on ownership issues, the EC's programme may actually be taking state enterprises to the limit of their usefulness. The implication of current EC initiatives is that utility-type industries should be operated competitively and that any distortions arising from ownership be removed. In many respects, therefore, the direction of Community policy is more in line with the efforts of the Conservatives to liberalize markets, policies which Labour may try to reverse.

[10] Though some that are sympathetic to the Labour Party have suggested that this acceptance of Brussels role would be unsustainable: conflicts would almost inevitably emerge. See Cowling and Sawyer (1990).

CONCLUSION

There has then been a major shift in Labour Party policy on ownership. The extent of that shift was made clearest when the Labour leader announced that nationalization was effectively a dead issue. What is at first sight surprising about the scope of the shift is that it has come from the Party when in opposition, traditionally a period when the Party has been more left wing in its policies. This change was of course part of a wider shift in policies reflecting the success of Thatcherism and the emergence of the then Liberal–Social Democratic alliance in British politics. The former had the effect of shifting the balance of British economic policy (and correspondingly the middle ground) to the right; the latter presented the threat of another party willing to fill that middle ground. For the leadership of the Party moreover, the sheer financial, logistical, and political cost of renationalization became steadily greater and greater. Rather as in the council house sales process, reversing the policy would have been too controversial and damaging as well as costly and difficult.

While the experience of a number of election defeats prompted a widespread review of policy (both formally and informally), there was in the case of public ownership probably a wider disillusionment with existing models. Morrisonian nationalization was regarded as over-centralized, inflexible, and unresponsive to consumer preferences. This view was not only held by the leadership and their advisers but also by a number of theoreticians on the Left of the Party (whose influence probably extended beyond their own acolytes). They pointed to more decentralized forms of state participation in the economy as models for future public ownership (though the basis for such experiments was debatable). Increasingly ideas of pluralistic structures in the economy came to the fore, arguably weaker than the old ideas of 'competitive public enterprises'. Arguably, however, the retreat from Morrisonian principles means a retreat from nationalization *per se*. Whatever the faults of the Morrisonian model, it did at least have the advantage of being implementable: more decentralized forms of ownership have proved more difficult to pursue effectively.

The shift in Labour policy on the question of public ownership has been the most surprising aspect of the new pragmatism (or opportunism) which has swept through the Party since 1983. It is a rather perverse tribute to the policy agenda of privatization that the opposition to it should have crumbled so drastically. Nor is the British Labour Party alone. Some socialist parties have always been less enthusiastic about public ownership and many others are currently adapting their policies to adjust to what appears to be a new orthodoxy.

Privatization has shaped a new consensus, which in a sense reflects

the old consensus surrounding the nationalized sector. In earlier governments, the development of the public enterprise was not unique to any
phase of economic policy-making in the UK. Governments of both parties presided over its expansion even though there have been real differences in their attitudes towards it. In terms of rhetoric Conservative
governments opposed nationalization while Labour governments supported it, yet in practice the situation was less clear. The first major state
corporations (such as the Central Electricity Board) were created by
Conservative governments to address market failures, while even earlier, Conservative politicians presided over local interventions in the economy. As a rule of thumb it is possible to say that while Labour
promoted public ownership, the Conservatives did relatively little to roll
it back. Now the Conservatives promote privatization while Labour
does relatively little to reverse it.

For the Labour Party itself the policy shift has been relatively untrau-
matic. Though there have been some, particularly on the left, who have
criticized the commitment to renationalization (in the same way as they
criticized the lack of commitment to extend public ownership in previous decades), most have recognized the difficulties in maintaining the
policy. A few have applauded the shift. For them, nationalization was an
issue which was blown out of all proportion to its importance in policy
terms (Pimlott 1987). Privatization has exposed the dilemma for all sections of the Labour Party: is ownership important or not? As has been
pointed out (Cobham 1987), if the debate on privatization has shown
that ownership does not necessarily matter to the performance of the
company, then why should such companies be renationalized? It also
implies that we ignore the particularly difficult issues which surround
privatizations of monopoly industries (or the monopoly components of
those industries) where some evidence suggests that public and private
ownership have been equally efficient.

In many ways the most powerful political element of the opposition's
strategy towards the Conservative government's policy was the dubious
conduct of many privatizations, which were implemented with scarcely
any regard to questions of equity. From that point of view, however,
bygones are bygones: the wrong done could not be effectively reversed
except at great cost nor could it be revived as a political weapon except
as part of a broader catalogue of misdeeds invoked rhetorically. Even if
the Labour Party were to address these problems by returning to public
ownership segments of industries on equity and even performance
grounds, it would hard to recreate the industries as they were, especially
after a further four or five years' operation of the new structures. The
development of competitive structures in many of these industries
would be difficult to dismantle at a UK level and would fly in the face of
initiatives being taken at a Community level.

Moreover these constraints apply not only to the question of ownership but also that of control. Some have argued that privatization and the attendant regulatory system has left a more defined (if smaller) space for governments to develop policy. However, it is not clear how a Labour government would have been able to conduct policies which did not test the boundaries of that space (for example restricting gas use in power generation). Perhaps it could have redefined the space by appointing 'sympathetic' regulators. Such a move would, however, undermine the independence of these agencies and could be politically counterproductive. Another possibility would be to strike a bargain with major players in the newly privatized industries; one could envisage a revision of the regulatory framework—perhaps away from competition—in exchange for acts of 'corporate citizenship' (such as increased consumption of locally produced coal or developing a fibre optic network, presumably both on a cost-plus basis). Such moves would, however, risk alienating regulators, consumer groups, and new entrants.

The Labour Party has accepted the reality of privatization; any future Labour government will have to bring forward new policies to replace those which hinged on public ownership and which can address the issue of control of privatized companies. There is an urgent need to consider how such policies will interact with the new competitive regimes in place in many of these industries and which will be even more entrenched by the time of the next election. Such a consideration is implicit in many of the debates on the consumer voice in socialism and on the role of regulation, though barring one or two exceptions, it has not been to the fore in Party statements. The result of the election means that the unresolved issues in Labour's policy will not now manifest themselves in the near future. This gives the Party the opportunity to consider further its policy on ownership competition and regulation as part of its efforts to win next time.

References

Bollard, A., and Buckle, R. (1987), *Economic liberalism in New Zealand*, Wellington: Allen & Unwin.

Cairncross, A. (1985), *Years of Recovery*, London: Methuen .

Chick, M. (1991), 'Competition, competitiveness and nationalisation 1945–51', in G. Jones, and M. Kirby (eds.), *Competitiveness and the State: Government and Business in Twentieth-Century Britain*, Manchester: Manchester University Press.

Cobham, D. (1987), 'There is no alternative', *New Statesman*, **113/2912**, 15.

Conference of Socialist Economists (1980), *The Alternative Economic Strategy*, London: CSE.

Cowling, K., and Sugden, R. (1990), *A New Economic Policy for Britain*: *Essays on the Development of Industry*, Manchester: Manchester University Press.

—— and Sawyer, M. (1990), 'Mergers and Monopoly Policy', in Cowling and Sugden, *New Economic Policy for Britain*.

—— and Tomann, H. (1990), *Industrial Policy after 1992*, London: Anglo-German Foundation.

Crosland, C. A. R. (1956), *The Future of Socialism*, London: Cape.

Dell, E. (1991), *A Hard Pounding*: *Political and Economic Crisis, 1974–6*, Oxford: Oxford University Press.

Easton, B. (1989), *The Making of Rogernomics*, Auckland: Auckland University Press.

Estrin, S., and Holmes, P. (1983), *French Planning in Theory and in Practice*, London: Allen & Unwin.

Forbes, I. (1986) (ed.), *Market Socialism—Whose Choice?*, Fabian Tract no. 516, London: Fabian Society.

Garnham, N. (1990), *Telecommunications Policy for the UK*: *A Policy for the 1990s*, Fabian Discussion Paper no. 1, London: Fabian Society.

Geroski, P. (1990), 'Procurement as a tool of industrial policy', *International Journal of Applied Economics*, 4/2, 182–98.

HM Treasury (1967), *Nationalised industries*: *A Review of Economic and Financial Objectives*, Cmnd 3437, London: HMSO.

—— (1978), *The Nationalised Industries*, Cmnd 7131, London: HMSO.

Hague, D., and Wilkinson, G. (1983), *The IRC*: *An Experiment in Industrial Intervention*, London: Allen & Unwin.

Hall, P. (1986), *Governing the Economy*, Cambridge: Polity .

Hannah, L. (1990), 'Economic ideas and government policy on industrial organization in Britain since 1945', in M. O. Furner and B. Supple (eds.), *The State and Economic Knowledge*, Cambridge: Cambridge University Press.

Hardach, P. (1960), *The Political Economy of Germany in the Twentieth Century*, Berkeley, Calif.: University of California Press.

Hare, P. (1985), *Planning the British Economy*, London: Macmillan.

Hatfield, M. (1978), *The House the Left Built*, London: Gollancz.

Hattersley, R. (1987), *Choose Freedom*, London: Michael Joseph.

Hayward, J. (1986), *The State and the Market Economy*, Brighton: Wheatsheaf.

Hodgson, G. (1981), *Labour at the Crossroads*, London: Robertson.

Holland, S. (1972), *The State as Entrepreneur*, London: Weidenfeld.

Katzarov, K. (1964), *The Theory of Nationalisation*, The Hague: Nijhoff.

King, A. (1973), 'Ideas, institutions and the policies of governments', *British Journal of Political Science*, 3/3–4, 291–315, 409–24.

Labour Party (1979), *The Labour Way is the Better Way* (election manifesto).

—— (1983), *The New Hope for Britain* (election manifesto).

—— (1987), *Britain Will Win* (election manifesto).

—— (1988), *Social Justice and Economic Efficiency*, London: Labour Party.

—— (1990), *Looking to the Future*: *A Dynamic Economy and a Decent Society Strong in Europe*, London: Labour Party.

—— (1991), *Citizen's Charter*, London: Labour Party.

—— (1992), *It's Time to Get Britain Working Again* (election manifesto).

Leadbeater, C. (1986), 'Social ownership has to put the customer first', *New Statesman*, **112/2898** (10 Oct.), 21.

Lewis, B. (1952), *British Planning and Nationalization*, New York: 20th Century Fund.

Linton, M. (1985), *The Swedish Road to Socialism*, Fabian Tract no. 503, London: Fabian Society.

Mauldon, R. G. (1988), 'Industry Policy, Tariffs and Deregulation', in I. C. Marsh (ed.) *Australia can Compete*, Melbourne: Longman Cheshire.

Maunder, P. (1979) (ed.), *Government Intervention in the Developed Economy*, London: Croom Helm.

Milner, H. (1989), *Sweden: Social Democracy in Practice*, Oxford: Oxford University Press.

Murray, R. (1987), 'Ownership, control and the market', *New Left Review*, **164** (July–Aug.), 87–112.

Parris, H., Pestieau, P., and Saynor, P. ,(1987) *Public Enterprise in Western Europe*, London: Croom Helm.

Persky, J. (1991), 'Lange and von Mises: large scale enterprises and the economic case for socialism', *Journal of Economic Perspectives*, **5/4**, 229–36.

Pimlott, B. (1987), 'Bryan Gould and social ownership: what is it supposed to achieve?' *New Statesman*, **114/2959** (11 Dec.), 5.

Pryke, R. (1971), *Public Enterprise in Practice*, London: MacGibbon.

—— (1981), *The Nationalised Industries: Policies and Performance Since 1968*, London: Robertson

Pusey, M. (1991), *Economic Rationalism in Canberra*, Cambridge: Cambridge University Press.

Rees, R. (1984), *Public Enterprise Economics*, London: Weidenfeld & Nicolson.

Schmalansee, R. (1979), *The Control of Natural Monopolies*, Lexington, Mass.: Lexington.

Shonfield, A. (1965), *Modern Capitalism*, Oxford: Oxford University Press.

Sloman, R. (1978), *Socialising Public Ownership*, London: Macmillan.

Smith, M. (1986), *The Consumer Case for Socialism*, Fabian Tract no. 513, London: Fabian Society.

Surrey, A. J., Buckley, C. M., and Robson, M. (1980), 'Heavy Electrical Plant', in K. Pavitt (ed.), *Technical Innovation and British Economic Performance*, London: Macmillan.

Verney, D. V. (1959), *Public Enterprise in Sweden*, Liverpool: Liverpool University Press.

Waterson, J. M. (1990), 'The Major Utilities' in Cowling and Sugden, *New Economic Policy for Britain.*

—— (1991), *Regulation and Ownership of the Major Utilities*, Fabian Discussion Paper no. 5, London: Fabian Society.

14

The Costs of Privatization in the UK and France

TIM JENKINSON* AND COLIN MAYER†

1. INTRODUCTION

Since 1979 around thirty-nine companies have been privatized by way of a sale of securities on the London Stock Exchange. In addition, a number of enterprises have been sold in other ways, such as being sold to their management or sold to other private-sector organizations. By 1991, most of the utilities in the UK had been privatized—telecommunications, gas, airports, water, and electricity—and railways are scheduled to be sold over the next few years. In addition, the vast majority of the enterprises that had been taken into the public sector have also been sold—such as BP, Cable and Wireless, Enterprise Oil, Jaguar, etc. The FT-SE 100 index currently includes seventeen privatized companies, and the combined market capitalization of the listed privatized companies was, in July 1992, over £80bn. Privatizations in the UK have dominated new issue activity in the UK in most recent years: for example, as Jenkinson and Trundle (1991) report, between 1985 and 1989 of the £23.6bn. raised on the Listed market in the UK, £16.6bn. was raised by privatizations.

Since 1986, the French government has sold ten companies on the Paris Bourse, raising FF77bn.[1] To give an idea of the scale of these issues, between 1983 and 1985 a total of FF22bn. was raised by private corporations on the Paris Bourse. French privatizations have therefore been a very significant part of overall stock market activity.

The privatization programmes in the UK and France have, therefore, involved exceptional expansions in the scale of new issue activity on the London and Paris Stock Exchanges. Other countries have privatized segments of their public sector, but in no other countries have privatiza-

* Stock Exchange Fellow in Economics, Keble College, University of Oxford.
† Professor of Economics and Finance, Warwick Business School.

This research was supported by a grant from the Nuffield Foundation. All errors are the sole responsibility of the authors.

[1] There is some question as to whether Elf Aquitaine should be treated as a privatization, as it has remained in the public sector. It has not been included in the FF77bn.

tions had such a dramatic impact on domestic stock exchanges. This article is an analysis of the privatization process in the two countries.

Privatizations are particular examples of a general class of issues by companies, usually coming to the market for the first time (unseasoned new issues). Techniques for making new issues differ across countries and Section 2 summarizes the procedures that are most commonly applied in France and the UK. It discusses the costs that are typically associated with different methods of making unseasoned issues.

Section 3 describes the costs that have been incurred in the privatization process. The analysis suggests that substantial difficulties have been encountered in one aspect of the privatization process—the setting of the issue price. Section 4 describes a widely cited theory of unseasoned new issues that goes some way to describing this and other features of the new issue process. The theory suggests that serious problems can be encountered in circumstances in which new issues involve a diverse range of investors. This clearly bears directly on the process of selling public assets, and Section 4 draws inferences from theory and practice for future privatizations.

2. INITIAL PUBLIC OFFERS

2.1 Procedures

There are essentially three methods by which firms can make initial public offers (IPOs). They can make offers for sale at a fixed price, offers for sale by tender, or placings. In the fixed price offer, applicants specify the number of shares to which they wish to subscribe at a pre-announced price. In tenders, applicants specify a price (at or above a minimum price) and a quantity of shares. Once applications have been received a strike price is set which determines the cut-off below which applications are rejected. If the market-clearing price is above the minimum tender price, then the strike price may be set at or below the clearing price. If it is below, then a system of rationing shares will be required. In a placing, shares are not made publicly available but will be sold via brokers to institutional investors and large private investors.

In the UK a majority of the large private issues are fixed-price offers for sale that are underwritten by the issuing bank. Smaller issues and companies coming to the Unlisted Securities Market (USM) are usually placed with institutional investors. In France IPOs on the official listing are almost exclusively tender offers. On the Second Manche tender offers are employed in approximately one-third of issues, the remainder being primarily fixed-price offers.

2.2 Costs of issue

There are two components to the costs of an IPO.[2] First there is the direct cost of employing the services of investment bankers, accountants, and solicitors, and the payment of taxes and listing fees. Direct costs comprise fixed and variable elements and typically decline as a percentage of the proceeds of the issue as the size increases. Jenkinson and Trundle (1991) found that the direct costs of an IPO constituted around 13.8 per cent on average of the proceeds of offers for sale raising less that £5m., although this figure steadily declined as the issue size increased so that for issues raising in excess of £10m the direct costs had fallen to around 6.9 per cent of the proceeds. Similar costs were found for placings: the average placing raising less than £5m. absorbed 11.4 per cent of the proceeds, whereas the direct costs of placings raising over £10m. averaged 5.9 per cent.

TABLE 14.1. Summary of estimated underpricing of IPOs

Country/Study	Type of offering	Sample period	Sample size	Underpricing (%)
UK				
Merrett, Howe, and	Fixed price	1959–63	149	14.2
Newbould (1967)	Tender	1963	15	3.8
	Placing	1959–63	193	19.2
Jackson (1986)	Fixed price ⎫		58	5.4
	Tender ⎬	1983–6	25	7.7
	Placing ⎭		14	5.7
Jenkinson and Trundle	Fixed price ⎫		100	8.5
(1991)	Placings ⎬	1985–9	112	14.3
	Privatizations ⎭		15	19.6
France				
Jacquillat, McDonald, and Rolfo (1978)	Tender	1966–74	60	4.8
Jacquillat (1986)	Tender	1972–86	87	4.8

The second cost comes from the underpricing of the new issues. Table 14.1 summarizes the results of previous studies of IPOs in the UK and France.

In the UK, placings are normally found to be the most underpriced form of issue, although the actual magnitude of the underpricing is quite sensitive to the different samples. Offers for sale have, since 1986, been exclusively at a fixed price; the UK tender offer seems to have suffered a mysterious death. This is despite the fact that studies frequently found

---

[2] No account is being taken here of the costs in terms of management time.

underpricing in tender offers to be quite moderate, as would, perhaps, be expected. The study by Jenkinson and Trundle (1986) reports results for privatizations separately, and shows that the UK privatizations included in their sample were significantly more underpriced than private-sector fixed-price offers. The latter are the most obvious comparator as a fixed-price offer has to be used for IPOs raising above £15m.

IPOs in France are typically by tender, and the two studies cited suggest that the extent of underpricing is quite modest for private-sector issues, being somewhat less than in the UK.

3. THE COSTS OF PRIVATIZATIONS

3.1 Direct Costs

Table 14.2 lists the UK privatizations and their direct costs. These have ranged from 1.9 per cent of the gross proceeds of the Jaguar offer in 1984 to 11.8 per cent in the (comparatively small) sale of Associated British Ports in 1983. But a large majority have been between 3 and 5 per cent. With the exception of the Associated British Ports issue, direct costs of privatizations in the UK have therefore been unexceptional in relation to those quoted above for private issues, although it should be remembered that many of the privatizations were orders of magnitude larger than the typical private sector offer for sale and so one would expect significant economies of scale.

3.2 Underpricing

Table 14.2 also records the extent of underpricing of the privatizations relative to their issue price. It measures underpricing by comparing the increase in the price of the shares relative to the market by the end of the first week of trading. All calculations are performed on a fully-paid basis, even though some of the shares were issued partly-paid. Table 14.3 reports discounts on French privatizations.

The first observation is the magnitude of the discounts on the fixed-price offers in London and Paris. The discounts have been particularly appreciable in France in relation to the low discounts that are commonly observed on private-tender issues. But they are also large in relation to fixed-price offers on the London market.

Second, the extent of underpricing is quite variable, although in recent years in the UK the rule of thumb seems to be that the shares trade at about a 20 per cent premium to their issue price by the end of the first week. Particularly low discounts on fixed-price offers were observed on the first privatization (British Petroleum), Jaguar, British Steel, Scottish

TABLE 14.2. Cost and pricing of privatizations in the UK

Company	Proceeds[a] (£m.)	Costs of issue[b] (% of proceeds)	Times subscribed	Underpricing[e] (end first week) (%)
Offers for sale				
British Petroleum (1979)	290	4.8	1.5	6
British Aerospace (1981)	149	3.8	3.5	15
Cable and Wireless (1981)	224	3.1	5.6	17
Amersham International (1982)	71	4.4	24.0	35
Assoc. British Ports (1983)	22	11.8	34.0	28
Jaguar (1984)	294	1.9	8.3	7
British Telecom (1984)	3916	3.9	3.0	33
British Gas (1986)	5434	3.2	4.0	10
Rolls Royce (1987)	1363		9.4	35
British Airports Authority (1987)	1225		8.1	16
British Airways (1987)	900			32
British Steel (1988)	2500		3.3	−1
10 Water Companies (1989)	5240		3.4	22
12 Regional Electricity Companies (1990)	5100	3.7	11.5	21
National Power (1991)	1341	3.7	5.4	23
PowerGen (1991)	822	3.7	5.4	23
Scottish Hydro-Electric (1991)	920		3.2	5
Scottish Power (1991)	1955		3.2	2
Tender Offers				
Britoil (1982)	549	2.3	0.3	−20
Enterprise Oil (1984)	392	2.8	0.4	2
British Airports Authority (1987)	363		6.0	−4

[a] Figures include the value of the sale of securities but not the value of any debt created in the company that is repayable to the government.

[b] Taken from National Audit Office reports, and not from the original prospectus. The latter tend to significantly underestimate the true costs of the privatizations. (Not all figures are available.)

[c] Calculated on the basis of the fully paid share price, and is calculated relative to movements in the FT-All share index over the first trading week.

Only the initial public offerings are included in Table 14.2 (many companies were sold in tranches with secondary issues occurring a few years after the IPO).

Hydro-Electric, and Scottish Power. Exceptionally large premiums were recorded in the sales of British Telecom, British Airways, Rolls-Royce, and Amersham International. In France, discounts were lower in the later issues: Havas, Compagnie Générale d'Electricité, and Télévision Française 1.

Third, tender offers have displayed significantly lower discounts. For example, the British Airports Authority sale in 1987 was interesting in that 75 per cent of the shares were sold via a fixed-price offer, whilst 25 per cent were allocated to a tender offer. The tender did not follow the normal procedure described above in so far as accepted offers paid subscription prices, rather than a strike price. The result was that whilst the fixed-price offer was discounted by some 16 per cent, the average price paid under the tender offer was actually slightly higher than the trading price at the end of the first week. However, in the two cases when a tender offer was used for the entire IPO, neither was fully subscribed, leaving the majority of the issue with the underwriters. It is probably for this reason that tender offers have not been used for privatizations since the British Aerospace issue.

TABLE 14.3. The French privatization programme

Company	Gross proceeds (FFbn.)	Underpricing (end first week) (%)
Elf Aquitaine (1986)	3.3	31
St. Gobain (1986)	13.5	19
Paribas (1987)	17.5	24
Sogenal (1987)	1.5	36
Banque de Travaux Publiques (1987)	0.4	23
Banque Industrielle et Mobilière Privée (1987)	0.4	21
Crédit Commercial de France (1987)	4.4	17
Havas (1987)	6.4	8
Compagnie Générale d'Electricité (1987)	8.0	11
Société Générale (1987)	21.5	6
Télévision Française 1 (1987)	3.5	8

An alternative way of estimating the costs associated with underpricing privatizations is to compute the government revenue forgone in relation to what would have been achieved if the privatizations had been priced in line with equivalent private-sector sales. Table 14.4 presents the costs of discounts in UK privatizations in relation to a range of typical discounts on private-sector sales. Relative to a typical private-sector discount of 10 per cent, the privatization process resulted in a revenue loss of around £2.5bn. Even taking the normal private-sector discount in the UK at 15 per cent, corresponding to the upper end of the mean estimates reported in Table 14.1, the revenue forgone by the UK privatizations is nearly £1bn. The remainder of the article is devoted to an attempt to explain these observations.

4. THE THEORY OF INITIAL PUBLIC OFFERS AND THE PRIVATIZATION PROCESS

A theory of the discounts on IPOs has been suggested by Rock (1986) that appears to bear directly on privatizations in Europe. This theory is

TABLE 14.4. Revenue forgone by underpricing UK
privatizations

Relative to discount of:	Revenue loss (£bn.)	% of proceeds
0%	5.7	18
5%	4.1	13
10%	2.5	8
15%	0.9	3

Note: This table takes the offers for sale included in Table
14.2 and computes the revenue loss (or gain in some
cases) relative to the various discounts.

based on differences in information available to investors in public
issues.

In the Rock model there are two classes of investors—informed and
uninformed ('insiders and outsiders'). The informed have information
about the future value of a share in an unseasoned public issue that is
unavailable to the uninformed. The uninformed hold unbiased probability distributions of the future value of an issue. The informed investors
have a fixed amount that they can invest in the issue and in the absence
of their participation issues are undersubscribed. However, their
demand does not on its own absorb the entire issue: participation by the
uninformed is also required. If the issue price fixed in advance of the
sale falls below informed investors' valuation then they subscribe, but if
it does not then they abstain from bidding.

As a consequence, uninformed investors face a winner's curse. If they
subscribe to an issue that is priced below its true value then informed
investors will bid. This increases the probability that the issue will be
oversubscribed and that shares will be rationed. On the other hand, if
the issue is overpriced then informed investors will not bid thereby
increasing the probability that the offer will be undersubscribed. Thus
uninformed investors are more likely to receive allocations of their
shares in over- than under-valued issues. To induce uninformed
investors to participate the issue has to be priced at a discount which
just yields an expected normal return, taking account of the probability
of rationing.

The UK privatizations illustrate this point rather clearly. While thirteen of the offers for sale displayed discounts of 10 per cent or more,
only British Telecom yielded an average capital gain (discount/times
oversubscribed) of more than 10 per cent. A majority lay between 0 and
5 per cent. However, the undersubscribed Britoil issue yielded a capital
loss to subscribers of 20 per cent.

Both the French and British privatizations have been the linchpin of a policy of extending private-sector share ownership to a wider segment of the population. The reasons for pursuing such a policy remain obscure. Plausible stories of a relation between individual share ownership and economic performance can be told—see Grout 1987 for an overview, and Merton 1987 for a rationale for broadening the investor base—but in large part political considerations have probably dominated. We abstract from a discussion of the desirability of the policy and merely consider whether it is appropriate to pursue it in the context of public-asset sales.

The implication of the above discussion is clear. Deficiencies of the new-issue process become most acute in circumstances in which asset sales of uncertain value are sold to investors with diverse information. Attempts to broaden share ownership are therefore directly in conflict with the realization of revenues that are close to asset valuations. It is not, therefore, surprising that the largest discounts on privatizations in the UK have been associated with the period during which wider share ownership rose to prominence (from the sale of British Telecom onwards).

A further implication of the Rock model is that if issues are hard to value, it may make sense to sell the company in tranches. A large discount may then be observed on the first tranche (the IPO), but smaller discounts would be necessary on subsequent issues. This is quite consistent with the evidence from the UK. Subsequent secondary issues by Cable and Wireless, British Petroleum, and Associated British Ports were all priced much more accurately than the original IPOs of each company.

A number of conclusions can be drawn:

(i) Privatizations are not the appropriate vehicles for extending share ownership.

(ii) Mispricings are best avoided by establishing traded security prices. This can be achieved by disposal of asset in stages. The first sale could be confined to institutions.

(iii) Where tenders can be arranged they should help to reduce mispricings.

On (i), the obvious alternative is the tax system. In the UK the costs of the privatization programme to date could have been used to subsidize a substantial extension of Personal Equity Plans (perhaps with fewer restrictions on equity investments via unit trusts and investment trusts). On (ii) it is interesting to note that a privatization to which we have not referred in this article, the sale by the Japanese Government of Nippon Telegraph and Telecommunication, involved an initial IPO by tender (restricted to institutions) for a relatively small proportion of the equity followed by subsequent secondary issues to which the public could subscribe. The subsequent collapse of the NTT share price (and the large number of individual investors who have incurred losses) should not detract from the attractiveness of such a procedure from the viewpoint of selling public assets at the correct price.

References

Jackson, P. (1986), 'New issue costs and methods in the United Kingdom', *Bank of England Quarterly Bulletin*, Dec.

Jacquillat, B. C. (1986), 'French auctions of common stock: methods and techniques of new issues, 1966–86', in *Going Public: An International Overview*, Euromobiliare Occasional Paper 2.

—— McDonald, J. G., and Rolfo, J. (1978), 'French auctions of common stock', *Journal of Banking and Finance*, **2**, 305–22.

Jenkinson, T. J., and Trundle, J. M. (1991), 'New equity issues in the United Kingdom', *Bank of England Quarterly Bulletin*, May, 243–52.

Merrett, A. J., Howe, M., and Newbould, G. D. (1967), *Equity Issues and the London Capital Market*, London: Longmans.

Merton, R. C. (1987), 'A simple model of capital market equilibrium with incomplete information', *Journal of Finance*, **42**, 483–510.

Rock, K. (1986), 'Why new issues are underpriced', *Journal of Financial Economics*, **15**, 187–212.

15

Popular Capitalism

PAUL GROUT*

1. INTRODUCTION

In 1979 the proportion of the adult population of the UK that directly owned shares in companies was 9 per cent. In the last thirteen years this has risen dramatically and it is estimated that 25 per cent of the adult population now own shares. In many ways this has been a spectacular change and one that, in 1979, would have appeared almost impossible to achieve. This seems to indicate that 'popular capitalism' has arrived in abundance and has been an unmitigated success. There is, however, another side to the story. In 1975 the percentage of the UK equity market in direct personal ownership was 37.5 per cent. By 1981 this had fallen to below 30 per cent and by the end of the decade was barely above 20 per cent.

So what has been achieved is a very thin spread of shares across a large proportion of the population. Of course, simple figures are misleading and behind these figures lie a series of diverse changes in ownership patterns and the results of several distinct policy thrusts. The main aim of this paper is to assess the effect of these changes and the policies that have brought them about. It is pointed out that in a perfectly competitive economy there is no reason to encourage wider share ownership, indeed the equilibrium should be characterized by the exact opposite. It is only in the presence of market failures that wider share ownership can play a significant role. The privatization programme has provided a major injection of new shareholdings which may improve economic welfare but is mainly aimed at satisfying other criteria. A main point of the paper is that this type of popular capitalism is unlikely to become a long-term important feature or to arrest the decline in private ownership since, even in the presence of economic benefits arising from such ownership, there are large externalities present and firms do not have strong incentives to promote this type of ownership. In contrast many of the gains are internalized in the case of employee share

* Professor of Economics, University of Bristol.

I am indebted to S. Valentine of ProShare for supplying information in Tables 15.1, 3, 4, and 6.

ownership and employee buy-outs, and it is reasonable to anticipate continued growth in this area provided minimal support is forthcoming from the government. It is suggested, therefore, that in the long run the privatization issues will prove to have played no more than a minor role in the promotion of sustainable and economically important private-share ownership.

It is conventional to think of the popular capitalism that has been promoted in the last decade purely as the promotion of share ownership by the man in the street. However, for the purposes of providing a careful analysis, it is beneficial to separate the share-ownership concept into several distinct categories and to define these by their relationship between the company and the shareholder. The most important distinction lies between ownership by what can genuinely be thought of as the man or woman in the street, which we will refer to as popular capitalism, and ownership by the man or woman in the work-place, which will be called employee share ownership. The former catorgory covers shareholdings where there is no specific relationship between the company and the shareholder other than perhaps a purchaser, on a very small scale, of final output. This has occurred mostly through the privatization process but to a lesser extent through the general policies of encouraging wider share ownership. In contrast, employee shareholding consists of holdings in the company where the owner of the shares also looks to the firm for the main source of income.

Popular capitalism, as defined here, arrived with a bang and fanfare whereas employee share ownership, with the exceptions of a few famous buy-outs, was a far quieter revolution in ownership habits. Both, however, have played a considerable part in the creation of the many small shareholdings in the years since 1979 and a full analysis of any potential impact of this widening of share ownership must recognize that they may have different impacts on the economy.[1] A common theme that runs through the analysis is the notion of market failure since without such failure, it is difficult to justify a policy that cuts across the efficient distribution of risk. Transactions costs, external effects, asymmetric information, and the problem of incentive-compatible contracts are all of significance, as is the presence of monopoly power and the consequences of the inability to precommit future government behaviour. The following section provides some background and is followed in Section 3 with a discussion of the notion of popular capitalism as defined above. Section 4 considers employee shareholding and employee buy-outs. Conclusions are drawn in Section 5.

---

[1] Privatizations alone have added hundreds of thousands of new employee shareholdings. In many of the privatizations the employee take-up of shares has been close to 100%. This is not surprising, of course, given that often a minimum number of free shares were distributed to each employee.

2. BACKGROUND

There are now approximately eleven million shareholders in the UK compared to around three million in 1979. With the exception of employee share ownership, the majority of these shareholders have been induced to hold shares as a result of the privatization programme during the last decade. An indication of the changes and how this relates to the programme can be seen from Table 15.1. The main reason for the popularity of such new issues has been the financial attraction of purchasing shares in privatizations. Table 15.2 outlines the difference between the (partly paid) price paid by the public in the various flotations and the price that the shares opened for trade. It is worth noting that not all of the additional demand for shares has been induced by privatization.[2] A second and far less dramatic effect on share ownership has come from the general policy to increase the fiscal attractiveness of owning shares, notably the use of personal equity plans (PEPs) which allow inveastors to receive tax-free dividends and to avoid capital gains tax providing they hold shares for a specified period. There is an upper bound on the amount that can be put into a PEP in each year and only a limited amount of the investment can be in the form of mutual funds, the objective being to increase the amount of direct ownership.

TABLE 15.1. Number of British individual shareholders

Year	No. of shareholders (millions)	Privatizations
1979	3 (approx.)	
1983	4 (approx.)	1979–83 small privatizations
1984	5	British Telecom
1985	5.6–6	None
1987	8.4	British Gas & TSB
1988	9	Br. Airways; BAA; Rolls-Royce; BP
1989	9	None
1990	10.8	Abbey National and Water issues
1991	11	Regional electricity companies

It has already been noted in the introduction that, although there are now a large number of shareholders, the typical holding of shares must be very small. Table 15.3 provides details of the composition of the ownership of shares in the UK by various sectors. It is clear that the general movement from personal ownership to mutual funds has continued

[2] See Estrin, Grout, and Wadhwani (1987) for details and analysis of these schemes.

TABLE 15.2. Opening prices, UK privatizations

Company	Offer price (p)	Opened at (p)
British Airports Authority (BAA) (July 1987)	100	146
British Airways (Feb. 1987)	65	109
British Gas (Dec. 1986)	50	68
British Petroleum (BP) (Oct. 1979)	150	154
British Steel (Dec. 1988)	60	63
British Telecom (Dec. 1984)	50	91
Regional Electricity Companies (Dec. 1990)		
Eastern	100	148
East Midlands	100	150
London	100	142
Manweb	100	166
Midlands	100	144
Northern	100	142
Norweb	100	152
Seeboard	100	142
Southern	100	150
South-Wales	100	164
South-Western	100	150
Yorkshire	100	160
English Electricity Generators (Mar. 1991)		
National Power	100	137
PowerGen	100	137
Scottish Electricity Generators (June 1991)		
Scottish Hydro-Electric	100	122
Scottish Power	100	116
Water Companies (Dec. 1989)		
Anglian	100	149
North-West	100	135
Northumbrian	100	157
Severn-Trent	100	131
South	100	141
South-West	100	147
Thames	100	136
Welsh	100	144
Wessex	100	154
Yorkshire	100	149

Note: For more detailed information, see Curwen and Holmes 1992.

TABLE 15.3. Percentage of UK-quoted equities owned by various sectors

	1957	1989
Personal	68.8	21.3
Pension funds	3.4	30.4
Insurance companies	8.8	18.4
Investment Trusts	5.2	1.6
Other financial institutions	—	1.6
Unit Trusts	0.5	5.9

almost unabated despite the dramatic increase in share owners. It follows immediately that the typical holding must involve few shares. In addition, it is also the case that the typical shareholder is not diversified in his/her direct ownership. Table 15.4 provides the percentage of shareholders according to the number of different companies in their portfolio. The majority of share owners have shares in only one company. Although part of this problem arises because of the growth of employee share ownership, the discussion of which is left to the following section, the privatization process itself has led to the growth in shareholders with few companies in the portfolio. It is interesting to note that despite the short-term advantages of privatization stocks, a surprising number of small shareholders retain the holdings. For example, Table 15.5 shows the proportion of British Gas shareholding by size and the interesting feature is that small holdings are reasonably robust over time, although obviously declining as they are slowly replaced by larger holdings. The experience of British Gas is fairly typical although perhaps rather more robust than most. Finally, in terms of background statistics it is useful to look at the method by which shareowners acquire shares. Table 15.6 gives this information (ignoring employee share ownership) and it is clear that the privatization new issues are of great importance.

This series of tables is sufficient to provide a good picture of the change in share ownership that has arisen as a result of the drive to

TABLE 15.4. Individual's portfolios

Percentage of shareholders having:	
1 holding	54
2 holdings	20
3 companies	9
4–10 companies	14
11 or more companies	3

Paul Grout

TABLE 15.5. Percentage of British Gas shareholding by size of holding

	Number of shares held by each individual			
	1–500	501–1,000	1,000–10,000	10,000
1987	73.5	19.3	7.1	0.1
1991	64.4	26.0	9.4	0.2

TABLE 15.6. Methods of share-purchase

Bought in new issue	71%
Through bank or broker	14%
Inheritance	7%
Gift	23%
Other	6%

Note: Shareholders may acquire by several methods.

popular capitalism. Many people have invested in shares that have never done so before but almost all of this additional ownership is the result of the large financial gains that have been available in the privatizations and very little of this has spilt over into more general active share dealings through banks or brokers. There is almost no attempt to build up even the most limited diversified portfolio (clearly impossible anyway in the light of the small sums involved and the transactions costs that apply to small investors). The introduction of PEPs may at best have slowed the movement towards investment in mutual funds and one suspects that, to date at least, few new investors have been brought into the pool via this route. While there exists a core of active investors with a series of companies in their portfolios this is likely to still be falling in number as the drive to mutual funds continues. Active share transactions from the personal sector through banks and brokers involve a disproportionately large percentage of sales compared to buys reflecting the slow movement out of privatized shares, often to be replaced with further privatized holdings at a later date.

3. POPULAR CAPITALISM

All of the evidence of the previous section when taken together suggests that it is actually quite difficult to promote active direct share ownership and to persuade investors to transfer from being a passive 'privatization' owner to becoming a 'real' investor in risky stocks. A sensible starting point to explain this phenomena is to consider the basic underlying theory of competitive equilibrium in the presence of risky assets. In the simplest model investors can be thought of as having prefences based on mean return and variance. Investors will wish to mix risk-free and risky assets to maximize their utility. However, as long as investors have homogeneous expectations, they will agree on the appropriate mix of risky assets that, when combined with a risk-free asset, provides the minimum variance for any given expected return. It follows that all investors will wish to hold the same mix of risky assets (the market portfolio) and will only differ in the proportion of risky to safe assets that they hold, which will depend on the degree of risk aversion. This feature of simple competitive equilibria with risky assets is referred to as two-fund separation, i.e. there are only two assets in the equilibrium, one risk-free asset and the other a composite asset made up of the set of risky assets. This is actually an extremely powerful result.[3] It not only indicates that shareholders will wish to diversify their portfolio but that they wish to diversify in exactly the same way. The implications for wider share ownership are quite clear. Individuals should, in equilibrium, hold a fully diversified set of risky assets but there is no reason for them to hold them directly. The correct mix of risky assets can be created in a mutual fund. Indeed, in the presence of transactions costs with economies of scale, the choice of mutual funds should drive direct ownership out of the market. At this simple level, the decline in direct ownership can be seen as an obvious consequence of the long-run changes in the distribution of wealth.

Theoretically, this competitive-equilibrium model describes the efficient allocation of risks given the implicit assumptions of the model. It follows that the policy to promote the direct ownership must be defended on the grounds that there exist market failures which prevent the efficient outcome being achieved in the absence of intervention. Arguments do exist of this form and we will discuss three types based around issues of control and information.

(i) The issue of control takes on several forms. One of the most important is the problem of control of management to achieve efficient allocation of resources. Market failures can arise from the desire of managers to follow objectives that are not totally consistent with those of the shareholders and this may lead to inefficient allocation of resources. The benefits arising from closer monitoring of management behaviour are spread amongst all shareholders whereas the costs fall on those conduct-

---

[3] See texts such as Brealey and Myers (1988) or Copeland and Weston 91988) for a discussion of these issues.

ing the monitoring. The monitoring process creates an externality for all shareholders and the result of this externality can be an inefficiently low level of monitoring. Any widening of the share base increases the difference between the aggregate benefit of monitoring and the benefit for any individual shareholder, suggesting that wider share ownership may increase the discretion of management to pursue ends at variance with profit maximization. There is clearly some sense in this argument although it is easy to overestimate it. Large mutual funds are not noted for their aggressive approach to weak management whereas small shareholders are well noted for exposing their views at shareholder meetings. Of course, small shareholders, by definition, cannot vote down proposals at meetings but can have a chastening effect on managerial proposals. Furthermore, the extent that any shareholders need to engage in individual monitoring behaviour is reduced if efficient compensation schemes are in place. There have been major changes in compensation packages in the UK and management compensation is now far more sensitive to financial performance than it was a decade ago. Indeed, many feel that there has been too much movement in this direction and this fear is itself inducing pressure for greater transparency in remuneration pachages. Such transprency further helps to reduce monitoring costs by reducing the cost of information for the shareholder.

It is often argued by management that the real effect of widening the share base for any individual company is in the opposite direction. Chief executives frequently claim that private shareholders are loyal to a company and more willing to take a long-term view. One has to be careful not to confuse loyalty with the fact that small shareholders face higher transactions costs and, to some extent, a conflict of interest is bound to emerge between shareholders that face radically different costs of transacting in the market. However, on average there does appear to be a genuine greater loyalty to a company from private shareholders and, more importantly for the chief executive, loyalty to individuals that have developed a company. Many chief executives will admit to being happy to put up with a costly share register for the extra commitment from such shareholders in the face of a hostile bid or attempted coup. Again, it is the vociferous nature of the small shareholder that is the useful element since even in aggregate they usually have no significant voting power. Of course, there is no reason why inefficient management should be protected by loyal shareholders with high transactions costs, and for the argument to make any sense one has to accept the other part of the story which is that financial markets are too short-term in their view. This is far from obvious although it has proved difficult to provide any totally convincing evidence in either direction.[4]

---

[4] Marsh (1990) provides a good discussion of this issue. See also Grout (1987) and references therein.

Looking at these arguments cynically, loyalty can be reinterpreted as a lack of control over management and the latter argument in favour of widening the share base could be viewed as the same as the preceding one but with the added twist that it is management not shareholders that are the true custodians of social welfare. Viewing the managerial-control issue in total it is difficult to believe that there is significant positive overall social benefit of this effect. There would have to be a considerable increase in the size of the shareholder base for the small private shareowners to have any real voting power and even then what positive gains that exist may be partly offset by the negative impact on managerial control. This suggests that it is necessary to look elsewhere if significant social gains are to be found.

(ii) The issue of control for the privatized industries is of a more fundamental nature. The impact of the change of control from the public to the private sector receives considerable analysis elsewhere in this volume and we will not attempt to summarize the costs and benefits of the policy here. What is an issue for the present discussion is the role that private shareholdings play in this process. Fear of insufficient demand for the first huge flotation, British Telecom, led the government to entice the small shareholder into the flotation. As indicated in Section 2, when viewed purely in terms of creating demand, the whole process proved to be an enormous success. This process has continued almost unabated. Does privatization play a particular deep role in the process of wider share ownership?

Privatization plays an obvious central role because such flotations are so large that they achieve in one day what may take years through PEPs and other favourable investment schemes. But even this is not obviously totally beneficial to the promotion of wider share ownership. It is common to hear those in favour of wider share ownership suggesting strongly that the privatization process actually damages the long-term prospects. The view is that the large initial gains made on privatizations give new shareholders the wrong impression of share ownership, viewing it as a short-term gamble and leading these new investors to become disenchanted with other shareholdings where it may be necessary to hold for many years to obtain any gain. There is clearly some sense in this view and, given the attitudes of some of the new shareholders, it is an unrealistic mission to attempt to convert all existing shareholders into long-term investors with a wide portfolio of shares.

A deeper concern is that the long-term future of such companies is not independent of the ownership structure. If private ownership is beneficial then it is essential that there is confidence in the future for such companies. A political party is less likely to renationalize a company if its assets are spread across voters. Thus a share register with large numbers of small holdings creates a safer climate for the companies. Furthermore, the assets are then of greater value to other shareholders both because the company can perform in a safer environment and the possibilty of nationalization at unattractive rates is reduced. This implies that the price that the goverment can attain from institutions is higher if private shareholders own a significant proportion of the shares. Thus part of the supposed give-away to private shareholders is clawed back through a higher price. Such a view suggests it is extremely difficult to assess with any accuracy what the true cost of the wider share ownership component of privatizations actually is (see Branco and Mello 1991).

This defence is rather sophisticated and surely secondary to the more immediate political mileage that is gained from the discounts on privatized shares. Nevertheless, the Labour Party's view of the potential for nationalization of privatized companies has changed considerably in the face of wide private ownership and this will certainly have fed into the price of shares. In summary though, it is surely the case that this effect is not sufficient to justify the gains given to small private holders and cannot be used as a major justification of the discount programme.

(iii) It is impossible to view the programme of wider share ownership in the 1980s independently of the complete change in economic and political changes. The vision of a share-owning and home-owning democracy was promoted as part of a change in attitudes that would move the UK away from the attitudes of the 1960s and 1970s. The whole process of share ownership makes individuals aware of the role of profits and encourages individuals to take a more rounded view of the economic process. At its best it may lead to more sensible negotiations in the work-place and may play a part in changing political attitudes. All the main political parties now talk positively about share ownership with the Liberal Democrats keen to point out that this has long been part of their policy in the work-place and the Labour party pointing out that the first large-scale employee share ownership programme was introduced by them in 1978.

Formally, the argument is that there are market failures, e.g. monopoly in the labour market and imperfect information, that have the effect of reducing efficiency. Wider share ownership by changing attitudes and improving the flow of information reduces these inefficiencies. Despite endless surveys on attitudes to share ownership, the real extent of such changes in attitudes and their impact on economic behaviour is unknown. It may in the long run be one of the greatest benefits of the whole process of wider share ownership but, if this is so, we can see that the seeds of failure are built into the whole programme. Theory indicates that there are good reasons why individuals should not hold nondiversified portfolios. Companies will have to go out of their way to make this attractive. On the other hand, the benefits of the type suggested here are spread across the whole economy. We have argued that the benefits that accrue directly to the company are likely to be small so that any company that tries to encourage small private shareholdings captures little of the benefit. Therefore, a programme is unlikely to succeed without government intervention to overcome the externality. In recent years the government has played this role on a grand scale. New shareholders have been sucked into the market because of large gains, but even here there are doubts about the attitude that this creates. Any such gains for shareholders are short lived and, as we see, such shareholding declines continually after flotation. There is nothing in this scenario that suggests that direct share ownership of this type will do anything other than decline in the long run even if such share ownership is indeed beneficial for the economy.

This may appear to be rather a gloomy picture but it is difficult to see how the external effects can be overcome. We are essentially arguing that not only are there market failures that create a situation where the structure of ownership does affect economic performance but additional market failures prevent wider share ownership playing its role in correcting part of this problem. It is for this reason that it is essential to separate out the various forms of ownership that have occurred over the last decade. The essential factor we have identified is that the effect of the externality must be minimized. We now turn to the forms of wide share ownership where such externalities may be internalized.

4. EMPLOYEE SHARE OWNERSHIP AND EMPLOYEE BUY-OUTS

One of the features of the growth in the number of share owners in the last decade has been the small number of shares in the typical portfolio. There are two main reasons for this. One is the privatization programme but the other is the enormous growth of employee share ownership. From our perspective an intriguing feature of this type of ownership is that far more of the benefits of share ownership are likely to be captured within the economic relationship. To the extent that benefits arise from the work force having greater awareness of the company's position and problems, these will be reflected in improvements in the negotiating process within the company and hence captured by the shareholders. The incentives to attract employees as shareholders is therefore stronger than the incentive to attract any other private shareholder. Again market failure is at the heart of the problem since in a perfectly competitive labour market the negotiating process will be independent of the ownership structure. These arguments can be formalized in various forms. For example, the most obvious is that wages are less likely to be raised (and share price reduced) if employees own a significant number of shares. In addition, a company may not be willing to make long-term expensive

commitments because the employees are likely to convert the consequent lack of flexibilty into higher remuneration. In most models of the
bargaining process the presence of employee share ownership reduces
the extent that wages rise when a firm is locked into expensive commitments and this suggests that firms with higher levels of share ownership
may be willing to invest more.[5] These models indicate that firms can
gain from encouraging employee share ownership in a way that will not
happen if they encourage more general direct shareholding.

There are two main causes of the growth in employee shareholdings.
One has been the provision of shares to all employees in virtually all of
the privatizations and the other has been the practice of most of the
major companies to take up the government schemes to provide shares
to employees. We have suggested that employees will generally require
some incentives for share ownership to offset the fact that their portfolio
is not diversified. This is particularly so in the case of employee share
ownership since the individual's income is tied up in the company.
Optimal investment policy indicates that the portfolio should be
invested in assets that are negatively correlated with the firm's performance. The decision to maintain part of the employees' wealth in the
same company aggregates risks rather than reducing them. Not surprisingly, therefore, the employee share ownership schemes that are available to most employees and have proved most successful have some
fiscal advantages.

Given the problems because of the bundling of risks, one would have
expected employee share ownership to be the least sturdy of the forms
of wider share ownership. This is far from the case. More employees
become involved with the schemes each year and more companies introduce schemes. The growth in employee share ownership and the effort
and money that firms put into the promotion of such schemes is an indication of the benefits that they perceive can be gained from employee
share ownership.[6] Because the benefits are internalized there is more
hope that any genuine form of welfare-enhancing share ownership will
come from this form of ownership than the more conventional form of
popular capitalism.

The most dramatic case when the problem of externality is avoided is
when the employees purchase a major part of the company. There have
been several very successful buy-outs in recent years. It is necessary to
be somewhat circumspect when interpreting the apparent success since
many of the spectacularly successful cases have involved purchase from
the government-controlled industries at extremely attractive prices, a situation not unlike that for private shareholders in the large privatizations. The most well known is the buy-out of National Freight (NFC),

---

[5] See Grout (1988).   [6] See CBI (1991) for evidence of attitudes.

led by Sir Peter Thompson, where the value of shares increased over 7,000 per cent in six years. One cannot deny the hard work that went into this company over the period but the progress was accompanied by huge reductions in personnel and sales of large quantities of land in a rising market. Another interesting example is the buy-out at Istel, initially part of the Rover Group. The company was owned roughly one-third by company executives, one-third by management and staff, with the remaining third going to financial institutions. The buy-out took place in June 1987 and the company was taken over by AT&T just over two years later (October 1989). Shares worth £1 in June 1987 were purchased by AT&T for £33.74. It is very difficult to believe that all this increase in value arose because of the impact of the change in ownership on the performance of the company.

Nevertheless the rate of return in most employee buy-outs has been well above average. (This has not been the case with management buy-outs.) Furthermore, these firms are continuing to work hard at increasing the share ownership of employees. For example, Unipart, another buy-out from the Rover Group where employees and management own 45 per cent of the shares, allow workers to purchase options at a 20 per cent discount on the underlying share price. It is clear that such firms believe that there are genuine gains to be obtained from encouraging greater employee ownership even when such sales have to be made at advantageous prices. There are indeed sensible theoretical reasons why firms with imperfect labour markets will gain from the introduction of large-scale employee ownership.[7] One obvious one is that the employees can now capture a significant part of the gain that can be achieved by reducing excessive employment and wages. As with the discussion of employee share ownership, the incentives to increase employee involvement are sufficient to offset the problems associated with the bundling of risks and such buy-outs appear to have a healthy long-term future after the government take a back seat in promoting this form of ownership.

5. CONCLUSIONS

An important part of our discussion has been to draw the distinction between general share ownership by private shareholders, which is probably the general notion of popular capitalism, and specific employee share ownership. The former has received an enormous push from the governemt, particularly for the purposes of moving large volumes of shares, to achieve political ends and possibly to precommit the

---

[7] See Grout and Jewitt (1988).

behaviour of future governments. Given the existence of market failures it is quite reasonable to argue that there may be real, albeit small, gains from such a programme, but these benefits are economy wide. There is no reason that any firm should be willing to sacrifice to achieve wider share ownership given that the benefits are external to the operation. One suspects that in the very long run, after the push from privatization has disappeared, that the popular capitalism process will recede and the decline in private share ownership will not be reversed. We have argued that these problems are less likely to hold for employee share ownership where the benefits of such ownership are mainly internal to the economic relationship between the employer and the firm. This suggests that progress will probably continue to be made in this area given the enthusiasm of companies, providing some government-based fiscal privilege remains. The implication is that as far as popular capitalism is concerned the privatization programme will have very little if any real impact on the economy but that the slower, less heralded growth in employee ownership is unlikely to wither away and will, with moderate continued support, flourish.

References

Brealey, R.A., and Myers, S. C. (1991), *Principles of Corporate Finance*, New York: McGraw-Hill.

Branco, F., and Mello, A. S. (1991), *A Theory of Partial Sales and Underpinning in Privatizations*, Alfred P. Sloan School of Management Working Paper, no. 3282-91-EFA, Cambridge, Mass.: MIT.

CBI (1991), *Report of the CBI Wider Share Ownership Task Force*, London: CBI.

Copeland, J. E., and Weston, J. F. (1988), *Financial Theory and Corporate Policy*, New York: Addison-Wesley.

Curwen, P., and Holmes, D. (1992), 'Returns to small shareholders from privatization', *Quarterly Review*, National Westminster Bank.

Estrin, S., Grout, P., and Wadhwani, S. (1987), 'Profit sharing and employee share ownership', *Economic Policy*, **2**, 13–62.

Grout, P. (1987), 'Wider share ownership and economic performance', *Oxford Review of Economic Policy*, **3**, 13–29.

—— (1988), 'Employee share ownership and privatisation: some theoretical issues', *Economic Journal* (suppl.).

—— and Jewitt, I. D. (1988), 'Employee buy-outs', *International Journal of Industrial Organisation*, **6**, 33–45.

Marsh, P. R. (1990), *Short Termism on Trial*, London: Institutional Fund Managers Association.

16

Management Buy-outs and Privatization

MIKE WRIGHT*, STEVE THOMPSON,† AND KEN ROBBIE‡

1. INTRODUCTION

Most discussion about privatization appears to assume, explicitly or implicitly, that it will be effected by stock market flotation to create a dispersed ownership PLC (Vickers and Yarrow 1988). This focus of attention has been despite the large number of other forms of sale, such as buy-outs and sales to third parties, which have taken place (Wright, Thompson, and Robbie 1989). The benefits to be derived from privatization may be extended if these other forms of private-sector ownership are considered. This chapter critically examines the merits of the management buy-out (MBO) and its close relations as a privatization device. It is suggested that agency-cost arguments, supported by a growing body of empirical evidence, indicate that the MBO form is effective in improving firm performance, at least in the short to medium term.

Section 2 presents a brief overview of the growth of MBOs in the UK and documents their already frequent use in privatizations. Section 3 examines the efficiency rationale for selling businesses to their managements. Section 4 considers some of the difficulties arising in public sector buy-outs, especially those relating to pricing, and reviews some safeguards to protect vendor interests. Section 5 examines three case-studies of buy-outs which have arisen on privatization: NFC (a buy-out of a complete state firm); NBC (which produced 39 buy-outs when it was broken up); and RFS Industries (which was a management-led employee buy-out of a subsidiary of British Rail). Section 6 provides a brief conclusion.

* Professor of Financial Studies, and Director of the Centre for Management Buy-out Research, School of Management and Finance, University of Nottingham.
† Senior Lecturer in Business Economics, UMIST, Manchester.
‡ Centre for Management Buy-out Research.

An earlier version of the first part of this chapter appeared as Thompson, Wright, and Robbie 1990. Financial support from Barclays Development Capital Limited and Touche Ross Corporate Finance is gratefully acknowledged.

2. THE GROWTH OF BUY-OUTS

Since the late 1970s the management buy-out market has shown considerable development with well over 400 buy-out transactions now being completed annually in the UK (Table 16.1), plus a further 100 or more management buy-ins, where an outside team of individual entrepreneurs acquire the firm (Robbie, Wright, and Thompson 1992). Buy-outs developed in the UK in the early 1980s and were frequently adopted by management as an alternative to the closure or sale of their business units (Wright and Coyne 1985). They subsequently became associated with the voluntary divestment of divisions or subsidiaries which either did not fit a parent's new strategic direction and/or were difficult to control (Thompson and Wright 1987). The start of the 1990s and recessionary conditions in the economy marked an important return to the role of buy-outs as a means of restructuring businesses in receivership (Wright, Thompson, Chiplin, and Robbie 1991). Buy-outs arising on the privatization of public-sector assets have been a significant element of the total buy-out market for the last decade (Table 16.1). The first half of the 1980s saw a high level of divestment of subsidiaries from state firms who were restructuring prior to their own privatization. In 1987 and 1988 the break-up of National Bus dominated privatization buy-outs. At the beginning of the 1990s, privatization buy-out activity involved remaining state enterprises such as Scottish Bus Group, BTG, ports and power-stations in Northern Ireland, but with most transactions concern-

TABLE 16.1. Privatization buy-outs and the UK buy-out market

Year	Buy-outs		Share	
	Total	Privatizations	By number (%)	By value (%)
1982	127	8	4.1	18.5
1983	235	8	4.0	5.9
1984	237	4	2.0	6.3
1985	263	7	3.0	2.7
1986	315	15	5.2	11.5
1987	344	34	10.4	11.3
1988	375	22	6.2	4.3
1989	374	17	4.6	2.1
1990	485	22	4.6	2.1
1991	444	10	2.3	7.0

Note: Excludes buy-ins and buy-outs of overseas subsidiaries.

Source: CMBOR, an independent research centre founded by Touche Ross & Co., and Barclays Development Capital Limited at the University of Nottingham.

ing local authority and other quasi-governmental sectors. To the end of December 1991, a total of 158 buy-outs and buy-ins of public-sector assets had been completed (Table 16.2). Buy-outs are considerably more numerous than stock market flotation as a means of privatization, of which there had been 45 including secondary sales of shares in the same period. Data on sales to third parties are difficult to obtain but it would appear that they have been completed in comparable numbers to MBOs. The size of public flotation in terms of both employees and transaction value far exceeds that of MBOs (Bishop and Kay 1988; Wright, Thompson, and Robbie 1989), with the total value of the former amounting to approximately £40 billion and the latter about £1.3 billion in current prices.

Privatization buy-outs occur in four main ways:

1. *Complete enterprise buy-outs*

These have been unusual in the UK, mainly because government policy has generally preferred to privatize complete enterprises through stock market flotation, often after they have been restructured. A well-documented example is the management-led employee buy-out at National Freight Corporation which is discussed in detail in the case-study section. In early 1992 the part of BTG which remained after the sale of many of the earlier National Enterprise Board investments was sold as a management buy-out.

2. *Break-up and disposal via multiple buy-outs*

The primary examples of this form of privatization buy-out are the National Bus Company (NBC), which is examined in detail in the case-study section, and the parallel organization in Scotland, Scottish Bus Group (SBG) (Mulley and Wright 1986). In addition, British Shipbuilders has effectively been broken up using buy-outs (and buy-ins) and sales to third parties.

3. *Buy-outs on divestment of non-core activities*

As part of the preparation for the privatization of their core activities, most of the larger state enterprises have divested themselves of businesses which were either peripheral to their principal interests or in some cases involved trading relationships. In many cases, these divested enterprises were not previously free-standing companies with records which would allow them to seek a flotation. The most intensive divestors are shown in Table 16.2. These state enterprises have also sold a number of subsidiaries to third parties where a combination of factors such as price, absence of independent viability, weak management, etc. have meant that a buy-out was not feasible (see Wright, Chiplin, and Robbie 1989 for discussion of this point).

TABLE 16.2. UK public sector buy-outs and buy-ins to December 1991

Source	Pre-82	1982	1983	1984	1985	1986	1987	1988	1989	1990	1991	TOTAL
British Aerospace	—	1	—	—	—	—	—	—	—	—	—	1
BL/Austin Rover	2	—	2	—	1	—	7	1	—	—	—	13
British Rail	—	—	1	1	—	—	2	1	1	1	—	7
British Shipbuilders	—	—	1	2	3	2	—	1	2	—	1	12
British Steel	2	3	2	—	—	—	2	1	—	—	—	10
BTG/NEB	2	3	2	1	2	1	1	—	—	—	—	12
National Bus Company	—	—	—	—	—	11	22	6	—	—	—	39
NFC	—	1	—	—	—	—	—	—	—	—	—	1
Scottish Bus Group	—	—	—	—	—	—	—	—	—	3	2	5
Local authorities—non-bus	—	—	—	—	—	1	—	6	10	10	2	29
Local authorities—bus	—	—	—	—	1	—	—	3	2	1	3	9
Other buy-outs	—	—	1	—	1	—	1	3	2	7	2	16
Buy-ins	1	—	1	—	1	—	1	—	—	—	1	4
TOTAL	7	8	9	4	7	15	35	22	17	22	11	158

Source: CMBOR, an independent research centre founded by Touche Ross & Co., and Barclays Development Capital Limited at the University of Nottingham.

4. *Buy-outs of local authority services, ancillary health services and governmental and quasi-governmental agencies*

Parallel to the break-up of NBC and SBG, local authority bus services are being privatized, some of them by means of buy-outs. In addition, other services are being privatized following The Local Government Act 1988 which introduced compulsory competitive tendering (CCT) as a means of producing further real efficiency improvements from extending forms of contracting-out (Cubbin, Domberger and Meadowcroft 1987). Although buy-outs may hold various attractions because they involve transfer to a known group of individuals who may be heavily dependent on the local authority for continuing revenue, they can involve serious conflicts of interest when managers who are responsible for divesting services are attempting a buy-out (Audit Commission 1990). Similar issues are raised with buy-outs from governmental or quasi-governmental agencies (NAO with CMBOR 1991). Means of dealing with these issues are discussed below.

3. SELLING TO MANAGERS: THE AGENCY COST ISSUES

The modern firm is frequently characterized as an agency problem involving a group of key managers (the agents) making decisions on behalf of the beneficial owners or shareholder principals (Jensen and Meckling 1976; Fama and Jensen 1983). The diluted or even non-existent equity involvement of the managers may bring the pursuit of non-profit goals. The agency theorists, following Jensen and Meckling (1976), point out that the recognition of this possibility leads to bonding and monitoring expenditures aimed at constraining the managers' behaviour. For example, the shareholders in a public limited company may be thought of as hiring non-executive directors to monitor the professional managers at boardroom level and auditors to check the truthfulness of the published financial information.

Following the work of Williamson (1975; 1979) it has been recognized that the internal structure of the firm plays an important role in checking managerial behaviour. Williamson argued that the multi-divisional (M-form) form of organization—characterized by a decomposition of the firm into a strategic headquarters and profit accountable divisions possessed superior efficiency properties for large, diversified companies. Among these M-form attributes, Williamson suggested that there was a reduced propensity for the managerial pursuit of non-profit goals: the headquarters staff constitute a relatively small part of the whole firm while middle managers, whose promotions and remuneration depend on divisional performance, have lower incentives to misdirect resources. Empirical work in the US and the UK (Cable 1988), has tended to support Williamson's hypothesis for optimally organized M-forms. However, this work also indicates that many divisionalized firms' organizational structures fail to meet Williamson's rules on resource allocation and incentives (see Stephen and Thompson (1988) for a review of the evidence). Various strands from organization and strategy theory, particularly that relating to organizational core competences, cultures, and learning systems would suggest that firms' management structures do not adapt in a deterministic fashion in response to various environmental characteristics (e.g. Prahalad and Hamel 1990; Teece *et al.* 1990; Arrow 1974). As a result divestment, perhaps through a management buy-out may be a feasible means of dealing with such problems.

Transferring the ownership of a firm from the state to a diffuse set of shareholders has implications for the monitoring of the firm and incentives within it. Public enterprises are subject to direct or indirect review by the political process. Critics of the public sector argue that this tends to be better suited to revealing gross misconduct than to monitoring the attainment of performance targets, which furthermore are frequently poorly defined (Jackson 1982). After a share flotation, performance is evaluated by the stock market, using the published reports of professional analysts. Disappointing results will lower the share price and raise the threat of a take-over. In the limit, any very poorly performing private-sector firm will go bankrupt. By contrast, bankruptcy is not usually allowed to happen to public enterprises.

The flotation of a state-owned business does nothing of itself to alter the reward structure of management; although in practice managers (and other employees) are usually offered shares on preferential terms and subsequent remuneration for directors is generally more closely related to performance and private-sector norms (although of course in natural monopoly type firms, it is possible that even with a regulatory regime, profitability may improve as a result of market power rather than managerial action). Such performance-related remuneration which does occur in the public sector usually relies on indirect indicators, such as unit costs.

It would appear, therefore, that a straightforward share flotation would raise the value of the firm, that is reduce agency costs, through one or more of the following: the clear specification of profit objectives; the introduction of a bankruptcy threat; the transfer of monitoring from the political process to the stock market; and the potential for improved managerial incentives.

However, these improvements may not necessarily materialize to any substantial extent (Vicker and Yarrow 1988). If the firm effectively remains as a monopolist, or at least enjoys a dominant market position, it may still pursue satisfactory rather than maximum profits. Maximizing profits may entail the risk of regulatory sanctions, but there are also indications that price-related regulatory formulae have been relatively lax (see e.g. Wright 1987). As such, the threat of bankruptcy may be low or non-existent. Similarly, the dispersion of shareholdings may weaken monitoring efforts by arbitrageurs and major market players. The size of some privatized undertakings probably prohibits their being taken over. Highly leveraged take-over bids are possible, but the subsequent unbundling which they often require so as to pay-down debt quickly may not be possible in a former state enterprise with a narrow spread of product areas. Break-up by regionalization may be an option. Government equity retentions and 'golden share' provisions may in some cases reduce or even eliminate the possibility of take-over, though there have been instances where government have declined to block acquisitions of privatized entities.

The buy-outs which have been completed in the UK indicate important features to reduce agency costs. In summary, the key elements may be identified as follows. First, in most cases especially smaller buy-outs, the management team receive a majority of the equity. Second, this level of equity is made possible by heavy reliance on debt and quasi-debt finance (Chiplin, Wright, and Robbie 1991). Third, managements' shareholdings are themselves frequently dependent upon the medium-term performance of the firm and may be adjusted up and sometimes down by means of a ratchet mechanism (Thompson and Wright 1991). Fourth, the principal financing institutions usually require regular information in greater detail than the outside market and/or representation on the board or even in the chair of the bought-out firm (Wright, Thompson, and Robbie 1992). Fifth, many buy-outs involve mature, cash-generating businesses where the lenders can appraise the firms' market potential relatively easily. Sixth, particularly in privatization buy-outs, the non-managerial employees have the opportunity to take shares, either directly or via an employee share-ownership plan (ESOP) which establishes a trust fund to buy the shares and subsequently distributes them as the enabling loan is paid off from the firms' profits (Wright, Chiplin, Thompson, and Robbie 1990).

The leveraged financial structure of the newly bought-out firm incorporates very strong effort and monitoring incentives. Not merely does the management team own a significant proportion of the equity, but this stake itself may vary with performance. It is not uncommon in the UK for such ratchets to enable management to obtain control of the enterprise, providing pre-specified targets are met (Thompson and Wright 1991). The corollary of the use of leverage is that the managers now find themselves bonded (or pre-committed) to generate those cash flow targets necessary to service outside funding. The managers' discretion to pursue other objectives is curtailed unless they risk jeopardizing their human and non-human capital investments. Thus the threat of bankruptcy is magnified (Jensen 1986).

Furthermore, it is not merely the managers who have an intensified incentive to monitor in the newly bought-out firm. The institutions providing the various types of external finance will typically have a significant degree of involvement in the new companies. This involvement is reflected in their frequent presence in the boardroom and their informational requirements and supports the contention of Stiglitz (1985) that less-than-fully-diversified lenders to the firm will play a more active role than diversified shareholders.

The typical vertical monitoring present in most firms is augmented in buy-outs as members of the managerial team may be considered to have an incentive to engage in the horizontal monitoring of their peers. Wider employee equity ownership may influence worker involvement to the benefit of performance (Wright, Chiplin, Thompson, and Robbie 1990).

The issue remains as to the organizational level at which a buy-out on privatization may be most appropriate. As noted earlier, buy-outs on privatization have involved whole state firms, parts of firms which are being completely dismantled, and parts of firms where the 'core' activity is to remain intact. If the main economic objective of privatization can be considered to be to improve all aspects of efficiency, there is a need to trade-off increased incentives and monitoring against market-power effects, and the presence of economies of scale and scope. Hence, relatively small firms in competitive markets may be privatized intact (such as NFC) whilst such firms which hold a dominant market position may need to be broken up, especially where economies of scale and scope are unimportant (such as in NBC). Where trading relationships exist between parts of a state-owned firm, divestment of a subsidiary may help resolve monitoring problems.

The purchasing side of the transaction is also important as care needs to be taken that the buyer does not in effect re-create adverse competition effects without more than offsetting economies of scale and scope. In such cases, sale to an existing firm in the same sector may be problematical and a buy-out may be preferred. Where there is a rationale for divesting activities with a trading relationship, a buy-out may offer attractions in preference to sale to a competitor or to a supplier, especially where the former subsidiary is heavily dependent on its erstwhile parent (Wright 1986). An element of retained ownership may enable the state-owned parent as trading partner to influence post-buy-out behaviour. There may be requirements that the vendor guarantees to maintain a certain level of trading for a specified period of time after the buy-out in order to ensure its viability. Bought-out firms tend subsequently to reduce their dependence upon their former parents in order to avoid being squeezed by their more powerful trading partners. The new relationship may not necessarily involve a pure spot market but may be some kind of managed-market relationship or network where there is a degree of asset specificity in the transaction (see the case of RFS Industries below). Certain sectors may be more attractive as candidates for management and/or employee buy-outs, especially where the performance of the firm depends heavily on their specific skills which can be best rewarded by the incentive arrangements contained in a buy-out. Other things being equal, however, including the viability of a buy-out attempt (see below), the highest price offered may be the deciding factor.

From a practical and institutional standpoint, of course, buy-outs are only feasible where sufficient external funding is forthcoming, which depends on the ability of the management team to manage an independent entity, some expected level of independent viability of the enterprise, and an ability to service such funding from stable cash flows (Wright, Thompson, Chiplin, Robbie 1991). In addition, many firms which are candidates for buy-outs may not fulfil the size and other criteria for stock-market flotation. These points have particularly applied to those smaller privatization buy-outs which were formerly subsidiaries of larger state firms and which did not have a separately identifiable track record of independent trading (Thompson, Wright, and Robbie 1990). Divested firms of this type may require intense managerial effort to build up certain functions previously undertaken by the parent. Where a straightforward buy-out is not feasible or viable, but where the contribution of employees' specific skills is important, a joint sale to a buy-out team and a third party may be a preferred route, as for example in the privatization of BREL from British Rail, and the involvement of established firms in joint bids with employees for contracts in the local authority sector.

In general the empirical literature appears to support the theoretical arguments for the MBO as a means of altering incentives and so raising firm performance. Recent studies of post-buy-out performance both in the USA and the UK indicate significant positive effects at least in the short to medium term. In the USA, leveraged buy-out transactions have been shown to produce improvements in market value, productivity, and profitability, with the effects on employment and R&D being mixed (see Palepu 1990 for a review of the US evidence). Evidence from the USA relating to smaller buy-outs which often arise on divestment indicates major reorganization occurs following buy-out which was not possible under the previous ownership regime (Malone 1989). A study of the medium-term performance effects of 182 private- and public-sector UK MBOs completed in the period mid-1983 to late 1986 demonstrated similar performance improvements to the Malone study but also noted a higher level of new product development (Wright, Thompson, and Robbie 1992). The longer-term performance effects of UK buy-outs are as yet unclear; the studies completed to date having produced conflicting results but also being based on non-random samples (Wong *et al*. 1991), although there is evidence to show that managerial equity stakes are the most important influence on post-buy-out increases in value (Thompson *et al*. 1992). Evidence relating to post-buy-out performance of buy-outs from the public sector in the UK is presented in the case-study section below.

4. THE BUY-OUT PROCESS: PRICING, EQUITY AND EFFICIENCY ISSUES

A key feature of the debate about the privatization process relates to the extent to which public assets may be sold too cheaply. This concern applies to sales to third parties and flotations as well as to buy-outs. The disposal of Austin Rover to British Aerospace in particular brought criticism that excessive inducements to buy had been given (NAO 1989). There is also extensive evidence that underpricing of stock-market flotations has been greater than for private-sector flotations (Buckland 1987; Mayer and Meadowcroft 1985; Buck, Thompson, and Wright 1991; and Menyah *et al*. 1990). Since MBOs involve sale to a closely held group of shareholders, there is no immediate market price for comparison. An internal share market may be established, but in most cases the shares are not marketable to outsiders until a subsequent public flotation, after several years. Two alternative methods of assessing the extent of underpricing are available. The first involves a comparison of the deal price with the accounting value of the company's assets at the time of the buy-out. The second requires an examination of the increase in value of a company from buy-out to subsequent flotation or sale to a third party. This latter method is imperfect in that part of any increase occurring over time may be attributable to managerial actions rather than underpricing, but significant gains achieved in a very short period may be taken as prima-facie evidence of underpricing.

Assessing whether any observed underpricing in buy-outs differs from that involving other forms of sale is difficult because of the diversity of public-sector sales. The only substantial homogeneous sample of privatizations which can be used for comparative purposes is that arising on the break-up of National Bus. Evidence from the National Audit Office (NAO) investigation of the sale reveals that a greater proportion of buy-outs than trade sales were sold at prices below the book value of assets, especially in the first half of the privatization process (Table 16.3). The average ratio of sale proceeds to book value of assets is higher for buy-outs than for trade sales, but these figures are influenced by a small number of sales at very high ratios. A much greater proportion of buy-outs involved only the management team as bidder, especially those in

TABLE 16.3. Features of the National Bus privatization

	Buy-outs	Trade sales
No. of bids		
1	15	3
>1	21	23
Mortgage change	7	7
Break-up value		
Positive	6	7
Negative	28	17
n.k. or zero	2	2
Proceeds/Book value of assets		
1. 1st 31 sales		
>1	5	2
<1	19	5
2. 2nd 31 sales		
>1	7	13
<1	5	6
3. Total		
>1	12	15
<1	24	11
4. Average	1.75	1.49

Source: National Audit Office 1990.

the earlier part of the disposal programme. It is important to bear in mind that in the earlier part of the sale process there was considerable uncertainty over the consequences of deregulation which contributed to the presence of fewer rivals to management in the bidding. The position changed considerably in the later period as the NAO report demonstrates. Overall, the NAO considers that the sale process was carried out in a satisfactory, cost-effective, and timely fashion with care being taken to safeguard the taxpayer by either selling property separately or through the use of claw-back provisions and with negotiators being effective at increasing bids. The concern highlighted in the NBC case, seems to have been taken account of in the subsequent bus buy-outs from Scottish Bus Group and West Midlands Travel where the process of privatization was carried out in a more transparent and public manner and where appropriate devices have been used in an attempt to ensure fair pricing. In the case of the buy-out of the Department of Employment's skills-training agencies, however, an expected net return on the sale of £18.9 million was in doubt because sales of the agencies' surplus properties, from which the government was entitled to claw back a proportion of the revenue, had been adversely affected by the recession (NAO 1991).

Besides claw-back mechanisms it is possible to allay some concerns about the underpricing of public-sector assets by the use of delayed payments contingent upon performance and/or by the vendor retention of an equity stake. For example, the initial sale price of VSEL from British Shipbuilders was £60 million but this rose to an eventual £100 million as a result of a profit-related price mechanism. Similarly, the sale of Unipart from Austin Rover included a price escalation clause which depended on profits and market capitalization on flotation. Several buy-outs from both Austin Rover and British Steel have left the vendor with a retained equity stake as a check on initial underpricing (Wright, Chiplin, and Robbie 1989).

The claw-back mechanism may be particularly useful in comparison to bidding up the price of assets when there is considerable uncertainty about asset valuation. Managers are required to make non-diversified investments in risky situations and hence seek some return for such risk-taking if they are to be persuaded to undertake a buy-out. The claw-back mechanism goes some way to meeting public interest issues relating to underpricing whilst at the same time not removing all the possibility of gain for managers.

The problem of management using 'inside' information to obtain transactions on favourable terms may be acute where such information is used where trading is to continue with the former parent or local authority after the buy-out. The Audit Commission (1990) have sought to establish ground rules to enable authorities to ensure that they have discharged their fiduciary duty to their chargepayers. These include, arm's-length negotiations between authorities and management teams, ensuring competitive bidding takes place, the establishment of an independent contract monitoring inspectorate, and close control of the length and nature of contracts. It may be difficult to ensure competitive bidding since outsiders are unlikely to bid at all or to put forward unrealistic tenders if they perceive little possibility of winning the contract. The length and number of contracts awarded is also important, as authorities need to be aware that long contracts may make them vulnerable to poor performance. The Commission has suggested independent valuation of assets, determination of the market value of assets through competitive bidding, claw-back arrangements, or retention of assets by authorities. Similar rules have also been proposed in respect of buy-outs of governmental agencies (NAO with CMBOR 1991).

The phenomenon of the life-cycle of the firm is well-established and has particular application to buy-outs from the public sector. There is some evidence that some privatization buy-outs are resold—via a flotation, trade sale, or secondary buy-out/buy-in—within very short periods at premiums considerably in excess of the buy-out price (Table 16.4) and exit more rapidly and to a greater extent than buy-outs generally

TABLE 16.4. Exits from privatization
buy-outs/buy-ins

	Number
Flotations	7
Trade sale	
from State Enterprise MBO	27
from MBI	2
from Local Authority MBO	5
Secondary buy-out/buy-in	6
Failures	
from State Enterprise MBO	6
from Local Authority MBO	1
from other	1
Restructuring	
from Local Authority	2
Recapitalization	
from State Enterprise	1
Total exit	58
No exit	100
TOTAL	158

Source: CMBOR, an independent research centre founded by Touche Ross & Co., and Barclays Development Capital Limited at the University of Nottingham.

(Thompson, Wright, and Robbie 1990). Question marks are raised where public-sector management are concerned over their capability to operate independently in a new commercial environment. In addition, the viability of the newly independent enterprise carrying out a contract is also important in ensuring continuity of service provision. Even the initially successful buy-outs may meet with subsequent problems, especially if they fail to diversify successfully. Exits from buy-outs may be deemed necessary from the point of view of the strategic development of the business. For growth to be achieved even where there is critical mass, there may need to be access to further capital to finance future expansion and to augment the internal share market. With a work-force which is relatively stable in size and with little staff turnover, there is a danger that the internal market of an employee buy-out would soon run out of sufficient liquidity to operate effectively (Ben-Ner 1988) (see the case of NFC below).

5. CASES

Discussion in the previous sections has outlined the rationale for management and employee buy-outs on privatization. In this section, three cases are discussed which cover the spectrum of these issues.

National Freight Company: Privatization of a Complete State-owned Firm by Employee Buy-out

The National Freight Corporation employee buy-out, which was completed in 1982, illustrates the efficiency improvements which may be derived where employee ownership provides the incentive for entrepreneurial activity throughout many layers of a large organization. However, questions are also raised concerning the extent to which assets were undervalued at the time of the sale.

National Freight Corporation (NFC) was a state-owned corporation from 1947 to 1982, experiencing significant losses for much of the later part of this period as it failed to adapt to a highly competitive market. After considerable debate as to how NFC might be privatized, the key role of management and employees in the running of the business was recognized in agreement to sell the firm intact as an employee buy-out. The key role of employees located in over seven hundred depots and the generally anti-privatization stance of the firm's nine trade unions strongly influenced a requirement by potential providers of equity finance for widespread employee commitment through shareholding in addition to that of the senior management team who had originally proposed the idea of a buy-out. Of the total purchase price of £53.5 million, government received less than £7 million, the difference going to fund a deficit on NFC's pension fund. Even the gross price represents a considerable discount on the book value of net assets which stood at £93.3 million. The 37.5 per cent of employees who initially bought shares held 82.5 per cent of the equity. The anti-privatization stance of the TGWU in particular led to a lower take-up of shareholdings in those depots where this union was strongest. Performance improvements and increases in the value of shares produced a substantial demand for shares from those depots which had previously heeded union advice not to buy shares. Post-buy-out performance improvements in NFC have been addressed in several studies (e.g. Wright and Coyne 1985; Bradley and Nejad 1989). Management methods were improved, a profit-sharing scheme was introduced together with a detailed employee appraisal system, the organization was rationalized from nine business units to four product-based divisions, and more specialist added-value services were developed which would have been difficult to conceive of in NFC in earlier years.

The effects of ownership on employee motivation were seen in improved concern for the provision of high-quality service and an increased informal feedback of market intelligence from employees to marketing personnel. Decentralized incentive schemes and wage negotiations have been introduced so as to relate salary and conditions packages more specifically to the different circumstances prevailing in each division. Major redundancy programmes have continued since the buy-out, with the policy that being a shareholder is not a guarantee of job security. Tensions between share-owning and non-share-owning employees were minimized by explicit attempts by management to deal with the issue and also because of the subsequent opportunities to allow employees who had not initially purchased shares to do so (Bradley and Nejad 1989). Profitability increased consistently after the buy-out up to 1990, partly as a result of employee ownership and participation as such, but also due to several other factors such as the general economic recovery of the mid-1980s onwards; the positive effect of privatization on the willingness of some customers to use NFC to deliver their products; a new-found flexibility that enabled management to switch the focus of activities from loss-making parcels operations to growth sectors including overseas activities; the benefits from the long process of restructuring that had occurred prior to privatization; and the disposal of large amounts of underused property. It is difficult to estimate the contribution of such land sales to NFC's post-privatization profits but they were substantial and lead one to the conclusion that NFC's assets were severely underpriced. After a period of continued growth, the year ending October 1991, produced a 4 per cent fall in pre-tax profits from £97.7 million to £93.7 million. After considerable internal debate about the merits of flotation, NFC became listed on the official market in London in 1989, at a market capitalization of £890 million. By the time of the flotation, average employee shareholdings of £600 in 1982 were worth £60,000. The proportion of employees with shares rose from 37.5 per cent in 1982 to 80 per cent upon flotation in 1989. Flotation gave access to further capital to finance future expansion and augmented the internal share market which had liquidity problems caused by a relatively stable workforce. The Stock Exchange gave exceptional permission for a special share to be created which would give employee shareholders double votes in the event of a hostile take-over bid, so helping to preserve employee control. Despite continuous incentives offered to employees to buy and hold NFC shares, it now seems clear that they are relatively unwilling to do so. In 1982, 84 per cent of NFC equity was held by NFC employees, pensioners and their families, but this percentage had fallen to 55 per cent after flotation in 1990, and to 48.6 per cent in March 1991. (Note that the double-voting rights attached to NFC employee shares means that these percentages understate the degree of employee control.)

National Bus Company: Privatization, Break-up, and Buy-outs

The buy-outs arising on the break-up of the National Bus Company illustrate the potential for entrepreneurial activity in local bus operations and the link between privatization and changes in industrial structure.

National Bus Company (NBC), which ran bus and coach services, was created in 1969. Local authorities also ran bus services which were not generally in competition with NBC prior to deregulation. Besides providing for deregulation the Transport Act 1985 also laid down that NBC was to be split up or privatized and that local authority bus transport companies were to be formed into separate passenger companies, operating at arm's length from the local authorities. Given the local nature of bus services and the low level of economies of scale in the industry (Glaister and Mulley 1983), break-up with a preference for management/employee bids appeared to offer the best possibility of meeting government privatization objectives of increasing efficiency (Mulley and Wright 1986). The substitution of market or quasi-market transactions for internal organizational relationships after break-up was both feasible and as will be seen below, cost-effective. The alternatives were sale as a whole to management and employees, which may have had adverse market-power consequences, or flotation on a stock market where the positive effects from employee ownership may have been weakened. The privatization of NBC resulted in a total of 73 sales, over half of which were in the form of buy-outs and only five of which were employee buy-outs with widespread employee share ownership. A further eleven involved purchase by companies previously having been bought-out. In the earlier part of the break-up process, by far the majority of sales were to management. This position changed in the latter part as trade buyers and earlier buy-outs became more important. Competition for ownership was in some cases very intense as noted earlier. Subsequent buy-outs in the local authority bus sector have involved both management-led employee buy-outs plus trade union-led employee bids jointly with employee buy-outs from the earlier privatization of NBC.

Case-study interviews of twenty of the NBC buy-outs, undertaken in the first year after buy-out by the present authors, found clear evidence that break-up had given a great deal of freedom to introduce more appropriate organization structures, to purchase appropriate fleet vehicles, to reduce costs bases, and to obtain fuel at lower costs than available through central purchasing. Privatization also provided scope for greater organic growth through diversification into related travel and leisure areas. The negative side was some loss of central co-ordination of new management training. Also in respect of NBC, break-up was reported to allow more localized and flexible remuneration structures which were seen as important in meeting increases in competition which came from the deregulation which accompanied the privatization process.

Sale of NBC in one unit, as originally envisaged, was considered to pose the threat of entry-forestalling action against possible new competition (Mulley and Wright 1986). Hence the decision to break up the company and allow market forces to decide the structure of the industry in the medium term, through a mixture of new entry and mergers. By early 1992, however, the incumbent firms were still dominant having seen off most new entrants and the deregulated markets remain highly concentrated. There has also been extensive merger activity, which was not unexpected (Elliott 1991). The maintenance of competitive market conditions has proved particularly difficult because of uncertainty about the contestability of local bus markets and the applicability of merger legislation to this market. Despite containing superficial characteristics of contestability (Baumol, Panzar, and Willig 1982), local bus markets are at best only imperfectly contestable. Incumbents can thwart actual and potential entry in a variety of ways including possession of sufficient financial strength to survive prolonged price wars. The subsequent reputation effect from fighting off a new entrant would then serve to deter further entry. Incumbents can also change price easily in the face of entry and surprise 'hit and run' entry is difficult as new entrants have to give 42 days notice in applying for a route licence. In order to preserve competitive conditions in local bus markets post-privatization, governments have had recourse to other policy tools most notably aspects of anti-competitive practices and merger policy. The application of such tools has been problematical. Although in the five-year period following deregulation the OFT received over a hundred complaints concerning predatory behaviour, such action is difficult to prove. Only four investigations of predatory behaviour were initiated, two of which did not find evidence of such action (Elliot 1991). Six investigations of bus mergers have been published (Table 16.5). In all but one case the mergers were found to be against the public interest, with divestment generally being recommended to remedy the situation if other undertakings between the parties could not be agreed. However, the application of merger policy in this area has been thrown into disarray with an Appeal Court ruling in November 1991 that bus mergers in the South Yorkshire area, which had been found by the MMC to be against the public interest, did not fall within the scope of the legislation as the area did not constitute a substantial part of the UK within the meaning of Section 64(3) of the Fair Trading Act 1973. This finding is of particular concern for the operation of policy since the optimal market structure of the industry remained unclear. Moreover, the Committee of Public Accounts (1991) has also commented that the Department of Transport, whilst having taken

TABLE 16.5. MMC reports on mergers in the bus industry

Merger	Date	Divestment action	Combined Market share (%)
Badger Line Holdings*/ Midland Red West Holdings*	Mar. 1989	BHL should be required to divest Cityline or MRWH as a whole if undertakings not to weaken competitive tendering could not be agreed (majority report)	82
S. Yorkshire Transport/ S & D/Groves/ Sheafline/SUT	Aug. 1990	Divest assets and business acquired as most effective means of restoring competition	50+
Stagecoach/Portsmouth City Bus (PCB)	July 1990	Divest PCB if undertakings to remove possibility of anti-competitive practices are not agreed	40+
Western Travel*/G & G Coaches	Oct. 1990	Not against public interest	34+
Stagecoach Holdings (inc. Southdown*)/ Hastings and District*	Dec. 1990	Against public interest but divestment would replace one dominant provider by another. MMC recommended measures to prevent retaliation by new entrants, etc., as a means of offsetting adverse effects of merger	36+
Caldaire Holdings/Blue Bird Securities	Jan. 1991	Against public interest but divestment would not restore competition to premerger levels. Undertakings on price and service levels, encouragement of competition, etc. required	38

* Buy-outs from NBC.

measures to promote competition at the time of the sale, did not subsequently regard themselves as responsible for judging the adequacy of competition but rather left it to competition policy. Whether or not local bus markets turn out to be a special case, the debacle does raise the issue of ensuring appropriate post-privatization monitoring structures exist. Utton (1991) has also questioned the OFT/MMC's approach to mergers in the bus industry but considers that it is correct to be sceptical about the level of mergers given uncertainty about the optimal structure of the industry.

Privatization by divestment buy-out with continuing trading: RFS Industries from British Rail

The RFS Industries buy-out provided increased scope and incentive to diversify, together with the extension of ownership to the wider body of employees.

Restructuring of BREL, itself a subsidiary of British Rail, began in the mid-1980s as part of a programme to improve efficiency as a prelude to its eventual sale. An element in the restructuring of BREL was to separate the parts into entities which themselves could be privatized. The attempt by British Rail to improve efficiency involved the contracting-out of manufacture and repair work, with a system of competitive tendering being introduced to allocate the work. As a result the role of BREL changed and with it the activities at the Doncaster works were reorganized. The site in Doncaster contained several activities. Manufacture and repair of railway wagons, wheelsets, and related components was reorganized to become Doncaster Wagon Works, later changing its name to RFS Engineering as part of the RFS Industries group. British Rail was to retain ownership of the National Supply Centre and the heavy maintenance depot as these were more dedicated to servicing the parent company. The sale process instigated by British Rail involved potential buyers bidding both for the wagon works business and for a maintenance contract with British Rail. The maintenance contract was significant enough to effectively underwrite most of the expected turnover in the first year. The need to obtain ministerial approval for the sale encouraged management to wish to secure employee commitment and to give undertakings that the business would not be closed or significantly reduced in size.

Performance of the company prior to buy-out was difficult to establish since until a short period before the sale it had been a cost centre within BREL with no separate revenue accounts. As a result it was problematical to establish a realistic price, and to make profit projections that would easily convince financiers that the company was viable as an independent entity. It was clear that even if the company was bought and the contract with British Rail won, little growth could be expected from existing activities and there was also the danger that with the introduction of tendering, the contract with British Rail could be lost in the future. Future growth, and reduction of dependence upon British Rail, would need to come from diversification based on existing skills.

In order to obtain work-force commitment and trade union co-operation in the deal an Employee Share Ownership Plan (ESOP) was introduced (Brennan 1989). The total equity stake held by managers and other employees was to depend upon cumulative profit performance over a three-year period. The transaction was completed in October

1987. In the first year following privatization, trading profit exceeded projections by a little over 40 per cent and turnover was 6 per cent greater than anticipated. The product range of RFS Industries Group has been developed through the creation of new activities and through diversifying acquisitions to add to the original activities which were bought-out, with a focus on specific segments of the European railway-traction and rolling-stock market. In the first three years after the buy-out dependence on British Rail was reduced to below a half of turnover. Overall, turnover and profits grew significantly in the first two years but the latter fell sharply in 1990 as a result of the recession which has also involved a major reorganization of management to obtain improved focus and control. Employment increased by over 50 per cent from the 650 at the time of the buy-out and includes the recruitment of a number of senior staff to provide a greater breadth and depth of experience. The ESOP is reported to have been important in changing the culture in the firm and the ratchet mechanism in the original buy-out structure has been triggered so that management and employees now have a majority of the equity.

6. CONCLUSIONS

This chapter has examined the role of management buy-outs in privatization. Agency-cost arguments suggest that the use of debt and other control mechanisms common to buy-outs may provide the basis for improved monitoring at least for those firms which have the appropriate characteristics. The discussion also demonstrated that governments wishing to privatize through buy-outs face a dilemma: reduce opportunism on the part of management by encouraging competing bids and by applying instruments that delay the payment of rewards for higher profits versus risk the loss of bids discouraged by this interference in the process, reduced sale proceeds, and perhaps the long-term, dynamic gains from private ownership. Given the evidence on performance improvements in buy-outs, the arguments presented here suggest that government should, while using protective mechanisms where appropriate, err on the side of encouraging managers to buy-out. Privatization of local government services has been heavily influenced by the political colour of individual authorities. If the right balance of mechanisms is introduced to deal with potential abuses of insider positions, the incentive mechanisms available in buy-outs ought to provide efficiency improvements which are not obtainable in the public sector. The re-election of a Conservative government in April 1992 seems likely to give further impetus to privatization in these sectors.

References

Arrow, K. (1974), *The Limits of Organization*, New York: Norton.

Audit Commission (1990), 'Management buy-outs: public interest or private gain', Management Paper no. 6.

Baumol, W., Panzar J., and Willig, R.(1982), *Contestable Markets and the Theory of Industrial Structure*, New York: Harcourt-Brace-Jovanovich.

Ben-Ner, A. (1988), 'The life-cycle of worker-owned firms in market economies', *Journal of Economic Behavior and Organization*, **10**, 287–313.

Bishop, M., and Kay, J. (1988), *Does Privatisation Work? Lessons From the UK*, London: London Business School Centre for Business Strategy.

Bradley, K., and Nejad, A. (1989), *Managing Owners: The NFC in Perspective*, Cambridge: Cambridge University Press.

Brennan, L. (1989), *Sharing the Family Silver with the Staff*, London: New Bridge Street Consultants.

Buck, T., Thompson, S., and Wright, M. (1991), 'Post-communist privatisation and the British experience: the role of management and employee buy-outs', *Public Enterprise*, Summer.

Buckland, R. (1987), The costs and returns of the privatization of the nationalised industries, *Public Administration*, **65**, 241–58.

Cable, J. (1988), 'Organisational form and economic performance', in S. Thompson and M. Wright (eds.), *Internal Organisation*.

Chiplin, B., Wright, M. and Robbie, K.(1989), *Realisations from Management Buy-outs: Issues and Prospects*, Nottingham: CMBOR.

—— —— —— (1991), *Management Buy-outs in 1991: The Annual Review from CMBOR*, Nottingham: CMBOR.

Committee of Public Accounts (1991), *National Bus, HC*, London: HMSO.

Cubbin, J., Domberger, S., and Meadowcroft, S. (1987), 'Competitive tendering and refuse collection: identifying the sources of efficiency gains', *Fiscal Studies*, **8**, 49–58.

Elliott, D. (1991), 'The role of the OFT following bus deregulation', mimeo, OFT.

Fama, E., and Jensen, M. C. (1983), 'Agency problems and residual claims', *Journal of Law and Economics*, **26**, 327–52.

Glaister, S., and Mulley, C. (1983), *The Public Control of the British Bus Industry*, Aldershot: Gower Press.

Jackson, P. (1982), *The Political Economy of Bureaucracy*, Deddington, Oxon.: Philip Allan.

Jensen, M. C.(1986), 'Agency costs of free cash flow, corporate finance, and take-overs', *American Economic Review*, May, 326–9.

—— and Meckling, W. (1976), 'The theory of the firm: managerial behaviour, agency costs and ownership structure', *Journal of Financial Economics*, **3**, 305–60.

McLachlan, S. (1983), *The NFC Buy-out*, London: Macmillan.

Malone, S. (1989), 'Characteristics of smaller company leveraged buy-outs', *Journal of Business Venturing*, **4/5**, 345–59.

Mayer, C., and Meadowcroft, S. (1986), 'Selling public assets: techniques and financial implications', *Fiscal Studies*, **6/4**, 42–56.

Menyah, K., Paudyal, K., and Inyangete, C. (1990), 'The pricing of initial offerings of privatised companies on the London stock exchange', *Accounting and Business Research*, **21/81**, 51–56.

Mulley, C., and Wright, M. (1986), 'Management buy-outs and the privatisation of National Bus', *Fiscal Studies*, Aug.

National Audit Office (1989), *DTI: Sale of Austin Rover to British Aerospace plc*, London: HMSO.

—— (1990), *National Bus*, HC 43, 1990/91, London: HMSO.

—— (1991), *Skills Training Agency*, HC, London: HMSO.

—— with CMBOR (1991), *Auditing Management Buy-outs in the Public Sector*, London: NAO.

Palepu, K. G. (1990), 'Consequences of leveraged buyouts', *Journal of Financial Economics*, **27**, 247–62.

Prahalad, C., and Hamel, G. (1990), 'The core competence of the corporation', *Harvard Business Review*, May/June, 79–91.

Robbie, K., Wright, M., and Thompson, S. (1992), 'Management buy-ins in the UK', *Omega*, **20/6**, 445–56.

Stephen, F., and Thompson, S. (1988), 'Internal organisation and investment', in S. Thompson and M. Wright (eds.), *Internal Organisation*.

Stiglitz, J. (1985), 'Credit markets and the control of capital', *Journal of Money Credit and Banking*, **17**, 133–52.

Teece, D., Pisano, G., and Shuen, A. (1990), Firm Capabilities, Resources and the Concept of Strategy, CCC Working Paper no. 90–8.

Thompson, S., and Wright, M. (1987), 'Markets to hierarchies and back again: the implications of management buy-outs for factor supply', *Journal of Economic Studies*, **14**, 5–22.

—— —— (1988) (eds.), *Internal Organisation, Efficiency and Profit*, Oxford: Philip Allan.

—— —— (1991), 'UK management buy-outs: debt, equity and agency cost implications', *Managerial and Decision Economics*, Feb.

—— —— and Robbie, K. (1990), 'Management buy-outs from the public sector: ownership form and incentive issues', *Fiscal Studies*, **11/3**, 71–88.

—— —— —— (1992), 'Management equity ownership, debt and performance: some evidence from UK management buy-outs, *Scottish Journal of Political Economy*, **39/4** (Nov.), 413–30.

Utton, M. (1991), *Competition Policy in the Deregulated Bus Market*, London: NERA.

Vickers, J., and Yarrow, G. (1988), *Privatisation: An Economic Analysis*, London: MIT Press.

Williamson, O. E. (1975), *Markets and Hierarchies: Analysis and Antitrust Implications*, New York: Free Press.

—— (1979), 'Transactions cost economics: the governance of contractual relations', *Journal of Law and Economics*, **22**, 233–62.

Wong, P., Wright, M., and Thompson, S. (1991), *The Market for Corporate Control: Recent Developments and a Review of the Evidence*, CMBOR Occ. Paper.

Wright, M. (1986), 'The make-buy decision and managing markets: the case of management buy-outs', *Journal of Management Studies*, **23/4**, 434–53.

—— (1987), 'Government divestments and the control of natural monopolies in the UK: the case of British Gas', *Energy Policy*, **15**, June, 193–216.

Wright, M. and Coyne, J. (1985), *Management Buy-outs*, Beckenham: Croom-Helm.

—— Thompson, S., Robbie, K. (1989), 'Privatisation via management and employee buy-outs: analysis and UK evidence', *Annals of Public and Cooperative Economy*, **60/4**, 399–429.

—— Chiplin, B., and Robbie, K. (1989), 'Privatisations by buy-out of state firms and elsewhere in the public sector', *Public Money and Management*, autumn.

—— —— Thompson, S., and Robbie, K. (1990), 'Management buy-outs, trade unions and employee ownership', *Industrial Relations Journal*, summer.

—— Thompson, S., Chiplin, B., and Robbie, K. (1991), *Buy-ins and Buy-outs: New Strategies in Corporate Management*, London: Graham & Trotman.

—— —— and Robbie, K. (1992), 'Venture capital and management-led leveraged buy-outs: European evidence', *Journal of Business Venturing*, Jan.

17

Privatization and the Labour Market: Facts, Theory, and Evidence

JONATHAN HASKEL* AND STEFAN SZYMANSKI†

1. INTRODUCTION AND SUMMARY

Privatization will probably be the most significant legacy of the Conservative/Thatcherite regime of the 1980s. Not only has it radically changed the landscape of British Industry, it has also influenced the policies of governments throughout the world, be they industrialized or industrializing, economies in transition or economies facing stagnation. In the UK the policy has affected the lives of most citizens, either through their dealings with utilities as customers or increasingly as owners of shares. Privatization has also created a whole new set of regulatory bodies to oversee those industries where monopoly abuse is possible. In many ways consumers are probably better informed as a result; for example much more information on the costs of nuclear power generation have become available as a result of privatization and the break-up of the CEGB. There remains a degree of controversy as to whether the consumer is better served as a result of privatization, much of it politically motivated. As time goes by a clearer picture is likely to emerge, but already there are a number of studies (e.g. Thompson and Whitfield 1990, Vickers and Yarrow 1988) which address this issue.

It is sometimes forgotten nowadays that privatization was, as Bishop and Kay (1989) put it, 'a policy devised in opposition by a section of the Conservative party . . . primarily as a means of reducing the power of public-sector trade unions'. The notorious 'Ridley Report' on the nationalized industries prepared in 1978, one year before the Conservatives came to power, discussed the possibilities of controlling wage demands. It argued that the government should consider denationalization since where industries 'have the nation by the jugular vein the only feasible option is to pay up'. A number of then ministers emphasized the

* Department of Economics, Queen Mary and Westfield College, University of London.
† Imperial College Management School, University of London.

Published in M. Bishop, J. Kay, C. Mayer, and D. Thompson (eds.) (1992), *Privatization and Regulation: The UK Experience*, 2nd edn., Oxford: Oxford University Press.

importance of the unions and the labour force in their public pronounce-
ments on the privatization programme. John Moore MP, then Financial
Secretary to the Treasury, is just one example:

Public Sector trade unions have been extraordinarily successful in gaining
advantages for themselves in the pay hierarchy by exploiting their monopoly
collective bargaining position . . . . Privatization . . . makes it possible to link pay
to success and to provide appropriate rewards. I believe that overall pay bargaining can be carried out much more responsibly and easily in companies freed
from government interference. We have consciously tried to place responsibility
on the management of nationalized industries and to make it clear that pay
negotiations are a matter for them and their employees. But public-sector trade
union experience of previous administrations has given their leaders a taste of
political power without responsibility. They are all too ready to seek to involve
the government in the interests of their political objectives. (John Moore MP,
quoted in Kay *et al.* 1986)

However, it is also clear that the Thatcher government effected enormous changes in the management of labour relations of public firms in
the run up to privatization, and in public corporations for which privatization remains a distant dream. Thus not only did significant shedding
of labour occur at British Steel before the 1988 sell-off, and major
changes in labour relations at the then British Leyland, but also the government was prepared to take on the miners during a year-long strike in
1984/5 even though British Coal remained in public ownership. In fact,
although many Conservatives prior to the 1979 election were gloomy
about the prospects for controlling nationalized industries effectively, it
seems clear that they were in practice highly successful in achieving control and exercising it in pursuit of their political agenda.

In general however very little has been written on privatization and
the labour market. For the most part the privatization literature has
focused on changes in management organization and incentives. This
chapter then looks at the effects of privatization on the labour market.
Our main focus is on wages and employment since productivity is the
concern of the chapter by Bishop and Thompson.

The outline of our review is as follows. In Section 2 we look at the
changes in wages and employment in the public/privatized sector.
Employment has generally fallen sharply over the 1980s. Average wages
have grown in line with the rest of the economy, although top managers
have seen above average wage increases. Section 3 reviews theoretical
explanations to account for these facts. The standard approach concerns
the monitoring relation between managers and owners, be they government or shareholders. We argue that this is an inadequate description of
the relation between managers and owners, which is better seen as an
employment setting and wage-bargaining relationship. Privatization can
be seen as delegation to tougher, more profit-maximizing managers,

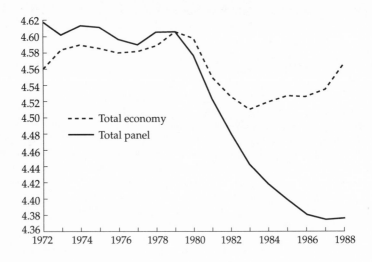

Fig. 17.1. Employment

who reduce employment and wages since they are firmer opposition to unions. Privatization, therefore, might be seen as an alternative to toughness on the part of the government in public-sector wage negotiations. In Section 4 we review the evidence on wages and employment in the UK. Privatization or changing public-sector objectives has reduced employment, but have had little effect on wages. But wages fall if there is liberalization so that firms lose market power. Section 5 concludes.

2. FACTS

Perhaps the greatest impact of privatization in the UK has been in the labour market. Many public-sector industries have experienced massive labour shedding both in the run up to and in the period after privatization. To get some idea of this we have assembled annual data, 1972–88, on a panel of 14 companies that were publicly owned in 1972.[1] These companies accounted for 76 per cent of pubic-sector employment in 1979 (we have not included the civil service, the NHS, or the education sector). Figure 17.1 shows employment in the companies with whole-economy employment as a reference. Although in the pre-1979 period

---

[1] The companies are British Airports Authority, British Airways, British Coal, British Gas, British Rail, British Steel, British Telecom, Electricity Supply Industry, North of Scotland Hydro-Electric Board, South of Scotland Hydro-Electric Board, London Regional Transport, Post Office, Regional Water Authorities, Scottish Transport Group.

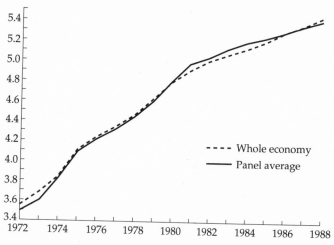

FIG. 17.2. Wages

there was a slight downward trend in employment levels in the public-sector, this accelerated sharply during the period that public industries prepared for and underwent privatization. Interestingly, the story for wages has been less dramatic. Figure 17.2 shows a close correlation between wage growth in firms going through the privatization process and the rest of the economy.

This aggregate data obscures changes within the panel of firms. Table 17.1 shows the variety of experience underlying Figures 17.1 and 17.2. There have been spectacular falls in employment in coal and steel, with rises in BAA and the Post Office. As for wages, BAA and the Post Office appear to lag rather behind the average, with BSC and BT showing above average increases. These data are similar to those reported by Bishop and Kay (1989) who also look at some other companies.

The picture for top managers' salaries is dramatic. Table 17.2, taken from Bishop and Kay (1989), shows that top managers' pay has accelerated sharply since 1979. On average, real wages have increased fourfold, whereas executive pay in the economy as a whole has doubled. As for productivity, Hartley *et al.* (1991) and Parker and Hartley (1991) have highlighted the large productivity increases associated with these employment reductions. Bishop and Kay (1989) and the chapter by Bishop and Thompson in this volume also show that public industries have improved their performance considerably since the 1970s.

There is rather little evidence on the impact of privatization on industrial relations. In a review, Ogden (1990) cites evidence from a case-study of the water industry and shows that there has been little change in union membership or the scope of bargaining following privatization. In other firms such as BT and electricity there appears to have been some movement towards more decentralized bargaining however. It should be noted that whilst the coal industry has seen the creation of a new union and separation of bargaining (Winterton 1990) it is a rather special case.

Privatization has influenced employee share ownership in the UK. All the major privatizations have offered generous terms to employees many of whom have enjoyed large capital gains as a result. For example, the employees of National Freight Corporation enjoyed capital gains of around 5400 per cent comparing the 1988 share price with the valuation in 1982 (Bishop and Kay 1989: 51).

3. THEORY

Whilst dealing with the labour market was undoubtedly an important factor in the early motivation of the government, it was not the only one. In fact, there are any number of possible reasons for privatization. In their influential book Vickers and Yarrow (1988) suggested seven:

  (i) improving efficiency;
 (ii) reducing the public-sector borrowing requirement;
(iii) reducing government involvement in enterprise decision-making;
 (iv) easing problems of public-sector pay determination;
  (v) widening share ownership;
 (vi) encouraging employee share ownership;
(vii) gaining political advantage.

In this chapter we choose to focus on what privatization actually changed in the corporations involved. Reducing the PSBR, widening share ownership, and gaining political advantage are beyond the scope of this study.

Most attention has been paid to the issue of efficiency. Usually a distinction is drawn between productive efficiency (ensuring that what is done is done at minimum cost) and allocative efficiency (ensuring that prices reflect costs accurately). In general there has been no presupposition that privatization will raise allocative efficiency. Indeed there has in general been an expectation that privatization will lead to inefficiency in this sense as privatized firms seek to exploit any market power which they might inherit. This problem has been recognized in the privatization process by the establishment of regulatory bodies to oversee pricing in industries where competition is limited, in particular Telecoms, Gas, Electricity, and Airports. In these cases private enterprise has not been permitted to operate unhindered since it was believed to be against the public interest. By contrast, in industries where competition was believed to be relatively strong (e.g. steel, airlines) there has been little or no intervention. This suggests that what is important for performance is not so much privatization *per se*, but liberalization, opening monopoly industries to competition. This point has been made by a number of writers e.g. Kay and Thompson (1986) and Vickers and Yarrow (1988).

3.1. *The agency approach*

The idea that privatization might raise productive efficiency has been extensively explored in the literature. Indeed, it has some claim to being the only real theory of privatization advanced hitherto. Agency theory is an approach to decision-making problems which focuses on the relationship between the person issuing instructions (the principal) and the person employed to carry them out (the agent). Normally this relationship is thought of in terms of an owner and a manager, but in the public-sector the parties can be the minister and enterprise manager. In general there is no agency problem if both parties are fully informed about the environment in which the task is carried out. Problems arise when the principal is less well informed than the agent. Suppose for example the principal can observe the output which results from the performance of a task, but not the agent's effort input. This is not a problem if the agent's reward can be made dependent on the outcome alone (e.g. sharecropping). However, typically this imposes a significant risk on the agent. There is normally a conflict between offering efficient incentives and sharing risk. For example, the managers of British Steel cannot bear the whole risk associated with a downturn in the steel industry but if their income is unaffected by poor performance they have no incentive to make any effort at all.

Agency problems can be to some extent mitigated by monitoring managerial performance. The agency approach to privatization is based on the view that the private sector is more effective when it comes to monitoring than the public-sector, e.g. Vickers and Yarrow 1988; Bos 1991; Rees 1988, etc. Thus privatization improves productive efficiency by ensuring that managers supply effort and keep down costs. At the same time it may be that privatized monopolies need to be regulated in order to ensure that prices are set at socially efficient levels (allocative efficiency). The problem with the agency approach is that it is circular. If the private sector is assumed to be better at monitoring than the public-sector then under certain conditions it can be shown that it will be more efficient. (See Vickers and Yarrow (1988: 34–6) for the basic model and Pint (1991) for a detailed exposition when such assumptions are not imposed). The basic assumption hardly seems warranted. First, it could plausibly be argued that a single owner might prove a better monitor than the public-sector, but in fact most privatizations have left ownership in the hand of a large numbers of shareholders, most of whom cannot expect to be as well informed as a government minister. No individual can have much say over the behaviour of the management and there are rarely opportunities for co-ordinated shareholder behaviour. Second, it is not very likely that the take-over mechanism acts as a threat to managers in most of the large privatized industries such as Telecoms, Gas, and Electricity. Third, there is every reason to suppose that individual ministers in charge of public industries were very well placed to monitor managerial behaviour and also well placed to take action.

Of course, it can be argued that managerial incentive schemes associated with privatization have helped to improve the performance of a number of privatized industries. However, there was no reason that such schemes could not have been introduced in public-sector industries. In all, the agency approach to privatization is based on an assertion which does not seem warranted in theory or justifiable in practice.

3.2. Privatization as Delegation

One of the most important changes brought about by privatization is a change in objectives. It is probably not so unrealistic to suggest that private firms pursue profit maximization in some broad sense (shareholder-value maximization might be more accurate, but under reasonable restrictions this should be equivalent). Public-sector firms rarely pursue profits exclusively. It is more reasonable to suppose that the broad objectives of public-sector organizations are set by the priorities of their political masters, and that politicians are motivated broadly by the pursuit of political power. A simple characterization of these relationships would be that the objective of a public firm is the maximization of a weighted average of the welfare of a collection of interest groups, the weights being determined by the importance of each interest group in getting political masters re-elected. So, the public-sector firm gives some weight to profits, consumer welfare (surplus) and the welfare of public-sector employees. By contrast private firms simply maximize profits. Thus the process of privatization involves shifting the objectives of the public-sector firm toward profit maximization. In fact, much of this process may take place before the formality of private ownership is brought about. It involves changing the attitudes of management whilst still in the public-sector.

These changes in objectives affect not only the employment decisions of managers but also the outcome of the wage bargain. We assume that the work-force bargains with the firm as a collective unit, i.e. a union. The bargaining structure itself is not changed by privatization, only bargaining outcomes. Under general conditions it can be shown (see Haskel and Szymanski 1991) that:

(i) the effect of changing objectives toward profit maximisation (the privatization/change in objectives effect) is to reduce both wages and employment;

(ii) any liberalization of markets has a tendency to reinforce the downward pressure on wages. But, employment would tend to rise as demand increases in firms reducing their prices (due to the loss of monopoly power).

These results are striking. Normally we would expect wages and employment to move in opposite directions: if wages fall employment rises and vice versa, as in the liberalization effect. However, the privatization effect puts downward pressure on both employment and wages. Employment falls for two reasons. First the public-sector has a bias toward high output because it favours consumers, and second because the public-sector attaches some weight to the well-being of employees. If both of these effects disappear (because of the privatization process) then employment will fall. Wages fall in our model because the private sector is willing to concede less to the work-force/union than the government. Because the government 'cares' about the work-force, the public-sector will not drive as hard a wage bargain with the union as the private sector, so that wages end up being higher in the public-sector.

One objection to this argument is that the Thatcher administration which was responsible for privatization did not care about the unions at all, and indeed passed legislation specifically aimed at reducing union power. Although this is probably true in a general sense it does not mean that the government could ignore the interests of employees *qua* voters (in key marginal constituencies, for example). Furthermore, even if the government of the day did not care for the unions, they could not guarantee that future governments would be as committed. Privatization can then be viewed as a way of committing the government to not paying high wages. In effect, privatization is a way of delegating authority over wage bargaining for a government which is unable to commit itself (or future governments) to bargaining at arm's length with the work-force/union.

In our formulation, privatization is characterized by a change of objectives. As we argued earlier, it is possible for objectives to change within the public-sector. It may happen, then, that in the run up to privatization a firm may start to behave like a private-sector firm (in fact we will argue below that this was in fact the case). However, it is difficult to shift the objectives of public-sector industry without the privatization process. This is because when it comes to bargaining with the unions, a government committed to public-sector industry will also find it hard to establish a credible negotiating stance. For example, the Labour government in the late 1970s found it hard to resist public-sector pay pressure whilst the Conservative government of the early 1980s was able to sit out lengthy strikes in the steel and coal industries. In the Labour case it was clear that ultimately the government would not allow public industry to collapse, whilst in the Conservative case it was clear that the government's ultimate goal was privatization. Changing the objectives of public-sector managers is only credible if there is a commitment to privatization. Where this is lacking firms will continue to be influenced by the objectives of political masters. Another example of this problem is provided by the recent difficulties faced by the government in turning hospitals into self-governing trusts. Given the government's insistence that it will not privatize the health service, the government will continue to be susceptible to political pressure in terms of employment and services provided by the trusts, undermining their attempts to impose tighter financial controls.

Whilst we argued above that privatization *per se* changes very little from a monitoring point of view, we have also to consider the possibility that privatization will be accompanied by liberalization of markets. If this is the case we will expect wages to fall, reflecting the lower profitability of the firm and therefore the smaller surplus over which the union can bargain; but we will also expect there to be increases in employment, as output rises in response to the higher demand associated with lower prices.

This is not a normative model of privatization. What it says is simply that privatization will reduce wages and employment in the absence of liberalization. Where there is liberalization we expect there to be a countervailing tendency of employment to rise.

Our argument above has considered a rather stark comparison between a public-sector and an unregulated private sector. Whilst this may be appropriate for British Airways and British Steel, industries such as BT, BAA, and British Gas have been subject to RPI–X regulation since privatization (see Beesley and Littlechild 1989 for discussion). A simple way to think of regulation is to regard it as a cap on the price that firms can charge, thus weakening the market power of firms which they would otherwise use to restrict output and raise prices. RPI–X therefore serves to moderate any fall in employment resulting from privatization and since it lowers market power it lowers wages.[2]

Lastly what of share ownership? What studies there have been have tended to look at the effects of profit-sharing in general rather than share

[2] Formally speaking RPI–X is a dynamic form of regulation and so raises extremely complicated issues concerning time-consistency and strategic behaviour by unions, firms, and regulators (see e.g. Grout 1982).

ownership and they have not found evidence of large impacts (e.g. Wadhwani and Wall 1990 and Bhargava 1991). This is not surprising. The income which employees receive from profit-sharing schemes, dividends, or capital gains are in most cases only a very small percentage of total income (although senior executives are frequently an exception). Employees are unlikely to perceive any direct correlation between their efforts and returns to share ownership.

4. EVIDENCE

Although a considerable amount of privatization has now taken place, we are still in the early post-privatization period. For this reason it has been difficult for researchers to assemble data on the effects of privatization. There have been a number of case-studies and general surveys (apart from books such as Vickers and Yarrow 1988; Veljanovski 1987; Bishop and Kay 1989; single studies include Ogden 1990; Watts 1991; Thompson and Whitfield 1990; Vickers and Yarrow 1991) but these have mostly dwelt on the mechanics of privatization or its impact on the product market.

As for the labour market, we are concerned here with the effects of privatization and liberalization on employment, wages, and productivity. Productivity has received attention in a number of papers. The most systematic evidence is reported in the work of Bishop and Thompson (1991) and Parker and Hartley (1991). Bishop and Thompson looked at productivity in 10 enterprises which were in the public-sector in the 1970s, some of which were privatized in the 1980s (BA, BAA, BT, British Coal, the ESI, British Gas, Post Office, British Rail, British Steel). In their paper they constructed productivity indices for each industry and compared performance in the 1970s and 1980s. Their main conclusions were that regulatory reform that affected these industries in the 1980s, whether privatized or not, significantly improved performance. They found that productivity improvements were greatest in Steel, Coal, BR, and the Post Office. In the first two of these the potential for entry had been significantly increased in the 1980s. However, it appears that in neither of the other two had there been significant privatization or entry, suggesting that other industry-specific or organizational factors had accounted for much of the improvement.

The Parker and Hartley study looked at the impact of organizational status and product-market conditions on labour productivity and employment in 10 organizations (Post Office, BT, NFC, Royal Ordnance, Royal Mint, HMSO, London Transport, BAE, Rolls-Royce, BA) over various periods stretching back as far as 1959 up to 1988. (However, most of their data went only up to the mid-1980s). They enumerated a number of changes in organizational status, not only nationalization and privatization but also internal reorganizations within the public-sector. Their findings suggested that organizational change was indeed associated with improvements in labour productivity growth: the greater the shift toward private ownership structures the greater the improvement in labour productivity. They also hypothesized that a move to private ownership would tend to reduce employment in the long run but their results were not strongly supportive of this relationship.

When looking at employment and wages there may be a host of other factors which have influenced them, as well as privatization. For example one might expect the liberalization of markets, the 1980–81 recession, and changes in the power of trade unions to have made an impact on wage and employment levels. To the best of our knowledge, Haskel and Szymanski (1991) is the only study that attempts to control for these factors. In it, we have undertaken a regression approach using the 14 companies we referred to above, matched to industry data.

The main hypotheses that we wish to investigate relate to privatization/changes in objectives and to liberalization. Privatization/changing objectives is expected to reduce employment and wages since the private sector cares less about high output and wages than the public-sector. Liberalization is expected to raise employment as competition reduces prices and increases output demand, and to lower wages as bargainers have less surplus to share out. Of course, to this we must add a number of other influences that would be expected to be important (for a formal justification of these see Haskel and Szymanski 1991). As for employment, we would also expect real wages, demand, and capital accumulation to be important. For wages our regressions also included outside wages, benefits, unions, and unemployment.

The effect of privatization/changes in objectives discussed above suggests that what mattered was the decision to privatize or to change the objectives of the public-sector firm; the shift of objectives towards profit maximization, rather than the actual date of privatization. We looked for the dates at which significant reorientations took place: for example the Energy and Water Acts of 1983 marked the start of the privatization process for the electricity supply and water industry, the reorganization of BA in 1982 marked a significant step toward privatization, and so on.[3]

To measure the effect of liberalization, a market-share indicator is required for each company. To take an example, the total route tonne-kilometres flown by British Airways is published in company accounts.

[3] The dates are BAA 1986 (Airports Act); BA 1982 (reorganization into three divisions); BC 1985 (end of strike and Coal Industry Act); BG 1982 (Oil and Gas Act); BR 1981 (reorganization into five divisions); BSC 1980 (end of strike, new management); BT 1984 (privatization); ESI, NSHEB, SSEB, 1983 (Energy Act); LRT, STG 1986 (competition in buses starts following Transport Act, 1985); PO 1985 (reorganization into three divisions); RWA, 1983 (Water Act).

Domestic market share is therefore taken as a proportion of total route tonne-kilometres flown by all UK airlines in and out of the UK; analogous market share indices were constructed for all our sample. However, many firms compete in international markets and so domestic market-share would give a misleading impression of market power. Therefore we adjusted the market-share variable by a factor reflecting the share of non-UK firms in the UK market. For example British Airways' domestic share can be corrected by the share of total passengers carried on flights to and from the UK by non-domestic airlines.

Our regression specifications and results involve some technical statistical considerations outside the scope of this chapter.[4] Concerning our two hypotheses of central interest our main findings can be summarized as follows.

Privatization/changes in objectives generally had a significant negative impact on employment, particularly in the coal and steel industries, although less so in the Post Office and BT. Our estimates suggested that employment was reduced by about 25 per cent on average in our industries due to this effect. This is almost exactly the average fall in employment since 1980 (see Table 17.1). There was some reduction in wages, but this was comparatively small; wages might be expected to fall by about 4 per cent.

As for liberalization, we found that where market share fell, implying

TABLE 17.1. Changes in wages and employment, 1980–1988 (%)

Company	Employment	Wages
British Airports Authority	15.9	68.6
British Airways	–4.5	79.0
British Coal	–61.7	82.1
British Gas	–23.2	62.3
British Rail	–27.8	85.4
British Steel	–62.4	120.1
British Telecom	–0.9	114.4
Electricity Supply Industry	–16.1	89.5
North of Scotland Hydro-Electric Board	–6.3	71.0
South of Scotland Hydro-Electric Board	–14.0	87.2
London Regional Transport	–31.2	101.6
Post Office: posts	10.7	42.9
Regional Water Authority	–23.6	81.0
Scottish Transport Group	–16.9	64.8
TOTALS	–25.6	81.5

Source: Authors' calculations from company accounts.

[4] We estimate employment and wage equations using SURE regression techniques. Details and robustness checks are reported in Haskel and Szymanski.

increased competition, wages also tended to fall. So for example British Steel which has been facing an increasingly competitive product market over the 1980s is expected to face downward pressure on wage costs. By contrast British Gas, which although privatized has not faced an intensification of competition, is expected to show little change in wages. In fact we found that the liberalization effect is small. For example, our results suggest that the effect on wages from Mercury attaining 2 per cent of BT's monopoly in a year is to slow wage growth by 1.5 per cent. This is small set against the average growth of 9 per cent in BT wages since reorientation. There was little effect of liberalization on employment.

In sum, our results suggest the following stylized story about the 1980s privatization process and the labour market in the UK. Privatization/changing objectives has led to large-scale labour shedding as companies have become more profit-oriented. The remaining workers have been quite successful in maintaining their wages relative to comparable groups. But where market power has fallen, as a result of liberalization for example, relative wages have been reduced.

This story has a number of interesting implications. Kay and Thompson (1986) argued that what matters, so far as efficiency is concerned, is not ownership but competition. If we think of efficiency as unit labour cost then efficiency is determined by wages divided by productivity. As far as wages are concerned the above findings suggest that increased competition reduces wages. But we also find that ownership (by changing objectives) affects wages. Our regression analysis enables us to quantify these effects; they do not appear to be large. Substantial economies in wage costs are only likely when there is considerable loss of market share.

Second, our results also seem to support 'Insider/Outsider' theories of wage and employment determination (e.g. Lindbeck and Snower 1990) popular in the labour economics literature. These suggest that those in employment within the firm exert a much greater influence on wage levels than those outside the firm (i.e. potentially competitive labour).

The effects of ownership on wages, whilst small, are in stark contrast to the rapid salary increases of the senior executives of privatized companies where salaries have risen very rapidly (Table 17.2 provides some figures, these come from Bishop and Kay 1989: 65–8). Although this phenomenon has been widely commented upon there is little real analysis to explain it. Partly it may reflect a catch-up effect since public-sector management wages tend to lag far behind those in the private-sector. It is also the case that private-sector executive salaries have risen rapidly in the 1980s (see e.g. Szymanski 1992). It is also possible that while unions may be weakened by privatization, the bargaining position of management may be enhanced by privatization. This is certainly an issue which warrants further research.

TABLE 17.2. Top-executive remuneration (1988) prices)

	1979 (£)	1988 (£)
Privatized		
Amersham	31,000	90,000
BAA	37,000	151,000
British Airways	45,000	253,000
British Gas	49,000	184,000
Cable & Wireless	31,000	208,000
National Freight Consortium	44,000	143,000
Rolls-Royce	95,000	130,000
Average	47,400	164,300
Public sector (1979)		
British Coal	49,000	145,000
British Rail	54,000	90,000
British Steel	58,000	134,000
Electricity Supply*	45,000	82,000
Post Office	48,000	84,000
Average	50,800	107,000
Average private sector†	115,000	213,000

* CEGB.

† Private-sector average is based on a sample of leading industrial companies, equivalent to those in the 1979 public sector.

Source: Bishop and Kay 1989: Table 36.

5. CONCLUSIONS

Much of the privatization literature is highly partisan. Usually it is assumed that privatization *per se* raises the efficiency of management, so that the only task for researchers is to measure the size of this effect. This type of analysis has tended largely to focus on product market effects, given its emphasis on management issues. We have looked at privatization from the point of view of the labour market. This approach is warranted by the fact that some of the most noticeable effects of privatization and its related reforms have been in that area. Rather than assume that private enterprise is superior we have focused on the objectives of public- and private-sector management and deduced the impact that these would have on wages and employment. We have suggested that privatization is likely to lead to falling employment and wages. Empirical research suggests that while privatization/changing objectives have had a large negative impact on employment, there has been a smaller impact on wages. However, liberalization does tend to reduce wages.

The impact of privatization on labour markets is an important issue, not just in the UK where only a relatively small section of the economy has been moved into the private sector, but also in regions such as Eastern Europe where a much deeper privatization process is now taking place. We are still in the early post-privatization period and there is still much research to be done in this area. We believe that it is important that researchers should in future focus more on the labour-market impacts of privatization. This goes not only for the UK but for other countries where privatization programmes are yet to be implemented.

References

Beesley, M., and Littlechild, S. (1989), 'The regulation of privatized monopolies in the UK', *Rand Journal of Economics*, **20/3**, 454–72

Bhargava, S. (1991), 'Profit-sharing and profitability: evidence from UK panel data', mimeo.

Bishop, M., and Kay, J. (1989), *Does Privatisation Work? Lessons from the UK*, London: Centre for Business Strategy, London Business School.

Bos, D. (1988), 'Public enterprises in theory and practice', *European Economic Review*, **32**, 469–514.

Grout, P. (1982), 'Investment and wages in the absence of binding contracts: a Nash bargaining approach', *Econometrica*, 449–60.

Hartley, K., Parker, D., and Martin, S. (1991), 'Organisational status, ownership, and productivity', *Fiscal Studies*, **12/2**, 46–60.

Haskel, J., and Szymanski, S. (1991), 'Privatization, liberalization, wages and employment: theory and evidence for the UK', Centre for Business Strategy, Working Paper no. 120, London Business School

Kay, J., and Thompson, D. J. (1986), 'Privatisation: a policy in search of a rationale', *Economic Journal*, **96**, 18–32.

—— Mayer, C., and Thompson, D. J. (eds.), (1986), *Privatization and Deregulation: The UK Experience*, Oxford: Oxford University Press.

Lindbeck, A., and Snower, D. (1990), *The Insider–Outsider Theory of Wages and Employment*, Cambridge, Mass.: MIT Press.

Ogden, S. (1990), 'Privatisation and industrial relations: the shock of the new?', University of Leeds, Discussion Paper, 90/12.

Parker, D., and Hartley, K. (1991), 'Organizational status and performance: the effects on employment', *Applied Economics*, **23**, 403–16.

Pint, E. (1991), 'Nationalisation versus Regulation of Monopolies: the Effects of Ownership on Efficiency', *Journal of Public Economics*, **44**, 131–163.

Rees, R. (1988), 'Inefficiency, public enterprise privatisation', *European Economic Review*, **32**, 422–31.

Szymanski, S. (1992), 'Director's pay and incentives in the 1980s: the UK experience', Centre for Business Strategy, Working Paper no. 125, London Business School.

Thompson, D., and Whitfield, A. (1990), 'Express coaching: privatisation, incumbent advantage and the competitive process', mimeo.

Veljanovski, C. (1987), *Selling the State*, London: Weidenfeld and Nicolson.

Vickers, J., and Yarrow, G. (1988), *Privatization: An Economic Analysis*, Cambridge, Mass.: MIT Press.

—— —— (1991), 'The British electricity experiment', *Economic Policy*, **12**, 187–231.

Wadhwani, S., and Wall, M. (1990), 'The effects of profit sharing on employment, wages, stock returns, productivity: evidence from micro-data', *Economic Journal*, **100**, 1–17.

Watts, C. (1991), 'British Leyland: the effects of managerial approach on performance', London Business School, mimeo.

Winterton, J. (1990), 'Private power and public relations: the effects of privatization upon industrial relations in British Coal', in G. Jenkins and M. Poole (eds.), *New Forms of Ownership*, London: Routledge.

18

Privatization in the UK: Internal Organization and Productive Efficiency

MATTHEW BISHOP* AND DAVID THOMPSON†

1. INTRODUCTION

Over the last decade the programme of privatization in the UK has changed both the shape and the nature of the public-enterprise sector. Whilst the motivations and objectives of these policies have been both multiple and shifting over time, a central concern has related to the efficiency of public enterprises. Outlining his objectives for the (then) new policy, Treasury Minister John Moore said in 1983 that 'our main objective is to promote competition and improve efficiency'.

A recurring theme in discussion and evaluation of enterprises' performance has been the role of 'corporate culture'. Thus the culture regarded as prevalent in the public-enterprise sector was seen as inappropriate to ensuring efficient performance and 'culture change' was seen both as a necessary prerequisite for improved performance and also as a powerful explanatory factor in shaping changes to performance which have been observed (see Bishop and Kay 1988).

Our objective in this paper is to examine slightly more specifically what 'culture change' might involve. An extensive literature (stemming from the work of Williamson and Coase) has examined the organizational characteristics of firms which are relevant to enhancing their performance in private markets (see, for example, R. S. Thompson and M. Wright 1988). The question we want to examine is whether publicly owned enterprises—in the form in which they existed in the UK at the

* Journalist with *The Economist*.
† Department of Education. At the time the paper was written David Thompson was a Senior Research Fellow at the Centre for Business Strategy, London Business School.

The financial support of the Gatsby Foundation in carrying out the research upon which this paper is based is gratefully acknowledged. Helpful comments on an earlier draft came from John Kay, Jone Pearce, Peter Ruys, David Starkie, and a referee; the usual disclaimer applies.

beginning of the 1980s—had adopted organizational features appropriate to enhancing performance. And, where this is not the case, we want to investigate whether regulatory reform has prompted changes to the internal organization of these enterprises.

The structure of the paper is as follows. Following this introduction, in Section 2 we outline the main features of the regulatory reforms implemented in the UK over the last decade. Whilst commonly associated with privatization, these reforms have also involved the deregulation of activities which were formerly public-enterprise monopolies (in some cases in conjunction with privatization, in some cases not) and changes to the regulation of enterprises remaining in the public sector.

In Section 3 we consider two important aspects of enterprises' internal organization. First we look at organizational form and we examine the characteristics of the multi-divisional, M-form, company and its incentive properties. Second we consider the role of performance pay, and management incentives, in attenuating the agency problem which arises from the separation of ownership and control in large corporations.

Our findings on the internal organization of the UK's publicly owned enterprises show that at the beginning of the 1980s performance pay was infrequent and organizational form most usually followed a unitary, U-form, structure with only limited delegation of responsibility for financial performance. Our findings also show that by 1990 this picture had changed substantially. Performance pay had become commonplace amongst senior and middle managers; and multi-divisional structures had also increased in importance.

In Section 4 we examine enterprises' productivity. Our analysis focuses on nine of the largest publicly owned enterprises (as they existed at the beginning of the 1980s, when each enjoyed significant market power). We measure changes in labour productivity and in total-factor productivity. Our results show a significant upturn in productivity growth rates during the course of the 1980s. In the final section we draw together our findings and conclusions.

2. REGULATORY REFORM IN THE UK

The regulatory reforms implemented in the UK over the last decade include privatization, changes in the regulation of publicly owned enterprises, and the deregulation of former state monopolies. In this part of the paper we give only a brief outline of the main reforms (see Vickers and Yarrow 1988 for a more detailed account).

During the 1970s publicly owned enterprises were regulated under a framework which established guidelines on pricing and investment policies (guidelines which followed the standard allocative rules) and which established financial targets; these were usually specified as a return on assets. The link between the rules for pricing investment and the financial targets was never clearly established—either in theory or in practice—and financial targets often proved to be flexible to unanticipated changes in costs or in pricing and investment policies. It has been argued (see for example Pryke, 1981 or NEDO 1976) that this framework offered few incentives to the achievement of productive efficiency. That, furthermore, asymmetries in information meant that the allocative rules were unenforceable in practice. And, in part because of this, enterprises' strategies were subject to *ad hoc*, and often short-term, political intervention. The consequence was that, unless it could be assumed that the managers of publicly owned enterprises acted as welfare maximizers, the expectation would be inefficient performance; this often turned out to be the case (again see Pryke 1981 and NEDO 1976).

Changes to this framework of control for publicly owned enterprises stemmed from a government White Paper in 1978. This introduced explicit targets for productivity and established financial performance as the enterprises' primary objective; financial targets were to drive pricing policy rather than vice versa. Subsequent changes to accounting policy (see HM Treasury 1986) aimed to align an enterprise's return on assets with the (average) return being earned on its investment projects. Performance pay for senior managers (board members) was also introduced, linked to the achievement of the financial and productivity targets.

Deregulation of state-monopoly activities commenced with the liberalization of entry controls on express-coach services in 1980 and has subsequently touched many of the former state monopolies. Privatization of state-owned enterprises began with smaller enterprises, typically already operating in competitive private markets, but the privatization of British Telecom at the end of 1984 marked a change in the direction of privatization policy. Subsequently many of the 'natural monopolies' have been privatized. In markets where these enterprises continue to hold market power prices have been subject to a regulatory ceiling, which limits price changes to a specified amount (which may be positive or negative) below the change in the consumer price index; this ceiling is reset at periodic intervals (for a discussion of the incentive properties associated with this framework see Littlechild 1983, or Vickers and Yarrow 1988). It can be seen that the framework bears some similarities to the methods of regulation introduced for publicly owned enterprises in the 1978 White Paper.

In the following parts of this paper we will focus our analysis upon nine of the largest publicly owned enterprises—as they existed at the beginning of the 1980s when each held significant market power. Table 18.1 summarizes how the regulatory reforms have affected these enter-

TABLE 18.1. The effects of regulatory reform

Enterprise	Privatized	Main changes to competitive environment
British Airways	Jan. 1987	Routes liberalized; North Atlantic (1977); UK (1982); Europe (1984 forwards)
BAA	July 1987	—
British Coal	—	Quasi-competitive contracts for supply to electricity generators; 1989
British Gas	Dec. 1986	Gas Act (1985); partial competition in supply to industrial customers
British Rail	—	—
British Steel	Dec. 1988	Unwinding of EC steel quotas (1980 forwards)
British Telecom	Nov. 1984	Liberalization of apparatus supply (1981); value added services (1981) and second fixed link carrier (1982)
Electricity Supply	Dec. 1990/ Spring 1991	Energy Act (1983); partial competition in supply. Electricity Act (1986); competition in supply (1990 forwards)
Post Office	—	Courier services deregulated (1981)

prises showing dates of privatization, where appropriate, and policy changes which have resulted in some of these firms facing more competitive product markets.

3. INTERNAL ORGANIZATION AND PERFORMANCE

We will focus on two aspects of internal organization which the literature suggests have particular relevance to the performance of firms in private markets:

- organizational form;
- the structure of management remuneration.

Companies in private markets can be structured in a wide variety of ways but the most common form of organization amongst large corporations—particularly in America and Europe—is the multi-divisional, or M-form, firm; what Williamson (1985) has described as 'the most significant organizational innovation of the twentieth century'. The essential characteristic of the M-form firm is that profit responsibility is decentralized to the level of individual product lines, individual brands or geographically distinct markets (or to some combination of these). Within each profit centre the organization is then segmented functionally into marketing, distribution, finance, etc., whilst corporate headquarters

monitors the performance of the decentralized profit centres, allocates
resources between them, and carries out strategic planning for the future
direction of the corporation as a whole (see Figure 18.1).

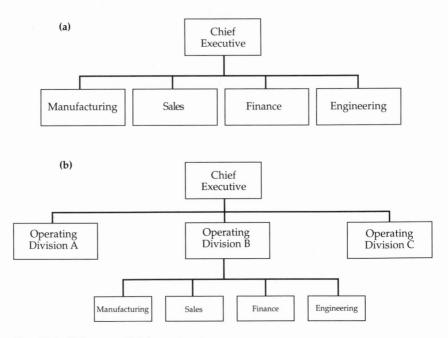

FIG. 18.1. U-form and M-form structures

M-form is seen as being superior to the more traditional U-form of
organization (where segmentation is along functional lines) in large,
diversified companies for several reasons (see Cable 1988). First, it facilitates more effective use of senior management time. In a U-form company senior management is necessarily involved in all (or at least most)
of the policy decisions which involve interaction between the various
functions. Whilst this may be effective in small or medium-sized companies, in large corporations it places high demands on senior management's capacity to absorb and evaluate the necessary information on
their business's performance (the problem of 'bounded rationality').
Second, M-form is more effective in inhibiting opportunistic behaviour
on the part of middle and junior management. In a large corporation U-
form implies a long hierarchy of control between the senior managers
responsible for determining strategies and the middle management
responsible for implementing them. The scope for opportunism by middle and junior management—behaviour which serves their own goals
but not necessarily those of the corporation—is increased in conse-

quence both of the long control span which arises and also because of the information overload on senior management.

The M-form resolves these problems by decentralizing profit responsibility (and hence responsibility for interaction between the functional specialisms) down to the level of identifiable economic markets, defined by product or geographic area. Empirical studies (see Cable 1988 for a review) suggest that, at least in the UK and North America, adoption of M-form is generally associated with more successful performance, although it appears that the effective decentralization of operational decisions is an important prerequisite for this to be the case (see Hill and Pickering 1986)). Nevertheless, M-form is not necessarily appropriate in all circumstances, particularly for smaller firms (where U-form is more appropriate), for process industries where the divisionalization of production imposes costs, or in industries where technological change is an important source of competitive advantage (see, for example, Goold and Campbell 1987).

The second feature of internal organization that we examine relates to management remuneration. An extensive literature has analysed the classic agency problem which arises once the ownership and control of a firm are separated (see, for example, Jensen and Mecklin 1976). Agency theory predicts that opportunistic behaviour by managers will be reduced, and their activities aligned more closely to the interests of shareholders, where remuneration is linked to their firm's performance. Incentive packages are a familiar feature of executive remuneration in private corporations. Empirical studies have generally found a positive link between pay and performance (see, for example, Jensen and Murphy 1990) although one which is estimated to be quantitatively smaller than might be expected from the widespread use of performance pay. Studies of the effect upon companies' market valuation of the introduction of incentive pay schemes have also shown a positive and significant impact (see R. S. Thompson (1988) for a review).

To investigate the characteristics of the internal organization of the nine enterprises in our study we use results from a survey of forty-six public enterprises carried out in conjunction with United Research; details of the findings for the other enterprises, which are consistent with the results reported here, are documented in United Research 1990.

Management Remuneration

In the private sector performance pay is widespread but in the UK's publicly owned enterprises it was almost wholly absent at the beginning of the 1980s (see Table 18.2). Over the following decade performance pay has been introduced extensively. However, the nature of the incentive schemes vary from enterprise to enterprise reflecting the familiar issues which arise where there is team-working. For example, the scheme introduced for management in the Post Office's Counters services involves two elements (see MMC 1988*a*). The first relates to measures of labour productivity and service quality achieved within the particular operating unit in which the manager works. This element clearly applies in equal measure to all managers within a particular operating unit and reflects the team characteristics of the output measures. In contrast, the second element is tailored to the individual. However, it is based upon a performance assessment made by line management, reflecting the absence of quantified output measures which can be related to the individual manager. Another example is British Steel where a small-scale bonus scheme for management was introduced in 1979, whilst from 1980 decentralized management have participated in the 'works lump-sum bonus' in which the pay of all employees is linked to the performance of the plant at which they work. Subsequently annual performance assessment for senior managers has also been introduced (see MMC 1988*b*). More generally the findings in Table 18.2 show that performance pay has been introduced for senior and middle management in most of the 9 enterprises over the last decade.

Organizational Structure

Perhaps the earliest example of structural reorganization along M-form lines is the case of British Steel (see MMC 1988*b*). At the beginning of the 1970s the recently (re)nationalized enterprise was organized along product lines with each of six product groupings acting as a profit centre. However, a functional structure at board level (with separate board members responsible for finance, marketing, personnel, engineering, etc.) provided overall 'head office' control of policy. Thus whilst decentralized profit centres existed, the enterprise's organizational structure more closely resembled a 'corrupted' M-form (as identified by Williamson and Bhargava 1972) in which the centre intervenes in the operational policy decisions of the divisions, and the performance incentives of full M-form are correspondingly attenuated (Hill and Pickering (1986) show that the performance of corrupted M-form firms conforms to this view).

In the mid-1970s British Steel was reorganized into a unitary form. The objective was to access perceived scale economies in production by co-ordinating, and in some cases integrating, the activities of many, geographically dispersed plants. A financial crisis in the late 1970s, prompted by the rapid fall in demand and prices after the first oil-price shock, resulted in a further reorganization in 1980. This involved implementing an M-form structure in which the enterprise's activities were divided into a series of businesses, each established as a profit centre.

TABLE 18.2. Performance-related pay

(a) Was pay related to performance in 1979?

	Senior management	Middle management	Employees
British Airways	Yes	No	No
British Airports Authority	No	No	No
British Coal	No	No	Yes
British Gas	No	No	No
British Rail	No	No	No
British Steel	No	No	Yes
British Telecom	No	No	No
Electricity	No	No	No
Post Office	No	No	Yes

(b) Has performance pay been introduced since 1979?

	Senior management	Middle management	Employees
British Airways	Prior to 1979	After 1979	After 1979
British Airports Authority	1987	1990	1990
British Coal	After 1979	After 1979	Prior to 1979
British Gas	1987	1987	No
British Rail	No	No	No
British Steel	1980	1980	Prior to 1979
British Telecom	1982	1989	No
Electricity	1986–90	1989–90*	No
Post Office	1986	1986	Prior to 1979

* In some companies.

Source: Centre for Business Strategy and United Research 1990.

The underlying objectives of the restructuring were to decentralize decision-making and to delegate accountability for performance to individual divisional managers. Corresponding to this aim head office 'line' control of commercial decisions was abolished and the activities of head office functional specialists were converted to a supporting role.

British Rail has implemented similar changes to its organizational structure during the 1980s (see MMC 1980 and 1987). At the beginning of the decade its railways activities had a unitary structure with board responsibilities divided functionally. In 1982 it divided its railways activities into five separate business sectors: Network South-East (commuter lines serving London), Inter City, Provincial (all other passenger services), Freight, and Parcels. Each sector became a profit centre responsible for specifying the nature and quality of its services, for defining products and marketing them, and for preparing investment projects relevant to their provision. Now it will be clear that the supply of the different business-sector products involves both common and joint costs. Reflecting this, responsibility for production—the operation and maintenance of both train services and infrastructure—remained initially with a regionally organized management structure. A system of internal contracts specified the terms under which the 'producers' supplied services to the five businesses. The essential features of these were that producers were only able to incur expenditure where contracted to do so by a business and that each business had ultimate profit responsibility for the performance of the services which it contracted. Subsequent organizational change has resulted in the five business sectors assuming a greater degree of responsibility for the operation of their services, with supply to other businesses on a contractual basis.

The Post Office has followed a similar path of establishing separate businesses for its different products (see MMC 1988*a*). In 1985 'Counters' was established as a separate business from 'Mails' (letters and parcels), being incorporated as a separate company on 1 October 1987, and more recently letters and parcels activities have been divided into two separate businesses. As in the case of British Rail, contracts have been established to determine the conditions under which one business supplies services to another (e.g. Counters selling stamps on behalf of letters or parcels).

Summary information on changes in organizational structure for the remaining six enterprises is set out in Table 18.3. It can be seen that in most cases there has been a substantial increase in the number of profit centres during the 1980s. This is not true, however, for British Airways whilst the results for British Coal show a decline in line with the size of the business. In this case, however, specification of products and their pricing and marketing is carried out centrally and the resulting structure might properly be regarded as a corrupted M-form.

These changes to internal organization have been associated with col-

TABLE 18.3. Changes in organizational structure

	Number of Profit Centres	
	1979	1990
British Airways	17	14
BAA	7	12
British Coal	219	73
British Gas	1	3
British Telecom	1	22
Electricity	11	28

Source: Centre for Business Strategy and United Research 1990.

lateral changes in the skill-mix of the senior management of the nine enterprises. Our findings show, in most cases, a shift in the composition of board members toward financial and marketing skills and, associated with this, an increased representation from members with previous experience in the private sector (see United Research 1990).

4. PRODUCTIVITY GROWTH IN THE PUBLIC UTILITIES

The performance of public enterprises can be measured against a range of criteria, financial, commercial, economic, or social, and an extensive literature has examined the properties of alternative indicators (see, for example, Marchand, Tulkens, and Pestieau 1984). In what follows we will focus upon the achievement of productive efficiency. Performance in relation to this will usually be central to determining whether other objectives are achieved, and we will examine two measures of productivity: labour productivity and total-factor productivity. Further details of the productivity measures, which are constructed from weighted indices for the quantities of the various outputs supplied by each of the nine enterprises and corresponding indices for the quantities of the various inputs used in their production, are provided in Bishop and Thompson 1992.

In Figure 18.2 we summarize our results on labour productivity. The graph aggregates together the results, appropriately weighted, for the nine enterprises (figures for each enterprise are detailed in Bishop and Thompson 1992). The graph also shows the trend in labour productivity in the UK economy as a whole. These results suggest three observations. First it can be seen that the growth in labour productivity was slower for the nine enterprises during the 1970s than for the UK economy as a whole. Second, it can be seen that labour productivity in the economy as a whole increased more rapidly during the 1980s than in the 1970s. The causes and consequences of this have been much debated (see, for example, Kay and Haskel 1990 for a discussion). Perhaps the most striking observation, however, is the relative increase in labour productivity growth for the nine enterprises.

In part, this upturn is a consequence of the substitution of other factors of production for labour. This can be seen from Figure 18.3 which presents corresponding results for total-factor productivity (t.f.p.). The trend in t.f.p. mirrors the trend in labour productivity, showing little change over the 1970s and an upturn through the 1980s. However, comparison of the two graphs shows that the growth in t.f.p. during the 1980s is considerably slower than the growth in labour productivity, a consequence of factor substitution (see Haskel and Szymanski (1990) and Rees (1989) for discussion of the changes in the bargaining positions

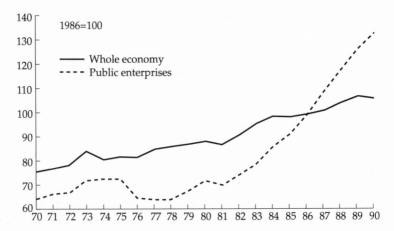

FIG. 18.2. Labour productivity

of enterprises and employees associated with regulatory reform and the implications for employment).

Now of course measured productivity growth will usually reflect a combination of causal factors. These are likely to include—in particular—scale effects, technological change, and short term disequilibria, as well as any changes to productive efficiency. Our analysis shows that these factors have been relevant in explaining observed productivity growth in individual industries (see Bishop and Thompson 1992). Thus,

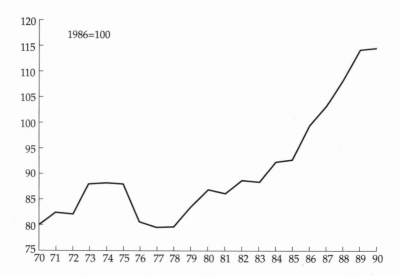

FIG. 18.3. Total-factor productivity

for example, the growth in demand for postal services (and the potential to exploit scale economies) has been greater during the 1980s than the 1970s, but in the case of British Gas the opposite is true. Similarly the speed of technical change has been greater, for example, for postal services during the 1980s but in the case of British Airways, and perhaps BT, technical change has been slower. Overall, however, we have found it difficult to identify any systematic change in the opportunities for exploiting scale economies or technical change between the two decades, although data in relation to the latter is particularly limited. This suggests that an important part of the upturn in productivity growth identified in our findings can be attributed to changes in productive efficiency; how large that part is, given the multi-causal nature of productivity growth, we cannot say with certainty. However, the conclusion that performance in relation to productive efficiency has improved is confirmed by the findings of efficiency studies carried out by the UK's competition authorities during the 1980s. In particular, sequential studies of British Coal (see MMC 1983 and 1989), and London's commuter rail services (see MMC 1980 and 1987) each identify relevant changes to performance over the course of the decade. These findings are also consistent with international comparative studies which show the UK's postal and rail services to be relatively efficient (see Perleman and Pestieau 1987) as do some studies of international airlines (see Windle 1991); comparative analysis of BT's performance shows more mixed results, however (see Foreman-Peck and Manning 1987).

5. CONCLUSIONS

Over the last decade there has been extensive discussion in the UK about the role of 'corporate culture' in determining the performance of publicly owned enterprises. 'Culture change' is often seen as an important requirement for improved performance whilst the regulatory reforms implemented over the last ten years are regarded as an important precursor to changes in culture. Thus, John Moore the Financial Secretary to the Treasury, in 1983: 'Tell any able manager to create and build up a prosperous efficient company and he will know what to do. Tell him at the same time to carry out a host of non-commercial functions and he will get hopelessly muddled.'

Our aim in this paper has been to examine slightly more specifically the nature of the changes to internal organization which have been induced by regulatory reform and to analyse associated changes in enterprises' performance. Our analysis of productivity (in Section 4) shows a marked upturn in performance in the period following the regulatory reforms. Whilst conclusions at this early stage must be provisional—the longer term impact of the regulatory changes upon the level and quality of investment remain to be seen—the observed upturn is consistent with the view that the changes to regulation have constrained the enterprises to perform more effectively, at least in relation to the achievement of productive efficiency. We also noted that this conclusion is consistent with other sources of evidence on the enterprises' performance and it is, of course, consistent with the view that performance is conditioned by the nature of the financial constraints which an enterprise faces (as suggested by Rees (1984) for example).

We discuss these issues further elsewhere (see Bishop and Thompson 1992); our particular interest in this paper is the role of organizational change in enabling enterprises to respond to the changed regulatory environment. We have shown that there have been important changes to two dimensions of internal organization, management remuneration and organizational form, although other aspects of 'culture change' have no doubt also been important.

In Section 3 we showed that, at the beginning of the 1980s, few of the UK's public enterprises had adopted a multi-divisional (M-form) organizational structure. The main advantages claimed for M-form are its more effective use of senior management time and the constraint on opportunistic behaviour by middle and junior management. Whilst there are circumstances in which M-form is not necessarily appropriate, for most large, diversified private corporations it is commonly associated with superior business performance. We show that during the 1980s there has been a shift in the publicly owned enterprises' organizational structures toward the adoption of M-form.

The second dimension of internal organization which we have considered relates to management remuneration. Amongst private corporations there is widespread use of performance-linked pay to attenuate the agency problem which arises from the separation of ownership and control. Yet we show that amongst the UK's publicly owned enterprises performance pay was infrequent at the beginning of the 1980s; our results show that, by the end of the decade, most enterprises had introduced performance pay for both senior and middle management.

Both of these shifts in internal organization relating to management remuneration and to organizational form would be expected to induce more effective performance.

References

Ashworth, M., and Forsyth, P. S. (1984), *Civil Aviation Policy and the Privatization of British Airways*, IFS Report Series no. 12, London: IFS.

Bishop, M., and Kay, J. A. (1988), *Does Privatisation Work? Lessons from the UK*, London: Centre for Business Strategy, London Business School.

—— and Thompson, D. J. (1992), 'Regulatory reform and productivity growth in the UK's public utilities', Centre for Business Strategy Working Paper, London Business School.

Cable, J. R. (1988), 'Organisational Form and Economic Performance', in R. S. Thompson and M. Wright (eds.) *Internal Organisation, Efficiency and Profit*.

Foreman-Peck, J., and Manning, D. (1988), 'How well is B.T. performing? An international comparison of telecommunications total-factor productivity', *Fiscal Studies*, **9/3**, 56–67.

Goold, M., and Campbell, A. (1987), *Strategies and Styles*, Oxford: Basil Blackwell.

Haskel, J., and Szymanski, S. (1991), 'Privatisation, liberalisation, wages, and employment: theory and evidence from the UK', Centre for Business Strategy Working Paper, London Business School.

—— and Kay, J. A. (1990), 'Productivity in British industry under Mrs Thatcher', Centre for Business Strategy Working Paper no. 74, London Business School.

Hill, C. W. L., and Pickering, J. F. (1986), 'Conglomerate mergers, internal organization and competition policy', *International Review of Law and Economics*, **6**, 59–75.

HM Treasury (1986), *Accounting for Economic Costs and Changing Prices*, London: HMSO.

Jensen, M. C., and Meckling, W. H. (1976), 'The theory of the firm: managerial behaviour, agency costs and ownership structure', *Journal of Business*, **52**, 469–506.

—— and Murphy, K. J., (1990), 'CEO Incentives—It's not how much you pay, but how', *Harvard Business Review*, **68/3**, 138–49.

Marchand, M. P., Pestieau, P., and Tulkens, H. (1984) (eds.), *The Performance of Public Enterprises*, Amsterdam: North Holland.

Monopolies and Mergers Commission (1980), *British Railways Board: London & South-East Commuter Services*, Cmnd 8046, London: HMSO.

—— (1983), *National Coal Board*, Cmnd 8920, London: HMSO.

—— (1987), *British Railways Board: Network South-East*, Cmnd 204, London: HMSO.

—— (1988a), *Post Office Counter Services*, Cmnd 398, London: HMSO.

—— (1988b), *British Steel Corporation*, Cmnd 437, London: HMSO.

—— (1989), *British Coal Corporation*, Cmnd 550, London: HMSO.

Moore, J. (1983), 'Why privatise?', HM Treasury Press Release 190/83.

National Economic Development Office (1976), *A Study of UK Nationalised Industries*, London: HMSO.

Perelman, S., and Pestieau, P. (1988), 'Technical performance in public enterprises', *European Economic Review*, **32**, 432–41.

Pryke, R. (1981), *The Nationalised Industries: Policies and Performance since 1968*, Oxford: Martin Robertson.

Rees, R. (1984), 'A positive theory of the public enterprise', in M. Marchand, P. Pestieau, and H. Tulkens (eds.), *The Performance of Public Enterprises*.

—— (1989), 'Modelling public enterprise performance', in D. R. Helm, J. A. Kay, and D. J. Thompson (eds.), *The Market for Energy*, Oxford: Clarendon Press.

Thompson, R. S. (1988), 'Agency costs of internal organisation', in R. S. Thompson and M. Wright (eds.), *Internal Organisation, Efficiency and Profit*.

—— and Wright, M. (1988) (eds.), *Internal Organisation, Efficiency and Profit*, Oxford: Alden Press.

United Research (1990), *Privatization: Implications for Cultural Change*, Morristown, NJ: United Research.

Vickers, J., and Yarrow, G. (1988), *Privatization: An Economic Analysis*, Cambridge, Mass.: MIT Press.

Williamson, O. E. (1985), *The Economic Institutions of Capitalism: Firms, Markets and Relational Contracting*, New York: Free Press.

—— and Bhargava, N. (1972), 'Assessing and classifying the internal structure and control apparatus of the modern corporation', in K. G. Cowling (ed.), *Market Structure and Corporate Behaviour*, London: Gray-Mills.

Windle, R. J. (1991), 'The world's airlines: a cost and productivity analysis', *Journal of Transport Economics and Policy*, **25/1**, 31–50.

INDEX